Informatics in Medicine

Informatics in Medicine

Edited by:

Jovan Pehcevski

ARCLER PRESS

www.arclerpress.com

Informatics in Medicine

Jovan Pehcevski

Arcler Press
224 Shoreacres Road
Burlington, ON L7L 2H2
Canada
www.arclerpress.com
Email: orders@arclereducation.com

ISBN: 978-1-77407-778-8 (Hardcover)

DECLARATION

Some content or chapters in this book are open access copyright free published research work, which is published under Creative Commons License and are indicated with the citation. We are thankful to the publishers and authors of the content and chapters as without them this book wouldn't have been possible.

ABOUT THE EDITOR

Jovan obtained his PhD in Computer Science from RMIT University in Melbourne, Australia in 2007. His research interests include big data, business intelligence and predictive analytics, data and information science, information retrieval, XML, web services and service-oriented architectures, and relational and NoSQL database systems. He has published over 30 journal and conference papers and he also serves as a journal and conference reviewer. He is currently working as a Dean and Associate Professor at European University in Skopje, Macedonia.

TABLE OF CONTENTS

LIST OF CONTRIBUTORS

Hugo Saldanha
University of Brasília, Brasil

Edward Ribeiro
University of Brasília, Brasil

Carlos Borges
University of Brasília, Brasil

Aletéia Araújo
University of Brasília, Brasil

Ricardo Gallon
University of Brasília, Brasil

Maristela Holanda
University of Brasília, Brasil

Maria Emília Walter
University of Brasília, Brasil

Roberto Togawa
Embrapa/Genetic Resources and Biotechnology, Brasil

João Carlos Setubal
University of São Paulo, Brasil

Shubhalaxmi Kher
Electrical Engineering, Arkansas State University, USA

Jianling Peng
Samuel Roberts Noble Foundation, USA

Eve Syrkin Wurtele
Department of Genetics, Development and Cell Biology, Iowa State University, USA

Julie Dickerson
Electrical and Computer Engineering, Iowa State University, USA

Harun Pirim
King Fahd University of Petroleum and Minerals

Şadi Evren Şeker
Istanbul University, Turkey

Estela S. Estape, M.T, Ph.D., FASAHP, DHL
Post-doctoral Master of Science in Clinical and Translational Research (MSc) and Hispanics in Research Capability (HiREC) Endowment Programs, School of Health Professions, Medical Sciences Campus-University of Puerto Rico

Mary Helen Mays, Ph.D., MPH, MBA, RD
Post-doctoral Master of Science in Clinical and Translational Research (MSc), School of Health Professions, and the Puerto Rico Clinical and Translational Research Consortium, Medical Sciences Campus – University of Puerto Rico

Elizabeth A. Sternke, Ph.D
Post-doctoral Master of Science in Clinical and Translational Research (MSc) School of Health Professions, Medical Sciences Campus-University of Puerto Rico

I. A. Sadkovsky
I.M. Sechenov First Moscow State Medical University, Moscow, Russia

O. Golubnitschaja
European Association for Predictive, Preventive and Personalized Medicine (EPMA), Brussels, EU
Rheinische Friedrich-Wilhelms-University of Bonn, Bonn, Germany

M. A. Mandrik
I.M. Sechenov First Moscow State Medical University, Moscow, Russia

M. A. Studneva
I.M. Sechenov First Moscow State Medical University, Moscow, Russia

H. Abe
International Society for Personalized Medicine (ISPM), Tokyo, Japan

H. Schroeder
Department of Medicine, Genetics and Comparative Pathology, University of Alabama at Birmingham (UAB), Birmingham, USA

E. N. Antonova
I.M. Sechenov First Moscow State Medical University, Moscow, Russia

F. Betsou
Université du Luxembourg and IBBL (Integrated BioBank of Luxembourg), Luxembourg, EU

T. A. Bodrova
National Research University "Higher School of Economics", Moscow, Russia

K. Payne
Institute of Population Health and Health Economics, University of Manchester, Manchester, UK

S. V. Suchkov
I.M. Sechenov First Moscow State Medical University, Moscow, Russia
A.I. Evdokimov Moscow State Medical & Dental University, Moscow, Russia
United Cultural Convention (UCC), Cambridge, UK

Dirk Lassner
Institute of Cardiac Diagnostics and Therapy, Berlin, Germany

Maria Rohde
Institute of Cardiac Diagnostics and Therapy, Berlin, Germany

Christine Sabine Siegismund
Institute of Cardiac Diagnostics and Therapy, Berlin, Germany

Uwe Kühl
Institute of Cardiac Diagnostics and Therapy, Berlin, Germany
Department of Cardiology and Pneumonology, Charité—University Medicine Berlin, Campus Benjamin Franklin, Berlin, Germany

Ulrich Michael Gross
Institute of Cardiac Diagnostics and Therapy, Berlin, Germany

Felicitas Escher
Institute of Cardiac Diagnostics and Therapy, Berlin, Germany
Department of Cardiology and Pneumonology, Charité—University Medicine Berlin, Campus Benjamin Franklin, Berlin, Germany

Carsten Tschöpe
Department of Cardiology and Pneumonology, Charité—University Medicine Berlin, Campus Benjamin Franklin, Berlin, Germany

Heinz-Peter Schultheiss
Department of Cardiology and Pneumonology, Charité—University Medicine Berlin, Campus Benjamin Franklin, Berlin, Germany

Adam Attarian
MIT Lincoln Laboratory, Lexington, MA, USA.

Hien Tran
Department of Mathematics, North Carolina State University, Raleigh, NC, USA.

Tae Min Hwang
School of Electronics Engineering, College of IT Engineering, Kyungpook National University, 80 Daehakro, Bukgu, Daegu, Republic of Korea

Seol Young Jeong
School of Computer Science and Engineering, College of IT Engineering, Kyungpook National University, 80 Daehakro, Bukgu, Daegu, Republic of Korea

Soon Ju Kang
School of Electronics Engineering, College of IT Engineering, Kyungpook National University, 80 Daehakro, Bukgu, Daegu, Republic of Korea

Youn-Sik Hong
Department of Computer Science and Engineering, Incheon National University, Incheon 406-772, Republic of Korea

Hui-Ru Cao
Nanfang College of Sun Yat-sen University, Guangzhou 510970, China

Choujun Zhan
Nanfang College of Sun Yat-sen University, Guangzhou 510970, China

Joanna Jaworek-Korjakowska
Department of Automatics and Biomedical Engineering, AGH University of Science and Technology, Krakow, Poland

Pawel Kleczek
Department of Automatics and Biomedical Engineering, AGH University of Science and Technology, Krakow, Poland

Mohammed A. Aseeri
National Centre for Sensors and Defense Systems Technologies (NCSDST), King Abdulaziz City for Science and Technology (KACST), Riyadh 11442, Saudi Arabia

Meshaal A. Alyahya
National Centre for Sensors and Defense Systems Technologies (NCSDST), King Abdulaziz City for Science and Technology (KACST), Riyadh 11442, Saudi Arabia

Hatim A. Bukhari
National Centre for Sensors and Defense Systems Technologies (NCSDST), King Abdulaziz City for Science and Technology (KACST), Riyadh 11442, Saudi Arabia

Hussein N. Shaman
National Centre for Sensors and Defense Systems Technologies (NCSDST), King Abdulaziz City for Science and Technology (KACST), Riyadh 11442, Saudi Arabia

Boris A. Kobrinskii
Pediatric Research Clinical Institute, Russian National Research Medical University, Moscow, Russia

Fen Miao
Shenzhen Institutes of Advanced Technology, Chinese Academy of Sciences, Shenzhen, China

Xiuli Miao
Taihe Hospital of Traditional Chinese Medicine, Fuyang, China

Weihua Shangguan
Shenzhen Institutes of Advanced Technology, Chinese Academy of Sciences, Shenzhen, China

Ye Li
Shenzhen Institutes of Advanced Technology, Chinese Academy of Sciences, Shenzhen, China

Janneke E. M. Aerts
Geestelijke Gezondheidszorg Westelijk Noord Brabant, Halsteren, The Netherlands.

Arno van Dam
Geestelijke Gezondheidszorg Westelijk Noord Brabant, Halsteren, The Netherlands.
Tranzo (Tilburg University), Tilburg, The Netherlands.

Sabato Manfredi
Faculty of Engineering, University of Naples Federico II, Napoli, Italy

Ali Al Musawi
College of Education, Sultan Qaboos University, Seeb, Oman

Wajeha Al-Ani
College of Education, Sultan Qaboos University, Seeb, Oman

Mohamed Al-Aghbari
College of Education, Sultan Qaboos University, Seeb, Oman

LIST OF ABBREVIATIONS

AODV	Ad-hoc On-Demand Distance Vector Routing Protocol
AWS	Amazon Web Services
BAN	Body area network
BLER	block error rate
BP	blood pressure
BSN	body sensor network
CLR	Context likelihood of relatedness
CMV	cytomegalovirus
CTCs	circulating tumor cells
DFD	data flow diagram
DGS	defected ground-plane structures
DTC	direct-toconsumer
EBI	European Bioinformatics Institute
ECG	electrocardiograph
EMBL	European Molecular Biology Laboratory
EMR	Elastic Map Reduce
EST	Expressed Sequence Tag
GO	Gene Ontology
GSM	Global system for mobile
GWAS	genome-wide association studies
HAART	Highly Active Antiretroviral Therapy (
HPLC	high performance liquid chromatography
IGCM	Idiopathic giant cell myocarditis
ISVs	independent software vendors
KATS	Korea Agency for Technology and Standards
LAN	(Local Area Network)
LCMS	long-term care management system
MST	minimum spanning tree

MTD	mobile teledermoscopy
PPD	personal portable devices
PPG	photoplethysmograph
RDF	Resource Description framework
RHC	receding horizon control
SGD	Saccharomyces Genome Database
SNPs	single nucleotide polymorphisms
SPI	serial peripheral interface
TDMA	Time Division Multiple Access
TRS	transformed radial stub
URI	Uniform Resource Identifier
WS	Web Services
XML	eXtensible Markup Language

PREFACE

The term medical informatics originates from the late 1970s, initially from the French term "informatique médicale", and today combines disciplines that are described as clinical informatics, medical computer science and medical information systems. The term health informatics is generally considered to be the application of information principles to the entire health and healthcare system, including administrative and economic services, and as such it is used to break down the areas covered by public health and social medicine. In this sense, the concept of medical informatics is more comprehensive and hierarchically superior.

For medical informatics, a set of procedures is applied to provide medical care to patients, including: (a) examination and history of patients, (b) diagnostics, and (c) treatment. The system is not simple and one-way, as it may at first glance be assumed, since the doctor works with each patient, and so here the disease differs from the overall patient average by at least some indicator. The doctor uses the information collected from the patient and creates the knowledge they can further process. The doctor's information activity in such a system is described by a diagnostic-therapeutic cycle, in which information circulates from a patient to the doctor and back to the patient, in the form of measured, interpreted and conclusive data. This cycle can be accomplished only once, but also repeated in terms of re-examination of the patient, or even changed in case actions are required due to an inappropriate response to treatment.

Disease data collection is based both on interviewing the patient (medical history) and on examination of the patient. The characteristic of this "observation" phase is that it collects an enormous amount of data over sometimes short periods of time (e.g. emergencies), among which only a fraction of this data might be important to get reliable conclusions. If possible, data should be read and stored immediately, using patient records or electronic data entry forms. Information topics related to these issues include data collection and processing, classification of medical data and medical language of communication, creation of formalized and informal medical records, as well as computer support for data processing and databases.

This edition covers different topics related to medical informatics, including bioinformatics methods, personalized medicine, IT solutions in medicine, and e-health and m-health trends in telemedicine. Section 1 focuses on bioinformatics methods, describing a hybrid federated cloud platform to efficiently execute bioinformatics workflows; hierarchical biological pathway data integration and mining; ensemble clustering for biological datasets; and molecular modelling to study interactions between molecules with biological activity.

Section 2 focuses on personalized medicine, describing translation in data mining to advance personalized medicine for health equity; PPPM (predictive, preventive and personalized medicine) as a new model of the national and international healthcare services; myocarditis – a personalized medicine by expanded endomyocardial biopsy diagnostics; and an optimal control approach to structured treatment interruptions for HIV patient from a personalized medicine perspective.

Section 3 focuses on IT solutions in medicine, describing wireless TDMA-based body area network platform gathering multi bio-signals synchronized with patient's heartbeat; smart care beds for elderly patients with impaired mobility; novel emergency healthcare system for elderly community in outdoor environment; eSkin – a study on the smartphone application for early detection of malignant melanoma; and a compact microstrip lowpass filter with low insertion loss for UWB medical applications.

Section 4 focuses on e-health and m-health, describing current state and future steps of e-health and telemedicine; a Mobi-healthcare system, which is a body sensor network based m-health system for healthcare applications; blended e-health in cognitive behavioral therapy and its usage intensity, attitude and therapeutic alliance in clinical practice; a performance evaluation study of healthcare monitoring systems over heterogeneous wireless networks.

SECTION 1
BIOINFORMATICS METHODS

CHAPTER

1

TOWARDS A HYBRID FEDERATED CLOUD PLATFORM TO EFFICIENTLY EXECUTE BIOINFORMATICS WORKFLOWS

Hugo Saldanha[1], Edward Ribeiro[1], Carlos Borges[1], Aletéia Araújo[1], Ricardo Gallon[1], Maristela Holanda[1], Maria Emília Walter[1], Roberto Togawa[2] and João Carlos Setubal[3]

[1] University of Brasília, Brasil

[2] Embrapa/Genetic Resources and Biotechnology, Brasil

[3] University of São Paulo, Brasil

INTRODUCTION

Current generation of high-throughput DNA sequencing machines [1, 35, 66] can generate large amounts of DNA sequence data. For example,

Citation: Hugo Saldanha, Edward Ribeiro, Carlos Borges, Aletéia Araújo, Ricardo Gallon, Maristela Holanda, Maria Emília Walter, Roberto Togawa and João Carlos Setubal (November 28th 2012). "Towards a Hybrid Federated Cloud Platform to Efficiently Execute Bioinformatics Workflows", Bioinformatics, Horacio Pérez-Sánchez, IntechOpen, DOI: 10.5772/50289.

the machine HiSeq 2000 from the company Illumina, a current workhorse of genome centers, is capable of generating 600 Giga base-pairs of sequence in one single run [35]. The Human Microbiome project (https://commonfund.nih.gov/hmp) and the 1000 Genomes project (http://www.1000genomes.org) are two examples of projects that are generating terabyte-scale amounts of DNA sequence.

Such vast amounts of data can only be handled by powerful computational infrastructures (also known as cyberinfrastructures), sophisticated algorithms, efficient programs, and well-designed boinformatics workflows. As a response to this challenge, a large ecosystem composed by different technologies and service providers has emerged in recent years with the paradigm of cloud computing [2, 58, 63, 71]. In this paradigm users have transparent access to a wide variety of distributed infrastructures and systems. In this environment, computing and data storage necessities are accomplished in different and unanticipated ways to give the user the illusion that the amount of resources is unrestricted.

In this scenario, cloud computing is an interesting option to control and distribute processing of large volumes of data produced in genome sequencing projects and stored in public databases that are widespread in distinct places. However, considering the constant growing of computational and storage power needed by different bioinformatics applications that are continouslybeeing developed in different distributed environments, working with one single cloud service provider can be restrictive for bioinformatics applications. Working with more than one cloud can make a workflow more robust in the face of failures and unanticipated needs. Cloud federation [11, 14, 15] is one such solution. Cloud federation offers other advantages over single-cloud solutions. Bioinformatics centers can profit from participation in a cloud federation, by having access to other center programs, data, execution and storage capabilities, in a collaborative environment. The federation can abstract cloud-specific mechanisms, thus potetially making the use of such a resource more user-friendly and easier to install and customize. This is particularly valuable for small and medium centers that can enlarge their hardware resources and software tools using machines and programs of other centers integrating a federated system.

In this work, we propose a hybrid federated cloud computing platform that aims at integrating and controlling different bioinformatics tools in a distributed, transparent, flexible and fault tolerant manner, also providing highly distributed processing and large storage capability. The objective is to make possible the use of tools and services provided by multiple institutions, public or private, that can be easily aggregated to the cloud. We also discuss a use case of this platform, a bioinformatics workflow for identifying differentially expressed genes in cancer tissues.

FEDERATED CLOUD COMPUTING

There are many distinct definitions of cloud computing. According to [29], cloud computing could be defined as *"a computational paradigm highly distributed, directed by a scale economy, in which the computational power, storing, abstract platforms and services, virtualized, managed and dinamically scalable are provided on demand by external users through the Internet*". [71], using all the characteristics collected from the literature, proposed a definition of clouds as *"a big pool of virtualized resources, easily usable. The resources can be reconfigured dinamically according to a variable load, allowing optimized using. This pool is typically explored by a pay-per-use model in which guarantees are offered by the infrastructure provider, following a service contract"*.

These authors attempted to define cloud computing using only common characteristics in cloud providers, but they did not find features that were mentioned by all providers. The most common were scalability, pay-per-use model and virtualization.

From these definitions we can state that the goal of cloud computing is to offer to users the idea that they have unrestricted resources, but they have to pay only for those effectively used (model pay-per-use). Another significant advantage of clouds is the management of the computational infrastructure, relieving users from concerns such as power failures and backups. The property of allocating computational resources depending on user needs is called elasticity.

Cloud services can be deployed by providers in different ways [48]:

- Private cloud: operated for the use of a single organization. It can be managed by the organization itself or by external ones.
- Community Cloud: shared by several organizations and used as a tool for a specific group of users with common interests.
- Public Cloud: available to the general public or a large corporate group that is part of the organization that sells this service.
- Hybrid cloud: composed of two or more clouds (private, community or public) that remain separate entities, but that are

bound together by standardized or proprietary technologies that enable portability of data and applications.

In clouds, one of the key technologies adopted to execute bioinformatics programs is the Apache Hadoop framework [6], in which the MapReduce [25] model and its distributed file system (HDFS) [13] are used as infrastructure to distribute large scale processing and data storage. In the MapReduce model parallelization does not require communication among simultaneously processed tasks, since they are independent from one another.

Bittman [11] claimed that the evolution of cloud computing market could be divided in three phases. In phase 1 (Monolithic), cloud computing services were based on proprietary architectures, or cloud services were delivered by megaproviders. In phase 2 (Vertical Supply Chain), some cloud providers leveraged services from other providers, i.e. independent software vendors (ISVs) developed applications as a service using an existing cloud infrastructure. Clouds were still proprietary, but ecosystems construction started. In phase 3 (Horizontal Federation), smaller providers would horizontally federate to gain economy of scale and efficient use of their assets. Projects would leverage horizontal federation to enlarge their capacibilities, more choices at each cloud computing layer would be provided, and discussion about standards would begin.

In general, cloud computing intends to increase efficiency in service delivery, dealing with services including infrastructure, platforms and software, and treating with distinct users like a single user, other clouds, academic institutions and large companies. Besides public clouds maintained by large organizations, hundreds of smaller heterogeneous and independent clouds, private or hybrid, are being developed. In this scenario, cloud federation becomes an interesting way to optimize the use of the resources offered by various organizations. In particular, in this chapter, we are interested in horizontal cloud federation, also called federated cloud computing, inter-cloud [14] or cross-cloud [15].

Federated cloud computing can be defined as a set of cloud computing providers, public and private, connected through the Internet [14, 15]. Among its objectives we distinguish the seemingly availability of unrestricted resources, independence of a single infrastructure provider, and optimization when using a set of distinct resource providers.

Thus, federation allows each cloud computing provider to increase its processing and storage capabilities by requesting more resources to other clouds in the federation when needed. This means that a local cloud provider is able to satisfy user requests beyond its capabilities, since idle resources from other providers can be used. Furthermore, if a provider fails, resources can be requested to another one, providing more fault tolerance.

Although the advantages of federated cloud computing are obvious, its implementation is not trivial, since the participating clouds present heterogeneous and frequently changing resources. Therefore, traditional models of federation are not useful [15]. Typically, federated models are based on *a priori* agreements among their members, noting that these agreements can be inappropriate according to the particular characteristics of a cloud provider. Thus, to make possible the creation of a federated cloud environment, it is necessary to achieve the following requirements [14, 15]:

- **Automatism:** a cloud member of the federation, using discovery mechanisms, should be able to identify the other clouds in the federation together with their resources, responding to changes in a transparent and automatic way;
- **Application behavior prediction:** the system implementing the federation has to be able to predict demands and behaviors of the offered applications, so that its load balancing mechanism can have its efficiency improved;
- **Mapping services to resources:** the services offered by the federation must be mapped to available resources in a flexible manner so that it can achieve the highest levels of efficiency and cost/benefit. In other words, the schedule must choose the best hardware-software combination to ensure the quality of service at lowest cost, taking into account the uncertainty of the availability of resources;
- **Interoperable security model:** federation must allow the integration of different security technologies so that a cloud member does not need to change its security policies when entering the federation;
- **Scalability in monitoring components:** considering the possible large number of participants, the federation must be able to handle multiple task queues and the largest number of requests, so that management can guarantee that the various cloud providers of the federation will mantain scalability and performance.

It is noteworthy that issues to choose an appropriate cloud provider and lack of common cloud standards hinder the interoperability across these federated cloud providers. Thus, nowadays the user is faced with the challenging problem of selecting the appropriate cloud that fits his or her needs. To address this problem, the BioNimbus platform offers to users a federated platform that can execute bioinformatics applications in a transparent and flexible manner. This is possible because BioNimbus offers standardized interfaces and intermediate services to manage the integration of different cloud providers. Moreover, as will be seen next, BioNimbus was designed to incorporate the requirements defined by [15].

BIONIMBUS: A FEDERATED CLOUD PLATFORM

As mentioned before, cloud computing is a promising paradigm for bioinformatics due to its ability to provide a flexible computing infrastructure on demand, its seemingly unrestricted resources, and the possibility to distribute execution in a large number of machines leading to a significant reduction in processing time due to the high degree of achieved parallelism. Some bioinformatics tools have been implemented in cloud environments belonging to several infrastructures of physically separated institutions, which makes it difficult for them to be integrated.

BioNimbus [12, 62] is a federated cloud platform designed to integrate and control different bioinformatics tools in a distributed, flexible and fault tolerant manner, providing rapid processing and large storage capabilities, transparently to users. BioNimbus joins physically separate platforms, each modelled as a cloud, which means that independent, heterogenous, private/public clouds providing bionformatics applications can be used as if they were a single system. In BioNimbus, resources of each cloud can be maximally explored, but if more are required, other clouds can be requested to participate, in a transparent manner. BioNimbusis thus able to satisfy further service allocation requests sent by its users. The objective is to offer an environment with apparently unrestricted computational resources given that computing and storage space demands are always provided on demand to the users.

BioNimbus architecture

All the components of BioNimbus architecture together with their funcionalities are defined such that it allows simplicity, speed and eficiency when a new cloud provider enters in the federation. Another key characteristic is the communication among the BioNimbus components that is realized through a Peer-to-Peer (P2P) [67] network, guaranteeing the following properties:

- Fault tolerance, since there is not a single fail point. Thus, even if some nodes fail, the others can work;
- Efficiency, since there is not a single bottleneck. Then, messages are end-to-end and not routed by a single node;
- Flexibility, since clouds can operate independently or in a coordinated manner;
- Scalability, since the use of a P2P network allows integration of thousands of interconnected machines.

BioNimbus (Figure 1) architecture enables the integration of different cloud computing platforms, meaning that independent, heterogeneous, private or public providers may offer their bioinformatics services in an integrated manner, while maintaining their particular characteristics and internal policies. BioNimbus is composed of three layers: application layer, core layer and cloud provider layer.

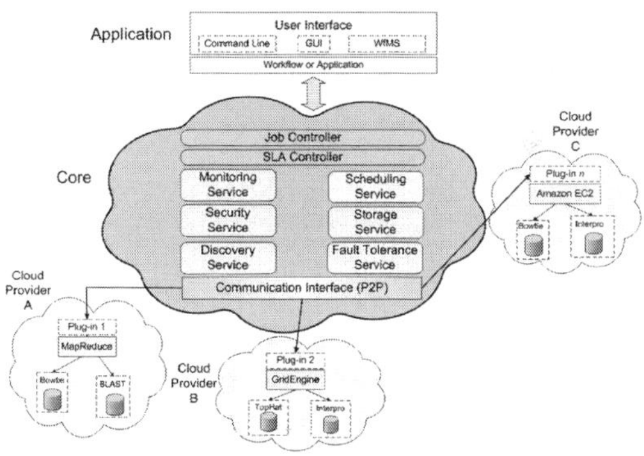

Figure 1: The architecture of BioNimbus hybrid federated cloud.

Application layer

This layer provides the service of interaction with users, which can be implemented by web pages, command lines, graphical interfaces (GUI) or workflow management systems (WfMS). Users can execute workflows or a single application, choosing among available services. Job controller service has the function of collecting user requests and sending the input data to the core layer. Moreover, this layer is responsible for showing to each user the current status of his running applications. Users can list the files stored in the federation, upload or download files, create and execute workflows in the BioNimbus cloud environment.

Cloud provider layer

This layer encompasses the cloud providers belonging to BioNimbus. The previous described core layer ensures a unified view of the cloud, which allows users to see all the resources available on each cloud as if they were one unified system.

A plug-in service is used to integrate a cloud provider (public or private) in the federation. Each plug-in service is an interface that aims at communicating the BioNimbus core with each cloud provider. Cloud providers can communicate among themselves also using the core layer. Each plug-in needs to map the requests sent by the core components to the corresponding actions that have to be realized in each cloud provider. This implies that each cloud requires a special plug-in service. Furthermore, to integrate distinct providers (public or private), each plug-in needs to treat three different kinds of requests: information about the provider infrastructure, task management and file transfer.

Core layer

This layer is responsible for managing the federated environment. Among their functions are: identification of new providers with their corresponding hardware and software resources; task scheduling and controlling; definition, establishment and monitoring of SLA (Service Level Agreement); storage and managing of input and output files; maintainance of the online environment; and the election of new coordinators for each requested service. To each function implemented in this layer, a controller service was included in the architecture, as described next.

Discovery service

This service identifies the cloud providers integrating the federation, and consolidates information about storage and processing capabilities, network latency, availability of resources, available bioinformatics tools, details of parameters and input and output files. To realize this, the discovery service waits for information published by providers about their infrastructure and available tools. To consolidate these data, the discovery service maintains a data structure that is updated whenever new data is received. Furthermore, the discovery service has a policy of controlling each provider, removing from the federation those providers not regularly sending updated information, which guarantees the correct and update task execution on the federated cloud. Regarding to the entrance of a cloud provider in BioNimbus, a priori, at any time a peer participating in the P2P network can start the process of publishing its resources (storage and processing capabilities) and available bioinformatics applications. However, for security and controlling purposes, permission to join the federation as a provider must be verified with the support of the security service whenever any information about a new provider arrives to the discovery service.

As can be seen from the above description, an efficient resource discovery mechanism plays a central role in our federated cloud, since the information gathered by this service is essential to other services to properly perform their functions. According to [49], in large-scale distributed services, a resource discovery infrastructure has to meet the following key requirements: it must be scalable so it can handle thousands of machines without being unavailable or losing performance; it must be able to handle both static and dynamic resources; and it must be flexible enough so its queries could be extended in order to handle different types of resources. Possible implementations of a resource discovery service could be developed using central or hierarchical approaches, but these are known to have serious limitations of scalability, fault-tolerance and network congestion [56].

In BioNimbus, we plan to use a publish/subscribe mechanism, in which providers publish information about their resources to a decentralised resource discovery system. This system will use a Distributed Hash Table (DHT) data structure [7] in order to achieve low management costs and network overhead, efficient resource searching and fault-tolerance. For resource information handling, we plan to use serializable and extendable formats such as the JSON format [23]. In this way it will be possible for the federated cloud to deal with different types of information, thus causing the least impact possible.

Job controller

The job controller links the core and the application layers of BioNimbus. It first calls the security service to verify if a user has permission (authentication) to execute jobs in BioNimbus and what are the credentials of this user. Moreover, the job controller's main function is to manage distinct and simultaneously running workflows, noting that the workflows may belong to the same or to different users. Thus, for each accepted workflow, the job controller generates an associated ID and controls each workflow execution using this ID.

SLA controller

According to [74], SLA is a formal contract between service providers and consumers to guarantee that consumers' service quality expectations can be achieved. In BioNimbus, the SLA controller is responsible for implementing the SLA lifecycle, which has six steps: discovers service providers, defines SLA, establishes agreement, monitors SLA violation, terminates SLA and enforces penalties for violation. A SLA template represents, among others, the QoS parameters that a user has negotiated with BioNimbus. The user can populate, through an user interface, a suitable template with required values or even define a new SLA from scratch in order to describe functional (e.g. CPU cores, memory size, CPU speed, OS type and storage size) and non-functional (e.g. response time, budget, data transfer time, availability and completion time) service requirements. In bioinformatics, functional requirements are number of cores, amounts of memory and storage, CPU speed, bioinformatics programs and databases and respective versions. Non-functional requirements are latency (transfer rate) and uptime (reliability, in the sense that it measures how frequently a cloud provider is running tasks or if it is not entering and leaving the federation).

The SLA controller has the responsibility to investigate whether the SLA template submitted by the user can be supported by the federated cloud platform. For this, the SLA controller retrieves the SLA level published through the provider plug-in (e.g. gold, silver or bronze SLA level).

So, if the service agreement required by the SLA template cannot be satisfied, a negotiation phase starts. The SLA negotiation phase is done as follows: the user submits a service request with the new SLA template to the job controller. Next, after parsing the SLA definition, the SLA controller asks the monitoring service if it could execute the service with the specified requirements. In order to respond to this request, the monitoring service requests the scheduling service to find the best suitable provider by matching the gathered resource properties to the service requirements by applying predefined scheduling algorithms. If none of the providers can be matched, the monitoring service enables the discovery service, which must seek new cloud providers to be integrated into the federated environment, aiming at satisfying the SLA template requested by the user. However, if this is not possible, the mentioned steps must be repeated for renegotiation, with a new SLA template, until reaching an agreement.

After establishing an agreement, the SLA controller generates an ID for the agreement, and sends the ID to the job controller, which records this ID agreement. Then, the job controller forwards both the request and the agreement ID to the monitoring service, which sends the tasks for the scheduling service. The monitoring service is responsible for checking if a violation of the agreement occurred and in this case it immediately has to inform the SLA controller, which terminates the SLA and enforce penalties for violation.

Monitoring service

This service verifies if a requested service is available in a cloud provider, searching for another cloud in the federation if it is not; receives the tasks to be executed from the job controller, and sends them to the scheduling service that will distribute them, guaranteeing that all the tasks of a process are correctly executed; and informs the job controller when a task successfully finishes its execution. To ensure the monitoring of all the requested tasks, this service periodically sends messages to the clouds that are executing tasks, and informs the user the current status of each submitted task.

To perform the activities described above, the monitoring service must be able to gather information about resource allocation and task execution, which depends on the application being executed [28]. Therefore, we have to establish some criteria about the frequency that data are obtained and their corresponding format, so that the decision-making process performed by this service can be made with reliability with respect to data timeliness and flexibility towards distinct applications. In BioNimbus, the monitoring service was planned to send messages at regular intervals to all the federation members or whenever needed. The latter case happens when a decision has to be taken for a specific federation member or when data update is necessary. All information exchange is done with timestamps so only the updated data are sent in order to save network bandwidth. We also plan to use an extensible and flexible format, such as JSON [23], like in the discovery service.

In federated clouds the monitoring service must have other characteristics, such as: scalability, to handle a large number of resources and tasks to be monitored; elasticity, to handle addition and removal of resources in a transparent manner; and federation, to handle entering and leaving providers [20]. In order to meet these requirements, we propose to use a decentralized information indexing infrastructure, which would be the same DHT available to the discovery service. Furthermore, as previously described, the monitoring service has to verify agreement violations.

Storage service

This service decides how to distribute and replicate data among the cloud providers integrating the federation [8, 39, 73], particularly model the storage strategy of the files consumed and produced by the jobs executed in BioNimbus. To realize this, the storage service can communicate with the discovery service to access information about the federation, since the discovery service knows the actual storage conditions of each provider integrating the federation.

Thus a storage policy is defined, so that this choice can be made based on receiving information about the file (FileInfo) and returns at least one cloud provider (PluginInfo) to store this file.

Some characteristics of biological data for bioinformatics applications are: large volume; it is not necessary to guarantee the ACID transaction properties since there are no users simultaneously updating data during execution; according to a particular bioinformatics application, fragmentation and replication can use different models; and data provenance is essential.

Considering these characteristics, the BioNimbus storage service proposal is based on the HBaseNoSQL (Not only SQL) database. Among distinct noSQL databases, like HBase [38], Dynamo [26], Bigtable [17], Cassandra [41], PNUTS [22], monogDB [19] and cloudDB [5], we adopted HBase since its basic data storage is Apache's Hadoop Distributed File System (HDFS) [13] and it is a column-oriented database [24, 50, 51], which allows joining data (biological data file) and sets of information (e.g. data provenance).

Replication will be done copying data to at most three clouds in order to ensure recovery in case of failure. Total or partial fragmentation depends on the biological data and the application. On the top of HBase, we propose to create an Analyzer module, which will decide where the replication has to be done.

The objective of the Analyzer module is to reduce data transfers among the cloud providers, based on three criteria: disk space, geographic position and data transfer speed. The most important analysis is the available space, which should be sufficient to store input and output. The geographic position criterion has the objective of reducing data transfer on the network, being the closer clouds used first if possible. Finally, the Analyzer module uses data transfer speed, which must be computed using the time to transfer packages.

Security service

This service guarantees integrity among the distinct tasks executed in the federated clouds. A federated cloud needs to include the security policies of each cloud provider while avoiding strong inter-dependency among the clouds. A security context can be partitioned into three main topics: authentication, authorization and confidentiality. We address those requirements using standard algorithms and protocols as described next.

- **Authentication:** The descentralized federated cloud infrastructure should not make a centralized authentication, which is a not a good choice because it limits the scalability and creates a strong interdependency among the clouds. We intend to use a Single Sign-On (SSO) protocol [52] so that no central authority is in charge of its users' authentication, which prevents a single point of failure and allows scalability according to the number of users. We chose the OpenID standard [57] as our SSO mechanism, since it has been used by corporate and academic sites around the world. OpenID allows each "site" (e.g. a cloud) to provide an authentication facility to its users so that they do not need to authenticate with each other cloud integrating the federation. Instead, each cloud provider acts as an identity provider for user credentials, so that each user should authenticate with its affiliated provider. Once this user is authenticated, each time his/her credentials are required, OAuth [10] allows a user's site to forward authorization without exposing the user account or login information.
- **Authorization:** The authorization of a federated cloud resource is provided by the Access Control Lists (ACLs) [69] provided by each cloud provider. An ACL determines who can access a given resource, e.g. disk storage, CPU cycles and bioinformatics services. Therefore, each cloud is able to determine access patterns so that it can control its resource's uses.
- **Confidentiality:** Communication between each two cloud providers is established using TLS/SSL [68] connection. The use of secure connections between two clouds in the federation is not enforced by our model, but it can be provided as well. As far as we know, few cloud systems provide secure intra-cloud communication. Each cloud should provide a certificate that will

be used by hosts in two clouds to establish a secure connection. As we improve BioNimbus, we plan to include audit trails so that each required resource can be available when needed.

Fault tolerance service and high availability

This service guarantees that all the core services are always available. In a cloud environment, machine failures occur, and it is well known among the cloud community that those failures are the norm rather than the exception. Thus, any federated cloud should be designed for fault recovering and system availability. Therefore, a fault tolerance service is an essential part of our federated cloud, and has the objective of providing high availability and resiliency against periodic or transient failures.

There are extensive studies in the literature on failure detection systems [16, 31, 45, 70]. On the other hand, few systems are designed to scale with a large number of nodes as those found on clouds.

Thus, an important requirement of our fault detection service is to be scalable with a large number of machines. We adopted a modified gossip based failure detector proposed by Renesse et al [70], which works as described. Each host runs the gossip failure detector service, which maintains a list of known hosts in the cloud. Every $T_{seconds}$, a host increases a heartbeat, and at random chooses a set of nodes for sending a list of known nodes. When received, each list is merged with the host current list, assuming the largest heartbeat for each node in the list. If a node does not update its heartbeat for a $T_{elapsed}$ time, then it will be marked as failed. Note that a node may be marked as failed due to slow network links or even in presence of a fractioned network. But our failure detection service is conservative so that it only purges a host from the list after a $T >= 2 * T_{elapsed}$.

Performing tasks in BioNimbus

Figure 2 shows how BioNimbus works. Initially (step 1), the user interacts with BioNimbus through an interface, which could be a command line or a web interface, for example.

The user informs details of the application (or workflow) to be executed, and these information are sent to the job controller in form of jobs to be executed. Then, the job controller verifies the availability of the informed applications and input files, sending a response message to the user accordingly. Afterwards, these jobs' features are analyzed by the security service (step 2), which verifies the user permission to access the resources of the federation, and sends a response to the job controller (step 3). If the requested jobs can be executed, a message is sent to the SLA Controller (step 4) that investigates whether the SLA template submitted by the user can be identified by BioNimbus.

If the user request can be executed, the SLA controller sends a message to the monitoring service (step 5), which stores the jobs in a pending task list. This service is responsible for informing to the scheduling service that there are pending jobs waiting to be scheduled.

Next (step 6), the scheduling service starts when the monitoring service informs that there are pending jobs. The scheduling policy adopted in BioNimbus can be easily changed, according to the characteristics of a particular application.

The scheduling service gets information about the resources using the discovery service (steps 9 and 10), which periodically updates the status of the federation infrastructure, and stores these information in a management data structure. This information is used to generate the list of ordered resources, and to assign the more demanding jobs to the best resources, according to the scheduling policy.

With the resource and job ordered lists, the scheduling service communicates with the storage service to ensure that all the input files are available to the providers chosen to execute the jobs (steps 7 and 8).

Next, the scheduler distributes instances of jobs (tasks) to be executed by the plug-ins and their corresponding clouds (steps 11 and 12).

The scheduling service decision is then passed to the monitoring service (step 13) so that it can monitor each job status until it is finished. When the jobs are all completed, the monitoring service informs the SLA Controller (step 14), which sends a message to the job controller (step 15). Finally, the job controller communicates with the user interface (step 16) informing that the jobs were completed, which closes one execution cycle in BioNimbus.

The BioNimbus architecture follows [3], who claims that high-throughput sequencing technologies have decentralized sequence acquisition, which increases demands for new and efficient bioinformatics tools that have to be easy to use, portable across multiple platforms, and scalable for high-throughput applications.

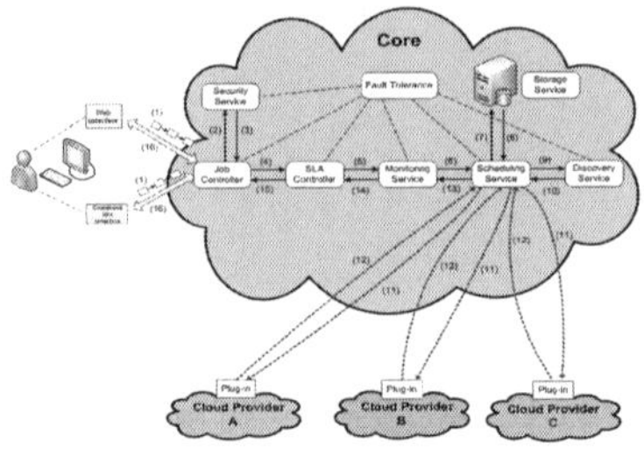

Figure 2: Example of a job execution in the BioNimbus hybrid federated cloud.

A CASE STUDY

A federation with two cloud providers, one nonpublic (University of Brasilia) and one public (EC2 Amazon), were created in order to study BioNimbus when applied to a simple workflow with real data.

A prototype of BioNimbus containing all the main controller services was implemented: *monitoring and scheduling service*, *discovery service* and a simple *storage service*, using an open source implementation of the Zab protocol [59], which allows a distributed consensus among a group of processes. We also implemented Hadoop infrastructure plug-ins. Each plug-in provides information about the current status of its respective infrastructure, like number of cores, processing and storage resources and bioinformatics tools that can be executed in BioNimbus, as well as information of input and output files. The interaction of the user and the platform was implemented by a command line that sends requests. Services and plug-ins communicate through a P2P network based on the Chord protocol [67].

In order to study the runtime performance of a workflow involving real biological data, we created a three-phase workflow in BioNimbus. The objective was to compare the time of a workflow running in a federated cloud to a single cloud.

Cloud providers

At the University of Brasilia, a Hadoop cluster was implemented with 3 machines, each one with two Intel Core 2 Duo 2.66Ghz (so a total of 6 cores), 4 GB RAM and 565 GB of storage. The Hadoop cluster executed Bowtie [44] with the HadoopMapReduce (Hadoop streaming), with storage implemented with the Hadoop Distributed FileSystem (HDFS).

In addition, at Amazon EC2, a Hadoop cluster ClusterHadoop was implemented with 4 virtualized machines, each one with two Intel Xeon 2.2 7Ghz (so a total of 8 cores), 8 GB RAM, and 1.6 TB of storage. The cluster also executed Bowtie.

Two Perl scripts implementing the workflow (SAM2BED and genome2interval) and the coverageBed program (integrating the BEDTolls suite [54]) were installed in each cloud provider.

Workflow, tools and data

Workflow

Now we describe the workflow used as our case study. The objective of the workflow was to identify differentially expressed genes in human kidney and liver cancerous cells [47, 60], with fragments of genes sequenced with Illumina technology [35]. The workflow consists of four phases (Figure 3): (i) mapping the input sequences onto the 24 human chromosome sequences; (ii) converting format from SAM (Bowtie) to BED (a specific format of the CoverageBED program); (iii) generating fixed intervals for all chromossomes based on their length, since this is the input for the CoverageBED program; and (iv) executing the CoverageBED program, which generates histograms showing the number of mappings for each interval.The *mapping phase* has the objective of identifying the region of a reference genome where each input sequence was located. A set of sequences mapping in the same region allows the inferences that these sequences have the same structural organization of the reference genome.The *CoverageBED*program [54] allowed the study of the expression level of the cancerous genes using histograms of the mapped input sequences onto the human reference genome, so that differentially expressed genes between kidney and liver cancer genes could be identified.

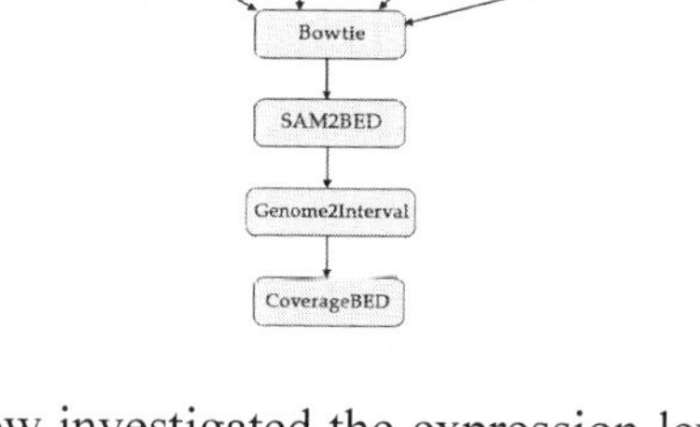

Figure 3: The workflow investigated the expression level of liver and kidney genes (generated by Illumina) mapping them to 24 human chromosome sequences.

Tools

Four tools were implemented in each cloud provider: Bowtie [44], SAM2BED (a Perl script), genome2interval (another Perl script) and coverageBed [54].

Data

The 24 human chromosome sequences were downloaded from HG19:

ftp://ftp.ncbi.nih.gov/genomes/H_sapiens/Assembled_chromosomes/seq/

The reference site is:

http://www.ncbi.nlm.nih.gov/genome/assembly/293148/

Finally, the names of the files followed the format:

hs_ref_GRCh37.p5_chr*.fa.gz.

Implementation details

A message module allowed the communication among the services, having been created using the Nettycommunication library [36], which is responsible for the TCP connection event manager. Messages were serialized using both JSON format [23] and Jackson library [21], and file transfer was accomplished through the HTTP protocol GET and PUT methods. Message and file communications were realized using an unique TCP port, which avoided the necessity to create complex firewall rules. Besides, the message module is capable of multiplexing both message and file traffic. A simplified version of the *Chord* [67] protocol was implemented for the P2P network and plug-ins. We developed plug-in prototypes for Apache Hadoop and SunGridEngine. Java was the language used to implement the BioNimbus prototype.

Next, we briefly describe somefeatures of the services implemented on our BioNimbus prototype (Figure 4):

- Discovery service: this implementation used two execution threads. The first one is responsible for updating and cleaning the data structure storing information about the cloud providers. The second thread waits for P2P network messages that have to be treated by the discovery service. A data structure map was used for storing information about each federated cloud provider using a unique identifier. Besides, each cloud has a timestamp for its last mapping. To update the infrastructure, the first thread is executed in intervals of 30 seconds in order to send messages to all the BioNimbus members. The response of each plug-in is treated by the second thread, which updates the mapping with the received new information and corresponding timestamp for each execution. The first thread removes from the map those pieces of information that did not have their date modified in the last 90 seconds, which indicates that those cloud providers left the federation. The second thread also treats the requisition about the federation clouds, using the map maintained by the discovery service.

- Monitoring and scheduling service: to realize the work of receiving, monitoring and scheduling user jobs, three main data structures of type map were used. The first one, called PendingJobs, maps each job identifier to its information and also represents those jobs waiting to be scheduled. The second one, named RunningJobs, maps each executing task identifier to its information and the job to which it belongs. The third data structure, called CancelingJobs, maps the task identifier to its corresponding job and to the user requiring its cancelation.

In the monitoring service, there is a thread responsible for waiting the user requests and responses received from other services of the infrastructure. When a request initiates a job (JobStartReq) is received, this thread generates an unique identifier for this job and saves this informaticon in the PendingJobsmap. Next, it calls the scheduling policy, which returns a mapping among the jobs and the plug-ins that can execute them. Thus, when the jobs are all scheduled, this thread sends requests in order to create tasks (TaskStartReq) that have to be executed in the cloud providers, and waits for their corresponding outputs (TaskStartReply). When an output is received, the service removes the job from the PendingJobsmap and creates an input in the RunningJobsmap, with information about the job and its corresponding tasks, removing a job when all its tasks finish. As previouly mentioned, a new *DynamicAHP*algorithm was implemented in BioNimbus [12], which is based on on a decision making strategy proposed by [61].

Another thread in the monitoring service, executed at intervals of 15 seconds, is responsible for following the jobs. First, it sends status requests (TaskStatusReq) to each job registered in RunningJobs. The response (TaskStatusReply), treated by the previous described thread, can again initiate the scheduling service according to some parameters. Cancelling messages

(TaskCancelReqand TaskCancelReply) will be sent, and the job will be reinserted in the PendingJobsmap and removed from the RunningJobs. This thread also verifies whether there are pending jobs in PendingJobs, initiating another scheduling process in this case, and sending query messages to the discovery service (CloudReq) and to the storage service (ListReq), whose responses (CloudReplyand ListReply) will be received by the first thread and used by the scheduling policy when needed.

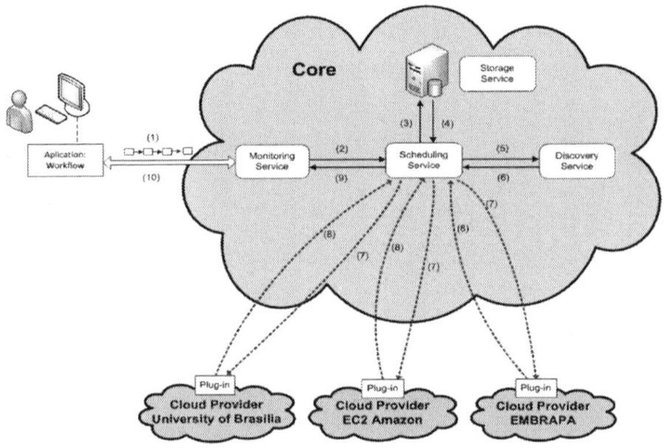

Figure 4: The services implemented for our case study, noting that we used two cloud providers in the BioNimbus prototype.

- Storage service: two threads were used for its implementation. The first one waits for the requests sent by other services. To treat the request of saving files (StoreReq), the storage service executes the storage policy adopted in BioNimbus. For this case study, we used a method based on a round-robin of the plug-ins that informed having enough space to store the file. When a cloud is chosen, a response (StoreReply) is sent to the service making the request, which will send the file to the cloud indicated by the storage service. When this transfer finishes, the plug-in receiving the file storage sends a special message (StoreAck), which contains information that will keep correct the federation file table.

In the case study, a simple backend was implemented to maintain the federation file table. Every time a new confirmation is received by the storage service, it adds an input in the map file with the file identifier containing information such as name, size and storage cloud. This mapping is stored in JSON format [23] in a file in the federation file system of the cloud where the service will be executed. When initiating its execution, the storage service verifies if the map file left and load in memory the federation file table last status.

The other two types treated by the first thread are file list (ListReq) and localization (GetReq). For the first case, the thread builds a response (ListReply) with the mapping loaded in memory. For localization, it builds a response (GetReply) searching for the cloud information in the map using the request identifier.

Finally, another thread is executed at intervals of 30 seconds requesting to the discovery service the current configuration of the federation (CloudReqmessage). The received information is used by the storage policy.

Results

We executed the workflow at the University of Brasilia and the Amazon EC2, and on both cloud providers (Table 1).

Table 1. Workflow execution time on each cloud and on the BioNimbus federated cloud.

Cloud Providers	hour:minute:second
University of Brasilia (UnB)	1:11:47
Amazon EC2	1:18:44
Both clouds (UnB and EC2)	1:09:07

We measured how the file transfer time affected the job execution total time. Table 2 and Figure 5 shows the total and file transfer times of the 18 longest jobs of the workflow, as well as the percentage of the file transfer time related to the total time. These percentages show that file transfer represents at least 50% of the total time of this job execution. This means that in federated clouds executing data-driven bioinformatics applications, storage services have to be especially designed to minimize as much as possible huge file transfers.

We also investigated how the time execution of a job was affected when sent to execution in a cloud provider, taking a long time, being cancelled and returning to the list of pending jobs to be executed again.

There were seven jobs cancelled, the first seven jobs in Table 2 with the longest times to be executed. When making an experiment without cancelling jobs, we obtained greater times, when compared to the experiment with cancelling since they were sent to clouds almost idle.

We mention now some points that can affect BioNimbus performance: (i) the scheduler does not consider jobs being transferred and identifies CPUs involved in these transfers as idle; (ii) the input files are all simultaneously downloaded, i.e. there are no priorities for downloads; (iii) jobs are now canceled based only on the wait time in the pending jobs list, i.e. the file transfering time is not considered; and (iv) jobs with small input files that were sent to a cloud provider after jobs with large input files got executed earlier, while the later were still downloading their input data.

Table 2. Total and file transfer times of the longest jobs executed in BioNimbus.

Total time (seconds)	File transfer time (seconds)	Percentage of file transfer time related to the total time
4230.297	2114.996	50.0 %
4123.492	2264.552	54.9 %
4098.571	2337.454	57.0 %
4030.492	2297.580	57.0 %
3807.501	2229.992	58.6 %
3145.645	2168.201	68.9 %
3113.729	2116.199	68.0 %
3066.488	2058.771	67.1 %
3032.701	2018.942	66.6 %
3001.165	2137.157	71.2 %
2952.875	2087.761	70.7 %
2849.506	2074.117	72.8 %
2801.489	2023.309	72.2 %
2680.382	1892.002	70.6 %
2587.076	2006.842	77.6 %
2579.184	1959.727	76.0 %
2533.254	1928.888	76.1 %
2405.470	1899.626	79.0 %

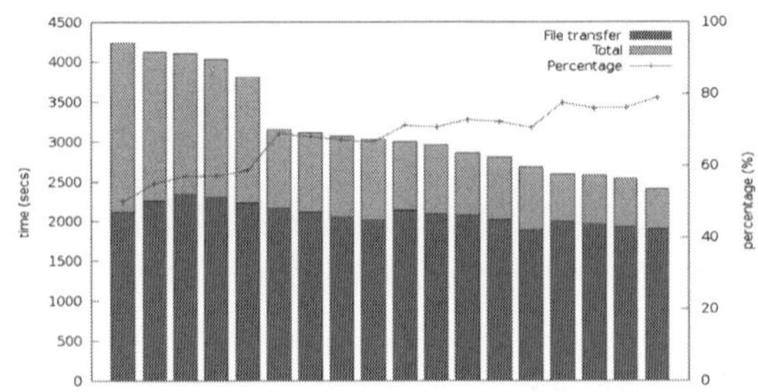

Figure 5. Comparing the total and file transfer times of the longest jobs executed in BioNimbus. The file transfer time is colored red, while its percentage related to the total time is shown in blue.

Table 3 and Figure 6 show the number of jobs executed in a single cloud provider and on both. Note that, including the transfer time, jobs with smaller inputs execute faster on two cloud providers, since the possibility to cancel delayed jobsthat are running and scheduling them again lowered the total execution time. Besides, when files are small, the time to transfer files is rapid, while when they are large the transfer time strongly affects the total execution time (as shown in Table 2). Thus, for large files, the storage policy has to be very carefully designed using replication and fragmentation in order to significantly decrease file transfer time.

Table 3: Number of executed jobs, where time includes the file transfer time.

Cloud Providers	until 200 seconds	between 200 seconds and 1000 seconds	above 1000 seconds
University of Brasilia	34	30	32
EC2 Amazon	37	27	32
UnB and EC2	64	8	24

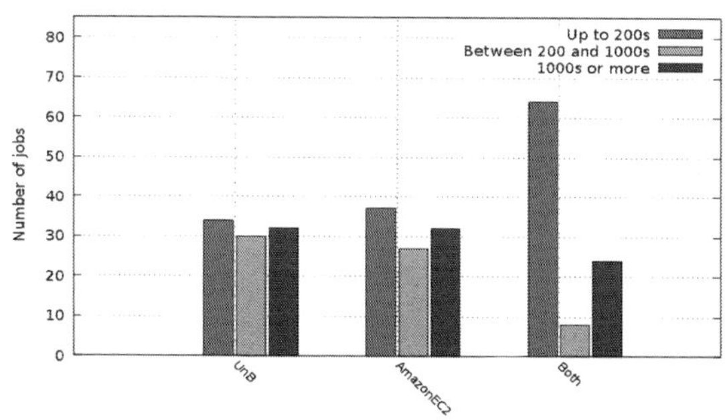

Figure 6: Comparing the number of executed jobs in BioNimbus, where time (in seconds) includes the file transfer time.

RELATED WORK

In this section, we discuss cloud projects designed to accelerate execution and increase the amount of storage available to bioinformatics applications. When compared to BioNimbus, these projects are dedicated to particular applications or are executed in a single cloud environment. BioNimbus intends to integrate public and private centers offering bioinformatics applications in one single platform using the hybrid federation cloud paradigm.

Cloudburst [64] parallel algorithm is optimized for mapping DNA fragments, also known as short read sequences (SRSs), to a reference genome. The execution time varies almost linearly with the increase in the number of processors. The mapping of millions of SRSs to the human genome, executed in 24 cores, is thirty times faster when compared to other non-distributed applications [44, 65]. CloudBurst uses the MapReduce model.

Crossbow [43] is a pipeline developed in the infrastructure provided by the Apache Hadoop streaming mode. It combines the Bowtie [43] SRS mapping tool, performed during the map phase, with the SOAPsnp [46] tool to identify SNPs, processed during the reduce phase. During the execution of the workflow, the SRSs are sent as input to the nodes of the Hadoop cluster, which executes the map phase. In this phase, the SRSs are mapped to a reference genome using Bowtie. Afterwards, the mappings are joined with parts of the reference genome, and each group is sent to a node that executes the reduce phase. The SOAPsnp tool is used to detect SNPs in the already analyzed parts of the genome. The execution time for about 2.6 billion SRSs and the entire human genome used as a reference took a little more than 3 hours in a 320 core cluster of the Amazon EC2 [2] infrastructure. The experiments cost less than US$ 100.

Myrna [42] identifies differentially expressed genes in large sets of sequenced data. The workflow combines a mapping phase with a statistical analysis phase, performed with R [55], which is able to analyze more than one billion SRSs in a little more than 90 minutes, using 320 cores and costing around US$ 75.

The RSD (Reciprocal Smallest Distance) comparative genomics algorithm, composed of different bioinformatics tools, was adapted to be executed in the Amazon EC2 infrastructure, having obtained expressive results [72].

[3] created the Cloud Virtual Resource (CloVR), a desktop application for automated sequence analysis using cloud computing resources. CloVR is implemented as a single portable virtual machine (VM) that provides several automated analysis pipelines for microbial genomics, whole genome and metagenome sequence analysis. The CloVR VM runs on a personal computer, uses local computer resources and addresses problems arising in constructing bioinformatics workflows.

[4] noted that genomic applications are limited by the "bioinformatics bottleneck", due to computational costs and infrastructure needed to analyze the enormous amounts of SRSs. They presented benchmark costs and

runtimes for microbial genomics applications, microbial sequence assembly and annotation, metagenomics and large-scale BLAST. They also analyzed workflows (also called pipelines) implemented in the CloVR virtual machine running in Amazon EC2, having achieved cost-efficient bioinformatics processing using clouds, and thereby claiming that this is an interesting alternative to local computing centers.

[53] adapted a particular peptide search engine called X!Tandem to HadoopMapReduce. Their MR-Tandem application runs on any Hadoop cluster, but it was especially designed to run on Amazon Web Services. They modified the X!Tandem C++ program and created a Python script for driving Hadoop clusters, which includes the Amazon Web Services (AWS) Elastic Map Reduce (EMR) used by the modified X!Tandem as a Hadoop streaming mapper and reducer.

[75] worked on pathway-based or gene set analysis of expression data, having developed a gene set analysis algorithm for biomarker identification in a cloud. Their YunBe tool is ready to use on the Amazon Web Services. YunBe performed well when compared to desktop and cluster executions. YunBe is open-source and freely accessible within the Amazon Elastic MapReduce service.

[27] ported two bioinformatics applications, a pairwise Alu sequence alignment application and an Expressed Sequence Tag (EST) sequence assembly program, to the cloud technologies Apache Hadoop and Microsoft DryadLINQ. They studied the performance of both applications in these two cloud technologies, comparing them with traditional MPI implementation. They also analyzed how non-homogeneous data affected the scheduling mechanisms of the cloud technologies, and compared performance of the cloud technologies under virtual and nonvirtual hardware platforms.

[32] used cloud computing for scientific workflows, and discussed a case study of a widely used astronomy application.

The Bio-Cloud Computing platform [9] was designed to support large-scale bioinformatics processing. It has five main bio-cloud computing centers, with a total peak performance up to 157 Teraflops, 33.3 TB memory and 12.6 PB storage.

Recently, many bioinformatics applications have been ported to clouds [33, 37, 40], noting that they offer user-friendly web interfaces and efficiency in the execution of tools that extensively use memory and storage resources.

CONCLUSION AND FUTURE WORK

In this work, we proposed a hybrid federated cloud computing platform called BioNimbus, which aims at integrating and controlling different bioinformatics tools in a distributed, transparent, flexible and fault tolerant manner, also providing highly distributed processing and large storage capability. The objective was to make possible the use of tools and services provided by multiple institutions, public or private, that could be easily aggregated to the federated cloud. We also discussed a case study in a prototype of BioNimbys including two cloud providers, in order to verify its performance in practice. We created a bioinformatics workflow for identifying liver and kidney cancerous differentially expressed genes, and measured its total time execution on each single cloud provider and on all of them.

The next step is to study different scheduling strategies for the scheduling service, in order to improve its efficiency when choosing a cloud provider to execute jobs. Our results showed that the execution time is strongly affected by the file transfer time, implying that we have to carefully design the storage service; we plan to use data replication and fragmentation to address this problem. A fault tolerance service to check the cloud providers and other services status will be developed and evaluated. We also plan to use an adaptive fault monitoring algorithm, as proposed by [18, 30] and [70], which are more adaptable to be used in a large-scale distributed environment. It is also important to include a security service and an SLA service in the federated platform. Finally, we will investigate the use of a Workflow Management System (WfMS) in BioNimbus.

ACKNOWLEDGEMENT

M.E.M.T.Walter would like to thank to FINEP (Project number 01.08.0166.00) and all the authors would like to thank Daniel Saad for having written the Perl scripts for the workflow.

REFERENCES

1. 454 2012.. 454 life sciences. roche diagnostics corporation, http://www.454.com/.
2. Amazon 2012.. Amazon Elastic Compute Cloud (Amazon EC2), http://aws. amazon.com/ec2/.
3. Angiuoli, S. V., Matalka, M., Gussman, A., Galens, K., Vangala, M., Riley, D. R., Arze, C. & White, J. R. 2011.. Clovr: A virtual machine for automated and portable sequence analysis from the desktop using cloud computing, BMC Bioinformatics 12(356): 1–15.
4. Angiuoli, S. V., White, J. R., Matalka, M., White, O. & Fricke, W. F. 2011.. Resources and costs for microbial sequence analysis evaluated using virtual machines and cloud computing, PLoS ONE 6(10): e26624.
5. Apache 2011.. The Apache Software Foundation: Apache, http://couchdb. apache.org/.
6. Apache 2012.. Apache Hadoop, http://hadoop.apache.org/.
7. Balakrishnan, H., Kaashoek, M. F., Karger, D., Morris, R. & Stoica, I. 2003.. Looking up data in p2p systems, Commun. ACM 46(2): 43–48. URL: http://doi.acm.org/10.1145/606272.606299
8. Bermbach, D., Klems, M., Tai, S. & Menzel, M. 2011.. Metastorage: A federated cloud storage system to manage consistency-latency tradeoffs, IEEE International Conference on Cloud Computing (CLOUD), IEEE, pp. 452–459.
9. BGI 2012.. Bio-Cloud Computing, http:www.genomics.cn/en/navigation/ show_navigation?nid=4143.
10. Bhandari, A. & Singh, M. 2010.. 2010 the oauth 1.0 protocol, internet engineering task force (ietf), rfc:5849. URL: http://tools.ietf.org/html/rfc5849
11. Bittman, T. J. 2008.. Th evolution of the cloud computing market, http://blogs.gartner.com/thomas_bittman/2008/11/03/ the-evolution-of-the-cloud-computing-market.
12. Borges, C. A. L., Saldanha, H. V., Ribeiro, E., Holanda, M. T., Araujo, A. P. F. & Walter, M. E. M. T. 2012.. Task scheduling in a federated cloud infrastructure for bioinformatics applications, in INSTICC (ed.), 2nd International Conference on Cloud Computing and Services Science (), CLOSER 2012, Porto, Portugal, pp. 1–7.
13. Borthakur, D. 2008.. The Apache Software Foundation: HDFS

Architecture, http:// hadoop.apache.org/common/docs/r0.20.2/hdfs_design.pdf.

14. Buyya, R., Ranjan, R. & Calheiros, R. N. 2010.. Intercloud: Utility-oriented federation of cloud computing environments for scaling of application services, Proceedings of the 10th International Conference on Algorithms and Architectures for Parallel Processing (ICA3PP 2010), Springer, pp. 21–23.
15. Celesti, A., Tusa, F., Villari, M. & Puliafito, A. 2008.. How to enhance cloud architectures to enable cross-federation, 3rd IEEE International Conference on Cloud Computing (IEEE Cloud 2010), Miami, Florida, USA, pp. 337–345.
16. Chandra, T. D. & Toueg, S. 1996.. Unreliable failure detectors for reliable distributed systems, Journal of the ACM 43: 225–267.
17. Chang, F., Dean, J., Ghemawat, S., Hsieh, W., Wallach, D., Burrows, M., Chandra, T., Fikes, A. & Gruber, R. 2008.. Bigtable: A distributed storage system for structured data, ACM Transactions on Computer Systems (TOCS) 26(2): 1–26.
18. Chen, W. 2000.. On the quality of service of failure detectors, IEEE Transactions on Computers 51: 561–580.
19. Chodorow, K. & Dirolf, M. 2010.. MongoDB: the definitive guide, O'Reilly Media, Inc.
20. Clayman, S., Galis, A., Chapman, C., Toffetti, G., Rodero-Merino, L., Vaquero, L. M., Nagin, K. & Rochwerger, B. 2010.. Monitoring Service Clouds in the Future Internet, Towards the Future Internet - Emerging Trends from European Research, IOS Press.
21. Codehaus 2012.. Jackson Java JSON-Processor, http://jackson.codehaus.org.
22. Cooper, B., Ramakrishnan, R., Srivastava, U., Silberstein, A., Bohannon, P., Jacobsen, H., Puz, N., Weaver, D. & Yerneni, R. 2008.. PNUTS: Yahoo!'s hosted data serving platform, Proceedings of the VLDB Endowment, VLDB Endowment, pp. 1277–1288.
23. Crockford, D. 2006.. The application/json Media Type for JavaScript Object Notation (JSON), RFC 4627 (Informational). URL: http://www.ietf.org/rfc/rfc4627.txt
24. da Silva, C. A. R. F. O. 2011.. Data modeling with NoSQL: How, When and Why, Master's thesis, University of Porto.

25. Dean, J. & Ghemawat, S. 2004.. MapReduce: simplified data processing on large clusters, 6th Conference on Symposium on Operating Systems Design & Implementation, USENIX Association, Berkeley, CA, EUA, pp. 10–10.
26. DeCandia, G., Hastorun, D., Jampani, M., Kakulapati, G., Lakshman, A., Pilchin, A., Sivasubramanian, S., Vosshall, P. & Vogels, W. 2007.. Dynamo: amazon's highly available key-value store, SIGOPS Oper. Syst. Rev. 41(6): 205–220. URL: http://doi.acm.org/10.1145/1323293.1294281
27. Ekanayake, J., Gunarathene, T. & Qiu, J. 2011.. Cloud technologies for bioinformatics applications, IEEE Transactions on Parallel and Distributed Systems 22(6): 998–1011.
28. Elmroth, E. & Larsson, L. 2009.. Interfaces for placement, migration, and monitoring of virtual machines in federated clouds, Proceedings of the 2009 Eighth International Conference on Grid and Cooperative Computing, GCC '09, IEEE Computer Society, Washington, DC, USA, pp. 253–260. URL: http://dx.doi.org/10.1109/GCC.2009.36
29. Foster, I., Zhao, Y., Raicu, I. & Lu, S. 2008.. Cloud Computing and Grid Computing 360-Degree Compared, Grid Computing Environments Workshop GCE '08, pp. 1–10.
30. Hayashibara, N., Défago, X., & Rami Yared, T. K. 2004.. The phi Accrual Failure Detector, 23rd IEEE International Symposium on Reliable Distributed Systems, pp. 66–78.
31. Hayashibara, N., Défago, X., Yared, R. & Katayama, T. 2004.. The φ accrual failure detector, RR IS-RR-2004-010, Japan Advanced Institute of Science and Technology, pp. 1–16.
32. Hoffa, C., Mehta, G., Freeman, T., Deelman, E., Keahey, K. a. B. B. & Good, J. 2008.. On the use of cloud computing for scientific workflows, 3rd International Workshop on Scientific Workflows and Business Workflows Standards in e-Science, SWBES 2008, IEEE Digital Library, pp. 640–645.
33. Hong, D., Rhie, A., Park, S.-S., Lee, J., Ju, Y. S., Kim, S., Yu, S.-B., Bleazard, T., Park, H.-S., Rhee, H., Chong, H., Yang, K.-S., Lee, Y.-S., Kim, I.-H., Lee, J. S., Kim, J.-I. & Seo, J.-S. 2012.. FX: an RNA-Seq analysis tool on the cloud, Bioinformatics 28(5): 721–723. URL: http://dx.doi.org/10.1093/bioinformatics/bts023
34. Hunt, P., Konar, M., Junqueira, F. P. & Reed, B. 2010.. Zookeeper:

wait-free coordination for internet-scale systems, USENIX conference on USENIX annual technical conference, USENIXATC'10, USENIX Association, pp. 11–11.

35. Illumina 2012.. Illumina life sciences, http://www.illumina.com.
36. Inc., R. H. 2012.. Netty - the Java NIO Client Server Socket Framework, http://www. jboss.org/netty.
37. Jourdren, L., Bernard, M., Dillies, M.-A. A. & Le Crom, S. 2012.. Eoulsan: A Cloud Computing-Based Framework Facilitating High Throughput Sequencing Analyses., Bioinformatics (Oxford, England) . URL: http://dx.doi.org/10.1093/bioinformatics/bts165
38. Khetrapal, A. & Ganesh, V. 2006.. Hbase and hypertable for large scale distributed storage systems, Dept. of Computer Science, Purdue University, http://www.uavindia.com/ankur/downloads/HypertableHBaseEval2.pdf.
39. Kossmann, D., Kraska, T., Loesing, S., Merkli, S., Mittal, R. & Pfaffhauser, F. 2010.. Cloudy: a modular cloud storage system, Proceedings of the VLDB Endowment, VLDB Endowment, pp. 1533–1536.
40. Krampis, K., Booth, T., Chapman, B., Tiwari, B., Bicak, M., Field, D. & Nelson, K. 2012.. Cloud BioLinux: pre-configured and on-demand bioinformatics computing for the genomics community, BMC Bioinformatics 13(1): 42+. URL: http://dx.doi.org/10.1186/1471-2105-13-42
41. Lakshman, A. & Malik, P. 2010.. Cassandra: a decentralized structured storage system, SIGOPS Oper. Syst. Rev. 44(2): 35–40. URL: http://doi.acm.org/10.1145/1773912.1773922
42. Langmead, B., Hansen, K. & Leek, J. 2010.. Cloud-scale RNA-sequencing differential expression analysis with Myrna, Genome Biology 11(8): R83.
43. Langmead, B., Schatz, M. C., Lin, J., Pop, M. & Salzberg, S. 2009.. Searching for SNPs with cloud computing, Genome Biology 10(11): R134.
44. Langmead, B., Trapnell, C., Pop, M. & Salzberg, S. 2009.. Ultrafast and memory-efficient alignment of short DNA sequences to the human genome, Genome Biology 10(3): R25.
45. Larrea, M., Fernandez, A., Arevalo, S., Carlos, J. & Carlos, J. 2002.. Eventually consistent failure detectors, Brief Announcement, 14th

International Symposium on Distributed Computing (DISC'2000), pp. 326–327.

46. Li, R., Li, Y., Fang, X., Yang, H., Wang, J., Kristiansen, K. & Wang, J. 2009.. SNP detection for massively parallel whole-genome resequencing, Genome Research 19(6): 1124–1132. URL: http://dx.doi.org/10.1101/gr.088013.108
47. Marioni, J. C., Mason, C. E., Mane, S. M., Stephens, M. & Gilad, Y. 2008.. Rna-seq: An assessment of technical reproducibility and comparison with gene expression arrays,Genome Research 18: 1509–1517. URL: http://genome.cshlp.org/cgi/content/full/18/9/1509
48. Mell, P. & Grance, T. 2009.. The NIST Definition of Cloud Computing, National Institute of Standards and Technology 53(6): 50. URL: http://csrc.nist.gov/groups/SNS/cloud-computing/cloud-def-v15.doc
49. Oppenheimer, D., Albrecht, J., Patterson, D. & Vahdat, A. 2004.. Scalable wide-area resource discovery, Technical Report UCB/CSD-04-1334, EECS Department, University of California, Berkeley. URL: http://www.eecs.berkeley.edu/Pubs/TechRpts/2004/5465.html
50. Orend, K. 2010.. Analysis and classification of nosql databases and evaluation of their ability to replace an object-relational persistence layer, Master's thesis, Fakultät für Infoormatik, Technische Universität München.
51. Padhy, R., Patra, M. & Satapathy, S. 2011.. Rdbms to nosql: Reviewing some next-generation non-relational databases, International Journal of Advanced Engineering Science and Technologies 11(1): 15–30.
52. Pashalidis, A. & Mitchell, C. J. 2003.. A taxonomy of single sign-on systems, Information Security and Privacy, 8th Australasian Conference, ACISP 2003, Springer-Verlag, pp. 249–264.
53. Pratt, B., Howbert, J. J., Tasman, N. & Nilsson, E. J. 2011.. MR-Tandem: Parallel X!Tandem using Hadoop MapReduce on Amazon Web Services, Bioinformatics 8: 1–12.
54. Quinlan, A. R. & Hall, I. M. 2010.. BEDTools: a flexible suite of utilities for comparing genomic features, Bioinformatics 26(6): 841–842. URL: http://bioinformatics.oxfordjournals.org/content/26/6/841.abstract
55. R Development Core Team 2011.. R: A Language and Environment for Statistical Computing, R Foundation for Statistical Computing, Vienna, Austria. ISBN 3-900051-07-0. URL: http://www.R-project.org

56. Ranjan, R., Chan, L., Harwood, A., Karunasekera, S. & Buyya, R. 2007.. Decentralised resource discovery service for large scale federated grids, Proceedings of the Third IEEE International Conference on e-Science and Grid Computing, E-SCIENCE '07, IEEE Computer Society, Washington, DC, USA, pp. 379–387. URL: http://dx.doi.org/10.1109/E-SCIENCE.2007.27
57. Recordon, D. & Reed, D. 2006.. Openid 2.0: a platform for user-centric identity management, Proceedings of the second ACM workshop on Digital identity management, DIM '06, ACM, New York, NY, USA, pp. 11–16.
58. Redkar, T. 2011.. Windows Azure Platform, Vol. 1, 2th edn, Apress, Berkeley, CA, USA.
59. Reed, B. & Junqueira, F. P. 2008. A simple totally ordered broadcast protocol, 2nd Workshop on Large-Scale Distributed Systems and Middleware, LADIS'08, ACM, New York, NY, USA, pp. 2:1–2:6.
60. Robinson, M. & Oshlack, A. 2010.. A scaling normalization method for differential expression analysis of RNA-seq data, Genome Biology 11(3): R25+. URL: http://dx.doi.org/10.1186/gb-2010-11-3-r25
61. Saaty, T. L. 1990.. How to make a decision: The analytic hierarchy process, European Journal of Operational Research 48(1): 9 – 26.
62. Saldanha, H. V., Ribeiro, E., Holanda, M., Araujo, A., Rodrigues, G., Walter, M. E. M. T., Setubal, J. C. & Davila, A. 2011.. A cloud architecture for bioinformatics workflows, in L. INSTICC (ed.), 1st International Conference on Cloud Computing and Services Science, CLOSER 2011, pp. 1–8.
63. Sanderson, D. 2009.. Programming Google App Engine: Build and Run Scalable Web Apps on Google's Infrastructure, 1st edn, O'Reilly Media, Inc.
64. Schatz, M. C. 2009.. CloudBurst: Highly Sensitive Read Mapping with MapReduce, Bioinformatics 25: 1363–1369.
65. Smith, A., Xuan, Z. & Zhang, M. 2008.. Using quality scores and longer reads improves accuracy of Solexa read mapping, BMC Bioinformatics 9(1): 128.
66. Solid 2012.. Life technologies & applied biosystems, http://www.appliedbiosystems.com/.
67. Stoica, I., Morris, R., Liben-Nowell, D., Karger, D. R., Kaashoek, M. F., Dabek, F. & Balakrishnan, H. 2003.. Chord: a scalable peer-to-peer

lookup protocol for internet applications, IEEE/ACM Trans. Netw. 11(1): 17–32.

68. Tanenbaum, A. S. 2002.. Computer Networks (International Edition), fourth edn, Prentice Hall.
69. Tolone, W., Ahn, G.-J., Pai, T. & Hong, S.-P. 2005.. Access control in collaborative systems, ACM Comput. Surv. 37(1): 29–41.
70. van Renesse, R., Minsky, Y. & Hayden, M. 1998.. A gossip-style failure detection service, Proceedings of the IFIP International Conference on Distributed Systems Platforms and Open Distributed Processing, Middleware '98, Springer-Verlag, London, UK, pp. 55–70.
71. Vaquero, L. M., Rodero-Merino, L., Caceres, J. & Lindner, M. 2008.. A break in the clouds: towards a cloud definition, SIGCOMM Comput. Commun. Rev. 39: 50–55.
72. Wall, D., Kudtarkar, P., Fusaro, V., Pivovarov, R., Patil, P. & Tonellato, P. 2010.. Cloud computing for comparative genomics, BMC Bioinformatics 11(1): 259.
73. Wang, J., Varman, P. & Xie, C. 2011.. Optimizing storage performance in public cloud platforms, Journal of Zhejiang University-Science C 12(12): 951–964.
74. Wu, L. & Buyya, R. 2010.. Service level agreement (sla) in utility computing systems, CoRR abs/1010.2881.
75. Zhang, L., Gu, S., Wan, B., Liu, Y. & Azuaje, F. 2011.. Gene set analysis in the cloud, Bioinformatics 13: 1–10.

CHAPTER

2

HIERARCHICAL BIOLOGICAL PATHWAY DATA INTEGRATION AND MINING

Shubhalaxmi Kher[1], Jianling Peng[2], Eve Syrkin Wurtele[3] and Julie Dickerson[4]

[1] Electrical Engineering, Arkansas State University, USA

[2] Samuel Roberts Noble Foundation, USA

[3] Department of Genetics, Development and Cell Biology, Iowa State University, USA

[4] Electrical and Computer Engineering, Iowa State University, USA

INTRODUCTION

Biological pathway data is the key resource for biologists worldwide. Interestingly, most of these sources that generate, update, and analyze

Citation: Shubhalaxmi Kher, Jianling Peng, Eve Syrkin Wurtele and Julie Dickerson (November 28th 2012). "Hierarchical Biological Pathway Data Integration and Mining", Bioinformatics, Horacio Pérez-Sánchez, IntechOpen, DOI: 10.5772/49974.

data are open source. One of the observations that motivated this research work is that, the repositories of data created by a variety of laboratories and research units worldwide represent same pathways with significant details. Generally, if the pathway data has resulted from experimentation, then it is expected that across different resources, under similar conditions, pathways would be exactly identical and biologists may pickup from any source. Interestingly, almost all of the biological data sources refer to data integration of some kind. It may involve rigorous integration mechanisms within the data source and the purpose of integration may change the perspective of looking at the integration. These efforts in integration may be either local to the source or lack details associated with integration within a pathway, across pathways, or from various data sources etc. Further, the key attributes or design criteria may not be well documented and or may not be readily available to the biologist. In other words, the integration may be achieved as vertical integration (within the data source), or horizontal integration (across data sources). Since most of the extensively integrated data sources (plants or humans) like BioCyc-level-I, Reactome are human curated, it is hard to identify the integration done by the sources like; BioCyc. Also, on a similar note, it may not be apparent to find exactly when the data was integrated looking at a pathway.Data in general refers to a collection of results, including the results of experience, observation, or experiment, or a set of premises and can be utilized at the maximum when made available to all in a common format. Different organizations and research laboratories around the world store the data in their own formats; this diversity of data sources is caused due to many factors including lack of coordination among the organizations and research laboratories. These intellectual gaps can be bridged by adopting new technology, mergers, acquisitions, and geographic coordination of collaborating groups [1.. For the open source biological databases, it is common for the biologists and researchers to refer to many databases in order to pursue inference or analysis; though it is one of the most challenging tasks. Biological pathway data integration is aimed to work with repositories of data from a variety of sources. As such, two or more databases may not provide identical information for a given pathway, but integrating these two databases may yield a richer resource for analysis. Additionally, the conditions under which data is collected, either by experimentation or by collecting evidence of the published material, in either case the supporting references play a crucial role and is of interest to the biologists in making the analysis more meaningful. At present there are over 200 biological pathway databases. However, very few of them are independently created. Some of these databases may be derived from different data sources. Unfortunately, the documentation often does not reveal details of the data collection, sources, and dates. Further, the research groups involved in analysis of the data usually selectively use data from a single data source. For example, for yeast studies, the Saccharomyces Genome Database (SGD) is the reference for most analyses [2..

In case of biological pathway data, rapid accumulation of genomic and proteomic data have made two major bioinformatics problems apparent.

- The lack of communication between different bioinformatics data resources; whether they are databases or individual analysis programs.
- Biological data are hierarchical and highly related yet are conventionally stored separately in individual database and in different formats.
- Additionally, they are governed more by how data is obtained rather than by what they mean.

Most commercially available bioinformatics systems perform functional analysis using a single data source; an approach that emphasizes pathway mapping and relationship inference based on the data acquired from multiple data sources. Each pathway modality in the data has its own specific representation issues which must be understood before attempting to integrate across modalities.

OVERVIEW

There has been a dramatic increase in the number of large scale comprehensive biological databases that provide useful resources to the community like; Biochemical Pathways (KEGG, AraCyc, and MapMan), Protein Interactions (biomolecular interaction network database), or systems like; Dragon Plant Biology Explorer and Pathway Miner for integrating associations in metabolic networks and ontologies [3-8.. Other databases such as Regulon DB, PlantCARE, PLACE, EDP:Eurokaryotic promoter database, Transcription Regulatory Regions Database, Athamap, and TRANSFAC store information related to transcriptional regulation[9-15..

The aim of molecular biology is to understand the regulation of protein synthesis and its reactions to external and internal signals. All the cells in an organism carry the same genomic data, yet their protein makeup can be drastically different; both temporally and spatially, due to regulation. Protein synthesis is regulated by many mechanisms at its different stages. These include mechanisms for controlling transcription initiation, RNA splicing, mRNA transport, translation initiation, post-translational modifications, and degradation of mRNA/protein. One of the main junctions at which regulation occurs is mRNA transcription. A major role in this machinery is played by proteins themselves that bind to regulatory regions along the DNA, greatly affecting the transcription of the genes they regulate [16.. Friedman introduces a new approach for analyzing gene expression patterns that uncovers properties of the transcriptional program by examining statistical properties of dependence and conditional independence in the data.

For protein interactions, it is intended to connect related proteins and link biological functions in the context of larger cellular processes [17.. The content of these data sources typically complements the experimentally determined protein interactions with the ones that are predicted from gene proximity, fusion, co-expressed data, as well as those determined by using phylogenetic profiling. Each pathway modality in the data has its own specific representation issues which must be understood before integration across modalities is attempted. At present, the bioinformatics database owner only develops private system to provide user with data query and analysis services; such as NCBI develops Entrez database query system which is used on GenBank. European Molecular Biology Laboratory (EMBL) develops Sequence Retrieval Systems. The EMBL Nucleotide Sequence Database maintained at the European Bioinformatics Institute (EBI), incorporates, organizes, and distributes nucleotide sequences from public sources [18.. The database is a part of an international collaboration with DDBJ (Japan) and GenBank (USA). Data are exchanged between the collaborating databases on a daily basis to achieve optimal synchrony. The key point is how to share the heterogeneous databases and make a common query platform for users [19.

Friedman [16. describes early microarray experiments that examined few samples and mainly focused on differential display across tissues or conditions of interest. Such experiments collect enormous amounts of data, which clearly reflects many aspects of the underlying biological processes. An important challenge is to develop methodologies that are both statistically sound and computationally tractable for analyzing such data sets and inferring biological interactions from them. Most of the analysis tools currently used are based on clustering algorithms. The clustering algorithms attempt to locate groups of genes that have similar expression patterns over a set of experiments. Such analysis has proven to be useful in discovering genes that are co-regulated and/or have similar function. A more ambitious goal for analysis is to reveal the structure of the transcriptional regulation process. This is clearly a hard problem. Not only the current data is extremely noisy, but, mRNA expression data alone only gives a partial picture that does not reflect key events such as; translation and protein (in) activation. Finally, the amount of samples, even in the largest experiments in the foreseeable future, does not provide enough information to construct a fully detailed model with high statistical significance.

Some conventional bioinformatics approaches identify hypothetical interactions between proteins based on their three dimensional structures or by applying text mining techniques. Emerging protein chip technologies are expected to permit the large scale measurement of protein expression levels. Corresponding structural data are stored in data source such as protein data bank and represent invaluable sources of understanding of protein structures, functions and interactions. Successful use of high throughput protein interaction determination techniques such as yeast two hybrids, affinity purification followed by mass spectrometry and phage display has shifted research focus from a single gene/protein to more coherent network perspectives. Large scale protein-protein interaction data and their complexes are currently available for a number of organisms and data are stored in several interaction data sources such as BIND [6., DIP [20., IntAct [21., GRID [22. and MINT [23. that is all equipped with basic bioinformatics tools for protein network analysis and visualization. INCLUSive is a web portal and service registry for microarray and regulatory sequence analysis [24.. This provides a comprehensive index for all data integration research projects.The integration and management technique of heterogeneous sequence data from public sequence data source is widely used to manage diverse information and prediction. It is important for the biologists to investigate these heterogeneous sources and connect the public biological data source and retrieve sequences which are similar to sequences they have, and the results of their retrieval are used in homology research, functional analysis, and predication. However, there are few software packages available to deal with the sequence data in most biological laboratories and they are stored in file formats. File formats is another important issue for biological pathway data sources. XMl, SBML (systems biology markup language), KBML (KEGG), BSML (Bioinformatic Sequence Markup Language) based on XML, and a variety of versions of XML are used for representing the complex and hierarchical biological data. Each flat file from public biological database has different format. Recent tools which convert formats among standards are implemented in JAVA or Perl module. The constraints associated with biological pathway formats are the following;

- Conversion among different formats needs different parsers to extract the user interesting field.
- Formats can be modified anytime.
- Understand the range of field, its value is difficult, and data types in the same field in each format can be different.

From the discussions above, one of the major challenges of the modern bioinformatics research is therefore to store, process, and integrate biological data to understand the inner working of the cell defined by complex interaction networks. Additionally, the integration mechanisms may not register the important details like, copies of inputs files and time of integration along with the integrated output file.

In this chapter, issues related to biological pathway data integration system are discussed and a user friendly data integration algorithm across data sources for biological pathway, particularly, metabolic pathway as a case is presented. i.e. the data integration (BPDI) algorithm that integrates pathway information across data sources and also extracts the abstract information embedded within them are addressed. Today, a bioinformatics information system typically deals with large data sets reaching a total volume of about one terabyte [25. Such a system serves many purposes;

- User can select the data sources and assign confidence to each selected data source
- It organizes existing data to facilitate complex queries
- It infers relationships based on the stored data and subsequently predicts missing attribute values and incoming information based on multidimensional data.
- Data marts (extension of data warehouse) support different query requests.

DATA MANAGEMENT AND INTEGRATION

The Pathway Resource List contains over 150 biological pathway databases and is growing [26.. Usually, first step for the user is to identify a subset of these data sources for integration. To consolidate all the knowledge for a particular organism, extract the pathways from each database need to be extracted and transformed into a standard data representation before integration. Representation of the pathway data in each data source poses another challenge as each pathway modality has its own specific representation issues which must be understood before attempting integration across modalities. For example, metabolic pathways, signal transduction pathways, protein-protein interaction, gene regulation etc. Commonly employed styles of data integration may be implemented in different contexts and under requirements, in order to reuse the data across applications for research collaboration. Some of the data integration and management efforts are presented in [27-32.. Several major approaches have been proposed for data integration, which can be roughly classified into five groups [33-34. namely; data warehousing, federated data basing, service oriented integration, semantic integration and wiki-based integration. Across all of these groups, to a significant extent, an increasingly important component of data integration is the community effort in developing a variety of biomedical ontologies to deal in a more specific manner with the technicality and globalist of descriptors and identifiers of information that has to be shared and integrated across various resources. Variety of approaches for data integration is discussed below.

Data Warehousing

The data warehouse approach offers a "one-stop shop" solution to ease access and management of a large variety of biological data from different data sources. The user does not need to access many web sites for multiple data sources. Despite its advantages, the data warehouse approach has a major problem; it requires continuous and often human-guided updates to keep the data comprehensive of the evolution of data sources, resulting in high costs for maintenance. Many biological data sources change their data structures roughly twice a year.

Data integration with Federated Approach

Unlike data warehousing (with its focus on data translation), federated data basing focuses on query translation. The federated database fetches the data from the disparate data sources and then displays the fetched data for its user base. Queries in federated databases are executed within remote data sources and results displayed in federated databases are extracted remotely from the data sources. Due to this capability, federated data basing has two major advantages.

- Federated databases can be regarded as an on-demand approach to provide immediate access to up-to-date data deposited in multiple data sources.
- Compared with data warehousing, federated data basing does not replicate data in data sources; therefore, it presents relatively inexpensive costs for storage and creation. However, federated data basing still has to update its query translation to keep pace with data access methods at diverse remote data sources.

Service –Oriented Approach

A decentralized approach is also being developed, in which individual data sources agree to open their data via Web Services (WS). The service-oriented approach enables data integration from multiple heterogeneous data sources through computer interoperability. The service-oriented approach features data integration through computer-to-computer communication via Web API and up-to-date data retrieval from diverse data sources. Heterogeneous data integration requires that many data sources should become service providers by opening their data via WS and by standardizing data identities and nomenclature to ease data exchange and analysis.

Semantic Web

Most web pages in biological data sources are designed for human reading. RDF provides standard formats for data interchange and describes data as a simple statement, containing a set of triples: a subject, a predicate, and an object. Any two statements can be linked by an identical subject or object. OWL builds on RDF and Uniform Resource Identifier (URI) and describes data structure and meaning based on ontology, which enables automated data reasoning and inferences by computers. Application of semantic Web technologies is a significant advancement for bioinformatics, enabling automated data processing and reasoning. The semantic integration uses ontologies for data description and thus represents ontology-based integration. [27. Reviews the current development of semantic network technologies and their applications to the integration of genomic and proteomic data. His work elaborates on applying a semantic network approach to modeling complex cell signaling pathways and simulating the cause-effect of molecular interactions in human macrophages. [31. Illustrates his approach by comparing federated approach versus warehousing versus semantic web using multiple sources.

Wiki-based Integration

A weakness common to all the above approaches is that the quantity of users' participations in the process is inadequate. With the increasing volume of biological data, data integration inevitably will require a large number of users' participations. A successful example that harnesses collective intelligence for data aggregation and knowledge collection is Wikipedia: an online encyclopedia that allows any user to create and edit content. It is infeasible to integrate such large amounts of data into a single point (such as a data warehouse). Data sources are developed for different purposes and fulfill different functions. Therefore, it is promising to establish an efficient way for data exchange among these distributed and heterogeneous data sources. However, a dozen of data sources are designed merely for data storage, but not for data exchange.

Survey of Pathway Databases and Integration Efforts

Table 1 below shows various data integration efforts and projects for biological pathways worldwide.

Table 1. Various Data integration Efforts

Biochemical pathways	Description
BRITE	Bio molecular Relations in Information Transmission and Expression
EcoCyc/MetaCyc	Encyclopaedia of E. coli genes and metabolism; Metabolic encyclopedia
EMP	Metabolic pathways
KEGG	Kyoto encyclopaedia of genes and genomes
Biochemical Pathways	Enzyme database and link to biochemical pathway map
Interactive Fly	Biochemical pathways in Drosophila
Metabolic Pathway	Metabolic pathways of biochemistry
Molecular interaction	Kohn molecular interaction maps
Malaria parasite	Malaria Parasite metabolic pathways
aMAZE	Protein function and biochemical pathways project at EBI
PathDB	Metabolic pathway information
UM-BBD	Microbial bio catalytic reactions and biodegradation pathways primarily for xenobiotic, chemical compounds
WIT	Function assignments to genes and the development of metabolic models
THCME Medical Biochemistry	Description of several metabolic and biochemical pathways
Signaling pathways	
Apoptosis	Pathways of apoptosis at KEGG
BBID	Database of images of biological pathways, macromolecular structures, gene families, and cellular relationships
BioCarta	Several signalling pathways
BIND	The bio molecular interaction network database

CSNDB	Cell signalling networks database
GeneNet	Information on gene networks, groups of co-ordinately working genes
GeNet	Information on functional organization of regulatory gene networks
SPAD	Signalling pathway database
STKE	Pathway information
TransPath	Pathways involved in the regulation of transcription factors
Protein-protein interactions	
Blue Print	Biological interaction database
CYGD	Protein-protein interaction map at Comprehensive Yeast Genome Database
CytoScape	Visualization and analysis of biological network
DIP	Database of interacting proteins
GenMAPP	Gene Map Annotator and Pathway Profiler
GRID	The General Repository for Interaction Datasets
Proteome Bio knowledge	Biological information about proteins comprise Incyte's Proteome Bio Knowledge Library
Protein Interaction Domains	Signal transduction
Reactome	A knowledgebase of biological processes
Yeast Interaction Pathway	PathCalling Yeast Interaction Database at Curagen

Other efforts towards designing new applications for data mining and integration at the K.U.Leuven Center for Computational Systems Biology include;

- aBandApart (2007): A software to mine MEDLINE abstracts to annotate human genome at the level of cytogenic bands.
- ReModiscovery (2006): An intuitive algorithm to correlate regulatory programs with regulators and corresponding motifs to a set of co-expressed genes
- LOOP (2007): A toll to analyze ArrayCGH loop designs. ArrayCGH is a microarray technology that can be used to detect aberrations in the ploidy of DNA segments in the genome of patients with congenital anomalies.
- SynTReN (2006): A generator of synthetic gene expression data for design and analysis of structure learning algorithms.
- BlockAligner (2005): Provides an API in R to query BioMart databases such as Ensemble.
- BlockSampler (2005): Finds conserved blocks in the upstream region of sets of orthologous genes.
- M@cBETH (2005) (a Microarray Classification Benchmarking Tool on a host server): Web service offers the microarray community a simple tool for making optimal two class predictions.
- TxTGate (2004): A literature index database designed towards the summarization and analysis of groups of genes based on text.

- Endeavour is a software application for the computational prioritization of test genes based on training genes using different information sources such as MEDLINE abstracts and LocusLink textual description, gene ontology, annotation, BIND protein interactions, and Transcription Factor Binding Sites (TFBS).
- TOUCAN2 (2004): A workbench for regulatory sequence analysis on metazoan genomes: Comparative genomics detection of significant transcription factor binding sites and detection of cis-regulatory modules in sets of coexpressed/ coregulated genes.
- INCLUSive (2003): A suit of algorithms and tools for the analysis of gene expression data and the directory of cis-regulatory sequence elements.
- Adaptive Quality-Based Clustering (AQBC) (2002): AQBC is a heuristic, iterative twostep algorithm to cluster gene expression data.
- MotifSampler (2001): Finds over represented motifs in the upstream region of a set of co-regulated genes.

Types of pathways

Biological networks are studied and modeled at different description levels establishing different pathway types, For example; metabolic pathways describe the conversion of metabolites by enzyme-catalyzed chemical reactions given by their stoichiometric equations, such as the main pathways of the energy household as Glycolysis or Pentose Phosphate pathway. Another pathway type is signal transduction pathways, also known as information metabolism, explaining how cells receive, process, and responds to information from the environment. A brief description about various types of pathways is given below.

A. **Metabolic Pathways** describe the network of enzyme-catalyzed reactions that release energy by breaking down nutrients (catabolism) and building up the essential compounds necessary for growth (anabolism). Experimentally determined metabolic pathways have established for a few model organisms, but most metabolic pathways databases contain pathway data that has been computationally inferred from the genomes annotations. Because most genome annotations are incomplete, metabolic pathway databases contain pathway holes which can only be addressed by experiment or computational inference. A good test of a reconstructed metabolic network is to ask if it can produce the set of essential compounds necessary for growth, given a known minimal nutrient set. To solve this problem, metabolism can be represented as a bipartite directed graph, where one set of nodes represents metabolites, the other set represents biochemical reactions with labeled edges used to indicate relationships between nodes (reaction X produces metabolite Y, or metabolite Y is-consumed-by reaction X.

B. **Gene Regulatory Networks** describe the network of transcription factors that bind regulatory regions of specific genes and activate or repress their transcription. Gene regulatory networks or transcription networks have been found to contain recurring biochemical wiring patterns, termed network motifs, which carry out key functions. How does one find the most significant recurring network motif in a given transcriptional network? To answer this question, transcription networks can be described as directed graphs, in which nodes are genes, and edges represent transcription interactions, where a transcription factor encoded by one gene modulates and transcription rate of the second gene.

C. Signaling Pathways describe biochemical reactions for information transmission and processing. Unlike metabolic pathways that catalyze small molecule reactions, signaling pathways involve the post translational modification of proteins leading to the downstream activation of transcriptional factors. They are often formed by cascades of activated/deactivated proteins or protein complexes. Such signal transduction cascades may be seen as molecular circuits which mediate the sensing and processing of stimuli. They detect, amplify and integrate diverse external signals to generate responses, such as changes in enzyme activity, gene expression, or ion channel activity. Integration of signaling pathways poses a greater challenge than with metabolic pathways because of diversity of representation schemes for signaling. Some Signaling databases like; PATIKA [35. and INHO [36. use compound graphs to represent signaling pathways, while other object oriented databases use inheritance to establish relationships between post translational modifications of proteins.

D. Protein-Protein Interaction: In proteomic analysis, target genes are used as bait in immuno-precipitation to identify potential binding patterns in cell lysate. The higher level databases such as; KEGG

[3., TRANSPATH [37., ReactomeSTKE [38., and MetaCyc [39. networks of interacting proteins with definite cellular processes including metabolism, signal transduction and gene regulation. These resources typically represent biological information in the form of individual pathway diagrams summarizing experimental results collected during years of research on particular cellular functions. Currently, no single method is capable of predicting all possible protein interactions and such integrative resources as SPRING and predictome combine multiple theoretical approaches to increase prediction accuracy and coverage. A problem with these networks is the high number of false alarms.

E. Ontology Vocabulary Mapping: Ontology provides a formal written description of a specific set of concepts and their relationships in a particular domain. GO ontology has three categories molecular function, biological process and cellular composition. Integration of signaling pathways poses a greater challenge than with metabolic pathways because of the diversity of representation schemes for signaling.

Integration issues

Biological plant pathway data integration is a multi-step process. It includes integration of various types of pathways, interactions, and gene expression. On another level, it includes various species and different databases. A hierarchical pathway data integration scheme is presented in Figures 1 and 2 below.

Each database also defines supporting evidence codes specifically defined to consider criteria for selection, however may not be explicitly illustrated and that may not be similar across various sources. This heterogeneity in evidence codes and their representation needs consideration [40. Since the evidence code may originate as a result of experimentation or as evidence from published text, integration of the plant pathway data across databases involves standardizing the evidence code prior to the integration.

The first step is to integrate the evidence codes for a given pathway across database. Biological databases are results of experiments carried out with different conditions and controls, mostly open source, and employs a variety of formats [41. Integrating such databases is a multi-step procedure and involves handling the complexities associated with heterogeneous data integration.

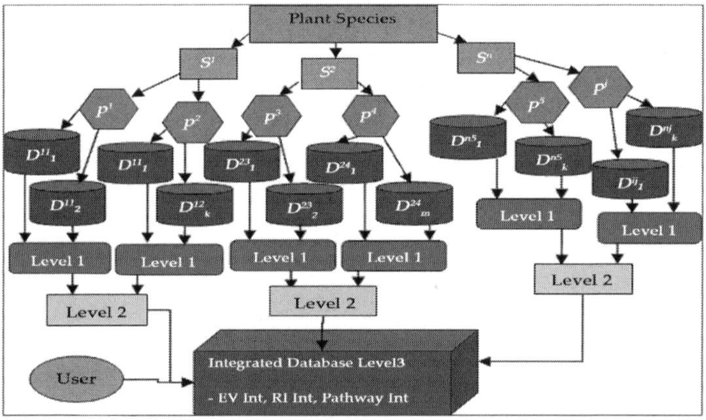

Figure 1. Hierarchical Pathway data Integration Scheme.

A. Ontology Development

Since isolation of ontologies complicates data integration, so in order to use ontologies at their full potential, concepts, relations, and axioms must be shared when possible. Domain ontologies must also be anchored to an upper ontology in order to enable the sharing and reuse of knowledge.

B. Synonym Integration

While integrating information about a pathway from a database, entities require independent approach. One such entity is synonym. Each database lists a set of synonyms that need integration to configure a pool of synonyms without causing duplication. In the data integration platform developed the synonym integration has issues like avoiding duplication and accommodating number of synonyms associated with one entity. Some pathways may include two compounds with different names but having same empirical formula. In such cases integration is challenging as biologists may be further interested in reviewing the chemical structure along with the integrated output. However, almost all biological pathways are vertically extendable and can associate further details. The point here is to include all the salient features (from a biologist's standpoint) of the pathway. There is no thumb rule to define biologist's interests.

C. Evidence Codes and issues

For defining an evidence code with an entity, granularity is another variable. Depending on the database, EV may be either for an entity within a pathway such as a gene, a compound, reaction or enzyme or for the pathway itself. In other words, many databases use the same evidence code for an entire pathway and map that code to each interaction in the pathway. Others assign different EV codes to each interaction and sometimes to each compound or gene.

The Gene Ontology (GO) defines a set of thirteen EVs that assign evidence to gene function. BioCyc defines a class hierarchy structure of four basic EVs with subclasses. MetNetDB incorporates four EVs [42.. KEGG defines only one EV. Ideally, the EVs also reflect on the individual nodes within a specific pathway. Figure 2 depicts the data integration platform highlighting multiple data sources and integration based on user inputs.

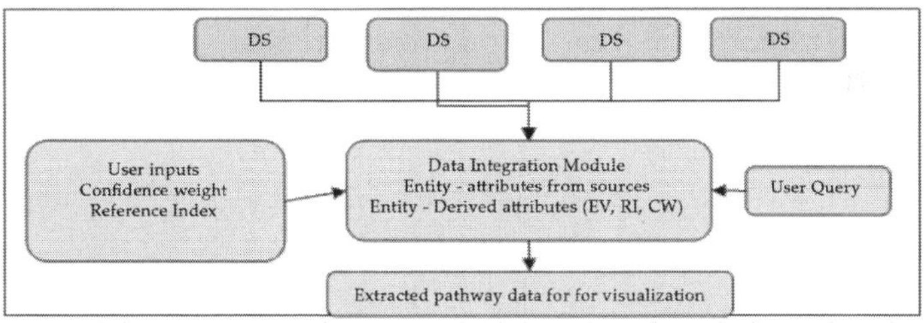

Figure 2. Data Integration Platform.

1. Many databases use the same evidence code for an entire pathway and map that code to each interaction in the pathway. Others assign codes to each interaction and sometimes each compound or gene. In other words, the granularity to which we can assign an EV may be either an entity such as a gene, a compound, reaction or enzyme within or across the pathway itself. The Gene Ontology (GO) defines a set of thirteen EVs that assign evidence to gene function [43.. BioCyc defines a class hierarchy structure of four basic EVs with subclasses [17.. MetNetDB incorporates four EVs. KEGG defines only one EV. Ideally, the EVs also reflect on the individual nodes within a specific pathway.
2. Since pathway information cannot be assessed with any reliability, it is hard to assign a measure of the orrectness/authenticity to any one database. We propose assignment to be user selective to resolve the issue. To combine the information, a heuristic rule set computes the composite EVs for the integrated database. The unification can be done using any one EV code set as a key. Since each database follows their own standard, it is likely that EVs may not find a perfect match among the databases or that there may be more than one likely match. To handle these situations, two

matching sets, a perfect match and a likely match are considered. The EVs to find a match for IEP and ND from GO in EV set above with those in BioCyc result in more than one likely match {GO: IEP → BioCyc: EV1, BioCyc: EV2}.

3. Integrated Evidence Code (EVint) for Perfect Matches: The EV codes encompass the quantitative information giving an insight into how the data was obtained. They define the conditions/constraint associated with obtaining the data.
4. Computing the Reference Index (RIint) For biological databases, the pathway information is mostly inferred by the curators based on experimental, computational, literature or other evidence. The references associated with the database are mostly accounted as a measure of support for the data. We introduce a qualitative approach to associate the references supporting the pathway or organism (or compounds or reactions). The reference index RIint is computed using a heuristic:
   1. For Rank = High, Ignore VF.
   2. For Rank = Low, Use only VF.
   3. For all other combinations of Rank and VF, compute the average.

Citations may be a robust way of supporting the claim in a database. However, some journals are ranked over other journals and citations from those journals will be valued more than citations in other sources. To accommodate this, we associate ranks with the journals. The Rank specifies the order of importance of journal as designated by the user. Additionally, we classify citations based on both the journal Rank and the value factor (VF). Finally, based on the Rank and VF, the Reference index (RI) is computed.

EVIDENCE CODES INTEGRATION ALGORITHM

Given: Set of n databases {D1, D2, D3, D4,……, Dn},

(For illustration, only three data sources namely, Bio-Cyc, KEGG and MetNetDB are considered)

User input: Confidence weight (CW)

List: Evidence Codes (EVi) for the object/entity (Ei) among the databases (Di), for example; D1/E1 {EV1}, D2/E1 {EV2},….

The steps below list the mapping process.

Step 1. For a given pathway/organism/entity,

List: EV codes across the databases. (See Tables III(a) and III(b))

Assign: Direct = 1.0; Indirect = 0.8; Computational =0.6; Hypothetical = 0.5.

Step 2. EV Unification (Rule Set –I)

BioCyc is a collection of 371 pathway/genome databases. Each pathway/genome database in the BioCyc collection describes the genome and metabolic pathways of a single organism. It considers a class hierarchy with four main classes. Since BioCyc and MetNetDB virtually use the same number of EV codes, the mapping is framed considering four major EV codes. KEGG uses only one EV for pathways namely 'manually entered from published materials'. The EV code for KEGG to Direct is mapped using the rules like;

If Di = BioCyc/AraCyc/MetaCyc, and EV = EV-Exp, then Change EV = Direct

Unification of the EV codes for the databases is based on the expert knowledge. EV code mapping is done with respect to a reference data source and unified according to the set of rules above

Step 3. Confidence Weight (CWi) Assignment

Researchers typically have databases that they treat as favored sources for different types of information. Since there is no precise rule for deciding which database is more correct and up to date, a user defined score, a confidence weight (CW) is applied. The EV mapping process is interactive and provides flexibility in choice for databases. Confidence is defined as,

CWi = {Very Strong, Strong, Moderate, Poor, Very Poor}

For example: CW KEGG: Strong, CWBioCyc: Normal

Step 4. EVint (Rule Set-II)

Using heuristic rules, integrated EVcode is calculated.

Step 5. Decode EVint value

The EV value from Step 4 is decoded using:

$EVint = \Sigma\ (CWi^{*}\ EV)/|i| = x$

Step 6. Rank Index

- Rank the journals in their order of importance.
- Make an ordered list of journals assigning Rank.
- Rank the conferences in order of their importance.
- Make an ordered list of conferences.
- - Assign:

If the publication in not in the list, Then, Rank = low

Else, Rank = as defined by the list

Step 7. Value Factor (VF)

The VF measures support for the entity using the publication evidence. This is a quantitative index with a temporal function.

For t = current year, compute VF (t) = |P (t-2)| / |P| where

|P (t-2)| = Number of publications in the last (t-2) years for Di, and

|P| = Total number of publications listed in Di.

Step 8. Reference Index (RIint)

- Compute RI for {D1,...Dn} given by,

RIi{t} = f {Rank, VF}

- Compute RIint for a pathway as;

RIint = max {RIi}

Integration models

Data integration aims to work with repositories of data from a variety of sources. As such, two databases may not provide identical information, and integrating these two databases may yield a richer resource for analysis.

The conditions under which data is collected and the supporting references play a crucial role in making the analysis more meaningful. So far, the integration approaches have focused on different types of pathways. The same pathway can have different representations in different databases.For example, a known pathway like Glycolysis is represented in different ways in KEGG and BioCyc as shown in Figure 3. A universal tool to integrate all types of pathways may not be a focus. Additionally, different databases employ various data representations that may not provide easy user access or user friendly. Figure 3(a) and 3(b) illustrate representational difference between two data sources for the same pathway. Various data integration models are defined below.

- Syntactic Networks: Syntactic networks adhere to the syntax of a set of words as given by the representation of the data and do not interpret the meaning associated. Syntactic heterogeneity is a result of differences in representation format of data.
- Semantic Networks (SN): Semantic heterogeneity is a result of differences in interpretation of the 'meaning' of data. Semantic models aim to achieve semantic interoperability, a dynamic computational capability to integrate and communicate both the explicit and implicit meanings of digital content without human intervention.
- Several features of SN make it particularly useful for integrating biological data include, ability to easily define an inheritance hierarchy between concepts in a network format, allow economic information storage and deductive reasoning, represent assertions and cause effect through abstract relationships, cluster related information for fast retrieval, and adapt to new information by dynamic modification of network structures [44.. An important feature of SN is the ease and speed to retrieve information concerning a particular concept. The use of semantic relationships ensures clustering together related concepts in a network. For example, protein synonyms, functional descriptions, coding sequences, interactions, experimental data or even relevant research articles can all be represented by semantic agents, each of which is directly linked to the corresponding protein agent.

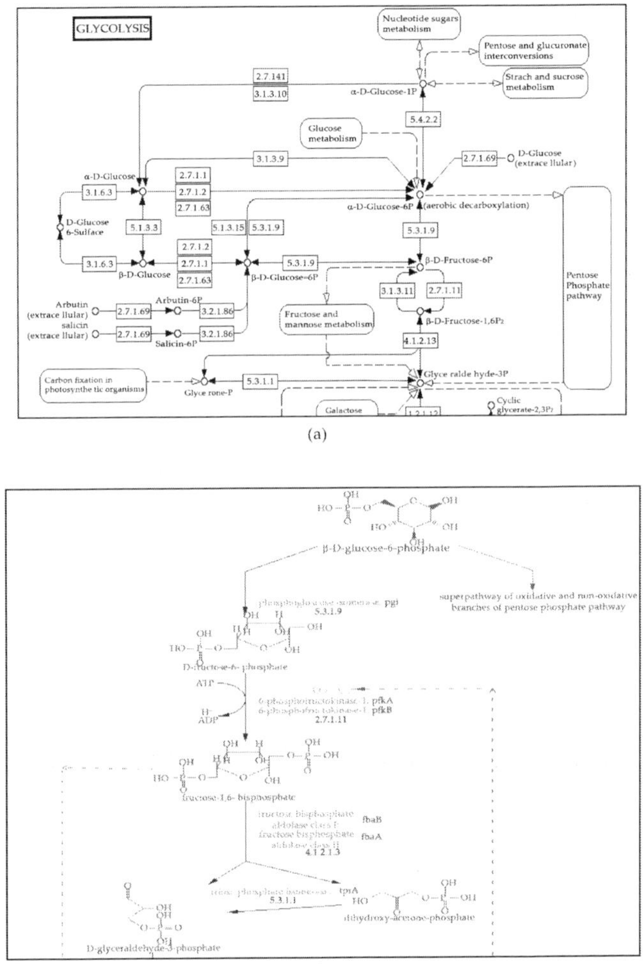

Figure 3. (a) Pathway from KEGG- Glycolysis (b) BioCyc- Glycolysis

Biological information can be retrieved effectively through simple relationship traversal starting from a query agent in the semantic network. Two approaches primarily in practice for SNs are;

1. memory-mapped data structure and
2. indexing flat files.

In the memory-mapped data structure approach, subsets of data from various sources are collected, normalized, and integrated in memory for quick access. While this approach performs actual data integration and addresses the problem of poor performance in the federated approach, it requires additional calls to traditional relational databases to integrate descriptive data. While data cleaning is being performed on some of the data sources, it is not being done across all sources or in the same place. This makes it difficult to quickly add new data sources. In the indexing flat files approach, flat text files are indexed and linked thus supporting fast query performance.

- Causal Models: A causal model is an abstract model that uses cause and effect logic to describe the behaviour of a system. Ex: Expression Quantitative Trait Loci: (eQTLs) eQTL analysis is to study the relationship between genome and transcriptome. Gene expression QTLs that contain the gene encoding the mRNA are distinguished from other transacting eQTLs. eQTL mapping tries to find genomic variation to explain expression traits. One difference between eQTL mapping and traditional QTL mapping is that, traditional mapping study focuses on one or a few traits, while in most of eQTL studies, thousands of expression traits get analyzed and thousands of QTLs are declared
- Context likelihood of relatedness (CLR): It uses transcriptional profiles of an organism across a diverse set of conditions to systematically determine transcriptional regulatory interactions. CLR is an extension of the relevance network approach. (http://gardnerlab.bu.edu/software&tools.html). [34. Presented architecture for contextbased information integration to solve semantic difference problem, defined some novel modeling primitives of translation ontology and propose an algorithm for translation.
- Bayes Networks (BN): Probabilistic graphical models that represent a set of variables and their probabilistic independencies. For example, a BN could represent the probabilistic relationships between diseases and symptoms. Given symptoms, the network can be used to compute the probabilities of the presence of various diseases. Bayes networks focus on score-based structure inference. Available heuristic search strategies include simulated annealing and greedy hill-climbing, paired with evaluation of a single random local move or all local moves at each step. [45. Bases his approach on the wellstudied statistical tool of Bayesian networks [46.. These networks represent the dependence structure between multiple interacting quantities (e.g., expression levels of different genes). His approach, probabilistic in nature, is capable

of handling noise and estimating the confidence in the different features of the network.

- Hidden Markov Models (HMM): HMM is a statistical model that assumes the system being modeled to be a Markov process with unknown parameters, and determines the hidden parameters from the observable parameters. The extracted model parameters can then be used to perform further analysis, for example for pattern recognition applications. An HMM can be considered as the simplest dynamic Bayesian network. HMMs are being applied to the analysis of biological sequences, in particular DNA since 1998 [47..

Need to use open grid service architecture ogsa-dai for data access and integration

Apart from the ubiquitous call for more functionality, bioinformatics projects with commercial users/partners are very anxious about the security of their data. The issue is further complicated by the lack of coherent security models with the evolving WS-RF and WS-I specifications which OGSA-DAI now supports. This issue needs to be resolved if bioinformatics projects with commercial users/partners are not to be deterred from adopting the product despite its utility. In contrast to the diversity of its data resources, a limited range of operations on these resources is typically required. For instance, one operation is to create a study data set by aggregating data from iterative searches of remote data collections using the same taxonomy object (representing a species or other group) as the search parameter [48..

Handling the heterogeneity in data representation among databases

For biological plant pathways, various databases incorporate information about an entity/reaction/pathway to a level of detail and define their own data format. This includes information like number of fields, column label/tag, pathway name(s), etc. At the outset, common information across the tables may look limited and hard to extract mainly because of the tag or synonyms (other names) of pathway. Before proceeding for integration of a pathway across data sources following steps need to be carried out. For biological pathway integration, following needs to be considered.

- What is the aim of integration? To query autonomous and heterogeneous data sources through a common, uniform schema (TARGET SCHEMA).
- How will the integrated data be used?
- Resolving various conflicts between source and target schema.
- Offering a common interface to access integrated information.
- Preserving the autonomy of participating systems.
- Easily integrating data sources without major modification.
- Is it within a single data source or across sources?
- Does it support web based integration?
- Does it encompass the dynamic nature of the data?
- What are the data, source, user models, and assumptions underlying the design of integration system?

Specific data integration problems in the biological field include:

- Some biological data sources do not provide an expressive language
- Derived wrapper (operate in two modes)
    1. Traditional wrapper
    2. Virtual source that buffers the execution result of a local application
- Data Model Inconsistencies requires complex data transformation coding
- Data Schema Inconsistencies
- Schema matching: error-prone task
- Mapping info: systematically managed
- Domain Expert participation
- Along with the data schema consistencies there may be data level inconsistencies such as:
- Data conflict as each object has its own data type, and may be represented in different formats
- Different Query Capabilities affect the query optimization of data integration system
- Miscellaneous: Network environment, Security

- **File formats:** For biological pathways, various data sources incorporate information about an entity/reaction/pathway to a level of detail and define their own data format. This includes information like number of fields, column label/tag, pathway name(s), etc. At the outset, common information across the tables may look limited and hard to extract mainly because of the tag or synonyms (other names) of pathway. One of the other important differences in the way these data sources are developed lies in the synonym representations. Some of the data sources limit the synonyms to 10 others may not result into may be over 40 synonyms. While we look at the data integration mechanism, if the names of the compounds do not match, then the search should be carried forward with the list of synonyms. In integrating different data bases this will take different search time. Also, since the field names (compound names) did not match, the search must unify the field names and generate a new list of synonyms.
- **Granularity of information**: Different pathway databases may model pathway data with different levels of details. This primarily depends on the process definition. For example, one database might treat processes together as a single process, while another database might treat these as separate processes. Also, one database might include specific steps to be part of the process, while another database might not consider these steps. Additionally, the levels of details associated with a certain data base necessitate pathway data modeling with different levels of granularity. Different pathway data formats (e.g., SBML and BIND XML) have been used to represent data with different levels of details. A semantic net based approach to data integration is proposed in [49..
- **Heterogeneous formats:** As the eXtensible Markup Language (XML) has become the lingua franca for representing different types of biological data, there has been a proliferation of semantically-overlapping XML formats that are used to represent diverse types of pathway data. Examples include the XML-derivatives KGML, SBML, CellML, PSI MI, BIND XML, and Genome Object Net XML. Efforts have been underway to translate between these formats (e.g., between PSI MI and BIND XML, and between Genome Object Net and SBML). However, the complexity of such a pair-wise translation approach increases

dramatically with a growing number of different pathway data formats. To address this issue, a standard pathway data exchange format is needed. While the Resource Description framework (RDF) is an important first step towards the unification of XML formats in describing metadata (ontologies), it is not expressive enough to support formal knowledge representation [50.. To address this problem, more sophisticated XML-based ontological languages such as the Web Ontology Language (OWL) have been developed. An OWL-based pathway exchange standard, called BioPAX, has been released to the research community [51..

BIOLOGICAL PATHWAY DATA INTEGRATION

An integration model may serve as a tool to the user for a specific type of pathway. An algorithm for integration is presented next.

Metabolic Pathways: Integrating pathways from different data sources for the same species extract similar structures in them as the first step; this step integrates vertically given pathway within a species across data sources. (Database is the variable) this includes sorting a graph G (V, E) for common V's and E's in G_i (V_i, E_i) and G_j (V_j, E_j). In the discussion that follows, integrating pathway as the TCA cycle given by two data sources namely; KEGG ($D^{ij}1$) and BioCyc ($D^{ij}2$) for E. coli K-12 is considered. For metabolic pathways the details associated with each graph include the nodes and edges as given below. For Protein-Protein interaction the nomenclature and associated fields for nodes and edges may change. However, it is possible to come up with a structure that can describe the Protein-Protein interactions or signal transduction pathways.

- Node: Biological Name, ID, Neighbor, Type, Context, Pathway, Data Source, PubList, SynList, empirical formula, Structure
- Edge: EdgeID, EdgeSource, EdgeDest, Reactiontype (Rev/ Irreversible), Data Source, Enzyme, Genes

Signal Transduction Pathways: The information contained in signal transduction pathways is not similar to the metabolic pathways. In signal transduction pathways, the interactions can be represented as a class hierarchy. Our aim is also to integrate a sample pathway like insulin from sources like KEGG, SPAD to see the performance of our algorithm. Interestingly, SPAD assigns evidence code to the edges (interactions) and KEGG assigns only one evidence code to the pathway (nodes and edges). The format of the table for integration is given above. Before integration information associated with every object (node) and edge (interactions) should be considered. Before proceeding for integration of a pathway across data sources following steps need to be carried out.

Step 1

- Check for the pathway name across the input pathways.

- If a synonym matches then, go to step 2 else, search for synonyms of pathway name.

Step 2

1. Choose the integrated output table format as the reference (number of columns, column tag)
2. Check for number of columns in the output table.
3. Match each of the column names in the output table with each of the column names in the input data files,
   - are same then continue, else see alternate tag for the column, and match them.
4. Match order in the output table format with the inputs from different sources

   - If the order matches, then continue, else reorder the columns as given in output table.
5. Check for number of columns in the output table,
   - If the number of columns is not same, then append the table with new columns.

Step 3

- Apply EV and Integration algorithms

The notations used in our algorithm are presented next.

NOTATIONS

- $S = \{s^1, s^2, s^3, \ldots s^n\}$ is set of species. (1)
- $P^{ij} = \{p^{i1}, p^{i2}, \ldots p^{ip}\}$ is a set of pathways within s^i (2)

Consider a tuple $(S^i, (P^{ij}, (D^{ij}_i))$ (3)

Where, $D^{ij}_k = \{d^{ij}_1, d^{ij}_2, d^{ij}_3, \ldots d^{ij}_k\}$ is a set of 'k' data sources for (S^i, P^{ij}) (4)

- $s^1 = \{(s^1, p^{1j} (D^{1j}_k)\} = \{(s^1, p^{1j}, d^{1j}_1\}) (s^1, p^{1j}, d^{1j}_2\}), \ldots (s^1, p^{1j}, d^{1j}_k)\}$ for '*k*' databases,

For example: s^1: *E.coli*; p^{1j}: TCA Cycle; d^{1j}_1= BioCyc, d^{1j}_2= KEGG.
Then, the tuple $(v^{11}_{1n}, e^{11}_{1m})$ gives *(node, edge)* in Biocyc for TCA cycle in *E.coli*, and the tuple $(v^{11}_{2p}, e^{11}_{2p})$ gives *(node, edge)* in KEGG for TCA cycle in *E.coli*

- $s^2 = \{(s^2, p^{2j} (D^{2j}_k)\} = \{(s^2, p^{2j}, d^{2j}_1), (s^2, p^{2j}, d^{2j}_2) \ldots\ldots, (s^2, p^{2j}, d^{2j}_r)\}$ *for 'r'* databases,

For example, s^2: *Arabidopsis*; p^{2j}: TCA Cycle; d^{2j}_1= BioCyc, d^{2j}_2= AraCyc
Then, the tuple $(v^{22}_{1p}, e^{22}_{1p})$ gives the *(node, edge)* in AraCyc for TCA cycle in *Arabidopsis*, and the tuple $(v^{22}_{2p}, e^{22}_{2p})$ gives the *(node, edge)* in KEGG for TCA cycle in *Arabidopsis*.

Each pathway p^{ij} *for a* d^{ij}_k is given by a graph $G\ (V^{ij}_k, E^{ij}_k)$, where,

- $P^{ij}_k = G\ (V^{ij}_k, E^{ij}_k)$ represents Pathway *'j'* from k^{th} datasourcesS for species *i'*... .(5)

Where, $V^{ij}_k = \{v^{ij}_{k1}, v^{ij}_{k2}, \ldots v^{ij}_{kn}\}$ = set of nodes in d^{ij}_k,. (6)

$E^{ij}_k = \{e^{ij}_{k1}, e^{ij}_{k2}, \ldots. e^{ij}_{km}\}$= set of edges in d^{ij}_k,. (7)

- ***SynList*** *{pathway name}* = ***SynList*** $\{P^{ij}\}$

- ***SynList*** *{entity name}* = ***SynList*** $\{v^{1j}_{kn}\}$
- $EV^{ij}_k = \{EV^{ij}_{k1}, \ldots. EV^{ij}_{kh}\}$ set of *'h'* EV Codes for $\{s^i, p^{ij}, d^{ij}_k\}$, for example;
  - EV^{1j}_1= {Set of EVcodes given by Biocyc for E.coli for TCA cycle}
  - EV^{1j}_2= {Set of EV codes given by KEGG for E.coli for TCA cycle}
  - EV^{2j}_3= {Set of EV codes given by AraCyc for Arabidopsis for TCA cycle}
  - EV^{2j}_2= {Set of EV codes given by KEGG for Arabidopsis for TCA cycle}
- RI^{ij}_k: Reference index for a database d^{ij}_k
- RI^{ij}_{int}: Reference index for the integrated pathway
- CW^{ij}_k: Confidence weight for a database d^{ij}_k
- CW^{ij}_{int}: Confidence weight of the integrated pathway p^{ij} within a species
- V^{ij}_{int}: Integrated node table for a species S^i, for a pathway p^{ij}
- E^{ij}_{int}: Integrated edge table for a species S^i, for a pathway p^{ij}
- $(v^{1j}_{kn}, e^{ij}_{km})$ = *(node 'n', edge 'm')* in d^{1j}_k of s^1 for p^{1j};

- ***ATT*** $\{(v^{1j}_{kn}, (A)\} = \{v^{1j}_{kn}, (A_1, A_2, A_3, A_4, \ldots A_s)\}$ = set of attributes of the node v^{1j}_{kn}
- ***ATT*** $\{(e^{ij}_{km}, (B)\} = \{(e^{ij}_{km}, (B_1, B_2, B_3, \ldots B_t)\}$ = set of attributes of edge e^{ij}_{km}
- ***DATT*** $\{v^{1j}_{kn}, (\delta A)\}$ = set of derived attributes of the node v^{1j}_{kn} (EV_i, CW_i, RI_i)
- ***DATT*** $\{e^{1j}_{kn}, (\delta B)\}$= set of derived attributes of the edge e^{1j}_{kn} (EV_i, CW_i, RI_i)
- δV^{ij}_k = Set of derived node attributes for Integrated pathway $\{EV_{int}, CW_{int}, RI_{int}\}$
- δE^{ij}_k= Set of derived edge attributes for Integrated pathway $\{EV_{int}, CW_{int}, RI_{int}\}$
- $V^{ij}_{int} = \{\Sigma\ V^{ij}_k\}_{for\ k=1\ to\ n}$
- $E^{ij}_{int} = \{\Sigma\ E^{ij}_k\}_{for\ k=1\ to\ n}$
- P^{ij}_{int} = Integrated pathway from multiple DSs = $\{\Sigma\ P^{ij}_k\}_{for\ k=1\ to\ n}$

BIOLOGICAL PATHWAY DATA INTEGRATION ALGORITHM

Following selections and inputs are defined by the user.

- User selected inputs: Species, Pathway, Data sources/database
- User inputs: Confidence assigned to each database
- User defined filters (UDF) for entities like substrate nodes, H_2O, CO_2 etc. for integrated pathway [$P^{ij}_{int} = G\ (V_{int}, E_{int}$).,

Step 1.

For each user selected pathway P^{ij} for a species s^i

List D^{ij} $(d^{1j}{}_{1},\ldots d^{nj}{}_{k})$, ***(KEGG, BioCyc, MetNetDB etc)***

Step 2.

Define rules to classify the interactions, for example;

- If the pathway is signal transduction, then use the classifier (Table 1)for interactions
- If the pathway is metabolic, then reaction is a general representation of the interaction **Sort** $(d^{1j}{}_{1},\ldots d^{nj}{}_{k})$ according to species $(s^i,d^{ij}{}_{1})$, $(s^j,d^{jj}{}_{1})$ etc.

Generate a set of (nodes, edges) from all the input data sources $\{(V^{ij}, E^{ij})\} = \{(V^{ij}{}_{1}, E^{ij}{}_{1}), (V^{ij}{}_{2}, E^{ij}{}_{2}).....(V^{ij}{}_{s}, E^{ij}{}_{s})\}$

where, $V^{ij}{}_{k}=\{v^{ij}{}_{k1}, v^{ij}{}_{k2}, \ldots .v^{ij}{}_{kt}\}$ and $E^{ij}{}_{1}=\{e^{ij}{}_{k1}, e^{ij}{}_{k2},\ldots .e^{ij}{}_{ku}\}$

Step 3.

For $k = 1, \ldots, q$ $(d^{1i}{}_{1},\ldots d^{1i}{}_{k})$,
For $s = 1,\ldots, n$, and $q = 1, \ldots m$,
List *ATT* $\{(v^{1i}{}_{ks}, (A)\}$
List *ATT* $\{(e^{ii}{}_{kq}, (B)\}$
Select $v^{ij}{}_{k1} \in V^{ij}{}_{k}$ **C** $d^{1i}{}_{k}$
For all $p = 1$ *to* n
Check *for* $v^{ij}{}_{k1} \in V^{ij}{}_{p}$ (node name match across data sources)
If *YES*, then **Apply** *EV* integration algorithm
Generate **DATT** $\{v^{1i}{}_{kn}, (\delta A)\}$, **DATT** $\{e^{1i}{}_{kn}, (\delta B)\}$.

Else, *For* $p = 1$ *to* n,
For $t = 1, z$
Check if $v^{ij}{}_{k1} \in$ ***SynList*** $\{v^{ij}{}_{pt}\}$ (node name(A) with Synlist(B))
If YES, then Apply EV integration algorithm.
Generate **DATT** $\{v^{1i}{}_{kn}, (\delta A)\}$, **DATT** $\{e^{1i}{}_{kn}, (\delta B)\}$.
Else,
Check if ***SynList*** $\{v^{ij}{}_{k1}\}$ has a match with $v^{ij}{}_{pt}$
If YES, then Apply EV integration Algorithm
Else,
Check if ***SynList*** $\{v^{ij}{}_{k1}\}$ has a match with ***SynList*** $\{v^{ij}{}_{pt}\}$
If $v^{ij}{}_{k1} = v^{ij}{}_{pt}$ *is TRUE*,
Then,
Include $v^{ij}{}_{pt}$ with the matched node name $v^{ij}{}_{k1}{}_{t} \in V^{ij}{}_{k1}$
Compute $(\delta V^{ij}{}_{k}, \delta E^{ij}{}_{k})$

This is the node name for the integrated database for the species. Level 1

Generate SynListInt = {SynList ($v^{ij}_{k,1}$) U Synlist ($v^{ij}_{p,l}$)U…} without duplication

Associate DOI (date of integration)

Generate P^{ij}_{int}

$$P^{ij}_{int} = \{\Sigma P^{ij}_k\}_{for\ k=1\ to\ n} = [\{V^{ij}_{int}, E^{ij}_{int}\} + \{\Sigma \delta V^{ij}_{kt}, \Sigma \delta E^{ij}_k\}_{for\ k=1\ to\ n}]_{at\ t=t1}$$
$$= \Sigma\{ATT[(v^{1ij}_{km}, (A)]\}, ATT[(e^{ij}_{km}, (B)]\} + \Sigma\{DATT\{v^{1ij}_{kn}, (\delta A), DATT\{e^{ij}_{kn}, (\delta B)\}_{for\ all\ n,m}\{\delta V^{ij}_k\ \delta E^{ij}_k\}$$

Step 4.

Repeat *Step 2-3 for $e^{ij}_k \in E^{ij}_k$ in (d^{ij}_1,… d^{ij}_k), for p^{ij}*

Include information associated with the edge, as given by 'edges' such as reaction, enzyme, by products and substrates along with attributes like evidence, reference publications, context etc.

** Outputs E^{ij}_{int} table for s^i using (d^{1ij}_1,… d^{1ij}_k), with EV^{ij}_{int}, CW^{ij}_{int} and RI^{ij}_{int}. **Level 1.** *

Step 5.

Generate integrated pathway by consolidating outputs G(V^{ij}_{int}, E^{ij}_{int}) for s^i

Step 6

For i =1,…n

Repeat steps 2- 4 to integrate P^{ij} for all species s^i

** This generates Table (V^j_{int}, E^j_{int}) = {(V^{ij}_{int}, E^{ij}_{int}) U (V^{ij}_{int}, E^{ij}_{int})U…} for S^i, for all i =1, ..n), for a p^{ij}. Level 2***

Step 7.

For (j = 1,….p)

Integrate for all P^{ij}

This generates output table (V_{int}, E_{int}) = (V^j_{int},E^j_{int}) U (V^k_{int},E^k_{int}) U….for all (j = 1,….p). Level 3*

Step 8.

Apply UDF (User defined filter)

QUERYING INTEGRATED PATHWAY

Once the data integration is accomplished, extracting information from the integrated data will be of interest to the biologist. There are various mechanisms to extract information from the integrated database generated.

Some of these are described below. Granular computing with semantic network structure captures the abstraction and incompleteness associated with biological plant pathway data. It is inspired by the ways in which humans granulate information and reason with coarse grained information. The three basic concepts underlying the human cognition are granulation, organization, and causation. Granulation involves decomposition of whole into parts, organization involves integration of parts into whole, and causation involves associations of cause and effects. The fundamental issues with granular computing are granulation of the universe, description of granules, and relationships between granules. The basic ideas of crisp information granulation have appeared in related fields, such as interval analysis, quantization, rough set theory, Demster Shafer theory of belief functions, divide and conquer, cluster analysis, machine learning, data bases and many others. Granules may be induced as a result of 1) equivalence of attribute values, 2) similarity of attribute values, and define the granules 3) equality of attribute value. We use granules for defining the user queries associated with the integrated pathway. Based on user (biologist) choice, granules can be defined to view the integrated pathway. This provides flexibility to the biologist for using the information.

Previous approaches towards metabolic network reconstruction have used various algorithmic methods such as name-matching in IdentiCS [52. and using EC-codes in metaSHARK [53. to link metabolic information to genes. The AUtomatic Transfer by Orthology of Gene Reaction Associations for Pathway Heuristics (AUTOGRAPH) method [54. uses manually curated metabolic networks, orthologue and their related reactions to compare predicted gene-reaction associations. Arrendondo [55. Proposes to develop a process for the continuous improvement of the inference system used, which is applicable to any such data mining application. It involves the comparison of several classifiers like Support Vector Machines (SVMs), Human Expert generated Fuzzy, and Genetic Algorithm (GA) generated Fuzzy and Neural Networks using various different training data models. In his approach, all classifiers were trained and tested with four different data sets: three biological and a synthetically generated mixture data set. The obtained results showed a highly accurate prediction capability with the mixture data set providing some of the best and most reliable results.

CONCLUSION

Biological database integration is a challenging task as the databases are created all over the world and updated frequently. For biological data sources that may be derived from an earlier existing data source, it is also important to identify the evidence of the data source represented by the evidence code, to be included as a candidate for integration. In most data integration algorithms the user does not participate thus leading to an integrated data source with any effective utility towards analysis. Large scale integration of pathway databases promises to help biologists gain insight into the deep biological context of a pathway. In this chapter, we presented algorithms that help user to select their choice of data sources and apply Evidence code algorithm to compute an integrated EV code and RI for the pathway data of interest. The ultimate goal is to generate a large-scale composite database containing the entire metabolic network for an organism. This qualitative approach includes aspects like user confidence scores for databases for mapping EV and generating RI for a given pathway. For the TCA pathway results show that generating such a mapping is helpful in visualizing the integrated database that highlights the common entities as well as the specifics of each database. As the database confidence weight selection is user specific, the integration yields different results for different users for the same database which will allow users to explore the effects of different hypotheses on the overall network. Once the integrated evidence code is generated, then data integration algorithm is applied to get the integrated pathway data. To best attempt integration of such data it is imperative to include user participation as user mostly identifies the associations and behavior of various compounds, reactions, genes in a given biological pathway leading to significant diagnosis.

REFERENCES

1. Akula, S.; Miriyala, R.; Thota, H.; Rao, A.; Gedela, S. Techniques for Integrating –omics Data, Bioinformation, Views and Challenges, 2009.
2. Saccharomyces genome database. http://www.yeastgenome.org/
3. KEGG: Kyoto Encyclopedia of Genes and Genomes. http://www.genome.jp/kegg/
4. TAIR- AraCyc: http://www.arabidopsis.org/biocyc/
5. Thimm, O; Blasing, O; Gibon, Y; Nagel, A; Meyer, S; Kruger, P; Selbig, J; Muller, L; Rhee, S; and Stitt, M. MAPMAN: a user driven tool to display genomics data sets onto diagrams of metabolic pathways and other biological processes, The Plant journal (2004) 37, pp 914-939. http://www.uky.edu/~aghunt00/PLS620/papers.htm/ Systems%20 approaches%20copy/MAPMAN.pdf
6. BIND: Biomolecular Interaction Network Database http://metadatabase.org/wiki/BIND_-_Biomolecular_Interaction_Network_Database
7. Bajic VB, Veronika M, Veladandi PS, Meka A, Heng MW, Rajaraman K, Pan H, Swarup S. Dragon Plant Biology Explorer. A text-mining tool for integrating associations between genetic and biochemical entities with genome annotation and biochemical terms list, Plant Physiol. 2005 Aug; 138(4):1914-25.
8. Pandey R, Guru R K, Mount D W. Pathway Miner: extracting gene association networks from molecular pathways for predicting the biological significance of gene expression microarray data, Bioinformatics. 2004 Sep 1;20(13):2156-8. Epub 2004 May 14.
9. RegulonDB database: Escheichia Coli k-12 transcriptional network. http://regulondb.ccg.unam.mx/
10. PlantCare a database. http://bioinformatics.psb.ugent.be/webtools/plantcare/html/
11. PLACE: a database of Plant Cis-acting regulatory netowrk. http://www.dna.affrc.go.jp/PLACE/
12. EPD: Eukaryotic promoter database. http://epd.vital-it.ch/
13. TRRD: transcription regulatory regions database http://wwwmgs.bionet.nsc.ru/mgs/gnw/trrd/
14. Athamap: http://www.athamap.de/
15. TRANSFAC: http://www.gene-regulation.com/pub/databases.html/

16. Friedman N, Linial, M; Nachman,I; and Pe'er, D. Using Bayesian Networks to Analyze Expression Data, Journal of computational biology, Volume 7, Numbers 3/4, 2000, pp. 601-620.
17. Schadt, et.al, An Integrative Genomics Approach to Infer Causal Associations Between Gene Expression and Disease, Nature Genetics, vol.37, number 7, July 2005, pp, 710-717.
18. The EMBL Nucleotide Sequence Database (http://www.ebi.ac.uk/embl/).
19. Liu, Y.; Wang, Y.; Liu, Y.;, Tan, Z. Data Integration of Bioinformatics Database Based on Web Services, International Journal of Web Applications, Volume 1, Number 3, 2009.
20. UCLA-DOE Institute for Genomics and Proteomics. http://dip.doe-mbi.ucla.edu/dip/Main.cgi
21. IntAct: open source database system and analysis tools for molecular interaction data.http://www.ebi.ac.uk/intact/
22. GRID: http://www.moldiscovery.com/soft_grid.php/
23. Zanzoni, A. Montecchi-Palazzi, L. Quondam, M. Ausiello, G. Helmer-Citterich, M. Cesareni, G. MINT: A Molecular INTeraction database. Elsevier FEBS Letters, 2002, Volume 513, Issue 1, Pages 135-140.
24. Coessens B. et.al, INCLUSive: A Web Portal and Service Registry for Microarray and Regulatory Sequence Analysis, Nucleic AciDS research, 2003, vol. 31, No.13. pp. 3468-3470. http://tomcatbackup.esat.kuleuven.be/inclusive/
25. Achard, F.; Vaysseix, G.; Barillot, E. XML, Bioinformatics, and Data Integration, Bioinformatics Review, Evry, France, 2001, pp. 115-125.
26. Pathway Data List. http://cbio.mskcc.org/prl
27. Hsing, M., Cherkasov, A. Integration of Biological Data with Semantic Networks, Current Bioinformatics, 2006, 1 000-000.
28. Chung, M., Lim, M., Bae, M., Park, S. Customized Biological Database Integration for cDNA Microarray, RECOMB 2005, Research in Computational and Molecular Biology, Cambridge, 2005.
29. Gopalcharyulu, P. Lindfors, E. et.al. Data integration and visualization system for enabling conceptual biology, BioInformatics, Vol.21, Suppl 1 2005, pp. i177-i185.
30. Rzhetsky, A et.al, GeneWays: A System for Extracting, Analyzing, Visualizing and Integrating Molecular Pathway Data, Journal of

Bioinformatics, 2004, 43-53.

31. Zucker, J.,Luciano, J., Brandes, A. Lin, X. Semantic Aggregation Integration and Inference: Three case studies, ISMB 2005.
32. Hu, Z., Mellor, J., Wu, J., Yamada, T., Holloway, D., DeLisi, C. VisANT: Data integrating visual framework for biological networks and modules, Nucleic AciDS research, 2005 vol. 33.
33. Zhang Z.; Bajic, V.; Yu, J.; Cheung, K.; Townsend, J. Data Integration in Bioinformatics: Current Efforts and Challenges. Bioinformatics: Trends and Methodologies, Intech, 2011.
34. Zhang, D. and Jing, L., Context based Numerical information, IEEE conference on Ecommerce Technology 2005Arredondo, T., Seeger, M., Dombrovskaia, L., Avarias, J., Calderón, F., Candel, D., Muñoz, F., Latorre, V., Agulló, L., Cordova, M., and Gómez, L.: "Bioinformatics Integration Framework for Metabolic Pathway Data-Mining". In: Ali, M., Dapoigny, R. (eds): Innovations in Applied Artificial Intelligence. Lecture Notes in Artificial Intelligence, Vol. 4031. Springer-Verlag, Berlin (2006) pp. 917-926.
35. PATIKA: http://www.iam.metu.edu.tr/research/groups/compbio/PATIKA_METU04.pdf
36. INHO: http://www.inoh.org/
37. TRANSPATH. http://www.ncbi.nlm.nih.gov/pubmed/12519957
38. ReactomeSTKE. http://stke.sciencemag.org/
39. MetaCyc. http://metacyc.org/
40. Kher, S; Jianling Peng; SyrkinWurtele, E.; Dickerson, J. A Symbolic computing approach to evidence code mapping for biological data integration and subjective analysis for reference associations for metabolic pathways, Annual Meeting of the North American Fuzzy Information Processing Society, 2008, NAFIPS 2008. NY 2008. pp. 1-6.
41. Kher, S; Dickerson, J; Rawat N. Biological pathway data integration trends, techniques, issues and challenges: A survey, Nature and biologically inspired computing, NaBIC 2010, Second World Congress, Fukuoka, Japan, 2010, pp.177 – 182.
42. MetNetDB. http://www.metnetdb.org/MetNet_db.htm
43. Karp, P. D., Paley, S., Krieger, C. J. An Evidence Ontology for Use in Pathway/Genome DS, Pacific Symposium on Biocomputing 2004, pp. 190-201, Singapore Bounsaythip, C., Lindfors, E., Gopalacharyulu,

P., Hollmen, J., and Oresic, M. Network Based Representation of Biological Data for Enabling Context Based Mining, Bioinformatics, vol.21, suppl 1. 2005, pp. 177-185.

44. Newman, M. E. J and Leicht, E. A Mixture Models and Exploratory Analysis in Networks, Physics, May 2007.
45. Pearl. J. (2000) Causality: Models, Reasoning, and Inference. Cambridge University Press, 2000.
46. Pearl, J. (1988). Probabilistic Reasoning in Intelligent Systems: Networks of Plausible Inference. San Mateo, CA, USA: Morgan Kaufmann Publishers.
47. Christopher Nemeth, STOR-I, Hidden Markov Models with Applications to DNA Sequence Analysis.
48. Crompton, S.; Matthews, B.; Gray, A.; Jones, A.; White, R. Data Integration in Bioinformatics Using OGSA-DAI, In Proceedings of Fourth All Hands Meeting, 2005.
49. Cheung Kei-hoi; Qi, P; Tuck,D; Krauthammer,M. A Semantic Web Approach to Biological Pathway Data Reasoning and Integration, Elsevier Vol. 4, issue 3, Sep 2006, pp. 207-215.
50. RDF-OWL. http://www.w3.org/RDF/
51. BioPAX: http://www.biopax.org/
52. Sun, J. and Zeng, A. , IdentiCS – Identification of coding sequence and in silico reconstruction of the metabolic network directly from unannotated low-coverage bacterial genome sequence, BMC Bioinformatics 2004, 5:112 doi:10.1186/1471-2105-5-112
53. Pinney, J.W., Shirley, M.W., McConkey, G.A., Westhead, D.R. (2005) MetaSHARK: software for automated metabolic network prediction from DNA sequence and is application to the genomes of Plasmodium falciparum and Eimeria tenella, Nucleic Acids Research, 33, 1399-1409.
54. Notebaart, R. A., F. H. van Enckevort, C. Francke, R. J. Siezen, and B. Teusink. 2006. Accelerating the reconstruction of genome-scale metabolic networks. BMC Bioinformatics 7:296
55. Arredondo, T., Seeger, M., Dombrovskaia, L., Avarias, J., Calderón, F., Candel, D., Muñoz, F., Latorre, V., Agulló, L., Cordova, M., and Gómez, L.: “Bioinformatics Integration Framework for Metabolic Pathway Data-Mining”. In: Ali, M., Dapoigny, R.(eds): Innovations in Applied Artificial Intelligence. Lecture Notes in Artificial Intelligence, Vol. 4031. Springer-Verlag, Berlin (2006) p. 917-926

CHAPTER 3

ENSEMBLE CLUSTERING FOR BIOLOGICAL DATASETS

Harun Pirim[1] and Şadi Evren Şeker[2]

[1]King Fahd University of Petroleum and Minerals

[2]Istanbul University, Turkey

INTRODUCTION

Recent technologies and tools generated excessive data in bioinformatics domain. For example, microarrays measure expression levels of ten thousands of genes simultaneously in a single chip. Measurements involve relative expression values of each gene through an image processing task.

Biological data requires both low and high level analysis to reveal significant information that will shed light into biological facts such as

Citation: Harun Pirim and Şadi Evren Şeker (November 28th 2012). "Ensemble Clustering for Biological Datasets", Bioinformatics, Horacio Pérez-Sánchez, IntechOpen, DOI: 10.5772/49956.

disease prediction, annotation of a gene function and guide new experiments. In that sense, researchers are seeking for the effect of a treatment or time course change befalling. For example, they may design a microarray experiment treating a biological organism with a chemical substance and observe gene expression values comparing with expression value before treatment. This treatment or change make researchers focus on groups of genes, other biological molecules that have significant relationships with each other under similar conditions. For instance, gene class labels are usually unknown, since there is a little information available about the data. Hence, data analysis using an unsupervised learning technique is required. Clustering is an unsupervised learning technique used in diverse domains including bioinformatics. Clustering assigns objects into the same cluster, based on a cluster definition. A cluster definition or criterion is the similarity between the objects. The idea is that one needs to find the most important cliques among many from the data. Therefore, clustering is widely used to obtain biologically meaningful partitions. However, there is no best clustering approach for the problem on hand and clustering algorithms are biased towards certain criteria. In other words, a particular clustering approach has its own objective and assumptions about the data.

Diversity of clustering algorithms can benefit from merging partitions generated individually. Ensemble clustering provides a framework to merge individual partitions from different clustering algorithms. Ensemble clustering may generate more accurate clusters than individual clustering approaches. Here, an ensemble clustering framework is implemented as described in [10] to aggregate results from K-means, hiearchical clustering and C-means algorithms. We employ C-means instead of spectral clustering in [10]. We also use different data sets. Two different biological datasets are used for each algorithm. A comparison of the results is presented. In order to evaluate the performance of the ensemble clustering approach, one internal and one external cluster validation indices are used. Silhouette (S) [31] is the internal validation index and C-rand [23] is the external one. The chapter reviews some clustering algorithms, ensemble clustering methods, includes implementation, and conclusion sections.

CLUSTERING ALGORITHMS

Clustering biological data is very important for identification of co-expressed genes, which facilitates functional annotation and the elucidation of biological pathways. Accurate predictions can serve as a guide for targeting further experiments and generating additional hypotheses. Furthermore, accurate predictions can facilitate identification of disease markers and targets for drug design [4]; clustering can also be used to determine whether certain patterns exist near viral integration sites[16].

Current algorithms used in gene clustering have some drawbacks. For example, K-means algorithm is sensitive to noise that is inherent in gene expression data. In addition, the solution (i.e. the final clustering) that the K-means algorithm finds may not be a global optimum since it relies on randomly chosen initial objects. However, K-means-based methods are prevalent in the literature such as [12, 17, 33]. K-means works upon randomly chosen centroid points that represent the clusters. The objects are assigned to the closest clusters based on distance calculation regarding centroid points. For example, the dataset illustrated in Figure 1 is assigned two centroids.

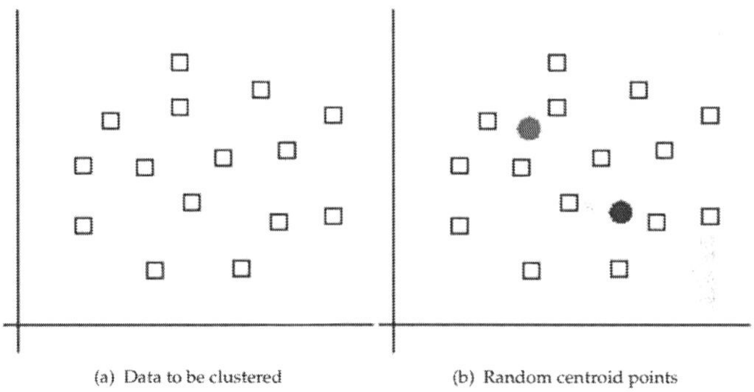

Figure 1. The dataset and two centroid points

The distance between any object from the dataset to both of the centroid points are calculated and the objects are assigned to the closest cluster represented by the closest centroid point as seen in Figure 2. Then new centroid points of clusters are calculated and objects are assigned to the closest clusters regarding the distance to new centroid points. Recalculation of centroid points and assignment of objects to new clusters goes on till centroids points remain the same as in Figure 3.

Another method, Self-organizing Map (SOM), is one of the machine-learning techniques widely used in gene clustering. A recent study is [14]. SOM requires a grid structured input that makes it ineffective.

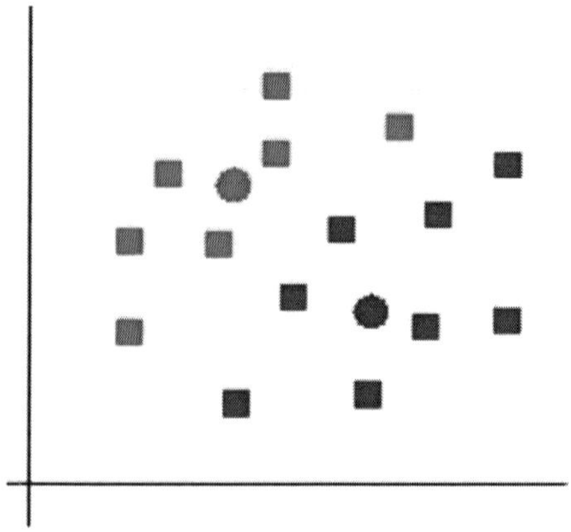

Figure 2. Initial clusters

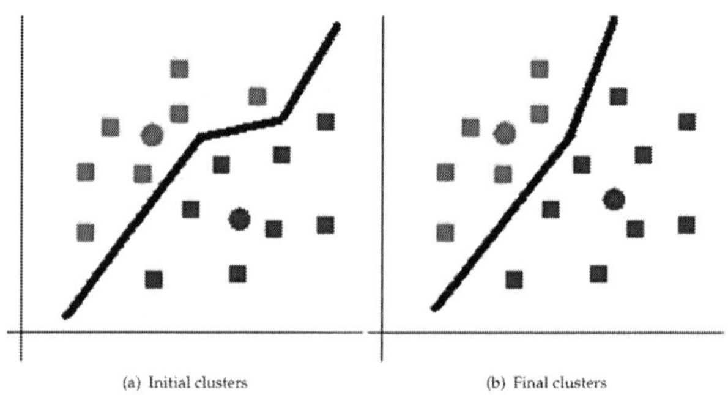

Figure 3. Iteration of K-means

Hierarchical clustering (HC) algorithms are also widely used and area of two types: agglomerative and divisive. In agglomerative approach objects are all in different clusters and they are merged till they are all in the same cluster as seen in Figure 4. Two important drawbacks of the HC algorithms are that they are not robust and they have high computational complexity. HC algorithms are "greedy" which often means that the final solution is suboptimal due to locally optimal choices being made in initial steps, which turn out to be poor choices with respect to the global solution. A recent study is [26].

Graph-theoretical clustering techniques exist in which the genomic data are represented by nodes and edges of a graph. Network methods have been applied to identify and characterize various biological interactions [13]. Identification of clusters using networks is often intractable, that is finding an optimal partition of a graph is an NP-hard problem [1]. NP-hard is a class of problems that are at least as hard as NP-complete problems. NP-complete is a class of problems that are in NP and reducible to an NP-complete problem in polynomial time. Some examples of graph theory-based clustering approaches are: [30] and [24].

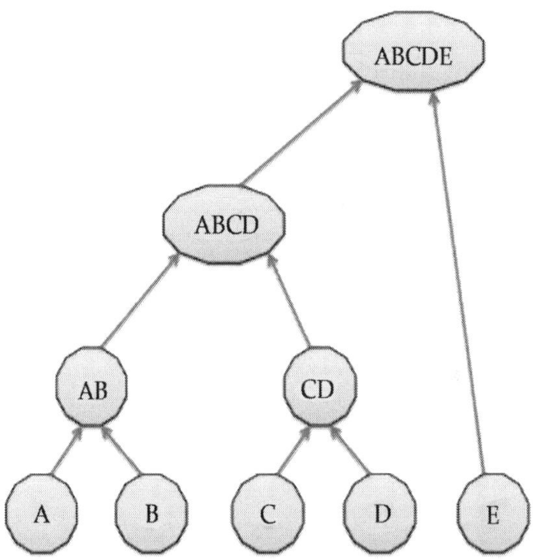

Figure 4. Agglomerative approach.

Model-based clustering approaches are the ones using probability distributions to predict the distribution of gene expression data. However, gene expression data does not have a unique distribution. Some examples are given in [19] and [34].

Sub-space clustering (biclustering) methods, which employ the reasoning that one gene may belong to multiple pathways or no pathways are also used in the literature as in [28]. There are also optimization-based algorithms as in [15], spectral algorithms as in [25], fuzzy algorithms as in [32], meta-heuristics as in [18] used for clustering genomic data.

ENSEMBLE CLUSTERING

Combining diverse partitions from different clustering algorithms may result in high quality and robust clusters, since ensemble approaches such as bagging and boosting used in classification problems have proven to be effective [22]. The fact that the objects have various features makes it difficult to find an optimal clustering of similar objects. In other words, objects may be classified based on different features such as size, color, and age. In that sense, ensemble clustering is a promising heuristic combining results based on different features.

Figure 5 represents a clustering ensemble framework. *CA*s are clustering algorithms, *P*s are partitions generated by them, *N* is number of clustering algorithms and partitions F_C is the consensus function and *CP* is the consensus partition.

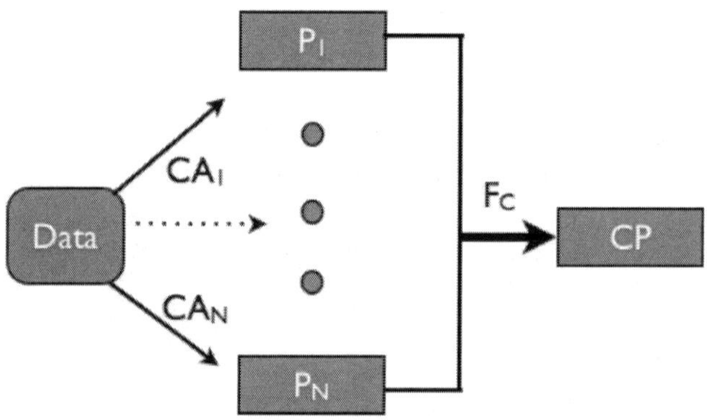

Figure 5. Ensemble clustering framework

Ensemble clustering requires the following tasks [2]:

1. selection of base clustering algorithms
2. definition of a consensus function
3. merging of individual partitions by the chosen consensus function

[2] apply an ensemble approach for clustering scale-free graphs. They use metrics based on the neighborhood which uses the adjacency list of each node and considers the nodes as having several common neighbors, the clustering coefficient, and the shortest path betweenness of nodes in the network. The scale-free graph used in the study is from a budding yeast PPI network that contained 15147 interactions between 4741 proteins. It is reported that ensemble clustering can provide improvements in cluster

quality for scale-free graphs based upon the preliminary results. [3] propose an ensemble clustering framework to extract functional modules that are relevant biologically in protein-protein interaction (PPI) networks. Their method attempts to handle the noisy false positive interactions and specific topological interactions present in the network. The method uses graph clustering algorithms, repeated bisections, direct k-way partitioning, and multilevel k-way partitioning, to obtain the base partitions. The method utilizes two topological distance matrices. One of the distance matrices is based on the clustering coefficient [36], and the other distance matrix is generated using the betweenness measure [29]. The proposed study demonstrates a soft ensemble method such that proteins are allowed to be assigned to more than one cluster. Empirical evaluation of the different ensemble methods in the study shows the superior performance of the proposed ensemble framework.

Fuzzy clustering algorithms are widely used with well-understood properties and benefits in various applications. Nevertheless, there has been very little analysis of using fuzzy clustering algorithms in regards to generating the base partitions in cluster ensembles. [35] compares hard and fuzzy C-means [7] algorithms in the well-known evidence-accumulation framework of cluster ensembles. In the study, it is observed that the fuzzy C-means approach requires much fewer base partitions for the cluster ensemble to converge, and is more tolerant of outliers in the data.

[5] propose a fuzzy ensemble clustering approach to address the issue of unclear boundaries between the clusters from the biological and biomedical gene expression data analysis. The approach takes into account their inherent fuzziness. The goal of the study is improving the accuracy and robustness of clustering results. After applying random projections to obtain lower dimensional gene expression data, the method applies the fuzzy K-means algorithm on the low dimensional data to generate multiple fuzzy base clusters. Then, the fuzzy clusters are combined using a similarity matrix where the elements of the matrix are generated by the fuzzy t-norms algorithm, and finally, the fuzzy K-means algorithm is applied to the rows of the similarity matrix to obtain the consensus clustering. It is demonstrated that the proposed ensemble approach is competitive with the other ensemble methods.

High throughput data may be generated by microarray experiments. If the dataset is very large, it is possible to generate an ensemble of clustering solutions, or partition the data so that clustering may be performed on tractable-sized disjoint subsets [20]. The data can then be distributed at different sites, for which a distributed clustering solution with a final merging of partitions is a natural fit. [20] introduce two new approaches to combining partitions represented by sets of cluster centers. It is stated that these approaches provide a final partition of data that is comparable to the best existing approaches and that the approaches can be 100,000 times faster while using much less memory. The new algorithms are compared with the best existing cluster ensemble approaches that cluster all of the data at once, and a clustering algorithm designed for very large datasets. Fuzzy and hard K-means based clustering algorithms are used for the comparison. It is demonstrated that the centroid-based ensemble merging algorithms presented in the study generated partitions which are as good as the best label vector method, or the method of clustering all the data at once. The proposed algorithms are also more efficient in terms of speed.

[11] propose evidence accumulation clustering based on dual rooted prim tree cuts (EAC-DC). The proposed algorithm computes the co-association matrix based on a forward algorithm that repeatedly adds edges to Prim's minimum spanning tree (MST) to identify clusters until a satisfying criterion is met. A consensus cluster is then generated from the co-association matrix using spectral partitioning. Here, a MST is a fully connected sub-graph with no cycles and a dual-rooted tree is obtained by finding the union of two sub-trees. They test their approach using the Iris dataset [8], the Wisconsin breast cancer dataset [27] (both obtained from [9]) and synthetic datasets, and presented a comparison of their results with other existing ensemble clustering methods.

[22] use a cluster ensemble in gene expression analysis. In the proposed ensemble framework, the partitions generated by each individual clustering algorithm are converted into a distance matrix. The distance matrices are then combined to construct a weighted graph. A graph partitioning approach is then used to generate the final set of clusters. It is reported that the ensemble approach yields better results than the best individual approach on both synthetic and yeast gene expression datasets.

[10] merge multiple partitions using evidence accumulation. Each partition generated by a clustering algorithm is used as a new piece of knowledge, to help uncover the relationships between objects. For this chapter, we adopt their ensemble approach. The core idea behind the

ensemble approach here is constructing the co-association matrix by employing a voting mechanism for the partitions generated using individual clustering algorithms. A co-association matrix C is constructed based upon the formulation below, where n_{ij} is the number of times the object pair (i, j) is assigned to the same cluster among the N different partitions:

$$C(i,j) = \frac{n_{ij}}{N}$$

After constructing the co-association matrix, [10] use single linkage hierarchical clustering to obtain the new cluster tree (dendrogram) and then use a cut-off value corresponding to the maximum life time (difference between merge points where branching starts) on the tree.

They also employ the same ensemble framework using K-means partitions with different parameters. They test their algorithms on ten different datasets, comparing the results with other ensemble clustering methods. They report that their ensemble approach can identify the clusters with arbitrary shapes and sizes, and perform better than the other combination methods.

IMPLEMENTATION

We employ the ensemble approach described in [10]. Different set of base clustering algorithms are chosen and implemented on protein and lymphoma datasets.

Protein dataset consists of 698 objects (corresponding to protein folds) with 125 attributes. The protein dataset contains 698 proteins from 125 samples. The real clusters correspond to the four classes of protein - folds: α, β, α/β and $\alpha+\beta$ protein classes. DLBCL - B is 2 - channel custom cDNA microarray dataset. This is a B cell lymphoma dataset with predefined three subtypes [21].

The ensemble clustering algorithm uses an array of vectors data structure for each of the file, in order to use the dynamic memory allocation and starts with initializing the file content in the vectors. The algorithm also processes the vectors and generates two temporary matrices with the dimension of maximum vector length. The ensemble clustering algorithm steps are as follows:

Algorithm 1 Ensemble Clustering Algorithm

Require: partitions

Ensure: distance matrix

```
for i = 0 to max(V[n]) do
  for j = 0 to max(V[n]) do
    for k = 0 to n do
      if V[k].elementAt(i) = V[k].elementAt(j)) then
        C[i][j] = C[i][j] + 1/n
      end if
      D[i][j] = 1 - C[i][j]
    end for
  end for
end for
```

Here, n is the number of files, $V[n]$ are the vectors holding the content of each file. $max(V[n])$ is the length of the longest vector, $C[i][j]$ is the co-association matrix and $D[i][j]$ is the distance matrix. The algorithm iterates through the two dimensional matrix via $i$and j loop variables inside a nested loop at lines 1 and 2 and for each member of the matrix, all the vectors are processed inside the loop via k loop variable at line 3. The condition of equality for the selected vector with the selected loop variables $i$and j, causes an increase on the co-association matrix elements at lines 4 and 5. Finally the distance matrix is calculated at line 7. After obtaining the distance matrix, hierarchial clustering with complete linkage is used to generate the dengrogram. The dendrogram is cut at a certain level to obtain consensus partition.

Ensemble approach is coded as a java application which is available upon request. The software allows addition of many partitions to generate the distance matrix of the corresponding ensemble. Files including the partitions can be added by clicking on the "Add File" button as seen in Figure 6. Distance matrix of the ensemble is generated by "Calculate" button.

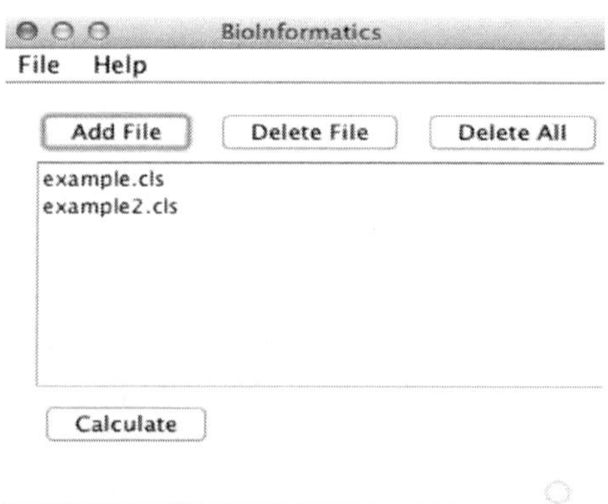

Figure 6. File input interface

The output is displayed on a separate screen as demonstrated on Figure 7. The output with csv format can be written into a file by clicking on the "Output CSV" button.

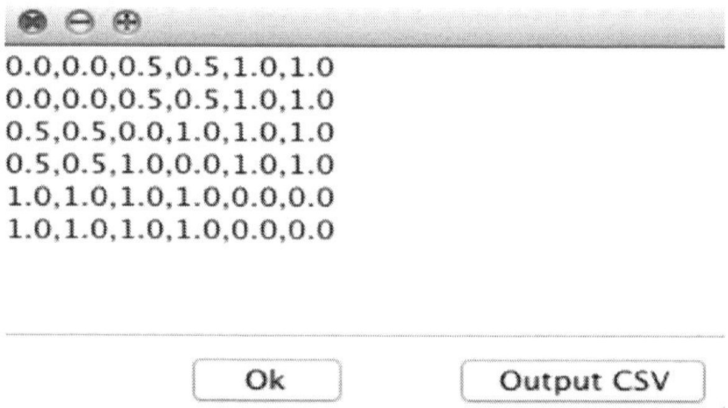

Figure 7. Example clusters

Considering two different partitions of a dataset with six objects which are (1, 1, 2, 1, 3, 3) and (2, 2, 2, 1, 3, 3), the algorithm's output is the distance matrix:

$$\begin{pmatrix} 0 & 0 & 0.5 & 0.5 & 1 & 1 \\ 0 & 0 & 0.5 & 0.5 & 1 & 1 \\ 0.5 & 0.5 & 0 & 1 & 1 & 1 \\ 0.5 & 0.5 & 1 & 0 & 1 & 1 \\ 1 & 1 & 1 & 1 & 0 & 0 \\ 1 & 1 & 1 & 1 & 0 & 0 \end{pmatrix}$$

The distance matrix is used in hierarchical clustering with complete linkage and the following dendrogram is generated. The dendrogram is cut at a level to give three clusters. The corresponding partition is (1, 1, 1, 2, 3, 3) which is the same as second partition (2, 2, 2, 1, 3, 3).

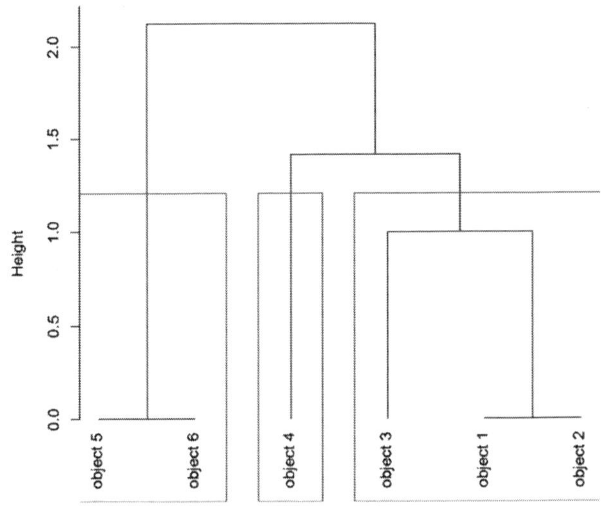

Figure 8. Example clusters.

We employ hierarchical clustering, K-means and C-means to obtain base partitions. K-means and hierarchical clustering algorithm are implemented using R base package, C-means is implemented using R e1071 package. Silhouette and C-rand indices are utilized to evaluate the performance of individual and ensemble algorithms. Silhouette and C-rand values are calculated using R clusterSim and flexclust packages respectively. Silhouette is an internal measure of compactness and separation of clusters [6]. The silhouette index values are between -1 and 1 representing worst and best values. C-rand is an external measure of agreement between two partitions. C-rand has maximum value of 1 and it can take negative values.

The silhouette and C-rand values found by the base and ensemble algorithms are given in Table 1. Ensemble approach improves clustering result both for the protein and DLBCL-B datasets. Ensemble approach finds better C-rand value, 0.157 than values by K-means and C-means, 0.127 for the protein dataset. Ensemble approach also finds the best C-rand value, 0.135 compared to values generated by individual clustering algorithms, 0.021, 0.063, 0.098. However, the ensemble approach makes S values worse in most cases.

Table 1. Index values for base and ensemble algorithms

Dataset	Method	Num. of clusters	S value	C value
Protein	HC K-means C-means Ensemble	4 4 4 4	0.344 0.379 0.379 0.078	0.199 0.127 0.127 0.157
DLBCL-B	HC K-means C-means Ensemble	3 3 2 3	-0.034 -0.015 -0.005 -0.017	0.021 0.063 0.098 0.135

CONCLUSION

Clustering groups of objects such that similar ones are placed in the same cluster, and in its application to biological datasets are very important in that it can help identification of natural groups of biological entities that might give insight about biomarkers. In this chapter, we review some clustering algorithms applied to biological data. Ensemble clustering approaches for biological data are also reviewed. Implementation of K-means, C-means and HC algorithms and merging of the algorithms using an ensemble frame work are presented using two different datasets. The datasets are protein and DLBCL-B. Two different cluster validation indices, adjusted rand and silhouette, are used for comparing the partitions from individual algorithms and ensemble clustering. Investigating Table 1, we conclude that merging individual partitions improves C-rand values meaning that ensemble approach finds partitions similar to the real partitions. Ensemble approach is coded as a Java application and available upon request.

ACKNOWLEDGEMENT

Authors thank DilipGautam for his contribution to this chapter. The work of ŞadiEvrenŞeker was supported by Scientific Research Projects Coordination Unit of Istanbul University, project number YADOP-16728.

REFERENCES

1. Arora, S., Rao, S. & Vazirani, U. 2009.. Expander flows, geometric embeddings and graph partitioning, Journal of the ACM 56(2): 1–37. URL: http://doi.acm.org/10.1145/1502793.1502794
2. Asur, S., Parthasarathy, S. & Ucar, D. 2006.. An Ensemble Approach for Clustering Scale-Free Graphs, KDD-2006 Workshop on Link Analysis, 12th ACM SIGKDD International Conference on Knowledge Discovery and Data Mining.
3. Asur, S., Ucar, D. & Parthasarathy, S. 2007.. An ensemble framework for clustering protein–protein interaction networks, Bioinformatics 23(13): 29–40. URL: http://dx.doi.org/10.1093/bioinformatics/btm212
4. Asyali, M. H., Colak, D., Demirkaya, O. & Inan, M. S. 2006.. Gene expression profile classification: A review, Current Bioinformatics pp. 55–73. URL: http://dx.doi.org/10.2174/157489306775330615
5. Avogadri, R. & Valentini, G. 2009.. Fuzzy ensemble clustering based on random projections for dna microarray data analysis, Artificial Intelligence in Medicine 45(2-3): 173–183. URL: http://dx.doi.org/10.1016/j.artmed.2008.07.014
6. Bandyopadhyay, S., Mukhopadhyay, A. & Maulik, U. 2007.. An improved algorithm for clustering gene expression data, Bioinformatics 23(21): 2859–2865.
7. Bezdek, J. C. 1981.. Pattern Recognition with Fuzzy Objective Function Algorithms, Kluwer Academic Publishers, Norwell, MA, USA.
8. Fisher, R. A. 1936.. The use of multiple measurements in taxonomic problems, Annals Eugen. 7: 179–188.
9. Frank, A. & Asuncion, A. 2010.. UCI machine learning repository. URL: http://archive.ics.uci.edu/ml
10. Fred, A. L. N. & Jain, A. K. 2005.. Combining multiple clusterings using evidence accumulation, IEEE Transaction on Pattern Analysis and Machine Intelligence 27: 835–850.
11. Galluccio, L., Michel, J.J., O., Comon, P., Hero, A. O. & Kliger, M. 2009.. Combining multiple partitions created with a graph-based construction for data clustering, Proceedings of IEEE International Workshop on Machine Learning for Signal Processing, Grenoble, France, pp. –.
12. Geraci, F., Leoncini, M., Montangero, M., Pellegrini, M. & Renda, M. E. 2009.. K-boost: a scalable algorithm for high-quality clustering of

microarray gene expression data, Journal of Computational Biology 16(6): 859–873.

13. Ghazalpour, A., Doss, S., Zhang, B., Wang, S., Plaisier, C., Castellanos, R., Brozell, A., Schadt, E. E., Drake, T. A., Lusis, A. J. & Horvath, S. 2006.. Integrating genetic and network analysis to characterize genes related to mouse weight, PLoS Genetics 2(8). URL: http://dx.plos.org/10.1371
14. Ghouila, A., Yahia, S. B., Malouche, D., Jmel, H., Laouini, D., Guerfali, F. Z. & Abdelhak, S. 2009.. Application of multi-som clustering approach to macrophage gene expression analysis, Infection, Genetics and Evolution 9(3): 328–336.
15. Glover, F. W. & Kochenberger, G. 2006.. New optimization models for data mining, International Journal of Information Technology and Decision Making 5(4): 605–609.
16. Gumus, E., Kursun, O., Sertbas, A. & Ustek, D. 2012.. Application of canonical correlation analysis for identifying viral integration preferences, Bioinformatics 28(5): 651–655.
17. Gungor, Z. & Unler, A. 2008.. K-harmonic means data clustering with tabu-search method, Applied Mathematical Modelling 32(6): 1115–1125.
18. He, Y. & Hui, S. C. 2009.. Exploring ant-based algorithms for gene expression data analysis, Artificial Intelligence in Medicine 47(2): 105–119.
19. Heath, J. W., Fu, M. C. & Jank, W. 2009.. New global optimization algorithms for model-based clustering, Computational Statistics and Data Analysis 53(12): 3999–4017.
20. Hore, P., Hall, L. O. & Goldgof, D. B. 2009.. A scalable framework for cluster ensembles, Pattern Recognition 42(5): 676–688. URL: http://dx.doi.org/10.1016/j.patcog.2008.09.027
21. Hoshida, Y., Brunet, J. P., Tamayo, P., Golub, T. R. & Mesirov, J. P. 2007.. Subclass mapping: Identifying common subtypes in independent disease data sets, PLoS ONE 2(11): 1195. URL: http://dx.plos.org/10.1371
22. Hu, X. & Yoo, I. 2004.. Cluster ensemble and its applications in gene expression analysis, Proc. 2nd conference on Asia-Pacific bioinformatics (APBC'04), Australian Computer Society, Inc., Darlinghurst, Australia, Australia, pp. 297–302.

23. Hubert, L. & Arabie, P. 1985.. Comparing partitions, Journal of Classification 2: 193–218. 10.1007/BF01908075. URL: http://dx.doi.org/10.1007/BF01908075

24. Huttenhower, C., Flamholz, A. I., Landis, J. N., Sahi, S., Myers, C. L., Olszewski, K. L., Hibbs, M. A., Siemers, N. O., Troyanskaya, O. G. & Coller, H. A. 2007.. Nearest neighbor networks: clustering expression data based on gene neighborhoods, BMC Bioinformatics 8(250): 1–13.

25. Kim, J. & Choi, S. 2006.. Semidefinite spectral clustering, Pattern Recognition 39: 2025–2035.

26. Langfelder, P., Zhang, B. & Horvath, S. 2008.. Defining clusters from a hierarchical cluster tree: the dynamic tree cut package for r, Bioinformatics Applications Note 24(5): 719–720.

27. Mangasarian, O. L. & Wolberg, W. H. 1990.. Cancer diagnosis via linear programming, 23(5): 1–18.

28. Mitra, S., Das, R., Banka, H. & Mukhopadhyay, S. 2009.. Gene interaction - an evolutionary biclustering approach, Information Fusion 10: 242–249.

29. Newman, M. E. J. & Girvan, M. 2004.. Finding and evaluating community structure in networks, Physical Review E 69(026113): 1–15.

30. Phan, V., George, E. O., Tran, Q. T. & Goodwin, S. 2009.. Analyzing microarray data with transitive directed acyclic graphs, Journal of Bioinformatics and Computational Biology 7(1): 135–156.

31. Rousseeuw, P. 1987.. Silhouettes: A graphical aid to the interpretation and validation of cluster analysis, Journal of Computational and Applied Mathematics 20(1): 53–65. URL: http://dx.doi.org/10.1016/0377-0427(87)90125-7

32. Saha, S. & Bandyopadhyay, S. 2009.. A new point symmetry based fuzzy genetic clustering technique for automatic evolution of clusters, Information Sciences 179(19): 3230–3246.

33. Tseng, G. C. 2007.. Penalized and weighted k-means for clustering with scattered objects and prior information in high-throughput biological data, Bioinformatics 23(17): 2247–2255.

34. Wang, S. & Zhu, J. 2008.. Variable selection for model-based high-dimensional clustering and its application to microarray data, Biometrics 64(2): 440–448.

35. Wang, T. 2009.. Comparing hard and fuzzy c-means for evidence-

accumulation clustering, Proceedings of the 18th international conference on Fuzzy Systems, FUZZ-IEEE'09, IEEE Press, Piscataway, NJ, USA, pp. 468–473. URL: http://dl.acm.org/citation.cfm?id=1717561.1717643

36. Watts, D. J. & Strogatz, S. H. 1998.. Collective dynamics of 'small-world' networks, Nature 393(6684): 440–442. URL: http://dx.doi.org/10.1038/30918

SECTION 2
PERSONALIZED MEDICINE

CHAPTER 4

TRANSLATION IN DATA MINING TO ADVANCE PERSONALIZED MEDICINE FOR HEALTH EQUITY

Estela S. Estape, M.T, Ph.D., FASAHP, DHL,[1] Mary Helen Mays, Ph.D., MPH, MBA, RD,[2] and Elizabeth A. Sternke, Ph.D.[3]

[1] Post-doctoral Master of Science in Clinical and Translational Research (MSc) and Hispanics in Research Capability (HiREC) Endowment Programs, School of Health Professions, Medical Sciences Campus-University of Puerto Rico

[2] Post-doctoral Master of Science in Clinical and Translational Research (MSc), School of Health Professions, and the Puerto Rico Clinical and Translational Research Consortium, Medical Sciences Campus – University of Puerto Rico

[3] Post-doctoral Master of Science in Clinical and Translational Research (MSc) School of Health Professions, Medical Sciences Campus-University of Puerto Rico

Citation: Estape, E. , Mays, M. and Sternke, E. (2016), "Translation in Data Mining to Advance Personalized Medicine for Health Equity". *Intelligent Information Management*, **8**, 9-16. doi: 10.4236/iim.2016.81002 .

ABSTRACT

Personalized medicine is the development of 'tailored' therapies that reflect traditional medical approaches, with the incorporation of the patient's unique genetic profile and the environmental basis of the disease. These individualized strategies encompass disease prevention, diagnosis, as well as treatment strategies. Today's healthcare workforce is faced with the availability of massive amounts of patient- and disease-related data. When mined effectively, these data will help produce more efficient and effective diagnoses and treatment, leading to better prognoses for patients at both the individual and population level. Designing preventive and therapeutic interventions for those patients who will benefit most while minimizing side effects and controlling healthcare costs, requires bringing diverse data sources together in an analytic paradigm. A resource to clinicians in the development and application of personalized medicine is largely facilitated, perhaps even driven, by the analysis of "big data". For example, the availability of clinical data warehouses is a significant resource for clinicians in practicing personalized medicine. These "big data" repositories can be queried by clinicians, using specific questions, with data used to gain an understanding of challenges in patient care and treatment. Health informaticians are critical partners to data analytics including the use of technological infrastructures and predictive data mining strategies to access data from multiple sources, assisting clinicians' interpretation of data and development of personalized, targeted therapy recommendations. In this paper, we look at the concept of personalized medicine, offering perspectives in four important, influencing topics: 1) the availability of 'big data' and the role of biomedical informatics in personalized medicine, 2) the need for interdisciplinary teams in the development and evaluation of personalized therapeutic approaches, and 3) the impact of electronic medical record systems and clinical data warehouses on the field of personalized medicine. In closing, we present our fourth perspective, an overview to some of the ethical concerns related to personalized medicine and health equity.

Keywords data mining; electronic medical records; translation; personalized medicine; biomedical informatics; heath equity; healthcare workforce

INTRODUCTION

In 2015, US President Barack Obama announced the Precision Medicine Initiative, to focus attention and resources towards the development of innovative technologies and infrastructure designed to improve individual and societal health and treatment of disease [1]. The President's Council of Advisors on Science and Technology (PCAST) defines personalized medicine (aka precision medicine) as the ability to tailor "medical treatment to the individual characteristics of the patient" [2]. Personalized medicine and precision medicine are terms that are often used interchangeably. There is mixed evidence on which term is the most correct, although the US National Research Council uses the term precision medicine. Some researchers prefer this term as they feel it more accurately represents the fact that therapies are recommended based on an individual patients characteristics as related to a similar population rather than constructed solely on the basis of individual characteristics [3]. The basis of personalized medicine is delivering information to the physician on the genetic, environment and lifestyle differences of an individual patient. The objective is to more effectively target their physiological and pharmacological responses to a specific treatment. Personalized medicine enables physicians and other care providers to treat individuals as unique, using observations from the individual patient as well as harnessing the power of aggregated data drawn from millions of other patients' data [4]. In so doing, "preventive or therapeutic interventions can then be concentrated on those who will benefit, sparing expense and side effects for those who will not" [2]. This ideal requires bringing together diverse data sources into an analytic paradigm.

Data used in creating a personalized medicine treatment plan are already routinely collected in day-to-day healthcare settings, for example, primary and specialty care offices, laboratories, imaging centers, pharmacies, and hospitals. Data can include patient sociodemographic and environmental information, family histories, personal monitoring device feedback, images and imaging results, phenotypes and genotypes, molecular and cellular data, disease traits, and treatment responses. Other healthcare and health-related data that are increasingly available include clinical trial data, claims data from health insurance providers, and research study data. Data, such as those available in electronic medical records (EMRs), will be in both structured and unstructured formats [4, 5]. Data from large projects, such as the Human Genome Project, have been used to highlight the importance of single nucleotide polymorphisms in human genetic variability and their association with disease and their role in understanding complex disease etiology [2, 6]. In short, there is now a superabundance of data which may be mined and analyzed to identify and support better clinical decisions as well as new treatment discoveries.

The principal difference in providing good clinical care today and into the future depends not only on mining "big data" but also on the "speed of change"; how quickly these changes and employing these data—dynamic, static, structured, and unstructured—can be implemented. Implementation will require a complex and advanced technological infrastructure that will allow data from many different sources and diagnostic disciplines to be integrated and presented to practitioners in ways that facilitate the interpretation of data and development of personalized interventions [7]. For example, personalized medicine reports may provide physicians with suggestions for pharmacological or biological interventions, targeting specific cells or, selecting interactive patient education that enables patients and providers to develop customized treatment plans for disease management[(8]. The development of systems that provide targeted outputs must focus on a variety of tools, including biologic, technical and computational strategies. These leveraged approaches support a greater understanding of the complexity and interrelated nature of disease, environment, and the person [4].

PERSPECTIVES

Bioinformatics and "Big Data"

These data, collectively recognized as "big data", are keys that can unlock doors to the potential of personalized medicine. These large, complex datasets will house structured data (e.g., numerical data for height, weight, blood pressure, glucose levels; categorical data such as yes/no for marital status; etc.) as well as unstructured data (e.g., physician notes). Such systems will need to be able to effectively aggregate and normalize data from across data sources (e.g., genomic data, patient data from EMRs, radiologic images, etc.). Systems such as those built on the "informatics for integrating biology and the bedside (i2b2)" framework are particularly useful and effective for integrating clinical and research data that may be used by investigators [9]. These clinical data repositories (i.e., databases) are often de-identified and often anonymized, allowing researchers to generate hypotheses and identify cohorts for study. These "big data" repositories can be queried by clinicians, using specific questions, with data used to gain an understanding of challenges in patient care and treatment.

The systematic mining of data in research has already shown to be of benefit to individuals and populations in a variety of diseases. In particular, cancer research has benefited greatly from the use of aggregated data in order to help assess which individuals may be more prone to developing cancers and which types of cancers could affect them. For example, research in breast and ovarian cancer led to the discovery of mutations in BRCA1 and BRCA2 which predispose women to these cancers [2]. Based on family and personal histories, physicians may now order testing for BRCA1 and/or BRCA2 for their patients and assist them in making decisions based on the results to mitigate their risk of developing breast or ovarian cancer [2]. Medications have also been developed using "big data," from chemotherapy designed to target specific cancers, to pharmacogenetic dosing algorithms for warfarin (an anticoagulant used to prevent heart attacks, strokes, and blood clots) [5]. There have also been strides in personalizing treatment for the onset of type 2 diabetes in children and young adults using genetic analyses. "Specific genetic variants that affect pancreatic beta cell function" have been discovered and are used to "add clarity to diagnosis" and treatment of this condition [2].

All these data have driven pharmacogenomics to an area that has expanded the most in molecular diagnostics with system-guided support. Such evidence has reduced the incidence of adverse events by checking for susceptible genotypes for drugs [10]. DNA testing for drug biomarkers is one area for data mining with more growth potential because of its pharmacogenetics applications for drug selection; drug dosing and drug interactions.

For example, the following inherited determinants for drug response have helped significantly in the treatment of disease: *1. Drug Metabolizing Enzymes*: Genotyping assays for allelic variants from CYP450 enzyme activity helps to identify Poor Metabolizers (PMs) from extensive metabolizers. One of the most significant first examples was with CYP2D6 in patients who had a 10-fold absorption and a 5-fold higher peak concentration to a given dose compared with Extensive Metabolizers to Atomoxetine HCl (Strattera), the first FDA-approved non-stimulant drug for attention deficit hyperactive disorder, NE uptake inhibitor [11]; *2. Drug Targets:* Specific disease–associated genes, allelic variants or gene products. A very well-known example is HER-2/neu oncogene and Herceptin for breast cancer [12]; *3. Transporters*: ATP – Binding proteins. An example is P-glycoprotein which blocks absorption in the gut, acting as gatekeeper for later P450 cytochrome actions (CYP3A4), multidrug resistance in tumors, responsible gene PGY-1 [13], and *4. DNA Processes* such as the methylation patterns on DNA, methyl guanine methyl transferase (MGMT) gene promoter alters response to treatment with alkylating agents [14].

An illustrative use of clinical data repositories to advance personalized medicine is often seen in the area of cancer research, such as Kathy Halamka's case reported by Strickland [15]. Diagnosed at the age of 49 with Stage III breast cancer, Kathy was faced with the choice of the conservative, standard-of-care protocol of mastectomy followed by chemotherapy. As a patient of Beth Israel Deaconess Medical Center, Kathy's medical team was able to query the clinical data repository comprised of data from the EMRs of five Harvard-affiliated hospitals, using the i2b2 platform. By searching for patients with certain characteristics (e.g., 50-year old, Asian females, stage III breast cancer, medications, outcomes), the medical team was able to identify variables which indicated that a different treatment protocol was more appropriate for Kathy. Choosing to not have surgery as a first treatment step, Kathy began with chemotherapy drugs that targeted the estrogen-sensitive tumor cells. By the completion of chemotherapy, the tumor was no longer visible on radiographs. Her treatment ended with a lumpectomy and a continuation of estrogen-blocking medication.

A New Paradigm in Medical and Health Professions Education: Team Science in Biomedical Informatics

In addition to the "grand challenge" of developing a systems approach in data mining to integrating "multiscale biological information intro predictive and actionable models", [4] there are many other challenges to the advancement of personalized medicine. For example, it has been suggested that training for physicians should shift "away from the current discipline-specific model to a vertically integrated nodes-and-connections framework" to give future physicians a more holistic view of biological processes [2, 4]. The sheer volume of information, and its rapid growth, will require such changes and new clinical decision support tools must be developed to support physicians in their work [8, 16]. Further educational outreach will be necessary to all principal stakeholders in the healthcare industry, including patients, healthcare organizations, pharmaceutical companies, and those who will develop research careers. These biomedical problems will best be solved by multi-disciplinary 'team science' groups, working through challenges using the diverse lens' clinical, healthcare, and informatics professionals [2, 4].

The incoming health workforce has been slowly transforming the way health care is delivered mainly through technological advances, innovative approaches and the need to make faster and better decisions in prevention, diagnosis, prognosis and treatment [17]. Experience has shown that achieving effective and efficient delivery of any type of solution to a challenge is done faster and more reliably if many minds work together in a team which has a common goal. Academic institutions have responded by providing healthcare professionals with education and training in the skills necessary to work effectively in multidisciplinary teams [18]. Delivering innovative health solutions at a faster pace, while providing the highest level of quality, requires that diverse, different and complementary health disciplines join expertise and establish clear and efficient patterns of communication [19]. There is an urgent need to integrate the experts in bioinformatics and technology (i.e., biomedical and health informaticians) with their end users (e.g., practitioners, researchers and health professionals), who will work with their data on a day-to-day basis. Communication among disciplines, by the use of technology, supports these stakeholders becoming partners for better health. These teams create a common pathway that allows them to network and understand each other's role in delivering targeted therapies.

Role of Electronic Medical Records in Translational Medicine

Translational medicine is a multidisciplinary form of science that bridges gaps that often exist between basic science, applied science, and clinical practice -- ultimately leading to more meaningful health outcomes at the individual as well as the population level. "Translation" is driven by the development of diagnostic tools, data analysis tools, medicines, policies and procedures, and education. The "gold standard" for translational medicine is that new products and therapies are incorporated into clinical practice as beneficial and may become part of accepted standards of care.

However, the use of new tests, implementation of diagnostic tools, approval of new medicines, and forward-thinking development of education, policies, and procedures is limited by the speed and accuracy of independent reviews for reliability and accuracy. Translational medicine has assisted in accelerating the movement of research into medical products and therapies, supported by funding into regulatory science. Westfall, Mold and Fagnan reported that it takes an average of 17 years for research evidence to reach clinical practice [20]. This lag has generally been applied to all forms of treatment modalities including pharmaceutical medications, therapeutic modalities, and outcomes related to interventions related to behavior change. As the burden of chronic disease continues to increase across the globe, increased wait times for more effective treatments to come to clinical practice is unrealistic. Case in point, over the past 50 years, advances in science and medicine have led to a dramatic increase in the average life expectancy in the United States (US). At the beginning of the 20th century, a child born in the US in 1900 rarely lived beyond the age of 50; by contrast, a child born in the US in 2000 had a life expectancy of 76 years [21]. With increased life expectancy, adults are living longer with a greater burden of chronic disease and the possibility of disabilities, such as neuropathy, a comorbidity of diabetes. In this paradigm, the US can expect to continue to spend between 70 and 75% of healthcare expenditures on the treatment of chronic diseases [22]. Translational medicine can shorten the time from 'bench to bedside' by focusing research in various aspects of clinical testing, such as biomarkers, new assay methods, and the role of genetics as mediators in response to treatment to drugs.

As the translational medicine pathway increasingly leads to a more effective and quicker delivery of products and therapies to clinical practice, clinicians have been faced with the implementation of information technology into the clinical care environment. The adoption and implementation of electronic medical records (EMRs) systems, providers are now faced with a plethora of patient information. These digital healthcare infrastructures are designed to improve how healthcare is delivered and improve the quality of healthcare provided, i.e., improve patient healthcare outcomes.

The concept of electronic health (medical) records was first introduced by Lawrence L. Weed in the 1960's. A physician, Weed believed that an automated system that would reorganize and improve access to patient information housed in medical records would improve patient care. His work was the nucleus for the PROMIS project at the University of Vermont in 1967 [23]. Project objectives were to develop an automated system that would provide physicians with timely and sequential information for a patient, enabling the rapid collection of data which could be analyzed and used for such endeavors as epidemiological studies to business audits. During this same time period, Mayo Clinic began work on developing an electronic medical record system as well. The decades of the 1970's and 1980's saw rapid development of early models of electronic medical record systems. Early EMR development was often driven by academic and research institutions. In addition to the PROMIS system from the University of Vermont, Harvard University developed the COSTAR EMR system for ambulatory care environments and Duke University pioneered "The Medical Record" as an early in-patient care EMR. In 1972, the Regenstrief Institute developed the Regenstrief Medical Record System, a physician-designed, integrated in-patient and out-patient information system, implemented in the Wishard Diabetes Clinic [24].

In 2004, George W. Bush released The President's Information Technology Plan [25], which set forward a bold plan to ensure that most Americans had an electronic health record within the next decade. This national commitment to the use of health information technology would be an innovation leading to reduced medical errors, controlling the rising costs of healthcare, and improving the quality of healthcare. The adoption of EMRs was stimulated by funding provided under the Health Information Technology for Economic and Clinical Health (HITECH) Act, a component of the American Recovery and Reinvestment Act of 2009 [26] under President Barack Obama. Not only did the HITECH Act promote adoption of EMRs, but it enacted sets of 'meaningful use' guidelines which would guide or help providers realize improvements in care [27]. By 2013, 94% of acute care hospitals were using EMR systems that were certified as meeting federal requirements for Meaningful Use objectives. And these facilities were increasingly using EMRs that were considered comprehensive systems, those that allowed providers to capture electronic clinical information (e.g., patient demographics, physician notes, medication lists, discharge summaries, etc.) as well as computerized provider order entry (CPOE) (e.g., lab reports, medications, radiology tests, nursing orders, etc.); results management (e.g., viewing of lab and radiology reports, view radiology images, view diagnostic images and results, etc.); and provided decision support (e.g., clinical guidelines, clinical reminders, drug allergy results, drug-drug interactions, drug dosing support, etc.) [28]. Each EMR system, in essence, is a small data repository of those patients receiving care from providers operating under a given healthcare system (i.e., hospital, clinic, etc.). Alone, these data repositories offer clinicians important insights into patient care, opening the door to personalized medicine. When combined with other data sources, resulting in large, "big data" repositories, the opportunity to further personalized medicine is increased exponentially.

Personalized Medicine and Health Equity

Hamburg and Collins commented that the investments made in basic science, particularly the Human Genome Project, laid the foundation for translational medicine and opened to door to the development of personalized medicine [29]. With the complete mapping of the human genome, researchers have identified genetic variations that contribute to disease. In turn, scientists have actively sought and continue to develop diagnostic tests and treatment modalities that improve an individual patient's response to therapy targeted toward their unique genetic profile. In this way, translational medicine can also provide a pathway to improve health equity across traditional barriers such as socioeconomic status, race/ethnicity, sex/gender, and geographical location [30].

Yet, personalized medicine and its impact on health equity is not without its concerns. Health disparities have often been linked to disparities in education, race, and income. In 2002, the Institute of Medicine (IOM) Committee on Understanding and Eliminating Racial and Ethnic Disparities in Health Care released its report on the quality chasm that existed between racial and ethnic minorities and the quality of healthcare they received [31]. Advocates of personalized medicine say that the healthcare system will realize lower total costs of care. This will be a result of the efficiency in clinical care that personalizes therapies. These savings could then be used for the care of uninsured and/or low-income patients.

Yet, there are concerns that the benefits of personalized medicine will go more to patients who are higher income, and who are often not people of racial and/or ethnic minority groups, thus increasing the health disparities healthcare now struggles with. Three strategies have been proposed to proactively optimize the benefits of personalized medicine, lessen the potential worsening of health disparities [32]. The foundation of these strategies is that health equity be included as a cornerstone in the development of personalized therapeutics. A brief summary of the strategies proposed by Ward [32] are:

1. Data must be collected in a systematic way from access to and use of personalized therapies, including how use varies by those patients of different socioeconomic status. This would include eligible users but who are not yet users of these therapies. A wide variety data sources should be included such as existing databases and registries including those maintained at the state and federal level as well as partners such as pharmaceutical companies and patient advocacy groups. Access to these multiple sources of data will require the development of public-private partnerships. These partnerships will need to not only support the extraction and translation of data out of information systems for use in developing personalize therapies, but will require feedback loops that inform providers about utilization of these therapies and their success.
2. Dissemination models for developed therapies should include strategies that include outreach to patients who are not likely to have access to medications and healthcare, e.g., uninsured vs.

insured. Strategies should serve to open access to patients who have been historically disadvantaged in access to healthcare and medical treatment without putting previously non-disadvantaged groups at risk for reduced access to personalized treatments.

3. Policies that foster the equitable development and access of medications, therapies, and devices that would be used in personalized medicine. Ward proposes that linking these developments to reimbursement and patent protections may establish a more level playing field for developers such as pharmaceutical companies may help assure that all patients may be eligible for personalized medicine approaches.

CONCLUSION

Through this review, we aimed to provide an overview of personalized medicine, offering perspectives in four important, influencing topics: 1) the availability of "big data" and the role of biomedical informatics in personalized medicine, 2) the need for interdisciplinary teams in the development and evaluation of personalized therapeutic app roaches, 3) the impact of electronic medical record systems and clinical data warehouses on the field of personalized medicine, and 4) strategies that will increase the impact of personalized medicine as a tool to promote health equity. Ongoing challenges to the translation of biomedical information into applied clinical practice of personalized medicine includes reclassification of disease states, scientific challenges such as determining which genetic markers have the most clinical significance, and policy regulation of genetic testing. Health informaticians are critical partners in overcoming these challenges, working with clinicians and researchers, to identify and implement data analytics, including the development of predictive data mining strategies, to enable the use of clinical data repositories for personalized therapies. Some have expressed concerns that personalized medicine may more significantly benefit those patients who have greater access to care, further deepening already existing health disparities and health inequities, However, there is a significant opportunity for personalized medicine to increase treatment accuracy and decrease social and scientific bias.

ACKNOWLEDGMENTS

This work was supported by the National Institute on Minority Health and Health Disparities of the National Institutes of Health under Award Numbers U54MD007587, S21MD001830 and R25MD007607. Its contents are solely the responsibility of authors and do not necessarily represent the official view of NIH.

REFERENCES

1. [Accessed: November 7, 2015];FACT SHEET: President Obama's Precision Medicine Initiative. 2015 https://www.whitehouse.gov/the-press-office/2015/01/30/fact-sheet-president-obama-s-precision-medicine-initiative. Last Updated: January 30, 2015.
2. National Research Council (US) Committee on a Framework for Developing a New Taxonomy of Disease. Toward Precision Medicine: Building a Knowledge Network for Biomedical Research and a New Taxonomy of Disease. National Academies Press; Washington, D.C: 2011. [Accessed: November 7, 2015]. http://www.ncbi.nlm.nih.gov/books/NBK91503/ Last Updated: 2015. http://dx.doi.org/10.17226/13284.
3. Katsnelson A. Momentum grows to make 'personalized' medicine more 'precise' Nature Medicine. 2013;19:249. http://dx.doi.org/10.1038/nm0313-249.
4. Hood L, Flores N. A personal view on systems medicine and the emergence of proactive P4 medicine: predictive, preventive, personalized and participatory. New Biotechnology. 2012;29:613–624. http://dx.doi.org/10.1016/j.nbt.2012.03.004.
5. Fernald GH, Capriotti E, Daneshjou R, Karczewski KJ, Altman RB. Bioinformatics challenges for personalized medicine. Bioinformatics. 2011;27:1741–1748. http://dx.doi.org/10.1093/bioinformatics/btr295.
6. Hindorff LA, Sethupathy P, Junkins HA, Ramos EM, Mehta JP, Collins FS, Manolio TA. Potential etiologic and functional implications of genome-wide association loci for human diseases and traits. Proceedings of the National Academy of Sciences. 2009;106:9362–9367. http://dx.doi.org/10.1073/pnas.0903103106.
7. Bates S. Progress towards personalized medicine. Drug Discovery Today. 2010;15:115–120. http://dx.doi.org/10.1016/j.drudis.2009.11.001.
8. West M, Ginsburg GS, Huang AT, Nevins JR. Embracing the complexity of genomic data for personalized medicine. Genome Research. 2006;16:559–566. http://dx.doi.org/10.1101/gr.3851306.
9. National Center for Biomedical Computing. [Accessed November 23, 2015];i2b2:Informatics for Integrating Biology and the Bedside. 2015 https://www.i2b2.org/. Last Updated: 2015.

10. Ma JD, Lee KC, Kuo GM. HLA-B*5701 testing to predict abacavir hypersensitivity. PLoS Currents Evidence on Genomic Tests. 2010;2:RRN1203. http://doi.org/10.1371/currents.RRN1203.
11. Sauer J-M, Ponsler GD, Mattiuz EL, Long AJ, Witcher JW, Thomasson HR, Desante KA. Disposition and Metabolic Fate of Atomoxetine Hydrochloride: The Role of CYP2D6 in Human Disposition and Metabolism. Drug Metabolism and Disposition. 2003;31:98–107. http://dx.doi.org/10.1124/dmd.31.1.98.
12. Ross JS, Fletcher JA. The HER-2/neu Oncogene in Breast Cancer: Prognostic Factor, Predictive Factor, and Target for Therapy. Stem Cells. 1998;3:413–428. http://dx.doi.org/10.1002/stem.160413.
13. Shugarts S, Benet LZ. The Role of Transporters in the Pharmacokinetics of Orally Administered Drugs. Pharmaceutical Research. 2009;26:2039–2054. http://doi.org/10.1007/s11095-009-9924-0.
14. Esteller M, Garcia-Foncillas J, Andion E, Goodman SN, Hidalgo OF, Vanaclocha V, Baylin SB, Herman JG. Inactivation of the DNA repair gene MGMT and the clinical response of gliomas to alkylating agents. New England Journal of Medicine. 2000;343:1350–1354. http://dx.doi.org/10.1056/nejm200011093431901.
15. Strickland E. Their prescription: big data. IEEE Spectrum. 2015;52:58–85. http://dx.doi.org/10.1109/mspec.2015.7115569.
16. Mirnezami R, Nicholson J, Darzi A. Preparing for precision medicine. New England Journal of Medicine. 2012;366:489–491. http://dx.doi.org/10.1056/NEJMp1114866.
17. Dougherty D, Conway PH. The "3Ts". Road Map to transform US Health Care. Journal of the American Medical Association. 2008;299:2319–2321. http://dx.doi.org/10.1001/jama.299.19.2319.
18. Estape E, Mays MH, Harrigan R, Mayberry R. Incorporating translational research with clinical research to increase effectiveness in healthcare for better health. Clinical and Translational Medicine. 2014;3:20–27. http://dx.doi.org/10.1186/2001-1326-3-20.
19. Estape E, Soto de Laurido LE, Shaheen M, Quarshie A, Frontera W, Mays MH, Harrigan R, White R. A Multi-institutional, Multidisciplinary Model for Developing and Teaching Translational Research in Health Disparities. Clinical and Translational Science Journal. 2011;4:434–438. http://dx.doi.org/10.1111/j.1752-8062.2011.00346.x.
20. Westfall J, Mold J, Fagnan L. Practice-based research – "Blue

Highways" on the NIH roadmap. Journal of the American Medical Association. 2007;297:403–406. http://dx.doi.org/10.1001/jama.297.4.403.

21. Child Trends Databank. [Accessed: November 14, 2015];Life expectancy. 2015 Available at: http://www.childtrends.org/?indicators=life-expectancy Last Updated: January, 2015.
22. Stanton MW, Rutherford MK. Research in Action Issue. Vol. 19. Rockville (MD): Agency for Healthcare Research and Quality; 2005. The high concentration of U.S. health care expenditures; pp. 1–12. AHRQ Pub. No. 06-0060.
23. Schultz JR. A history of the PROMIS Technology: An effective human interface. In: Goldberg A, editor. A History of Personal Workstations. Reading, MA: AMC Press; 1988. pp. 1–48.
24. Regenstrief Institute. Historical timeline. 2015 Retrieved from https://www.regenstrief.org/files/7713/6741/7221/Regenstrief_Timeline_v7.pdf.
25. The White House. Promoting Innovation and Competitiveness: President Bush's Technology Agenda. 2004 Retrieved from http://georgewbush-whitehouse.archives.gov/infocus/technology/economic_policy200404/chap3.html.
26. Health Information Technology for Economic and Clinical Health (HITECH) Act, Title XIII of Division A and Title IV of Division B of the American Recovery and Reinvestment Act of 2009 (ARRA), Pub. L. No. 111-5, 123 Stat. 226 (Feb. 17, 2009), codified at 42 U.S.C. §§300jj et seq.; §§17901 et seq.
27. Blumenthal D. Launching HITECH. New England Journal of Medicine. 2010;362:382–385. http://dx.doi.org/10.1056/nejmp0912825.
28. Charles D, Gabriel M, Furukawa MF. Adoption of Electronic Health Record Systems among U.S. Non-federal Acute Care Hospitals: 2008–2013. ONC Data Brief. 2014;16
29. Hamburg MA, Collins FS. The Path to Personalized Medicine. New England Journal of Medicine. 2010;363:301–304. http://dx.doi.org/10.1056/nejmp1006304 https://www.healthit.gov/sites/default/files/oncdatabrief16.pdf.Last Updated: May 2014. Accessed: November 14, 2015.
30. Dankwa-Mullan I, Rhee KB, Stoff DM, Pohlhaus JR, Sy FS,

Stinson N, Ruffin J. Moving Toward Paradigm-Shifting Research in Health Disparities Through Translational, Transformational, and Transdisciplinary Approaches. American Journal of Public Health. 2010;S1:S19–24. http://dx.doi.org/10.2105/ajph.2009.189167.

31. Smedley BD, Stith AY, Nelson AR, editors. Institute of Medicine (US) Committee on Understanding and Eliminating Racial and Ethnic Disparities in Health Care. Unequal treatment: Confronting racial and ethnic disparities in health care. Washington, DC: National Academy Press (US); 2002. http://dx.doi.org/10.17226/10260.
32. Ward MM. Personalized Therapeutics: A Potential Threat to Health Equity. Journal of General Internal Medicine. 2012;27:868–870. http://dx.doi.org/10.1007/s11606-012-2002-z.

CHAPTER 5

PPPM (PREDICTIVE, PREVENTIVE AND PERSONALIZED MEDICINE) AS A NEW MODEL OF THE NATIONAL AND INTERNATIONAL HEALTHCARE SERVICES AND THUS A PROMISING STRATEGY TO PREVENT A DISEASE: FROM BASICS TO PRACTICE

I. A. Sadkovsky[1], O. Golubnitschaja[2,3], M. A. Mandrik[1], M. A. Studneva[1], H. Abe[4], H. Schroeder[5], E. N. Antonova1, F. Betsou[6], T. A. Bodrova[7], K. Payne[8], S. V. Suchkov[1,9,10]

[1] I.M. Sechenov First Moscow State Medical University, Moscow, Russia

[2] European Association for Predictive, Preventive and Personalized Medicine (EPMA), Brussels, EU

Citation:Sadkovsky, I., Golubnitschaja, O., Mandrik, M., Studneva, M., Abe, H., Schroeder, H., Antonova, E., Betsou, F., Bodrova, T. , Payne, K. and Suchkov, S. (2014), "PPPM (Predictive, Preventive and Personalized Medicine) as a New Model of the National and International Healthcare Services and Thus a Promising Strategy to Prevent a Disease: From Basics to Practice". *International Journal of Clinical Medicine*, **5**, 855-870. doi: 10.4236/ijcm.2014.514115.

[3] Rheinische Friedrich-Wilhelms-University of Bonn, Bonn, Germany

[4] International Society for Personalized Medicine (ISPM), Tokyo, Japan

[5] Department of Medicine, Genetics and Comparative Pathology, University of Alabama at Birmingham (UAB), Birmingham, USA

[6] Université du Luxembourg and IBBL (Integrated BioBank of Luxembourg), Luxembourg, EU

[7] National Research University "Higher School of Economics", Moscow, Russia

[8] Institute of Population Health and Health Economics, University of Manchester, Manchester, UK

[9] A.I. Evdokimov Moscow State Medical & Dental University, Moscow, Russia 10United Cultural Convention (UCC), Cambridge, UK

ABSTRACT

Nowadays the system of public health is constructed in such a manner so that its main objective is the recovery of an already sick person, while prediction and prevention receive little attention. Meanwhile the development of these aspects of medicine can lead to the ability to control morbidity among the population, to identify chronic and genetic diseases in the early stages of development, and thus to prevent their further progression. This will reduce traditionally high costs of sick people treatment and the number of disabled population, and improve the quality and duration of life. The elaboration of new fields of science that are working on the study and interpretation of data obtained during laboratory and clinical research, creation of new methods for diagnosis, prognosis and treatment, provides an opportunity now to implement a new strategy, called PPPM, and gets promising results, which should lead to further development of an existing medicine.

Keywords Predictive, Preventive, and Personalized Medicine, Biomarkers, Subclinical, Metabolomics, Genomics, Proteomics, Bioinformatics, Public Health, Predisposition

INTRODUCTION

Over the course of its history, medical science was much more focused on the treatment of clinical illnesses that have already arisen, than on detecting and preventing their occurrence. Practical experience over many years has shown that this approach is often ineffective against a number of diseases, and also requires a great deal of expenses [1.-[3.. Medicine and thus healthcare services are now undergoing a major revolution that will transform the nature of healthcare from reactive and palliative to preventive and guaranteed [4.. The changes will be catalyzed by a new system approach to disease that will trigger the emergence of PPPM (Predictive, Preventive and Personalized Medicine)—a medicine that focuses on the integrated diagnosis, treatment and prevention of disease in individual patients (Figure 1). Predicting the future is not a new calling neither even a new challenge. But unlike the predictions of the oracles of antiquity or new-age fortunetellers, PPPM is based on the science achievements that help to prevent the development of disease before symptoms appear. Most of the chronic disorders develop gradually over a period of time. It may take years to reach a point to be diagnosed definitively [3.-[5.. To achieve the practical implementation of PPPM concept, it is necessary to create a fundamentally new strategy based upon the pre-early (subclinical) recognition of biomarkers of hidden imbalances long before the illness clinically manifests itself. This strategy would give a real opportunity to secure preventive measures whose personalization could have a significantly positive influence on demographics! NIH (National Institutes of Health) has added PPPM to a list of the five most prioritized branches of the development in 21st century. PPPM is also being actively supported and promoted by the European Commission, by FDA and by CDC

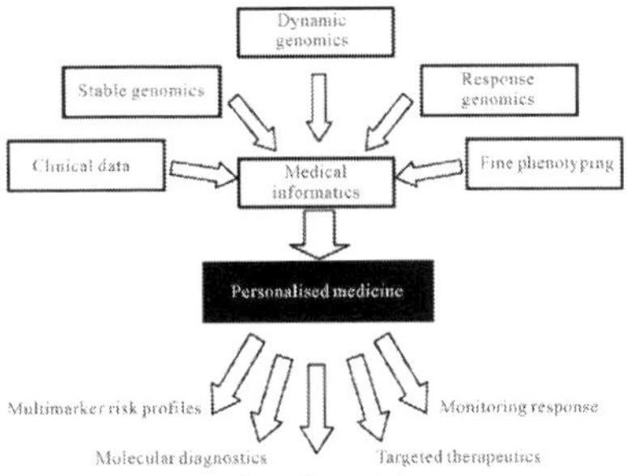

Figure 1. The scheme depicts the underpinnings of personalized medicine and principle approaches to be included into the PPPM protocols.

PPPM actively employs the latest scientific achievements, which help prevent disease, and thereby avoid a failure of performance, quality of life and life expectancy. Within this framework, a key role is given to the prediction and prevention diseases. Therefore, the search for new methods of diagnosis which would allow identifying the disease at an early stage, before the formation of the pathological process and the development of effective means of drug-based prevention have become the main objectives of the medical science of the 21st century (Figure 2). Thus, the main task PPPM includes:

- Determination of signs of the disease at the stage of preclinical pathology in conjunction with the identification of targets for adequate prevention;
- Targeted correction of the violations with the goal of pharmacological prevention, which belongs to the category of preventive measures that contribute to the suppression of the pathological process in the preclinical stage [3..

FUNDAMENTALS OF PPPM

PPPM as the big change to forecast, to predict and to prevent is rooted from the achievements of genomics, proteomics, metabolomics and bioinformatics which are being implemented into the daily practice to secure visualizing of lesion foci that was previously unknown to clinicians. The change mentioned is rooted in new science covering systems biology and biomedicine and utilizing a new generations of translational tools to implement the new concepts and technologies into clinical practice. And therefore it is necessary to create a new strategy that takes into account individual features of the organism. Complete diagnostics of the organism, the creation of individual genetic passports, development and correction of treatment strategies based on the individual features of genetics, metabolism, microbiota of particular organism—all these tasks are belongs to PPPM. However, holding such a colossal amount of expensive and complicated research would be impossible without translation of the latest scientific achievements into practical medicine [3. [6.-[8. (Figure 3).

Genomics

Genomics deals with the common principles of genome composition and function by analyzing DNA structure and function using a combination of sequencing and genetic polymorphism assays. The latter has revealed single nucleotide polymorphisms (SNPs) as families of genomic biomarkers that account for some of the genetic variability between individuals, and made possible the exploitation of genome-wide association studies (GWAS) to identify genetic variations and to thus define risks for common diseases (Figure 4). In reality, genomics as a set of molecular tools to probe genome and to thus identify and to select genomic biomarkers has allowed for identifying newer genes and newer genetic variations that affect health to form subclinical risks to be screened and unveiled, then the subclinical pathology to be diagnosed, monitored and terminated to prevent illness [3. [9..

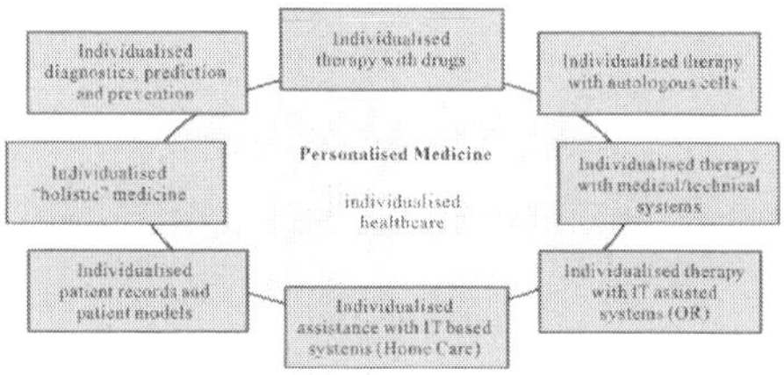

Figure 2. The overarching idea of personalized (individualized) medicine with basic branches aimed at subclinical diagnosis and preventive measures.

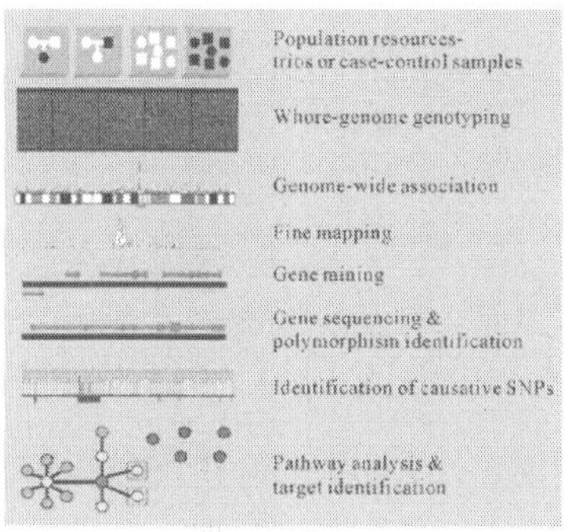

Figure 3. Ways to implementation of the main tasks of genomic diagnostics for new target identification and screening of causative mutations.

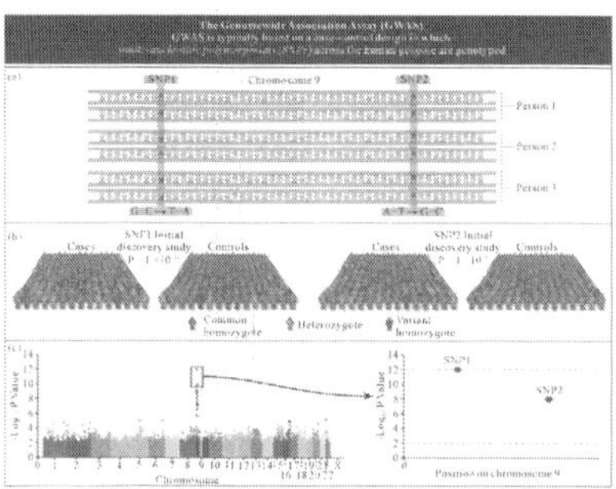

Figure 4. Bioinformatics as a valuable tool for processing of large data values in indicative research, genome-wide analysis and large-scale population studies (a). Simultaneous genotyping of more than 500,000 - 1,000,000 SNPs (b). Initial discovery study with large patient and control sample collection (c).

Statistical analysis (probability plot for association with a certain disease) and independent replication of top results.

Among the best-validated genomic biomarkers are cancer-related and autoimmunity-related ones to be broadly known (Figure 5 and Figure 6). As an allied portion of genomics and thus an area of study to examine the impact of genetic variations on the response to medications is pharmacogenomics.

The latter is aimed at tailoring drug therapy at a dosage that is most appropriate for an individual patient, with the potential benefits of increasing the clinical efficacy and safety. Pharmacogenomics will thus guide therapeutic decisions and monitor the response to therapy on one hand and speed the development of novel therapeutics, on the other one [10.. Genomic information is now increasingly available out-side traditional medical settings to suit the model of PPPM.

Patients can now instigate their own testing and often know more than their clinicians about particular genetic topics. Indeed, healthcare providers are increasingly bypassed altogether, as patients embrace direct-toconsumer (DTC) genetic tests and turn to social networks for help in interpreting their results.

Development of genomics pathologies, including autoimmune, not only provides their molecular genetic diagnostics, but also allows determining the intensity of RNA and protein synthesis (collectively-transcriptome) associated with the occurrence and development of disease.

The study of transcriptomics also referred to as expression profiling, examines the expression level of mRNAs in a given cell population, often using high throughput techniques based on DNA microarray technology. Also, recent advances in RNAi screening and next-generation sequencing technologies enable a synergistic application of all of these genomic technologies to the discovery of predictive biomarkers [3. [5..

Thus comparison of the transcriptome of normal and pathological samples allows to identify new biomarkers and biopredictors, control changes in their expression levels in time and, therefore, to make conclusions about the dynamics of disease and efficiency of treatment, predicting its outcome (Figure 7). Genes can say a lot about an individual's predisposition to a disease, but cannot reveal what is happening in cells at the protein level.

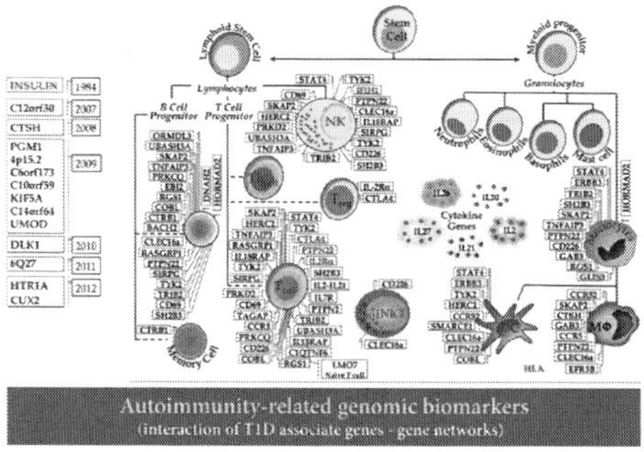

Figure 5. Autoimmunity-related genomic biomarkers (interaction of T1D associated genes-gene networks).

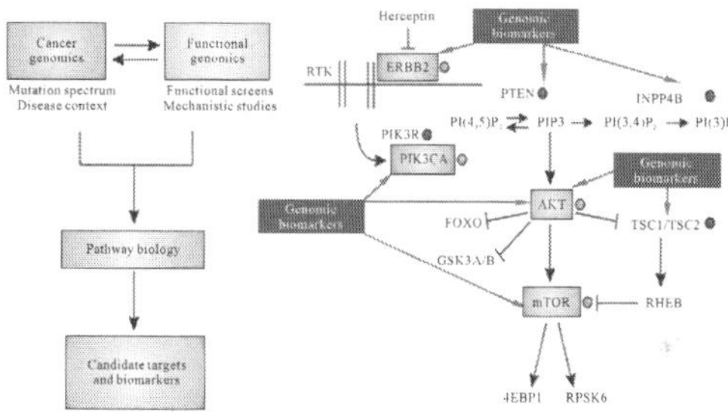

Figure 6. Genomic biomarkers and their impact into pathway-targeted cancer therapies. (a) Routine sequencing of cancer genomes will identify many new genes that are involved in cancer. (b) Detailed mechanistic studies will be required to determine how these genes contribute to tumorigenesis and how they influence therapeutic efficacy. Black arrows and lines illustrate the gene interactions in signaling pathways of cancerogenesis. Black arrows mean induction and lines mean repression.

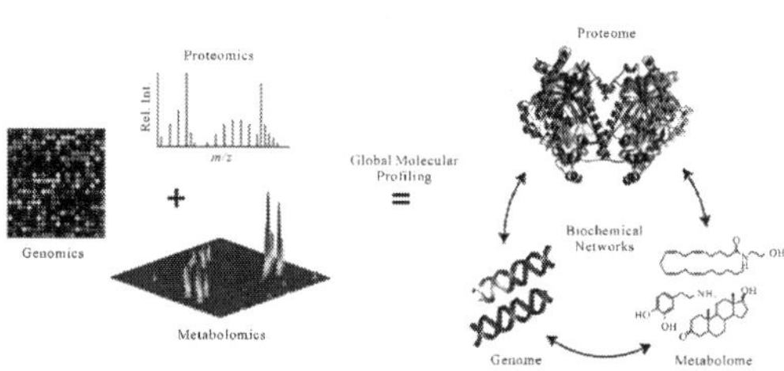

Figure 7. The interrelations between the basis of PPPM (genomics, proteomics, and metabolomics) and their application for global molecular profiling.

The latter would attribute to proteomics to identify within interactomes individual proteins and their epitopes to be valuable for predictive diagnosing and thus may eventually have a great impact on PPPM.

Proteomics

Proteomics provides opportunity to characterize the cell within the framework of current point of time by fixing all of its RNA transcripts and proteins in real time. Proteomic analysis is focused on the simultaneous study of many individual proteins and consequently researches include immunochemical tests, micro sequencing of proteins, high performance liquid chromatography (HPLC) and mass-spectrometry as well as application protein microarrays with various types of detection. Such approach allows to detect subclinical defects and imbalances that are suitable for preventive intervention, including cancer- and autoimmunity-related ones [3.. A combination of genomic and proteomic biomarkers are becoming of great significance to predict risks of the chronization and thus of the disabling since chronic diseases are preceded by a long subclinical (symptomfree) phase or a period of latency (Figure 8). At this point, most of the FDA approved targeted therapeutics are directed at proteomic, not genomic biomarkers. And protein-based assays were the first "companion diagnostic" assays to comprise both diagnostic and therapeutic resources and to be approved by FDA (Figure 9).

Metabolomics

Metabolomics shows the functional state of the cell in real time at the level of its metabolism, requiring use of the term "metabolome", which reflects the totality of all the metabolic pathways in the cell at a given time, which makes metabolomics highly effective means of early detection of disease, monitoring of treatment outcomes and toxic impact on the body (Figure 10). Metabolomics is based on combined application of the methods of physical chemistry (HPLC, gas chromatography, etc.) and computer analysis (pattern recognition). Progress in this field has led to the creation of methods such as metabolic fingerprinting (classification bioassay based on the characteristics of involved metabolites) and metabolic profiling (analysis of metabolites belonging to the same chemical class or a specific biochemical pathway), which allow to define thousands of metabolites in the bioassay. In fact, metabolomics today is development of global profile of metabolite concentrations in the sample in order to detect metabolic changes that are inherent to the point of initiation of the disease and its dynamics as well as regularities metabolic response to therapy. However, for correlation data with the overall picture of metabolism and prediction of the nature of the interlayer interaction based on the received regularities, we need to implement their data integration and visualization. Bioinformatics is designed to solve this task using mathematical modeling.

Bioinformatics

Over the past 40 years, science has accumulated tremendous amount of experimental and theoretical material in the field of molecular biology.

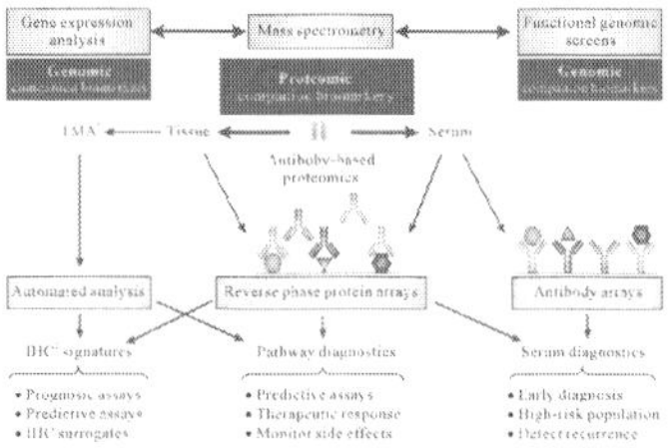

Figure 8. Discovering of proteomic companion biomarkers. IHC[1]: immunohistochemistry. TMAs[2]: tissue microarrays.

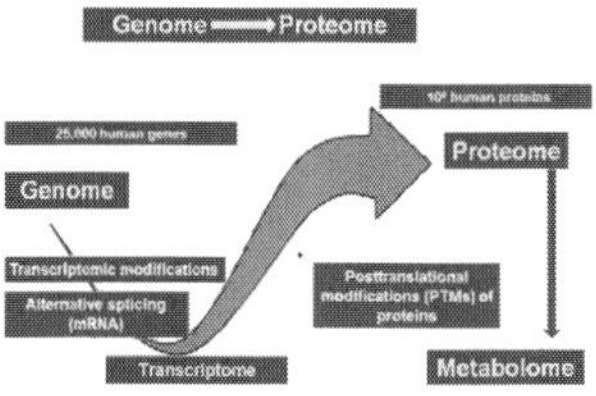

Figure 9. In reality, proteomics per se is the continuation of functional genomics and, at the same time, a prologue to metabolomics.

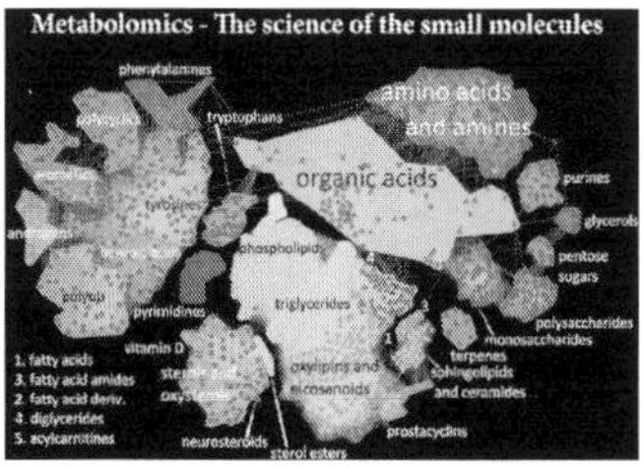

Figure 10. Metabolomics-the science of the small molecules.

Huge amount of data on the structure and functioning of biological molecules (proteins and nucleic acids) require advanced computer methods for their analysis and development of databases on the basis of the received information. Therefore a new science has appeared—bioinformatics, combining methods and approaches of computational molecular biology (Figure 11). Depending on the task, bioinformatics can be divided into several areas:

Sequence Analysis

Development of effective methods of decoding the nucleotide sequences resulted in automation of research and the accumulation of large amounts of information, in which it is impossible to find or compare (align) any parts of nucleotide sequences without application of computer methods.

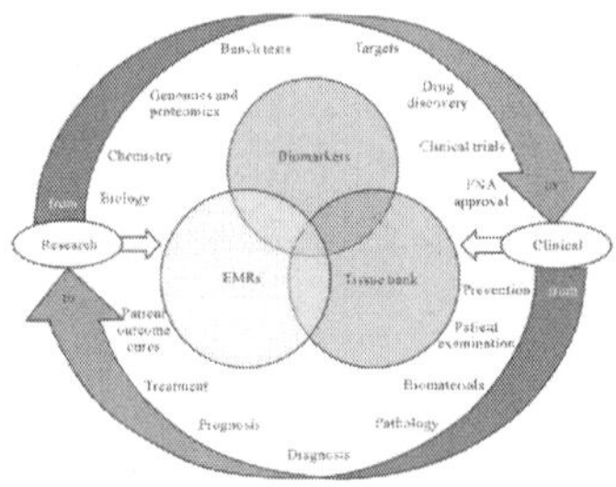

Figure 11. Knowledge received from scientific researches, as well as from clinical practice is exposed to careful processing and interpretation through bioinformatics.

Structural Bioinformatics

The unique spatial structure of a protein is one of its most important characteristics. Since the most drugs are chemicals whose molecules are able to form complexes with protein molecules, thereby influencing their action, the study of protein structure, finding binding sites to determine the structure of protein complexes with drug molecules are important objectives of bioinformatics.

Computer Genomics

Definition of full nucleotide sequence is only step to understanding the functioning of the cell. Application of computer analysis can significantly accelerate these studies that promotes to effectively search of potential drug targets, and studying of the metabolic pathways that can be used in biotechnology of future.

Biobanks

Biobanks would provide the proper information about a patient's proteomic, genetic and metabolic profiles to be used to tailor medical care due to the individual's needs and personalized scenarios. An under-standing of the factors underlying the burden of a disorder and later on of the clinical illness would provide policymakers, healthcare providers and medical educators with an opportunity to guide preventive initiatives at both individual and community levels. Prevention cannot be imagined without the use of a personalized approach, which involves the creation of individual databases that should be fully structured and analyzed by bioinformatics tools (Figure 12).

PPPM AS A TECHNOLOGICAL ARMAMENTARIUM OF A NEW GENERATION TO GET IT INTO THE PRACTICE IMPLEMENTED

Currently, there is an integration of fundamentals of PPPM, which described above, in clinical practice. PPPM uses a new generation of diagnostic tests, based in particular on the knowledge of genomic, proteomic and metabolomicsbiomarkers that allow us to individually determine the health status of a person predisposed to the disease and to reveal the agents of the probable or the already existing pathology. Predictive branch of PPPM is mainly designed to meet the interests of healthy individuals, its purpose being to determine whether susceptibility to a particular disease is increased or not.

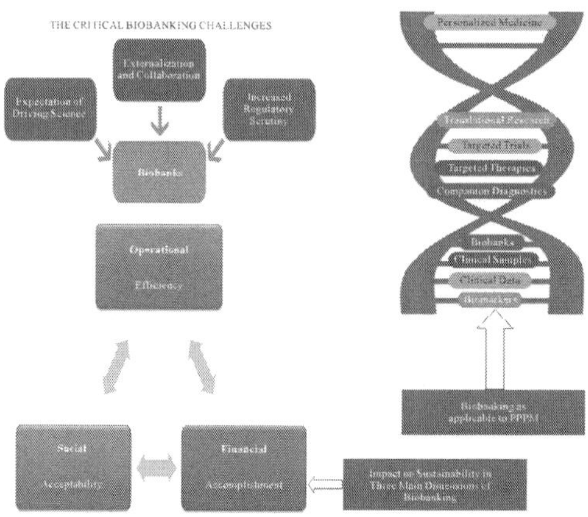

Figure 12. Biobankingas applicable to PPPM.

Preventive branch is aimed at taking measures to avoid development of clinical manifestations rather than cure or treat it on manifestation.

Personalized medicine proposes the customization of healthcare tailored to the individual patient and/or to the person-at-risk by the mutual integration of family history, medical records and other information including genomic, proteomic and metabolomic biomarkers-based profiles to be integrated via bioinformatics [11. [12..

In general, key benefits of PPPM to the patient, person-at-risk and the system would include new abilities to:

- Detect disease at an earlier stage, when it is easier and less expensive to treat effectively;
- Stratify patients into cohorts that enable the selection of optimal and preventive therapy;
- Improve the selection of new targets for drug discovery;
- Shift the emphasis from reaction to prevention and from disease to wellness.

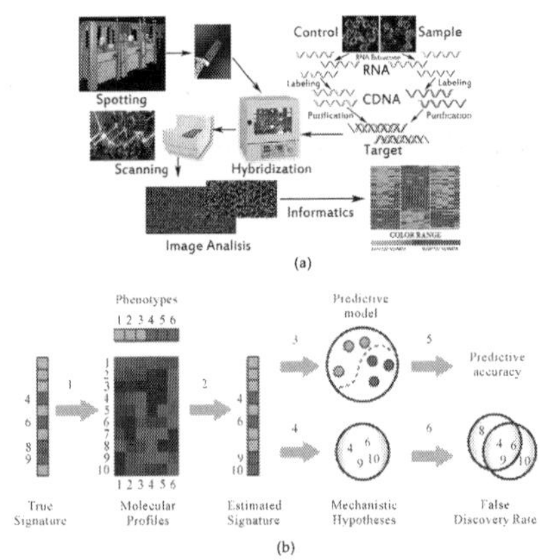

Figure 13. The fundamentals of BioChip methodology.

Generally, there is a multilevel infrastructure to demonstrate and to operate three levels desirable for providing optimal subclinical and clinical medical care services:

It includes:

1). Determining genetic predisposition to a defined pathology to utilise updated protocols of genotyping. This step requires the use of such technologies as genetic polymorphism testing and DNA sequencing, as well as the analysis of information available from the genealogical tree, anamnesis morbi, and anamnesis vitae (Figure 13(a) and Figure 13(b). Technologically, those goals can be accomplished by BioChip methodology (every disease has individual fingerprints and/or molecular signatures: changes in gene expression/transcription levels that are indicative of a nosology) [3. [13..

2). Survey using the target group phenotypic biomarkers (phenotyping protocol) of patients selected at the first stage.

3). Application of preventive measures including monitoring of dynamic changes in the levels of biomarkers and biopredictors and precise control of physiological reactions in response to drug-based preventive measures. We illustrate the ability to predict based on the diagnostic tests, regardless of basic mechanism of disease:

a) HLA-related biomarkers in combination with autoAbs to monitor chronic autoimmune disorders (T1D, MS, SLE).

b) genomic biomarkers in combination with cancer-associated antigens to monitor cancerogenesis. For chronic autoimmune diseases there are two typical examples that best illustrate the specificity of the topic: T1D and MS.

The basis of autoimmune diseases is a universal degenerative and inflammatory process, which comprises a number of stages, including the stage of subclinical pathology. Each stage is proved to be determined by a set of specific parameters, i.e.:

a) Appearance of anti-islet autoAbs and an upsurge in the autoAbs titers in T1D, the most important biopredictive factor of T1D at the subclinical stage.

b) Gene expression products of the key (e.g., functional transcripts) and anti-myelinautoAbs with proteolytic activity directed towards myelin antigens (Abs-proteases) [2..

It was found that the main factor of the clinical manifestations of chronic underlying disease is postinfectious autoimmune syndrome (PIFAS), which was then proposed as a universal model of autoimmune disease (Figure 14). From HLA-related biomarkers most informative genetic markers that increase the risk of developing T1D are DR4, DR3, DQ, DR2, DR6, and DR7, as their certain combinations promote the progression of PIFAS as a biopredictor of T1D-related clinical illness at a subclinical stage. Concerning MS, the most important and informative gene combinations that have to date been associated with MS include 509 TGFB1, C DRB*18(3), CTLA4*G and 238TNF*B1, 308TNF*A2, and CTLA4*G. Such combinations support the formation of PIFAS-related signs at the subclinical stage, which are highly informative biopredictors to monitor a process of demyelination signs at the subclinical stage, which are highly informative biopredictors to monitor a process of demyelination [3. [14.-[16.. Applicable to predictions of autoimmune diseases, proteomics is not less important than genomics (Figure 15). It is known that T1D patients begin expressing auto Abs as early as 5 - 10 years before the clinical onset of the disease. Most of the data available indicate that this phenomenon also occurs in SLE, RA, Addison's disease, celiac disease, and MS [3. [7.. A combination of these data with the geno-and phenotyping of persons having both categories (genomics-and proteomics-related ones simultaneously) allows to significantly increase the predictive index (up to 85% - 90%), thereby improving the selection of persons for further drug-based therapeutic prevention. With regard to cancer diseases, it is known that tumor initiation is provided by oncogenic mutations and inactivation of tumor-suppressor genes and depends on the stepwise acquisition of specific functions by cancer stem cells (CSC) and circulating tumor cells (CTCs) which may be defined by genomic tailoring approach on one hand and proteomic and immunonomic approaches, on the other hand (see Figure 6). A strategy of preventive treatment should contain, at least, two critical steps.

For chronic autoimmune and/or infectious diseases:

1) Quenching of autoaggression or blocking the infectious process;
2) Restoration of the tissue affected

For cancerogenesis:

1) Killing the malignancy and prevention of metastatic formation;

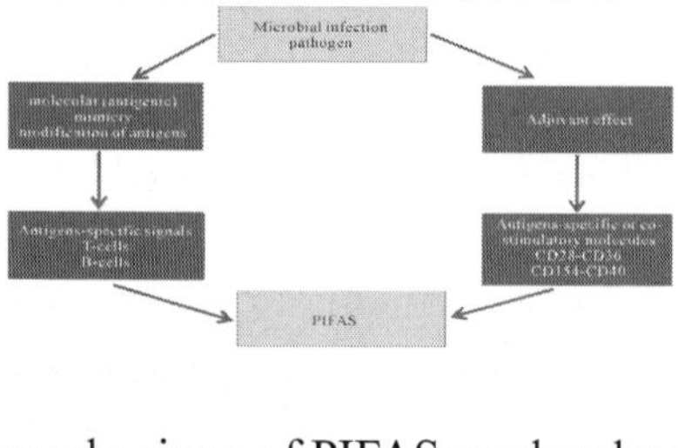

Figure 14. Two major mechanisms of PIFAS: molecular mimicry and adjuvant effect that are usually the common causes of most autoimmune diseases.

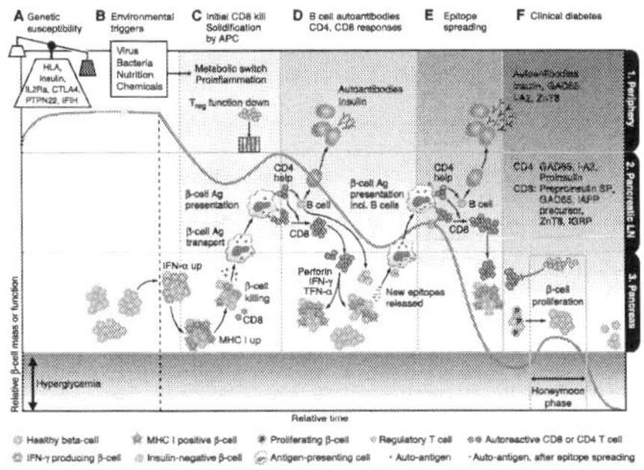

Figure 15. Autoantibodies and diabetes risk.

2) Restoration of the primary tissue affected. The latter can successfully be achieved through the practical realisation of a number of strategies, particularly cell- and/or gene-based therapy, allogenic or xenogeneic transplantation, and stem cell technologies. In addition, a principally new technology that holds promise in modern medicine is the application of Abs-proteases as novel tools for drug-based therapeutic prevention [3. [17..

CONCLUSIONS

21 century marked the beginning of a global transformation in medicine, which characterized by a changing in the fundamental principles of treatment and prevention of diseases. Translation of the advanced discoveries of fundamental sciences directly into clinical practice not only provides creating of new methods and the campaigns which are designed for "protection of individual health", but also allows focusing on diagnostics of diseases, that have not yet arisen, and consequently gives an opportunity to prevent them. PPPM is a new healthcare model that notifies people of the health conditions they're disposed to and it reveals the biomarkers and thus the agents to improve and to thus secure the health and individual biosafety. Meanwhile, implementation of PPPM would require the adjusted technology for proper interpretation of diagnostic and predictive data before the current model "physician-patient" could be gradually displaced by a "medical advisor-healthy persons-at-risk" model. This approach should be based on postulates which will change the incarnate culture and social mentality [3.. First of all, it is the impact of human responsibility for the own health and for the health of their children, and active involvement into the preventive measures for strengthening of the public health and country's biosafety. Secondly, a creation

of legal basis to satisfy all society needs for the protection of individual health—regulations of the state insurance in the PPPM. And, for sure, it's necessary to radically change the system of medical training, and designing novel ap- proaches to build the academic schools of new generations. Due to our viewpoint, all healthcare professionals of the future should be educated to deliver patient-centric care as members of inter-disciplinary teams, emphasizing evidence-based practice, quality improvement approaches and bioinformatics. That concerns the need for novel training programs since the society is in bad need of large-scale dissemination of novel systemic thinking and minding. And upon construction of the new educational platforms in the rational proportions, there would be not a primitive physician created but a medical artist to be able to enrich flow-through medical standards with creative elements to gift for a patient a genuine hope to survive but, in turn, for a person-at-risk—a trust for being no diseased. So, the existing medical education would strongly need to be restructured to involve along with traditional graduate and post-graduate training, pre-graduate preliminaries to disclose for schoolchildren the mysteries of the evidence-based medicine and PPPM as the entity. Currently, many of countries are stressing their national goal to establish a continuous and intensive system of education throughout life consciously. In addition to basic educational programs, it is important to include in the training program of additional education, which provides an individualization of educational process and assists the children to build their own pathway to learn and to know, whilst disclosing their own talents. The process of vocational training of highly skilled specialists in the new generation involves 10 - 12 years of the general and 4 - 5 years of vocational training. Thus, a multistep procedure of forming a competent specialist should not be restricted by the post-university internship training, but be broadened at a pre-university (secondary school) stage, in other words, simultaneously with the profiling seminars and workshops to secure the positive mental motion. In this regard, we suggest creating classes, which will specialize on medicine and biology at schools where students are aimed at the participation in health care modernization. The system of selection of talented youth and its involvement in scientific activity is important at a pre-university level.

The training of specialists who are able to build the interdisciplinary structure of health protection will be based on the new generation principles, taking into consideration the following:

- Peculiarities of introduction of school-university partnership onto international educational ground;

- Role of extra-classes education as the basis for such ground;
- Project principles in the framework of extra-classes education and design of research and engineering games;
- Tough necessity of multi-level testing and dialogues in the partnership student-teacher, their personal features considered, while forming vocationally self-sufficient, promising and highly-skilled specialist with personality for the future;
- Importance of innovation-related risks of educational process and possibility to manage those risks in crises.

The integration of science, education and production has an important role in the quality improvement of science staff training at the undergraduate and postgraduate levels. Such cooperation gives the unique opportunity to combine training on the basis of the fundamental knowledge received at university, with practical experience of production work. At the same time association of the large integrated production structures with universities will allow solving a problem of shortage of experts at the enterprises and in the scientific organizations of a high-tech complex. So, one of the most effective forms of science and education integration is the creation of basic professional chairs at the enterprises and the research laboratory in higher education institutions. Based on current trends and own experience, we have tried a non-canonical approach towards reshuffling the traditional educational tandem "school-university" to create a team of talented and gifted teenagers to be engaged into PPPM-related areas. The team has been given a roof under the aegis of European Association of Predictive, Preventive and Personalized Medicine (EPMA), Brussels, EU, and started up to move ahead now. Our global challenge is that the new guidelines should create the robust juristic and economic platforms for advanced medical services utilizing the cost-effective models of risk assessments followed by tailored preventive treatments focused on the precursor stages of chronic diseases.

COMMENTS

Individuals to be under regular monitoring that helps to detect pathological shifts at subclinical stages have a higher life expectancy and are able-bodied up to 8 - 15 years more than those under traditional treatment. This means that the society would save more than US $20,000 - 40,000 per person annually [18.. At the community level, the annual savings from each individual may vary from several thousands to several tens of thousands US dollars. In the area of oncology, for instance, the latter means that as little as a 10 percent reduction in cancer would translate into a savings of 4.4 trillion US dollars to society. As you might feel, besides the scientific and clinical challenges, there are economic hurdles. So, PPPM promises to sharply reverse the ever-escalating costs of healthcare-introducing diagnosis to stratify patients and disease, decrease high cost of approaches to drug discovery, preventive medicine and wellness. Already now, the implementation of aspects of PPPM improves the results of treatment, as well as expands the powers of the physician and the patient's ability. To ensure the widespread introduction of PPPM it is necessary to eliminate the key technical and societal (ethical, societal, policy, legal, economic, etc.) barriers, that requires a total and comprehensive transformation of Health Care System. On the speed they will be implemented with depends the quality and duration of life not only of the future but also of the present generations. The opportunity arises for unusual and, even extraordinary, strategic partnerships between governments, academic and business sectors. The healthcare industry, public policy sector, and consumer industries will be required to develop new and creative business models and products. And, no doubt, next generations will speak about the XXI century as a time, when medicine became preventive and personified, and its outcomes—predictive and guarantied.

REFERENCES

1. Ray, R. (2012) The Future of Medicine. American Journal of Medicine, 125, 236-239. http://www.ncbi.nlm.nih.gov/pubmed/22340917 http://dx.doi.org/10.1016/j.amjmed.2011.06.035
2. Gabibov, A.G., Paltsev, M.A. and Suchkov, S.V. (2011) Antibody-Associated Proteolysis in Surveillance of Autoimmune Demyelination: Clinical and Preclinical Issues. Future Neurology, 6, 303-305. http://www.futuremedicine.com/toc/fnl/6/3 http://dx.doi.org/10.2217/fnl.11.17
3. Bodrova, T.A., Kostyushev, D.S., Antonova, E.N., Slavin, S., Gnatenko, D.A., Bocharova, M.O., Legg, M., Pozzilli, P., Paltsev, M.A. and Suchkov, S.V. (2012) Introduction into PPPM as a New Paradigm of Public Health Service: An Integrative View. EPMA Journal, 3, 16. http://www.epmajournal.com/content/3/1/16
4. Golubnitschaja, O. and Costigliola, V. (2010) Common Origin but Individual Outcomes: Time for New Guidelines in Personalised Healthcare. Personalized Medicine, 7, 561-568. http://www.futuremedicine.com/doi/abs/10.2217/pme.10.42 http://dx.doi.org/10.2217/pme.10.42
5. Nair, V.S., Maeda, L.S. and Ioannidis, J.P. (2012) Clinical Outcome Prediction by microRNAs in Human Cancer: A Systematic Review. Journal of the National Cancer Institute, 104, 528-540. http://jnci.oxfordjournals.org/content/early/2012/03/06/jnci.djs027.full http://dx.doi.org/10.1093/jnci/djs027
6. Jones, T. and Price, P. (2012) Development and Experimental Medicine Applications of PET in Oncology: A Historical Perspective. Lancet Oncology, 13, e116-e125. http://www.ncbi.nlm.nih.gov/pubmed/22381934 http://dx.doi.org/10.1016/S1470-2045(11)70183-8
7. Patel, N.R., McPhail, M.J., Shariff, M.I., Keun, H.C. and Taylor-Robinson, S.D. (2012) Biofluid Metabonomics Using (1)H NMR Spectroscopy: The Road to Biomarker Discovery in Gastroenterology and Hepatology. Expert Review of Gastroenterology and Hepatology, 6, 239-251. http://www.ncbi.nlm.nih.gov/pubmed/22375528 http://dx.doi.org/10.1586/egh.12.1
8. Hood, L., Balling, R. and Auffray, C. (2012) Revolutionizing Medicine in the 21st Century through Systems Approaches. Biotechnology Journal, 7, 992-1001. http://www.ncbi.nlm.nih.gov/pubmed/22815171 http://dx.doi.org/10.1002/biot.201100306
9. Tran, B., Dancey, J.E., Kamel-Reid, S., McPherson, J.D., Bedard,

P.L., Brown, A.M., Zhang, T., Shaw, P., Onetto, N., Stein, L., Hudson, T.J., Neel, B.G. and Siu, L.L. (2012) Cancer Genomics: Technology, Discovery, and Translation. Journal of Clinical Oncology, 30, 647-660. http://www.ncbi.nlm.nih.gov/pubmed/22271477 http://dx.doi.org/10.1200/JCO.2011.39.2316

10. Scott, S.A. (2011) Personalizing Medicine with Clinical Pharmacogenetics. Genetics in Medicine, 13, 987-995. http://www.ncbi.nlm.nih.gov/pubmed/22095251 http://dx.doi.org/10.1097/GIM.0b013e318238b38c
11. Saubermann, A.J. and Lagasse, R.S. (2012) Prediction of Rate and Severity of Adverse Perioperative Outcomes: "Normal Accidents" Revisited. Mount Sinai Journal of Medicine, 79, 46-55. http://www.ncbi.nlm.nih.gov/pubmed/22238038 http://dx.doi.org/10.1002/msj.21295
12. Lemke, H.U. and Berliner, L. (2011) Patient Specific Modeling and Model Guided Therapy. EPMA Journal, 2, 181- 182. http://www.ncbi.nlm.nih.gov/pmc/articles/PMC3405420/
13. Farra, N., Manickaraj, A.K., Ellis, J. and Mital, S. (2012) Personalized Medicine in the Genomics Era: Highlights from an International Symposium on Childhood Heart Disease. Future Cardiology, 8, 157-160. http://www.ncbi.nlm.nih.gov/pubmed/22413975 http://dx.doi.org/10.2217/fca.12.3
14. Kostyushev, D., Tsarev, I., Gnatenko, D., Paltsev, M. and Suchkov, S. (2011) Myelin-Associated Serological Targets as Applicable to Diagnostic Tools to Be Used at the Preclinical and Transient Stages of Multiple Sclerosis Progression. Open Journal of Immunology, 1, 80-86. http://www.scirp.org/journal/PaperInformation.aspx?paperID=16662#.U3_Xavnud8E
15. Jain, K.K. (2012) Role of Nanodiagnostics in Personalized Cancer Therapy. Clinics in Laboratory Medicine, 12, 15-31. http://www.ncbi.nlm.nih.gov/pubmed/22340841 http://dx.doi.org/10.1016/j.cll.2011.10.001
16. Khitrov, A.N., Shogenov, Z.S., Tretyak, E.B., Ischenko, A.I., Matsuura, E., Neuhaus, O., Paltsev, M.A. and Suchkov, S.V. (2007) Postinfectious Immunodeficiency and Autoimmunity: Pathogenic and Clinical Values and Implications. Expert Review of Clinical Immunology, 3, 323-331. http://www.ncbi.nlm.nih.gov/pubmed/20477676 http://dx.doi.org/10.1586/1744666X.3.3.323

17. Robinton, D.A. and Daley, G.Q. (2012) The Promise of Induced Pluripotent Stem Cells in Research and Therapy. Nature, 481, 295-305. http://www.ncbi.nlm.nih.gov/pubmed/22258608 http://dx.doi.org/10.1038/nature10761
18. Sheiman, I. and Shishkin, S. (2010) New Challenges and New Objectives Problems of Economic Transition. Russian Health Care, 52, 4-49. http://connection.ebscohost.com/c/articles/49240513/russian-health-care-new-challenges-new-objectives

CHAPTER

6

MYOCARDITIS–PERSONALIZED MEDICINE BY EXPANDED ENDOMYOCARDIAL BIOPSY DIAGNOSTICS

Dirk Lassner[1], Maria Rohde[1], Christine Sabine Siegismund[1], Uwe Kühl[1,2], Ulrich Michael Gross[1], Felicitas Escher[1,2], Carsten Tschöpe[2], Heinz-Peter Schultheiss[2]

[1]Institute of Cardiac Diagnostics and Therapy, Berlin, Germany

[2]Department of Cardiology and Pneumonology, Charité—University Medicine Berlin, Campus Benjamin Franklin, Berlin, Germany

ABSTRACT

Myocarditis and dilated cardiomyopathy (DCM) are acute or chronic disorders of myocardium. The gold standard for final confirmation of causative reasons of these heart muscle diseases is the endomyocardial biopsy (EMB) analysis. Due to focal pathology, diagnostics are failing if the EMB does not contain the area of

Citation: Lassner, D. , Rohde, M. , Siegismund, C. , Kühl, U. , Gross, U. , Escher, F. , Tschöpe, C. and Schultheiss, H. (2014), "Myocarditis - Personalized Medicine by Expanded Endomyocardial Biopsy Diagnostics". *World Journal of Cardiovascular Diseases*, **4**, 325-340. doi: 10.4236/wjcd.2014.46042.

interest. Personalized medicine comprises the genetic information together with the phenotypic and environmental factors to yield a tailored healthcare for each individual and removes the limitations of the "one-size-fits-all" therapy approach. This provides the opportunity to translate therapies from bench to bedside, to diagnose and predict disease, and to improve patient-tailored treatments based on the unique signatures of a patient's disease. Furthermore, novel treatment schedules can be identified which have eventually the chance to enhance long-term survivals. Global biomarkers such as specific gene expression signatures or miRNA profiles not only have the potential to reduce this problem but also add valuable information for individualized therapy decisions. In future, multiplex approaches allowing rapid and absolutely reliable identification of inflammatory or virally-induced myocardial diseases will replace singleplex methods such as direct detection of viral genomes in one single biopsy. Gene or miRNA profiles are upcoming diagnostic biomarkers for cardiomyopathies which are not only detectable in tissue samples but in body fluids as well. Consequently, a systemic diagnostic approach by determination of distinct expression pattern in e.g., peripheral blood samples will support the characterization of distinct cardiomyopathies by means of non-invasive methods.

Keywords: Cardiomyopathy, Endomyocardial Biopsy, Personalized Medicine, Biomarker, MicroRNAs

INTRODUCTION

Cardiovascular disease is a leading cause for both hospitalization and death in Western European Countries. Its prevalence is rather increasing with the broad implementation of standardized evidence-based treatment algorithms for heart failure [1] -[4] .

Myocarditis and dilated cardiomyopathy (DCM) are acute or chronic disorders of myocardium. According to surveys of the European Society of Cardiology (ESC), 12 million European patients are suffering from heart failure including two million with non-ischemic dilated cardiomyopathy. DCM is the leading cause of heart transplantation (45%) of heart failure patients below 60 years of age in the US. The incidence of DCM is 5 to 8 per 100.000 and the prevalence is about 36 per 100.000 in United States [5] . These data are based on post-mortem studies regardless of the more frequent findings of DCM in endomyocardial biopsies (EMB). Based on this assumption, the worldwide incidence of DCM is at least above 50 million patients and thereby higher as the official number for human immune deficiency virus (HIV) (35 Mill. patients worldwide) as a well-known global health problem (UNAIDS Report 2012).

The individual patient's clinical symptoms, medical and family history, and data from laboratory and imaging evaluations are in the focus of traditional clinical diagnosis to confirm and treat illnesses.

Improvements in human genetics have enabled a more detailed understanding of the impact of genetics in disease. Large collaborative research projects e.g., the Human Genome Project brought forward the understanding of the roles of genes in normal human development and physiology, revealed single nucleotide polymorphisms (SNPs) that account for some of the genetic variability between individuals, and made the use of genome-wide association studies possible to examine genetic variation and risk for many common diseases [6] [7] . In consideration of the continuously expanding field of biomarker discovery in terms of proteomics, metabolomics and transcriptomics, physiological biomarkers like miRNA or gene expression profiles are belonging to personalized medicine as well, in our opinion.Personalized medicine is a kind of medicine that uses the patient's individual genomic information to improve diagnosis, prevention and therapy. In this review, we discuss the personalized management of myocarditis and DCM as monogenic or multifactorial disorders which require multistep diagnostics for an optimized treatment decision [8]

ACUTE MYOCARDITIS

The term myocarditis describes inflammatory disorders of the heart muscle of varied infectious and non-infectious origin. It can be caused by any kind of infection, drugs, toxic substances, or be associated with autoimmune conditions. Infectious etiologies include a vast number of viruses, bacteria, protozoa or fungi, but most frequently the myocardial inflammatory process is directed against viral pathogens. Viruses are the main cause in industrialized countries while bacteria or other infectious agents predominate the etiology of myocarditis in developing countries [9] . In common, the histological patterns of myocarditis are categorized by the predominant inflammatory cells and can be divided into lymphocytic (including viral and autoimmune forms), neutrophilic (bacterial, fungal, and early forms of viral myocarditis), eosinophilic (hypersensitivity myocarditis or hypereosinophilic syndrome), and granulomatous (cardiac sarcoidosis and giant cell myocarditis). The actual incidence of virus induced myocarditis or virus-associated cardiomyopathy is not well established because viral heart diseases can be unapparent, are difficult to diagnose and can vary with different viruses as a function of circulating virus populations (Figure 1).

Outcome and prognosis of myocarditis depend on etiology, clinical presentation, and disease stage. In acute phase, the clinical presentation can range from asymptomatic ECG alterations with or without echocardiographic abnormalities, to infarct-like presentation, global cardiac dysfunction, arrhythmias or progressive heart failure and cardiac decompensation [1] -[4] .

In contrast, the symptoms in subacute myocarditis and inflammatory cardiomyopathy are more subtle and insidious, often presenting as dilated cardiomyopathy with fatigue, reduced physical capacity and dyspnea.

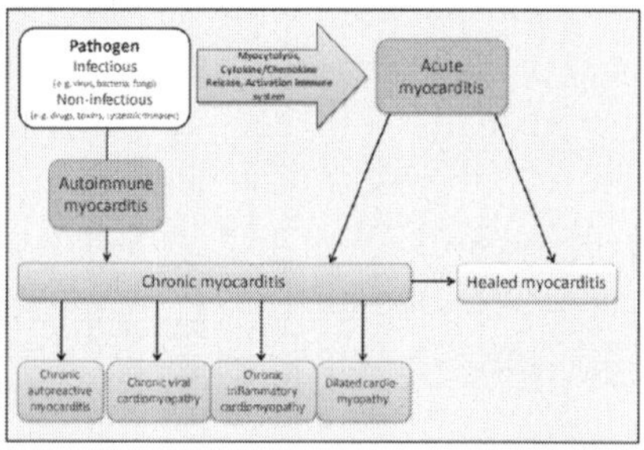

Figure 1. Pathogenesis and evolution of acute myocarditis to dilated cardiomyopathy (adapted from [2]).

Under specific circumstances acquired diseases are indistinguishable from hypertrophic (HCM), restrictive (RCM) or arrhythmic right ventricular cardiomyopathy (ARVC), clinically.

In about 50% of cases, acute myocarditis resolves in the first 4 - 12 weeks, but approx. 25% will develop persistent cardiac dysfunction and 12% - 25% may acutely deteriorate and either die or progress to end-stage DCM with a need for heart transplantation [1] [2] . Biventricular dysfunction at presentation has been reported as the main predictor of death or transplantation. Fulminant myocarditis is said to differ from (sub)acute lymphocytic myocarditis in its mode of onset, degree of hemodynamic compromise, and better outcome, but data are relatively scarce in adult patients.

Idiopathic giant cell myocarditis (IGCM), acute eosinophilic myocarditis and granulomatous inflammatory processes such as cardiac sarcoidosis (CS) are rare but clinically important acute inflammatory heart muscle diseases of often unknown etiology [10] . The majority of patients present with acute heart failure upon first encounter. These myocarditis subtypes have a high mortality if not diagnosed and treated in time. Drugs may induce myocardial inflammation by either direct toxic effects on heart tissue or by inducing hypersensitivity reactions which are often associated with an eosinophilic myocarditis [11] . Eosinophils are also observed in myocardial inflammatory processes which are associated with Churg-Strauss vasculitis or hypereosinophilic syndromes, vaccination for several diseases or caused by helminthic and parasitic infections [1] [2]. Chronic myocardial inflammation may be caused by persisting organ infections, toxic agents or distinct physical conditions, persist as a post-infectious condition, or be associated with systemic autoimmune conditions.

Because of the non-specific symptoms and clinically indistinguishable etiological factors the prevalence of infectious and non-infectious causes of myocarditis is not known. Biopsy of the myocardium is the only way to reach a treatment relevant diagnosis [2] [12] -[14] .

PATHOGENESIS OF MYOCARDITIS AND INFLAMMATORY DCM

Viral infections of the heart are progressing within distinct pathologically phases. A direct virus-related cytolysis of cardiomyocytes is already detected before any inflammatory infiltrate develops and appears to be decisive in fulminant cases of myocarditis [14] -[18] . Resulting myocyte necrosis may cause a significant loss of contractile tissue which is accompanied by rapidly developing cardiac failure and early death of the host. Early antiviral defence mechanisms of the innate immune system additionally contribute to early myocardial lesions and impaired myocardial function.

The activation of antigen-specific cell mediated immunity initiates the second phase of virus clearance. Virus-infected cells are destroyed by immune effector cells of the emerging acquired inflammatory response; therefore virus clearance will occur at the expense of further loss of infected myocytes. The ensuing myocardial damage depends on the scale of the cellular virus infection and increases with growing virus dispersion which, in addition to the early virusand immune-mediated injury, contributes to tissue remodelling and possible progression of the disease (Figure 1). The healing process therefore results primarily from a partial destruction of myocardial tissue that is not capable of regeneration. This finally may account for a clinical picture that is consistent with an often irreversible dilated cardiomyopathy. When myocardial inflammation persists despite virus clearance, a chronic myocarditis or inflammatory cardiomyopathy is present (Figure 1). It is generally accepted that viral myocarditis plays a major role in the development of inflammatory cardiomyopathy [2] [13] [19] .

In the third remodelling phase, virus infection may have been cleared completely and antiviral immune responses may have been resolved regularly. The extent of the myocardial damage determines the further clinical course of these patients whose biopsy results at that time will be that of idiopathic DCM. A post-infectious disease (healed myocarditis and DCM) can only be diagnosed if history or previous diagnostics had proven a preceding infectious or inflammatory state. On the other hand, latent virus infection, virus-associated low-grade immune reactivity and/or autoimmune processes may continuously assert negative effects on myocardial performance. Biopsy would then be consistent with inflammatory cardiomyopathy or persisting viral heart disease. Without sophisticated diagnostic analyses, the clinical picture is indistinguishable from that of DCM.

Long-term follow-up studies of patients presenting an acute myocarditis have shown that approximately 21% of them develop DCM. Additionally, the presence of a viral genome was demonstrated by polymerase chain reaction in the myocardium in up to 67% of patients with idiopathic left ventricular dysfunction [15] [20] . Thus, DCM can occur as a late stage following cardiac infection and inflammation. In contrast to acute myocarditis, which often presents with a preserved left ventricular size and normal or even increased wall thickness due to edema, inflammatory cardiomyopathy is characterized by the presence of chronic inflammatory cells associated with left ventricular dilatation, wall thinning and reduced ejection fraction, with or without viral persistence [16] [19] . Different mechanisms have been suggested for this evolution from acute disease to DCM [15] [21] -[23] .

INFECTIOUS CAUSES OF DCM

The major causes of myocarditis and inflammatory cardiomyopathy (DCMI) in acquired "idiopathic" diseases of the heart muscle [9] [24] are infectious agents and while practically any microbial agent can cause myocardial inflammation and dysfunction, non-viral infections are rare in these conditions, at least in developed countries. Nowadays viral forms are considered to be the most common cause of acquired DCMI [19] [24] .

In pediatric as well as in adult myocarditis and chronic heart muscle disease, coxsackieviruses [14] [17] and, to a lesser extend adenoviruses [17] [25] , are well established. Additionally, with varying degrees of frequency distinct genotypes of erythroviruses including parvovirus B19 (B19V), human herpesvirus type 6 (HHV6A/B) and its chromosomally integrated form (ciHHV6 A/B), HIV, cytomegalovirus (CMV), herpes simplex type 2 virus, Epstein-Barr virus (EBV) and hepatitis C virus, among many others, have been identified in cardiac tissues [26] -[29] .

Using molecular biological techniques including nested polymerase chain reaction (nPCR), viral genomes have been identified in myocardial tissues of approximately 30% to 73% of patients who underwent EMB in order to clarify the etiology of heart failure. Some more recent studies from Western Europe and the US have demonstrated a decrease in the prevalence of enteroviruses and adenoviruses as pathogens while erythroviral and herpesviral genomes became detectable in higher frequencies with erythroviruses B19V as the most frequent viruses detected in EMBs [15] [18] [25] [30] [31] . Concerning the higher frequencies of erythrovirus and herpesvirus, it has to be kept in mind that these viruses lead to a lifelong persistence after childhood infection [32] [33] . Therefore this detection in different tissues particularly in adults often represents latent infections. Virus-associated symptomatic diseases are normally caused by reactivation of persisting pathogens [1] [24] . Persistent latent infection of B19V occurs in the vascular endothelium of different organs including the heart with localisation of the virus in endothelial cells of venuoles, small arteries or arterioles of patients with fulminant myocarditis or sudden onset heart failure [34] -[36] . Reactivated erythrovirus is often associated with symptomatic endothelial dysfunction whereas latent infection is, in the majority of cases, asymptomatic [37] .

Another widespread latent virus infection frequently detected in EMBs is HHV6 [15] which consists of two genetically related but biologically distinct groups—HHV6A and HHV6B. After primary infection in childhood the virus persists in more than 70% of the adult populations [38] . In addition to lymphocytes, HHV6 also infects a variety of other cell types including cardiomyocytes and endothelial cells [39] [40] . Another interesting fact is that HHV6 can integrate into the telomeres of human chromosomes. ciHHV6 affects 0.4% - 0.8% of the whole population and is transmitted via the germline [33] [41] . Chromosomal integration with permanent virus reactivation may cause rarely recognized symptomatic diseases including cardiomyopathies. HHV6 and ciHHV6 become frequently reactivated with subacute clinical presentations.

Given the fact that a qualitative similar spectrum of viruses is detected in EMB of patients with acute and chronic myocarditis as well as in EMB of patients with DCM/DCMI, these diseases are considered to be different stages of one acquired disease rather than different disease entities [5] [15] . Virus persistence is associated with a progression of heart failure whereas patients improve clinically when viruses are cleared spontaneously or upon antiviral treatment [20] .

DIAGNOSIS AND PROGNOSIS OF MYOCARDITIS AND INFLAMMATORY CARDIOMYOPATHY

Myocarditis can manifest like a myocardial infarction with sudden-onset angina pectoris, arrhythmias, and/or heart failure developing within days. Most patients with myocarditis initially have such non-specific symptoms that these are often categorized in the context of the preceding infection and not as being of cardiac origin [16] [19] [20] [26] [42] . Cardiac involvement is often considered as the differential diagnosis only when cardiac symptoms, such as palpitations, angina, and/or exertional dyspnea, persist for a long period after the initial infection has resolved, or if they develop de novo in the course of the recovery. At this point in time, the electrocardiography results and laboratory chemical findings that are characteristic of acute myocarditis (changes of the ST segment, raised cardiac enzymes that are typical for acute myocardial involvement) are no longer present. Diagnostic evaluation starting at this point can only collect data on the extent of myocardial injury, even when using imaging methods (echocardiography, angiography, magnetic resonance imaging [MRI]); exclude specific cardiac disorders such as ischemic cardiomyopathy or valve deficiencies; or provide clues for a suspected diagnosis of infectious myocarditis. However, it cannot diagnose the cause of the existing disorder. While 60% to 70% of patients improve clinically and hemodynamically, the remaining patients will develop chronic heart failure or dilated cardiomyopathy within months or years [22] [43] .

An unequivocally confirmed bioptic diagnosis is the crucial prerequisite for differential diagnostic evaluation and the specific treatment strategies derived from this. As the pathophysiological changes of infectious and non-infectious myocarditis occur at a cellular and subcellular level, confirmation of a specific pathogen or inflammation requires a direct examination of myocardial tissue, which can be obtained without problems by means of a biopsy [26] [44] . In terms of therapeutic considerations it needs to be taken into account that a positive treatment effect will occur only if treatable causes such as viral infections, inflammatory processes, or cardiodepressive autoantibodies are present and the myocardium still has regenerative potential [4] . If irreversible myocardial damage already occurred, for which no specific treatment options exists such as in postinfectious or postinflammatory dilated cardiomyopathy, the development or progression of heart failure in the long term cannot be prevented.

Acute myocarditis mostly does not sufficiently respond to symptomatic medication for heart failure and mortality is still high despite treatment. The long-term disease course depends on the pathogen, the extent and type of inflammation, and the degree of injury to the myocardium. Focal borderline myocarditis often undergoes spontaneous clinical healing if no serious heart failure has developed initially. The early mortality of fulminant lymphocytic myocarditis requiring intensive care is greater than 40% in the first month [45] . Untreated IGCM and eosinophilic myocarditis also have an extremely poor prognosis, with a 4 year survival rate of 11% [10] . Granulomatous necrotizing myocarditis is fatal if overlooked and untreated. Non-fulminant active myocarditis has a mortality rate of 25% to 56% within 3 to 10 years, owing to progressive heart failure and sudden cardiac death, especially if symptomatic heart failure manifests early on [46] -[48] . In addition to impaired left ventricular (LV) and right ventricular (RV) function, virus persistence, chronic inflammation, and cardiodepressive autoantibodies are independent predictors of a poor prognosis [46] [49] [50] .

Damage of cardiomyocytes is not only caused by cytopathic effects of the virus but also by the attracted immune effector cells. Adenovirus and enterovirus are infecting myocytes. Even under optimal heart failure treatment, progression of myocardial injury cannot be prevented [14] [17] [21] . Myocardial function is affected by virus associated inflammation in case of vasculotropic viruses, e.g., erythrovirus or herpesvirus. Infarct like symptoms in these diseases are often induced by injury of the vascular endothelium [28] [34] [51] [52] .

Post-infectious inflammation affects myocardial tissue if the inflammatory process does not resolve after successful elimination of the infectious agent [12] [50] [53] [54] . Inflammation in association with collagenosis, rheumatic disorders or CS is less frequent than virus associated or postinfectious inflammation. Immunosuppression can significantly improve outcome of these diseases and the failing in recognition is fatal in untreated cases. Myocardial damages can be induced by toxic substances or drugs if treatment is not stopped immediately.

If the primary causes of acquired cardiomyopathies, e.g., inflammation or infection have resolved, the etiology of the disease remains unclear (idiopathic) because the causing agents are no longer detectable. In these cases, a specific treatment is impossible. These cardiomyopathy stages cannot be discriminated from other idiopathic or genetic cardiomyopathies [1] -[3] .

ENDOMYOCARDIAL BIOPSY DIAGNOSTICS

Since pathophysiological changes of acquired infectious and non-infectious heart muscle diseases, that can be treated specifically by anti-viral or anti-inflammatory medication, occur at cellular and subcellular levels, imaging techniques such as CMR or echocardiography can only provide non-invasive tissue characterization but fail in revealing the true underlying causes that determine prognosis of the disease [55] -[57] .

Invasive removal of a sufficient number of tissue samples by EMB is always necessary when an exact diagnosis cannot be obtained by other clinical methods and is influencing the following treatment [26] [27] [44] [58] .

EMB is mandatory in suspected myocarditis and DCM of unknown etiology since the diagnosis of myocarditis and other inflammatory diseases (inflammatory cardiomyopathy, cardiac sarcoidosis, giant cell myocarditis), viruses or storage diseases (amyloidosis) is impossible without their direct proof in myocardial tissue [1] [2] [4] [25] [49] [58] . The use of LV EMB to investigate cardiomyopathies is currently discouraged because it is considered riskier than and as contributive as RV biopsy. On the other hand, a recently published study on 4221 patients which underwent diagnostic EMB during a 28-year period confirmed however that even biventricular EMB has a low major complication rate (perforation with or without cardiac tamponade, embolization) of 0.33% for LV EMB and 0.45% for RV EMB. No patient died [27] . These data were in line with a formerly published study (no patient died, major complication rate 0.12%) in which 3048 diagnostic procedures (RV EMB) were taken during an 11-year period [44] . According to these studies, LV or RV EMB is a safe procedure with very low transient complications.

The histological examination of paraffin sections by different staining protocols (HE, EvG, PAS, Azan) detects myocardial cell death, scars, fibrosis, disarrays, cardiomyocyte changes, pathological vascular conditions, granulomas, and inflammatory cell differentiation. Storage disorders such as amyloidosis [26] [59] , iron deposits, glycogen and others can be excluded or specified by additional staining, e.g., immunohistochemical differentiation of amyloid subtypes and optional electron microscopical analyses. The

EMB diagnosis of myocarditis was based on histomorphological criteria according to the Dallas classification [26] [60] .

Routine immunohistochemical diagnostics are based on the application of antibody-supported detection of inflammatory infiltrates (lymphocytes, macrophages, memory cells, B-cells) and enhanced expression of tissue activation marker like adhesion molecules (HLA, ICAM, VCAM) or fibrotic proteins like collagens on cryofixed tissue section, following quantitative digital imaging analysis [26] [61] [62] .

Microbial genomes are determined, quantified and sequenced using PCR-based methods.

The use of these sensitive techniques detecting the most common cardiotropic viruses (such as enteroviruses, adenoviruses, erythrovirus, human herpesvirus 6, Epstein-Barr virus and in the Far East also hepatitis C) reveals a virus infection in up to 73% of patients who are biopsied under the clinical suspicion of myocarditis or DCM. The clinical significance is clearly demonstrated only for some cardiotropic viruses [2] [15] [17] [20] [25] [51] .

CURRENT BIOPSY-BASED TREATMENT DECISIONS

Despite expanding knowledge based on molecular and cellular pathophysiology and management of cardiomyopathy, it still remains difficult to accurately distinguish between patients who will someday develop progression of the disease requiring cardiac transplantation from those with excellent long-term prognosis. Of equal importance, current medical practice does not include strategies to tailor therapies to patient's most favorable benefit, while at the same time seeking predictors of poor or adverse responsiveness [63] .

During the last decade, the therapeutic management of patients with left ventricular systolic dysfunction has improved by administration of an optimal symptomatic heart failure medication.

The major goals of the treatment are the reduction of mortality and morbidity, the improvement of symptoms, and if possible the induction of reverse remodeling of the left ventricle.

The mainstay of treatment for myocarditis presenting as DCM is an optimal heart failure medical regimen according to the current American Heart Association/American College of Cardiology Foundation and ESC guidelines for the management of heart failure [3] [10] [19] .

Virus-negative chronic inflammation (post-infectious or auto-immune inflammatory processes) responds well to immunosuppression or immunoadsorption [5] . If an immunosuppressive treatment is administered in time before irreversible myocardial damages have developed, progression of heart failure can be avoided [49] [58] . Since heart failure of virus positive patients deteriorates upon anti-inflammatory treatment, it is of utmost importance that viral infections are excluded before any immunosuppression is administered.

For antiviral treatment currently two approaches exist: immunomodulation supporting intrinsic immune response and antiviral drugs that affect the life cycle of corresponding virus. Patients with chronic heart failure due to persisting enterovirus and adenovirus infections of the myocardium respond well to a six months' interferon-beta (IFN-β) treatment, whereas untreated patients have a poor prognosis with a mortality rate above 50% [64] [65] . Virus clearance is paralleled by a hemodynamic improvement and an amelioration of heart failure symptoms. The long-term mortality of patients is significantly reduced by the treatment [64] .

Other viruses, e.g., B19V or HHV-6, respond less well upon IFN-β treatment with respect to virus clearance. Despite incomplete virus clearance, these patients improve clinically in association with reduction of virus load due to improvement of endothelial function [52] .

In 15% - 20% of erythrovirus positive patients, an active virus replication is detectable by measurement of viral RNA or specific miRNA pattern [37] [66] . Transcriptionally active erythrovirus is associated with higher rate of angina, fatigue syndrome or dyspnea. Clinical symptoms of these patients often improve shortly after antiviral treatment with virus replication inhibitors. Whether this also improves outcome is currently unknown.

HHV-6 is the second frequent virus and detectable in over 14% of all EMBs with low viral loads. Its clinical relevance with respect to heart failure is still uncertain [15] [20] . In about 1% of all EMBs, HHV6 could be detected with persistent high viral loads (over 50.000 copies per μg myocardial DNA) characteristic for ciHHV-6. Cardiac complaints and general physical disability improve upon antiviral medication that reduces HHV6 reactivation [28] [33] .

In patients with DCM, a possible pathophysiological role for circulating autoantibodies against cardiac proteins has been suggested [50] [53] [54] . Incremental research on this topic particularly in the past few years has significantly contributed evidence to the hypothesis that autoimmune reactions against certain myocyte antigens may play a crucial role in the initiation and/or progression of DCM. Transfer experiments in animals performed by various groups and some preliminary clinical data even indicate that a few of these autoantibodies are indeed pathogenic, inferring that they can actually cause cardiac dysfunction and heart failure by their own. Dependent on the individual genetic predisposition such harmful autoimmune reactions are supposed to emerge as a consequence of heart muscle damage induced by viral triggers, ischemia or exposure to cardiotoxins leading to myocyte apoptosis (and/or necrosis) and subsequent liberation of a critical amount of self-antigens previously hidden to the immune system [53] .

LIMITED VALUE OF GENETIC TESTING FOR CARDIOMYOPATHIES

The detection of a gene mutation responsible for a monogenic disorder is the greatest effort of genetic testing. Current guidelines recommend genetic screening (evidence level A) for ARVD/C, HCM and DCM with conduction abnormalities or extra cardiac manifestations [67] . The majority of these mutations were identified by family screening tests, where one or more members were suffering from identical cardiac problems or died at younger age for unknown reason. Most genetic and clinical testing for cardiomyopathies has the drawback of trusting on imaging techniques as primary cardiological diagnostics. A differential diagnosis of infiltrative processes of myocardium or wall hypertrophy in acute inflammatory diseases caused by edema is requested, because in biopsies of patients suspicious for genetically determined cardiomyopathies as HCM or ARVD a massive infiltration of inflammatory cells or viral genomes are often seen, undetectable by echocardiography, CMR or computer tomography (CT).

Recent studies have identified a massive overrepresentation of previously described cardiomyopathy-related genetic variants in a healthy control cohort with genotype prevalence thousand fold higher than in diseased patients [68] . This finding makes genetic testing without prior clinic-diagnostically definition questionable [26] [69] .

In contrast, a 32-basepair deletion in the CC chemokine receptor 5 (CCR5, RANTES) gene (CCR5del32 polymorphism) was confirmed as a prognostic marker for acquired cardiomyopathies. This deletion leads to deficiency of this receptor for various proinflammatory cytokines. Homozygosity additionally results in reduced susceptibility to HIV infections [70] . This polymorphism is furthermore associated with an improved outcome in diabetes and coronary heart disease [71] .

The long-term effect of the CCR5 genotype in patients with clinically suspected myocarditis or DCM revealed a reduced mortality of patients with a 32-basepair deletion of the CCR5 receptor. The data showed that CCR5del32 polymorphism is an independent genetic factor that influences outcome in patients with clinically suspected myocarditis and DCM, not associated with myocardial inflammation, diabetes or viral infections. As shown for CCR5, only endomyocardial biopsy supported genetic studies can identify genetic markers which are associated with clinical occurrence of genetically determined cardiomyopathies, while simultaneously excluding myocardial inflammation or microbial infections as a reason for preceding heart muscle disease [69] [72] .

BIOMARKER BASED DIAGNOSTICS FOR PERSONALIZED MEDICINE

Detection of monogenic causes for current presentation and long term prognosis of cardiomyopathies such as cardiotropic viruses, inherited base of viral infection (ciHHV-6) or CCR5del32 genotype are still limited but possible by measurement of only one diagnostic parameter. Diagnosis of complex mechanisms like individual immune response on different inflammatory or viral induced processes and thereon based treatment options request multiparametric determination of corresponding biomarkers.

Regardless of individual determined genetic background, nearly all multistep diagnostics could be accounted as part of personalized medical approach. After the first clinical confirmed hint by digital imaging techniques (echocardiography, CMR or CT) Morbus Fabry can be diagnosed by additional laboratory and cardiac enzyme tests or tissue biopsies. Morbus Fabry, confirmed by the reduced alpha-galactosidase activity of leukocytes, can be treated by enzyme replacement therapy. If amyloidosis has been proven histologically, further immunohistological classification of the corresponding subtype is required to distinguish an age-related from a genetically determined ATTR-form. The latter of which would require family counseling [59] [69] .

Combination of currently available diagnostic findings in EMBs, with distinct immunohistological and virological profiles, support the selection of patients with active lymphocytic myocarditis or with circulating cardiac autoantibodies which will most likely benefit from immunosuppression as the optimized treatment decisions. Immunosuppression demands the exclusion of virus positive patients because these will deteriorate by application of immunosuppressive drugs [49] .

Novel biomarkers such as miRNA or gene expression profiles of myocardial tissue will improve diagnosis of specific cardiac disease entities by overcoming biopsy-based sample error due to their non-focal expression pattern in the near future (Figure 2) [26] [37] [66] . They can be used for primary diagnosis but also for therapy monitoring, due to the fact that they change their profiles during therapy indicating an alteration of molecular markers at the focal or systemic level. All diagnostic biomarker should improve currently applied diagnostics for the exact diversification of cardiac patients which profit from proposed treatment options (Figure 3).

It is now possible to simultaneously assess the expression of tens of thousands of gene transcripts, providing a resolution and precision of phenotypic characterization not previously possible [73] . Multiparametric diagnostic systems, measuring differentially expressed genes or miRNAs, may thus become a valuable diagnostic tool of the future due to its high predictive value in respect to clinical course, treatment decisions and therapy monitoring [74] .

Positive diagnostic findings in examined biopsies are confirming the myocardial condition, but negative results will not exclude infections, intramyocardial inflammation or other pathophysiological conditions. To reduce the biopsy-dependent sampling error an increased number of biopsies is required but could never overcome it completely. Therefore global and stable biomarkers to identify disease entities in the effected organ are urgently needed.

Of note, deregulation of myocardial gene expression is not limited to focal biopsy area. This allows the identification of specific disease situations by analyzing of neighbouring biopsies [75] [76] . Diagnosis of complex diseases by only one parameter is quite difficult hence current diagnostic biomarker panels are consisting of only few deregulated genes. With the help of novel biomarkers, viral infections or focal infiltration of inflammatory cells in myocardium can be diagnosed in neighbouring tissue samples without direct histological confirmation of these agents (Figure 2).

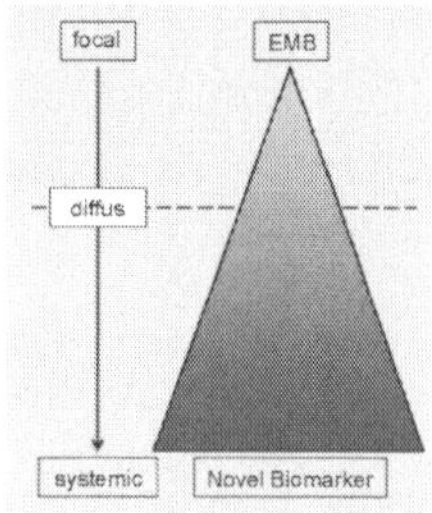

Figure 2. Increased diagnostic accuracy and reduction of biopsy-based (EMB) limitations by introduction of novel biomarker for personalized medicine of DCM patients.

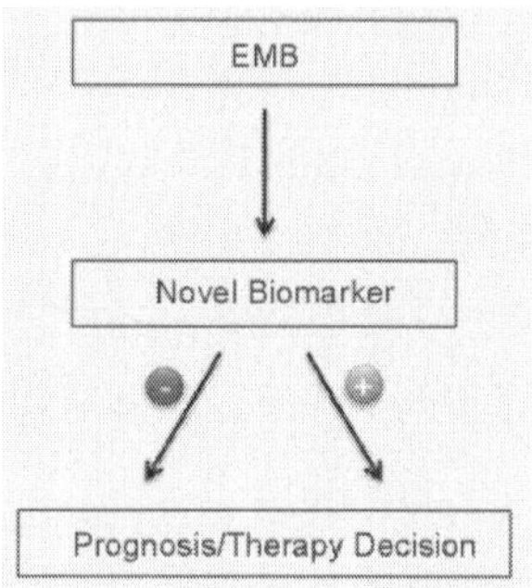

Figure 3. Biomarker support personalized treatment options after biopsy-based (EMB) diagnosis of different cardiomyopathies and various disease stages.

The identification and differentiation of IGCM and CS, two fatal myocardial diseases, is rather difficult and based on differential patterns of inflammatory cell infiltration and non-caseating granuloma. Since both multinuclear giant cells and granuloma are easily missed by conventional histological evaluation, an improved method to reliably identify those entities independent from histology is desirable [75] [76] . In this respect, the application of diagnostic gene expression profiling can predict multinucleated giant cells without their direct histological proof and thus differentiate IGCM from CS, active myocarditis or an inflammation-free myocardium [75] . According to the exact classification a personalized therapy can be administered (Table 1).

The application of immunoadsorption for removing circulating autoantibodies can significantly improve heart failure of patients with autoimmune DCM (Table 1). The selection of patients likely to respond to immunoadsorption has been established by comparison of the genetic expression profiles in samples from endomyocardial biopsies of patients with DCM and controls [50] [53] [54] . Responders could be discriminated from non-responders by their differentially expressed genes in myocardial tissue [77] -[79] .

Table 1. Personalized therapy options for different forms of myocarditis and DCM.

Disease	Subform	Applicable Drugs
Acute Myocarditis	Lymphocytic, Eosinophilic, Giant-Cell Myocarditis, Cardiac Sarcoidosis	Ciclosporin, Prednisolon
Chronic Inflammatory cardiomyopathy		Prednisolon, Azathioprin
Chronic Viral Cardiomyopathy	Enteroviruses, ADV, Parvovirus B19, HHV6A/B, CMV, EBV, HSV, VZV, Hepatitis C, RSV	Interferons, Val-/Ganciclovir, Ribavarin, Telbivudine, Cidovir, Aciclovir, Foscanet
Chronic Autoreactive Myocarditis		Immunoadsorption

As shown for enterovirus positive patients some patients are able to eliminate this virus spontaneously by intrinsic immune response with hemodynamic improvement and better long-term outcome [64] . Whereas patients with enterovirus persistence have an increased 10-year mortality [64] [65] . The use of novel biomarkers like gene expression or miRNA profiles allows the identification of enterovirus positive patients who will improve spontaneously by elimination of the virus, and those patients who will need a supportive interferon-β treatment (Figure 3) [64] [65] .

The role of miRNAs in physiologic and pathologic processes and the capability to correlate expression changes with distinct disease states highlights their value as novel molecular biomarkers [80] -[82] . Currently available miRNA profiles allow the identification of preceding cardiotropic infection even in PCR-negative biopsies. The clinical course of such patients becomes predictable at the point of primary biopsy and a disease-specific therapy can be initiated immediately to prevent ongoing myocardial injuries [26] [64] -[66] .

Symptomatic erythrovirus-associated heart disease may be caused by virus reactivation [26] [37] [66] . Measurement of characteristic signatures of mRNA and cardiac miRNAs allows the differentiation between latent and reactivated infection [37] [66] . Patients with transcriptionally active erythrovirus infection benefit from antiviral treatment (Table 1) [26] .

Viral infection or intramyocardial inflammation is not only isolated to heart muscle tissue but also affecting the whole body as well. This process is attracting peripheral blood cells or inducing changes of cellular metabolism in other organs by soluble systemic mediators like cytokines or chemokines or releasing specific miRNAs in body fluids. Based on their high biostability, miRNAs are also present in body fluids such as serum, plasma or liquor protected from endogenous RNase activity by inclusion in exosomes or protein complexes. Molecular signatures of miRNAs are influencing the systemic response on organ-specific alterations (Figure 4).

Disease-specific miRNA signatures in tissues differ significantly from those in blood cells, serum or other body fluids of the same patient and therefore have their own specificity for the present condition [26] [74] .

As shown for Takotsubo cardiomyopathy, a potentially life-threatening disease, which is clinically indistinguishable from acute myocardial infarction, circulating miRNAs are found which allow a differentiation of Takotsubo cardiomyopathy and myocardial infarction [83] .

These findings emphasize the potential of circulating miRNAs as stable blood-based markers for the detection of cardiomyopathies. The investigation of miRNA expression profiles in body fluids opens a new diagnostic approach to detect and characterize focal diseases by systemic markers with an easily taken and abundant sample [26] [75] [76] [80] . Application of diagnostic miRNA profiling can improve EMB analysis by predicting the clinical course of disease, resulting in faster therapy decisions and monitoring of applied treatments.

Therefore it could reduce the currently performed extensive workflow. Additionally, the signature of circulating miRNAs in blood or other body fluids will allow the diagnosis of organ-specific or systemic alterations by a minimal-invasive approach [74] .

Beside diagnostics, the confirmation of differentially expressed genes or miRNAs, associated with various forms or states of cardiomyopathies are possible candidates for new therapeutic targets. In contrast to gene transcripts, the miRNAs are more favorable targets.

Blocking of one miRNA influences one or more cellular pathways in the desired direction. Application of antagomir against translation of diagnostically applied biomarkers in pharmacologically usable drugs will broaden the currently existing treatment options [81] .

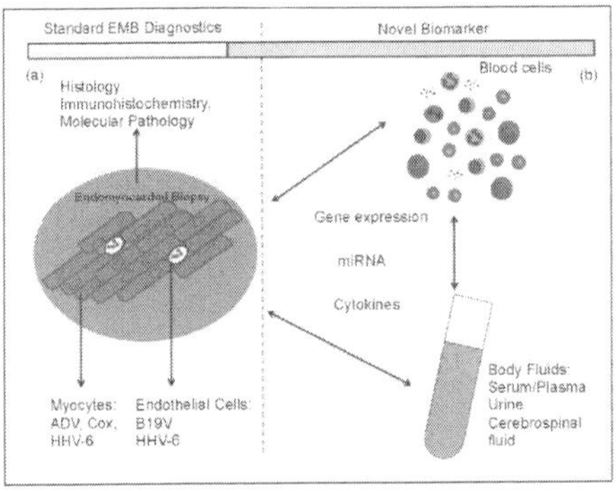

Figure 4. Novel biomarker like gene expression signatures and microRNA profiles improve current biopsy-based (EMB) diagnosis of different cardiomyopathies and various disease stages.

Nevertheless, the ultimate potential application of transcriptome-based molecular signature analysis is the individualization of the management of patients with heart failure, whereby an accurate assessment of prognosis and how individualized medical therapy could affect his or her outcome can be offered to patients with newly diagnosed cardiomyopathy [63] [73] .

FUTURE PERSPECTIVE

General guidelines for diagnosis, treatment and corresponding quality analyses for myocarditis and acquired cardiomyopathies are still missing because unambiguous successful treatments proven by large randomized studies are rare. Positive outcome from treatment has only been established for some subgroups including enteroviral cardiomyopathy, giant cell myocarditis, sarcoidosis, or acute persisting acute-lymphocytic-myocarditis. One major problem is the identification of suitable patients for a distinct treatment option. In this regard, therapy guiding diagnostics must be standardized and supervised. This approach cannot be reached by clinical diagnosis but by biopsy-based information with complete histological, immunohistochemical, and molecular workup of tissue samples. Although EMB diagnostics are revealing only an extract of heart's current situation, this is still the gold standard for final confirmations of causative reasons of cardiomyopathies. The introduction of novel biomarkers like miRNAs or specific gene expression profiles as global organ-specific or systemic markers will reduce the EMB associated sampling error and will define an individualized therapy for each patient. This personalized approach allows an optimal application of available treatment options. Antiviral or immunomodulatory drugs (interferon, ganciclovir, telbivudine) improve survival or symptoms in the most frequent cardiotropic virus infections (adenovirus, enterovirus, erythrovirus and HHV6/ciHHV6) and immunosuppressive strategies are available for important infiltrative disorders such as chronic myocarditis, idiopathic giant cell myocarditis or cardiac sarcoidosis.

ACKNOWLEDGEMENTS

Dirk Lassner#, Maria Rohde*, Christine Sabine Siegismund, Uwe Kühl, Ulrich Michael Gross, Felicitas Escher,, Carsten Tschöpe, Heinz-Peter Schultheiss (DFG), Transregional Collaborative Research Centre "Inflammatory Cardiomyopathy—Molecular Pathogenesis and Therapy" (SFB TR19, Z1), and two grants of the Federal Ministry of Education and Research (BMBF, Germany) for KMU innovative program (No.616 0315296, 0316141A).

REFERENCES

1. Schultheiss, H.-P., Kühl, U. and Cooper, L.T. (2011) The Management of Myocarditis. European Heart Journal, 32, 2616-2625. http://dx.doi.org/10.1093/eurheartj/ehr165
2. Caforio, A.L.P., Pankuweit, S., Arbustini, E., Basso, C., Gimeno-Blanes, J., Felix, S.B. and Elliott, P.M. (2013) Current State of Knowledge on Aetiology, Diagnosis, Management, and Therapy of Myocarditis: A Position Statement of the European Society of Cardiology Working Group on Myocardial and Pericardial Diseases. European Heart Journal, 34, 2636-2648. http://dx.doi.org/10.1093/eurheartj/eht210
3. Cooper, L.T., Baughman, K.L., Feldman, A.M., Frustaci, A., Jessup, M., Kuhl, U. and Virmani, R. (2007) The Role of Endomyocardial Biopsy in the Management of Cardiovascular Disease: A Scientific Statement from the American Heart Association, the American College of Cardiology, and the European Society of Cardiology. Circulation, 116, 2216-2233. http://dx.doi.org/10.1161/CIRCULATIONAHA.107.186093
4. Liu, P.P. and Schultheiss, H.P. (2008) Myocarditis. In: Baunwald, Ed., Heart Disease, W B Saunders Co., Philadelphia, 1775-1792.
5. Cooper, L.T. (2005) The Natural History and Role of Immunoadsorption in Dilated Cardiomyopathy. Journal of Clinical Apheresis, 20, 256-260. http://dx.doi.org/10.1002/jca.20045
6. Meder, B., Rühle, F., Weis, T., Homuth, G., Keller, A., Franke, J. and Katus, H.A. (2013) A Genome-Wide Association Study Identifies 6p21 as Novel Risk Locus for Dilated Cardiomyopathy. European Heart Journal, 35, 1069-1077. http://dx.doi.org/10.1093/eurheartj/eht251
7. Schierding, W., Cutfield, W.S., and O'Sullivan, J.M. (2014) The Missing Story Behind Genome Wide Association Studies: Single Nucleotide Polymorphisms in Gene Deserts Have a Story to Tell. Frontiers in Genetics, 5, 39. http://dx.doi.org/10.3389/fgene.2014.00039
8. Mestroni, L., Merlo, M., Taylor, M.R.G., Camerini, F. and Sinagra, G. (2011) Heart Failure and Personalized Medicine. Journal of Cardiovascular Medicine (Hagerstown, Md.), 12, 6-12. http://dx.doi.org/10.2459/JCM.0b013e32833e8b0d
9. Blauwet, L.A. and Cooper, L.T. (n.d.) Myocarditis. Progress in Cardiovascular Diseases, 52, 274-288. http://dx.doi.org/10.1016/j.pcad.2009.11.006
10. Cooper, L.T., Berry, G.J. and Shabetai, R. (1997) Idiopathic Giant-

Cell Myocarditis—Natural History and Treatment. Multicenter Giant Cell Myocarditis Study Group Investigators. The New England Journal of Medicine, 336, 1860-1866. http://dx.doi.org/10.1056/NEJM199706263362603

11. Taliercio, C.P., Olney, B.A. and Lie, J.T. (1985) Myocarditis Related to Drug Hypersensitivity. Mayo Clinic Proceedings, 60, 463-468. http://dx.doi.org/10.1016/S0025-6196(12)60870-2
12. Magnani, J.W. and Dec, G.W. (2006) Myocarditis: Current Trends in Diagnosis and Treatment. Circulation, 113, 876-890. http://dx.doi.org/10.1161/CIRCULATIONAHA.105.584532
13. Cooper, L.T., Baughman, K.L., Feldman, A.M., Frustaci, A., Jessup, M., Kuhl, U. and Virmani, R. (2007) The Role of Endomyocardial Biopsy in the Management of Cardiovascular Disease: A Scientific Statement from the American Heart Association, the American College of Cardiology, and the European Society of Cardiology Endorsed by the Heart Failure Society of America and the Heart Failure Association of the European Society of Cardiology. European Heart Journal, 28, 3076-3093. http://dx.doi.org/10.1093/eurheartj/ehm456
14. Dec, G.W., Palacios, I.F., Fallon, J.T., Aretz, H.T., Mills, J., Lee, D.C., and Johnson, R.A. (1985) Active Myocarditis in the Spectrum of Acute Dilated Cardiomyopathies. Clinical Features, Histologic Correlates, and Clinical Outcome. The New England Journal of Medicine, 312, 885-890. http://dx.doi.org/10.1056/NEJM198504043121404 .
15. Kühl, U., Pauschinger, M., Noutsias, M., Seeberg, B., Bock, T., Lassner, D. and Schultheiss, H.-P. (2005) High Prevalence of Viral Genomes and Multiple Viral Infections in the Myocardium of Adults with "Idiopathic" Left Ventricular Dysfunction. Circulation, 111, 887-893. http://dx.doi.org/10.1161/01.CIR.0000155616.07901.35
16. Felker, G.M., Boehmer, J.P., Hruban, R.H., Hutchins, G.M., Kasper, E.K., Baughman, K.L. and Hare, J.M. (2000) Echocardiographic Findings in Fulminant and Acute Myocarditis. Journal of the American College of Cardiology, 36, 227-232. http://dx.doi.org/10.1016/S0735-1097(00)00690-2
17. Pauschinger, M., Bowles, N.E., Fuentes-Garcia, F.J., Pham, V., Kühl, U., Schwimmbeck, P.L. and Towbin, J.A. (1999) Detection of Adenoviral Genome in the Myocardium of Adult Patients with Idiopathic Left Ventricular Dysfunction. Circulation, 99, 1348-1354. http://dx.doi.org/10.1161/01.CIR.99.10.1348 .

18. Breinholt, J.P., Moulik, M., Dreyer, W.J., Denfield, S.W., Kim, J.J., Jefferies, J.L. and Towbin, J.A. (2010) Viral Epidemiologic Shift in Inflammatory Heart Disease: The Increasing Involvement of parvovirus B19 in the Myocardium of Pediatric Cardiac Transplant Patients. The Journal of Heart and Lung Transplantation: The Official Publication of the International Society for Heart Transplantation, 29, 739-746. http://dx.doi.org/10.1016/j.healun.2010.03.003
19. Elliott, P., Andersson, B., Arbustini, E., Bilinska, Z., Cecchi, F., Charron, P. and Keren, A. (2008) Classification of the Cardiomyopathies: A Position Statement from the European Society of Cardiology Working Group on Myocardial and Pericardial Diseases. European Heart Journal, 29, 270-276. http://dx.doi.org/10.1093/eurheartj/ehm342
20. Kühl, U., Pauschinger, M., Seeberg, B., Lassner, D., Noutsias, M., Poller, W. and Schultheiss, H.P. (2005) Viral Persistence in the Myocardium Is Associated with Progressive Cardiac Dysfunction. Circulation, 112, 1965-1970. http://dx.doi.org/10.1161/CIRCULATIONAHA.105.548156
21. Kawai, C. (1999) From Myocarditis to Cardiomyopathy: Mechanisms of Inflammation and Cell Death: Learning from the Past for the Future. Circulation, 99, 1091-1100. http://dx.doi.org/10.1161/01.CIR.99.8.1091
22. D'Ambrosio, A., Patti, G., Manzoli, A., Sinagra, G., Di Lenarda, A., Silvestri, F. and Di Sciascio, G. (2001) The Fate of Acute Myocarditis between Spontaneous Improvement and Evolution to Dilated Cardiomyopathy: A Review. Heart (British Cardiac Society), 85, 499-504. http://dx.doi.org/10.1136/heart.85.5.499
23. Figulla, H.R. (2004) Transformation of Myocarditis and Inflammatory Cardiomyopathy to Idiopathic Dilated Cardiomyopathy: Facts and Fiction. Medical Microbiology and Immunology, 193, 61-64. http://dx.doi.org/10.1007/s00430-003-0205-y
24. Kühl, U. and Schultheiss, H.P. (2010) Myocarditis in Children. Heart Failure Clinics, 6, 483-496. http://dx.doi.org/10.1016/j.hfc.2010.05.009 .
25. Bowles, N.E., Ni, J., Kearney, D.L., Pauschinger, M., Schultheiss, H.P., McCarthy, R. and Towbin, J.A. (2003) Detection of Viruses in Myocardial Tissues by Polymerase Chain Reaction. Evidence of Adenovirus as a Common Cause of Myocarditis in Children and Adults. Journal of the American College of Cardiology, 42, 466-472. http://

dx.doi.org/10.1016/S0735-1097(03)00648-X

26. Lassner, D., Siegismund, C.S., Stehr, J., Rohde, M., Escher, F., Tschöpe, C. and Schultheiss, H.P. (2013) Recent Advances in Molecular Diagnostics and Treatment of Heart Muscle Diseases. Journal of Analytical Sciences, Methods and Instrumentation, 3, 98-109. http://dx.doi.org/10.4236/jasmi.2013.32012 [Citation Time(s):12]
27. Chimenti, C. and Frustaci, A. (2013) Contribution and Risks of Left Ventricular Endomyocardial Biopsy in Patients with Cardiomyopathies: A Retrospective Study over a 28-Year Period. Circulation, 128, 1531-1541. http://dx.doi.org/10.1161/CIRCULATIONAHA.13.001414
28. Lassner, D., Krueger, G.R.F., Buja, L.M. and Kuehl, U. (2014) HHV-6 and HHV-7 in Cardiovascular Diseases and Cardiomyopathies. In: Flammand, L., Lautenschlager, I., Krueger, G.R.F. and Ablashi, D.V., Eds., Human Herpesviruses HHV-6A, HHV-6B, and HHV-7: Diagnosis and Clinical Management, 3rd Edition, Elsevier B.V., Amsterdam, 267-280.
29. Kühl, U., Lassner, D., Pauschinger, M., Gross, U.M., Seeberg, B., Noutsias, M. and Schultheiss, H.P. (2008) Prevalence of Erythrovirus Genotypes in the Myocardium of Patients with Dilated Cardiomyopathy. Journal of Medical Virology, 80, 1243-1251. http://dx.doi.org/10.1002/jmv.21187
30. Towbin, J.A., Ware, S.M. and Jefferies, J.L. (2010) Heart Transplants in Pediatric Patients: Viral Infection as a Loss Predictor. Future Cardiology, 6, 735-741. http://dx.doi.org/10.2217/fca.10.105
31. Kandolf, R. (2004) Virus Etiology of Inflammatory Cardiomyopathy. Deutsche Medizinische Wochenschrift (1946), 129, 2187-2192. http://dx.doi.org/10.1055/s-2004-831863
32. Norja, P., Hokynar, K., Aaltonen, L.M., Chen, R., Ranki, A., Partio, E.K. and Hedman, K. (2006) Bioportfolio: Lifelong Persistence of Variant and Prototypic Erythrovirus DNA Genomes in Human Tissue. Proceedings of the National Academy of Sciences of the United States of America, 103, 7450-7453. http://dx.doi.org/10.1073/pnas.0602259103
33. Pellett, P.E., Ablashi, D.V., Ambros, P.F., Agut, H., Caserta, M.T., Descamps, V. and Razonable, R.R. (2012) Chromosomally Integrated Human Herpesvirus 6: Questions and Answers. Reviews in Medical Virology, 22, 144-155. http://dx.doi.org/10.1002/rmv.715 .
34. Bültmann, B.D., Klingel, K., Sotlar, K., Bock, C.T., Baba, H.A.,

Sauter, M. and Kandolf, R. (2003) Fatal Parvovirus B19-Associated Myocarditis Clinically Mimicking Ischemic Heart Disease: An Endothelial Cell-Mediated Disease. Human Pathology, 34, 92-95. http://dx.doi.org/10.1053/hupa.2003.48

35. Bock, C.T., Klingel, K., Aberle, S., Duechting, A., Lupescu, A., Lang, F. and Kandolf, R. (2005) Human Parvovirus B19: A New Emerging Pathogen of Inflammatory Cardiomyopathy. Journal of Veterinary Medicine. B, Infectious Diseases and Veterinary Public Health, 52, 340-343.

36. Klingel, K., Sauter, M., Bock, C.T., Szalay, G., Schnorr, J.J. and Kandolf, R. (2004) Molecular Pathology of Inflammatory Cardiomyopathy. Medical Microbiology and Immunology, 193, 101-107. http://dx.doi.org/10.1007/s00430-003-0190-1

37. Kuhl, U., Lassner, D., Dorner, A., Rohde, M., Escher, F., Seeberg, B. and Poller, W. (2013) A Distinct Subgroup of Cardiomyopathy Patients Characterized by Transcriptionally Active Cardiotropic Erythrovirus and Altered Cardiac Gene Expression. Basic Research in Cardiology, 108, 372. http://dx.doi.org/10.1007/s00395-013-0372-y

38. Di Luca, D., Mirandola, P., Ravaioli, T., Bigoni, B. and Cassai, E. (1996) Distribution of HHV-6 Variants in Human Tissues. Infectious Agents and Disease, 5, 203-214.

39. Caruso, A., Rotola, A., Comar, M., Favilli, F., Galvan, M., Tosetti, M. and Di Luca, D. (2002) HHV-6 Infects Human Aortic and Heart Microvascular Endothelial Cells, Increasing Their Ability to Secrete Proinflammatory Chemokines. Journal of Medical Virology, 67, 528-533. http://dx.doi.org/10.1002/jmv.10133

40. Krueger, G.R.F., Rojo, J., Buja, L.M., Lassner, D. and Kuehl, U. (2008) Human Herpesvirus-6 (HHV-6) Is a Possible Cardiac Pathogen: An Immunopathological and Ultrastructural Study. Hospital General, 71, 187-191.

41. Arbuckle, J.H., Medveczky, M.M., Luka, J., Hadley, S.H., Luegmayr, A., Ablashi, D., Lund, T.C., Tolar, J., De Meirleir, K., Montoya, J.G., Komaroff, A.L., Ambros, P.F. and Medveczky, P.G. (2010) The Latent Human Herpesvirus-6A Genome Specifically Integrates in Telomeres of Human Chromosomes in Vivo and in Vitro. Proceedings of the National Academy of Sciences of the United States of America, 107, 5563-5568. http://dx.doi.org/10.1073/pnas.0913586107

42. Caforio, A.L.P., Calabrese, F., Angelini, A., Tona, F., Vinci, A., Bottaro,

S., Ramondo, A., Carturan, E., Iliceto, S., Thiene, G. and Daliento, L. (2007) A Prospective Study of Biopsy-Proven Myocarditis: Prognostic Relevance of Clinical and Aetiopathogenetic Features at Diagnosis. European Heart Journal, 28, 1326-1333. http://dx.doi.org/10.1093/eurheartj/ehm076

43. Baboonian, C. and Treasure, T. (1997) Meta-Analysis of the Association of Enteroviruses with Human Heart Disease. Heart (British Cardiac Society), 78, 539-543.
44. Holzmann, M., Nicko, A., Kühl, U., Noutsias, M., Poller, W., Hoffmann, W. and Pauschinger, M. (2008) Complication Rate of Right Ventricular Endomyocardial Biopsy via the Femoral Approach: A Retrospective and Prospective Study Analyzing 3048 Diagnostic Procedures over an 11-Year Period. Circulation, 118, 1722-1728. http://dx.doi.org/10.1161/CIRCULATIONAHA.107.743427
45. McCarthy, R.E., Boehmer, J.P., Hruban, R.H., Hutchins, G.M., Kasper, E.K., Hare, J.M. and Baughman, K.L. (2000) Long-Term Outcome of Fulminant Myocarditis as Compared with Acute (Nonfulminant) Myocarditis. The New England Journal of Medicine, 342, 690-695. http://dx.doi.org/10.1056/NEJM200003093421003
46. Why, H.J., Meany, B.T., Richardson, P.J., Olsen, E.G., Bowles, N.E., Cunningham, L., Freeke, C.A. and Archard, L.C. (1994) Clinical and Prognostic Significance of Detection of Enteroviral RNA in the Myocardium of Patients with Myocarditis or Dilated Cardiomyopathy. Circulation, 89, 2582-2589. http://dx.doi.org/10.1161/01.CIR.89.6.2582
47. Mason, J.W., O'Connell, J.B., Herskowitz, A., Rose, N.R., McManus, B.M., Billingham, M.E. and Moon, T.E. (1995) A Clinical Trial of Immunosuppressive Therapy for Myocarditis. The Myocarditis Treatment Trial Investigators. The New England Journal of Medicine, 333, 269-275. http://dx.doi.org/10.1056/NEJM199508033330501
48. Magnani, J.W., Danik, H.J.S., Dec, G.W. and DiSalvo, T.G. (2006) Survival in Biopsy-Proven Myocarditis: A Long-Term Retrospective Analysis of the Histopathologic, Clinical, and Hemodynamic Predictors. American Heart Journal, 151, 463-470. http://dx.doi.org/10.1016/j.ahj.2005.03.037
49. Frustaci, A., Chimenti, C., Calabrese, F., Pieroni, M., Thiene, G. and Maseri, A. (2003) Immunosuppressive Therapy for Active Lymphocytic Myocarditis: Virological and Immunologic Profile of

Responders versus Nonresponders. Circulation, 107, 857-863. http://dx.doi.org/10.1161/01.CIR.0000048147.15962.31 .

50. Caforio, A.L., Goldman, J.H., Haven, A.J., Baig, K.M., Libera, L.D. and McKenna, W.J. (1997) Circulating Cardiac-Specific Autoantibodies as Markers of Autoimmunity in Clinical and Biopsy-Proven Myocarditis. The Myocarditis Treatment Trial Investigators. European heart journal, 18, 270-275.
51. Bock, C.T., Klingel, K. and Kandolf, R. (2010) Human Parvovirus B19-Associated Myocarditis. The New England Journal of Medicine, 362, 1248-1249. http://dx.doi.org/10.1056/NEJMc0911362
52. Schmidt-Lucke, C., Spillmann, F., Bock, T., Kühl, U., Van Linthout, S., Schultheiss, H.P. and Tschöpe, C. (2010) Interferon Beta Modulates Endothelial Damage in Patients with Cardiac Persistence of Human Parvovirus b19 Infection. The Journal of Infectious Diseases, 201, 936-945. http://dx.doi.org/10.1086/650700
53. Jahns, R., Boivin, V., Schwarzbach, V., Ertl, G. and Lohse, M.J. (2008) Pathological Autoantibodies in Cardiomyopathy. Autoimmunity, 41, 454-461. http://dx.doi.org/10.1080/08916930802031603 .
54. Schulze, K., Becker, B.F., Schauer, R. and Schultheiss, H.P. (1990) Antibodies to ADP-ATP Carrier—An Autoantigen in Myocarditis and Dilated Cardiomyopathy--Impair Cardiac Function. Circulation, 81, 959-969. http://dx.doi.org/10.1161/01.CIR.81.3.959
55. Lurz, P., Eitel, I., Adam, J., Steiner, J., Grothoff, M., Desch, S. and Thiele, H. (2012) Diagnostic Performance of CMR Imaging Compared with EMB in Patients with Suspected Myocarditis. JACC: Cardiovascular Imaging, 5, 513-524. http://dx.doi.org/10.1016/j.jcmg.2011.11.022
56. Escher, F., Kasner, M., Kühl, U., Heymer, J., Wilkenshoff, U., Tschöpe, C. and Schultheiss, H.P. (2013) New Echocardiographic Findings Correlate with Intramyocardial Inflammation in Endomyocardial Biopsies of Patients with Acute Myocarditis and Inflammatory Cardiomyopathy. Mediators of Inflammation, 2013, Article ID: 875420. http://dx.doi.org/10.1155/2013/875420
57. Kasner, M., Sinning, D., Escher, F., Lassner, D., Kühl, U., Schultheiss, H.P. and Tschöpe, C. (2013) The Utility of Speckle Tracking Imaging in the Diagnostic of Acute Myocarditis, as Proven by Endomyocardial Biopsy. International Journal of Cardiology, 168, 3023-3024. http://dx.doi.org/10.1016/j.ijcard.2013.04.016

58. Frustaci, A., Russo, M.A. and Chimenti, C. (2009) Randomized Study on the Efficacy of Immunosuppressive Therapy in Patients with Virus-Negative Inflammatory Cardiomyopathy: The TIMIC Study. European Heart Journal, 30, 1995-2002. http://dx.doi.org/10.1093/eurheartj/ehp249 .
59. Lassner, D., Rohde, M., Gross, U.M., Escher, F., Schultheiss, H.P., Linke, R.P. and Kühl, U. (2011) Classification of Four Chemically Different Amyloid Types in Routine Endomyocardial Biopsies by Advanced Immunohistochemistry. Amyloid: The International Journal of Experimental and Clinical Investigation: The Official Journal of the International Society of Amyloidosis, 18, 76-78. http://dx.doi.org/10.3109/13506129.2011.574354027
60. Thomas Aretz, H. (1987) Myocarditis: The Dallas Criteria. Human Pathology, 18, 619-624. http://dx.doi.org/10.1016/S0046-8177(87)80363-5
61. Noutsias, M., Pauschinger, M., Ostermann, K., Escher, F., Blohm, J.H., Schultheiss, H. and Kühl, U. (2002) Digital Image Analysis System for the Quantification of Infiltrates and Cell Adhesion Molecules in Inflammatory Cardiomyopathy. Medical Science Monitor: International Medical Journal of Experimental and Clinical Research, 8, MT59-MT71.
62. Silverio, J.C., de-Oliveira-Pinto, L.M., da Silva, A.A., de Oliveira, G.M. and Lannes-Vieira, J. (2010) Perforin-Expressing Cytotoxic Cells Contribute to Chronic Cardiomyopathy in Trypanosoma cruzi Infection. International Journal of Experimental Pathology, 91, 72-86. http://dx.doi.org/10.1111/j.1365-2613.2009.00670.x
63. Kittleson, M.M. and Hare, J.M. (2005) Molecular Signature Analysis: The Potential of Gene-Expression Analysis in Cardiomyopathy. Future Cardiology, 1, 793-808. http://dx.doi.org/10.2217/14796678.1.6.793
64. Kühl, U., Lassner, D., von Schlippenbach, J., Poller, W. and Schultheiss, H.P. (2012) Interferon-Beta Improves Survival in Enterovirus-Associated Cardiomyopathy. Journal of the American College of Cardiology, 60, 1295-1296. http://dx.doi.org/10.1016/j.jacc.2012.06.026
65. Kühl, U., Pauschinger, M., Schwimmbeck, P.L., Seeberg, B., Lober, C., Noutsias, M. and Schultheiss, H.P. (2003) Interferon-Beta Treatment Eliminates Cardiotropic Viruses and Improves Left Ventricular Function in Patients with Myocardial Persistence of Viral Genomes

and Left Ventricular Dysfunction. Circulation, 107, 2793-2798. http://dx.doi.org/10.1161/01.CIR.0000072766.67150.51 .

66. Kühl, U., Rohde, M., Lassner, D., Gross, U.M., Escher, F. and Schultheiss, H.P. (2012) miRNA as Activity Markers in Parvo B19 Associated Heart Disease. Herz, 37, 637-643. http://dx.doi.org/10.1007/s00059-012-3656-3
67. Hershberger, R.E., Lindenfeld, J., Mestroni, L., Seidman, C.E., Taylor, M.R.G. and Towbin, J.A. (2009) Genetic Evaluation of Cardiomyopathy—A Heart Failure Society of America Practice Guideline. Journal of Cardiac Failure, 15, 83-97. http://dx.doi.org/10.1016/j.cardfail.2009.01.006
68. Andreasen, C., Nielsen, J.B., Refsgaard, L., Holst, A.G., Christensen, A.H., Andreasen, L. and Olesen, M.S. (2013) New Population-Based Exome Data Are Questioning the Pathogenicity of Previously Cardiomyopathy-Associated Genetic Variants. European Journal of Human Genetics: EJHG, 21, 918-928. http://dx.doi.org/10.1038/ejhg.2012.283
69. Schultheiss, H.P. (2013) Genetic Testing Is Superior to Biopsy of the Myocardium in Cardiomyopathy—No. Deutsche Medizinische Wochenschrift (1946), 138, 599. .
70. Hütter, G., Nowak, D., Mossner, M., Ganepola, S., Müssig, A., Allers, K. and Thiel, E. (2009) Long-Term Control of HIV by CCR5 Delta32/Delta32 Stem-Cell Transplantation. The New England Journal of Medicine, 360, 692-698. http://dx.doi.org/10.1056/NEJMoa0802905
71. Muntinghe, F.L.H., Gross, S., Bakker, S.J.L., Landman, G.W.D., van der Harst, P., Bilo, H.J.G. and Zuurman, M.W. (2009) CCR5Delta32 Genotype Is Associated with Outcome in Type 2 Diabetes Mellitus. Diabetes Research and Clinical Practice, 86, 140-145. http://dx.doi.org/10.1016/j.diabres.2009.08.013
72. Lassner, D., Kuehl, U., Rohde, M., Siegismund, C.S. and Schultheiss, H.P. (2014) CCR5del32 Polymorphism Is a Protective Factor for Mortality in Non-Ischemic Cardiomyopathy. International Journal of Cardiology, 173, 561-562. http://dx.doi.org/10.1016/j.ijcard.2014.03.123
73. Kittleson, M.M. and Hare, J.M. (2005) Molecular Signature Analysis: Using the Myocardial Transcriptome as a Biomarker in Cardiovascular Disease. Trends in Cardiovascular Medicine, 15, 130-138. http://dx.doi.org/10.1016/j.tcm.2005.05.007

74. Siegismund, C.S., Rohde, M., Kühl, U. and Lassner, D. (2014) Multiparametric Diagnostics of Cardiomyopathies by microRNA Signatures. Microchimica Acta, in press. http://dx.doi.org/10.1007/s00604-014-1249-y .
75. Lassner, D., Kuhl, U., Siegismund, C.S., Rohde, M., Elezkurtaj, S., Escher, F. and Schultheiss, H.P. (2014) Improved Diagnosis of Idiopathic Giant Cell Myocarditis and Cardiac Sarcoidosis by Myocardial Gene Expression Profiling. European Heart Journal, epub ahead of print. http://dx.doi.org/10.1093/eurheartj/ehu101
76. Elezkurtaj, S., Lassner, D., Schultheiss, H.P. and Escher, F. (2014) Vascular Involvement in Cardiac Giant Cell Myocarditis: A New Pathophysiological Aspect. Clinical Research in Cardiology: Official Journal of the German Cardiac Society, 103, 161-163. http://dx.doi.org/10.1007/s00392-013-0638-2 .
77. De Groote, P., Pinet, F. and Bauters, C. (2013) New Technologies, New Therapies: Toward Personalized Medicine in Heart Failure Patients? European Heart Journal, 34, 636-637. http://dx.doi.org/10.1093/eurheartj/ehs432
78. Ameling, S., Herda, L.R., Hammer, E., Steil, L., Teumer, A., Trimpert, C. and Felix, S.B. (2013) Myocardial Gene Expression Profiles and Cardiodepressant Autoantibodies Predict Response of Patients with dilated Cardiomyopathy to Immunoadsorption Therapy. European Heart Journal, 34, 666-675. http://dx.doi.org/10.1093/eurheartj/ehs330
79. Staudt, A., Dörr, M., Staudt, Y., Böhm, M., Probst, M., Empen, K. and Felix, S.B. (2005) Role of Immunoglobulin G3 Subclass in Dilated Cardiomyopathy: Results from Protein A Immunoadsorption. American Heart Journal, 150, 729-736. http://dx.doi.org/10.1016/j.ahj.2004.11.002
80. Ikeda, S., Kong, S.W., Lu, J., Bisping, E., Zhang, H., Allen, P.D. and Pu, W.T. (2007) Altered microRNA Expression in Human Heart Disease. Physiological Genomics, 31, 367-373. http://dx.doi.org/10.1152/physiolgenomics.00144.2007
81. Thum, T., Catalucci, D. and Bauersachs, J. (2008) MicroRNAs: Novel Regulators in Cardiac Development and Disease. Cardiovascular Research, 79, 562-570. http://dx.doi.org/10.1093/cvr/cvn137
82. Corsten, M.F., Papageorgiou, A., Verhesen, W., Carai, P., Lindow, M., Obad, S. and Heymans, S. (2012) MicroRNA Profiling Identifies microRNA-155 as an Adverse Mediator of Cardiac Injury and

Dysfunction during Acute Viral Myocarditis. Circulation Research, 111, 415-425. http://dx.doi.org/10.1161/CIRCRESAHA.112.267443

83. Jaguszewski, M., Osipova, J., Ghadri, J.R., Napp, L.C., Widera, C., Franke, J. and Templin, C. (2014) A Signature of Circulating microRNAs Differentiates Takotsubo Cardiomyopathy from Acute Myocardial Infarction. European Heart Journal, 35, 999-1006.

CHAPTER

7

AN OPTIMAL CONTROL APPROACH TO STRUCTURED TREATMENT INTERRUPTIONS FOR HIV PATIENTS: A PERSONALIZED MEDICINE PERSPECTIVE

Adam Attarian[1], Hien Tran[2]

[1]MIT Lincoln Laboratory, Lexington, MA, USA.

[2]Department of Mathematics, North Carolina State University, Raleigh, NC, USA.

ABSTRACT

Highly Active Antiretroviral Therapy (HAART) has changed the course of human immunodeficiency virus (HIV) treatments since its introduction. However, for many patients, long term continuous HAART is expensive and can include problems with drug toxicity and side effects, as well as increased drug resistance. Because of these reasons, some HIV infected patients will voluntarily terminate HAART. Some of these patients will also

Citation: Attarian, A. and Tran, H. (2017), "An Optimal Control Approach to Structured Treatment Interruptions for HIV Patients: A Personalized Medicine Perspective". Applied Mathematics, 8, 934-955. doi: 10.4236/am.2017.87074.

interrupt the continuous prescribed therapies for short or long periods. After discontinuing HAART, patients will usually experience a rapid increase in viral load coupled with an immediate decline in CD4+ counts. The canonical example of a patient undergoing unsupervised breaks in HAART is that of the "Berlin patient". In this case, the patient was able to control viral load in the absence of treatment by cycling HAART on and off due to non-related infections. Due to this patient, interest in the use of structured treatment interruptions (STI) as a mechanism to regulate an HIV infection piqued. This paper describes an optimal control approach to determine STI regimen for HIV patients. The optimal STI was implemented in the context of the receding horizon control (RHC) using a mathematical model for the in-vivo dynamics of an HIV type 1 infection. Using available clinical data, we calibrate the model by estimating on a patient specific basis, a best estimable set of parameters using sensitivity analysis and subset selection. We demonstrate how customized STI protocols can be designed through the variation of control parameters on a patient specific basis.

Keywords:-Personalized Medicine, HIV Model, Sensitivity Analysis, Subset Selection, Parameter Estimation, Structured Treatment Interruptions, Receding Horizon Control

INTRODUCTION

There are few diseases in our society today that are more polarizing, politicized, and personal than human immunodeficiency virus/acquired immune deficiency syndrome, or HIV/AIDS. According to the Joint United Nations Programme on HIV and AIDS (UNAIDS), there were 34 million people living with HIV/AIDS in 2010, 22.9 million of which live in sub-Saharan Africa. Despite the prevalence and availability of effective treatment of HIV, even as late as 2010 the best practices for management of acute HIV infection are still unknown [1]. The time to initiate treatment and the manner of treatment are still the subject of many ongoing clinical trials that are investigating the treatment benefits versus risks.

Throughout the last few decades, mathematical models have been developed to further the understanding of the progression of the virus as it replicates in-host. These models focus on the interaction between the virus and the $CD4^+$ cells of the immune system, one of the virus' primary targets [2] [3] [4] . The early models of progression were critical in the understanding of the virus and the development of early treatments, as the science and understanding were lagging behind the impact of the spreading epidemic.

The models of in-vivo dynamics are most often formulated as a system of nonlinear ordinary differential equations (ODE), though recently several size structured partial differential equation models have been developed. These models allow for variations in viral production rates as a function of time, since it is thought that as infected cells age their overall fitness decreases [5] [6] . The ordinary differential equation models that we utilize are based on a compartmental and mass-balance analysis of the biological system. These models are developed to incorporate as many relevant physiological principles as possible, though at the cost of increased model complexity.

A primary goal of using modern models of HIV is to influence treatment decisions and construct better treatment protocols for infected patients. The construction of optimal control methodologies has been investigated by many authors, [7] - [16] , however in almost all of these cases the authors worked with simulated data and were not patient specific in nature. To use these dynamic models in a patient specific capacity, the models must first be calibrated to each individual patient. While much attention has been paid to the forward simulation problem over the years, less attention has been focused on the so-called inverse problem. Inverse problems are formulated when we wish to determine the parameters that characterize the system using measurements. One of the main obstacles in solving the inverse problem is that biological and physiological models are often nonlinear and contain many parameters. Additionally, the data for validation is often sparse, or possibly representative of only a portion of the model. Before parameter estimation methods can be applied to an ODE model, an investigation into the identifiability of the parameters, given available data, must be performed.

The investigation into parameter identifiability is not unique to the mathematical sciences, and many papers in engineering, statistics, and biomedical engineering have shed light into this area [17] [18] . Identifiability in an HIV model context has been examined in [19] [20] where structural and observer perspectives were used with a less complex model. In this paper we consider the parameter identifiability of a seven state, twenty two parameters HIV model based on clinically obtained measurements of both $CD4^+$ count and viral load. We utilize both sensitivity analysis and identifiability analysis methods to compute patient specific best-estimatable subsets of parameters. In [21] an identifiability analysis was conducted on an identical model, however the authors used a different, ad-hoc subset selection procedure.

Finally, the paper investigates the construction of optimal control and treatment therapies in a patient specific context, i.e. in the setting of personalized medicine or precision medicine. We develop treatments known as structured treatment interruptions (STI), wherein the effective treatment is terminated at specified times and then restarted in an attempt to increase an in-host immune response and provide a drug holiday for the patient. These treatment methods have been studied in detail, though a lack of double-blind, randomized clinical trials has lead to a lack of consensus on the effectiveness of these types of treatments [22] [23] [24] [25] . We implement the optimal STI using the receding horizon control (RHC) methodology [12] . Since RHC is a feedback control, it allows for adjustment for unexpected perturbations to the treatment schedule, e.g. the patient decides to go off-treatment for a period of time not otherwise prescribed.The organization of the paper is as follows. Section 2 describes the mathematical model of the HIV dynamics, including the control mechanisms. This section also describes the a-priori identifiability analysis, the available data and its incorporation into the parameter estimation problem, and the results of the model validation. In particular, we show how the model can well-fit both the $CD4^+$ count and viral load clinical data. The optimal control formulation to compute optimal treatment strategies of an STI type is considered in Section 3. In this section we also provide computed optimal control simulations along side the clinical data and discuss the relevance.

AN HIV MODEL

There have been numerous advances in modeling HIV viral dynamics in recent years. An excellent general overview of the modeling challenges of HIV, especially with regards to treatment protocols and stability analyses is given in [3] . In this section, we consider a model developed in [26] .

The dynamics of the HIV model are described by the system of nonlinear ordinary differential equations

$$\begin{aligned}
&\dot{T}_1 = \lambda_1 - d_1 T_1 - (1-\varepsilon_1) k_1 V_I T_1,\ \dot{T}_2 = \lambda_2 - d_2 T_2 - (1 - f\varepsilon_1) k_2 V_I T_2 \\
&\dot{T}_1^* = (1-\varepsilon_1) k_1 V_I T_1 - \delta T_1^* - m_1 T_1^* E,\ \dot{T}_2^* = (1 - f\varepsilon_1) k_2 V_I T_2 - \delta T_2^* - m_2 T_2^* E \\
&\dot{V}_I = (1-\varepsilon_2) N_T \delta (T_1^* + T_2^*) - (c + (1-\varepsilon_1)\rho_1 k_1 T_1 + (1 - f\varepsilon_1)\rho_2 k_2 T_2) V_I \\
&\dot{V}_{NI} = \varepsilon_2 N_T \delta (T_1^* + T_2^*) - c V_{NI},\ \dot{E} = \lambda_E + b_E \frac{T_1^* + T_2^*}{T_1^* + T_2^* + K_b} E - d_E \frac{T_1^* + T_2^*}{T_1^* + T_2^* + K_d} E - \delta_E E,
\end{aligned} \tag{1}$$

with an initial condition vector

$$\left[T_1(0)\ T_2(0)\ T_1^*(0)\ T_2^*(0)\ V_I(0)\ V_{NI}(0)\ E(0)\right]^{\mathrm{T}}.$$

The model compartments are T_1 (type 1 target cells, e.g. $CD4^+$ T-cells, cells/ ml blood), T_2 (type 2 target cells, e.g. macrophages, cells/ml blood), V_I (infectious free viron particles, RNA copies/ml blood), V_{NI} (non-infectious free viron particles, RNA copies/ml blood) and EE (cytotoxic T-lymphocytes (CTL), cells/ml blood). A superscript asterisk denotes infected cells. This model has two important features.

The presence of a second target cell type, T_2 satisfies a modeling requirement suggested in [4] : a reasonable HIV model predicts a non-zero steady-state viral load even in the presence of effective therapy. Because of this, one cannot expect the viral load to be driven to zero, only to be reduced significantly. This HIV specific immune response state EE consists of CTLs lysing antigens to HIV infected cells, killing them at rates m1m1 and m2m2 for each class of target cell. The immune response model used in this work does not directly clear viral particles, and so there is no interaction between the immune compartment and the virus compartments. In [27] the authors extended the model by adding a second immune effector state that represents CTL cells with memory. While that model incorporates a greater degree of HIV dynamics, it is shown in [21] that the model used in this paper is sufficient for clinical data fitting and model prediction.

External mechanisms by which the virus is controlled are incorporated into the model. We allow for therapeutic treatment by reverse transcriptase inhibitors (RTIs) and protease inhibitors (PIs). RTIs interfere with the viral RNA to DNA synthesis; when reverse transcriptase is inhibited HIV can enter a cell but the host cell will not become infected. PIs cause infected cells to produce non- infectious virions.

Thus when considering treatment that includes PIs, we consider both infectious and noninfectious viral particles. Noninfectious viral particles can remain present even in the absence of PIs. The prevailing paradigm of HIV treatment is to prescribe a highly active antiretroviral therapy (HAART) consisting of both PIs and RTIs. The treatment factors are given as $\varepsilon_1(t)=\bar{\varepsilon}_1 u(t)$ and $\varepsilon_2(t)=\bar{\varepsilon}_2 u(t)$, consisting of efficacy $\bar{\varepsilon}_1 \in [0,1]$ corresponding to a reverse transcriptase inhibitor and $\bar{\varepsilon}_2 \in [0,1]$ modeling the effectiveness of a protease inhibitor with a time dependent function $u(t), 0 \le u(t) \le 1$. We assume that the treatment has a reduced efficacy for the population of T_2, where the efficacy is $f\varepsilon_1(t), f \in (0,1)$. Treatment protocols are always implemented as a combination of both PIs and RTIs, so monotherapy is not considered.

The model (1) contains 22 biologically relevant parameters that must be specified before numerical simulations can be performed. We evaluate the model at a nominal set of parameter values that is justified through literature and past clinical studies; these values are given in Table 1. The parameter values are taken primarily from work done by [4] [28] . Several of the parameters are not available from human or animal data. The nominal values for $\lambda_1, k_1, \lambda_2$ and k_2 are chosen so that several conditions on viral load and target cell equilibria are satisfied.

Table 1. HIV model parameters and their nominal values.

Index	Parameter	Value	Units	Description
1		10	cells/ mm^3 day	Target cell type 1 source rate
2		0.03198	cells/ mm^3 day	Target cell type 2 source rate
3		0.01	1/day	Target cell type 1 death rate
4		0.01	1/day	Target cell type 2 death rate
5			mm^3/virions day	Population 1 infection rate
6		0.1	mm^3/virions day	Population 2 infection rate
7		0.01	mm^3/cells day	Immune-induced clearance rate for population 1
8		0.01	mm^3/cells day	Immune-induced clearance rate for population 2
9		1	virions/cell	Average number virions infecting a type 1 cell
10		1	virions/cell	Average number virions infecting a type 2 cell
11		0.7	1/day	Infected cell death rate
12		13	1/day	Virus natural death rate
13				Treatment efficacy reduction in population 2
14		100	virions/cell	Virions produced per infected cell
15		.001	cells/ mm^3 day	Immune effector production (source) rate

16		0.1	1/day	Natural death rate for immune effectors
17		0.3	1/day	Maximum birth rate for immune effectors
18		0.25	1/day	Maximum death rate for immune effectors
19		100	cells/ml	Saturation constant for immune effector birth
20		500	cells/ml	Saturation constant for immune effector death
21				RTI efficacy
22				PI efficacy

These conditions are actually not reflected in our model since we have omitted the chronically infected state from the Callaway-Perelson model, though it is believed that small adjustments to the parameter values will obtain the same qualitative behavior [26].

The parameters used in the immune response state are not well known, and are chosen primarily to exhibit expected model behavior in the simulations.

The parameters m_1,m_2 represent the effectiveness that the immune response EE clears the infected cells of the target populations. The commonly used values are taken from [4] .

Because the range of both the state variables and parameter values can vary over several orders of magnitude, we use a $\log_{10}$ transformed system for the state variables. We define the new state variable $x_i(t,q)=\log_{10}\bar{x}_i(t,q)$, , where $\bar{x}_i$ represents the original, non-log transformed state. We also log-transform the parameters, $q\rightarrow\log_{10}q$,as they also varying widely in magnitude (see Table 1). The new system of equations are then given by

$$\dot{x}_i(t,q)=\frac{10^{-x_i}}{\ln 10}f\left(10^{x_i(q)},10^{q}\right) \tag{2}$$

where f is the right hand side of (1). Performing this substitution puts both the states and parameters within an order of (log) magnitude of each other, allowing for a more robust estimation procedure. This transformation also resolves issues of physically unrealistic negative solutions that occur due to round- off error.

Sensitivity and Identifiability Analysis

A first step in the a-priori identifiability analysis of a system is to determine which parameters contribute greatest to the output of the system. For our model, the output of the system is $y_1 = T_1 + T_1^*$ representing the CD4$^+$ count and $y_2 = V_I + V_{NI}$ representing the viral load. Sensitivity analysis has traditionally primarily been used in the analysis of the forward problem when one needed to understand the effects of parameter perturbation on the output. In recent years sensitivity analysis has become an important component of inverse problem analysis, partly because it directly aids in uncertainty analysis. When physiologically based mathematical models are developed, the parameters typically have biological relevance, and thus one may wish to estimate these parameters from data. If these parameters are insensitive then they could be difficult to estimate despite their relevance. Sensitivity analysis determines the degree to which parameters affect system output. Sensitivity analysis can also aid in the optimal design of experiments and data collection [29], possibly maximizing parameter sensitivity.

Sensitivity analysis constitutes a subset of techniques within identifiability analysis. An excellent survey of methods for identifiability in ODE models is given in [30] . In that paper, the authors define a system to be identifiable if the parameter qq can be uniquely determined from the system input u(t) and the measured system output y(t) . The system is said to be unidentifiable if q cannot be uniquely identified. A wide variety of techniques have been developed for identifiability analysis, including power series expansions and similar transforms, the use of differential algebras, and the implicit function theorem. These methods are not dependent on experimental observations, and are termed methods of structural identifiability. We concern ourselves primarily with practical identifiability analysis, which combines both the model structure information and experimental observations to determine which parameters are able to be identified. For a detailed discussion of our implementation of the practical identifiability analysis we refer the reader to [31] .

Clinical Data

The data available have come from a clinical study at Massachusetts General Hospital of over 100 adults with acute HIV infection between 1996 and 2004. The data collected consists of CD4$^+$ T-lymphocyte count (cells/ml) and RNA viral load (RNA copies/ml) represented by $y_1 = T_1 + T_1^*$ and $y_2 = V_I + V_{NI}$, respectively. The viral load is quantified through different assay techniques;

the standard assay can detect viral loads in the range of 400 to 750,000 copies/ml, while an ultra-sensitive assay has a detection range of 50 to 100,000 copies/ml. The ultra-sensitive assay is used when a measurement is below the 400 copies/ml lower detection limit for the standard assay. This can often be the case when patients are successfully suppressing the virus due to HAART.

Due to the range sensitivity limits of the assays, the clinical viral load effectively have upper and lower limits of quantification. The upper limit of quantification is addressed by repeatedly diluting the sample until it falls within the detection range. The lower limit, or left censoring point, directly affects the collected data and how it is used within the inverse problem. When a datum is returned at a censor point, L_1=400 copies/ml or L_2=50 copies/ml, the only available knowledge is that the true measurement is between zero and the left quantification limit. These limits are illustrated in the longitudinal data set from patient identified by the number 1, shown in Figure 1. The data points appearing directly on the horizontal reference lines are said to be censored.

In addition to the data being censored at certain time values, the data are also collected at different time intervals. These intervals also differ between patients. This is visible in Figure 1 as well; the observations of viral load and $CD4^+$ may not have been made at the same time points. In general for patient j , we have $CD4^+$ data pairs $\left(t_1^{ij}, y_1^{ij}\right), i=1,\cdots,N_1^j$ and possibly different viral RNA pairs $\left(t_2^{ij}, y_2^{ij}\right), i=1,\cdots,N_2^j$.

Model Validation

Before we use the HIV model given in (1) to design the optimal treatment for

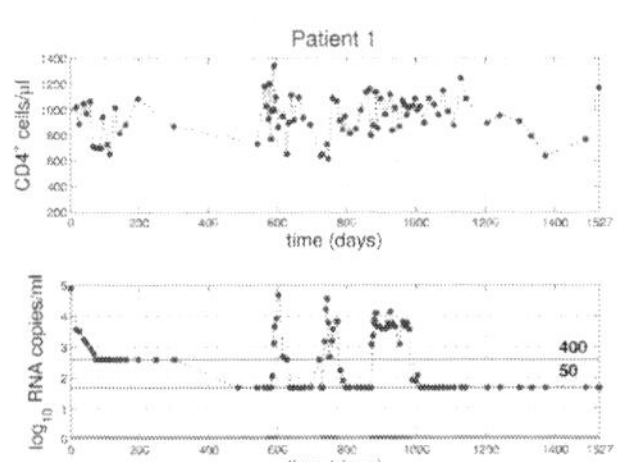

Figure 1. Patient 1 data set, with the censor points indicated by horizontal lines, L_1=$\log_{10}$400, L_2=$\log_{10}$50 . The green and red bars on the axis indicate patient treatment adherence and non-adherence, respectively.

HIV patients in the context of personalized medicine, we first calibrate the model parameters to the clinical data through the parameter estimation formulation.

The parameter estimation problem is patient specific; we use data from a single patient j in order to estimate the patient specific parameter value qjqj . A common approach for conducting parameter estimation in ODE models is through minimization of an ordinary least squares cost function [33] . To this end, we let $z_s\left(t_s^{ij}\right), s=1,2$ denote the model observation for patient j, output s, at time index i. That is, $z_1\left(t_1^{ij}\right)=T_1\left(t_1^{ij}\right)+T_1^*\left(t_1^{ij}\right)$ and $z_2\left(t_2^{ij}\right)=V_I\left(t_2^{ij}\right)+V_{NI}\left(t_2^{ij}\right)$ We define the cost function

$$J(q)=\sum_{s=1}^{2}\frac{1}{N_s^j}\sum_{i=1}^{N_s^j}\left|z_s\left(t_s^{ij};q\right)-y_s^{ij}\right|^2, \quad (3)$$

over an admissible parameter space $\Omega\subseteq\mathbb{R}^l$, where l is the number of parameters being identified by the practical identifiability analysis. The parameter estimation problem is to compute the unique minimizer of $q^{*j}=\operatorname{argmin} J(q)$, if it exists. Note that uniqueness of the minimizing parameter vector is an issue addressed by the identifiability analysis. Assuming the data are uncensored and produced by the model with additive and independent Gaussian noise, the ordinary least squares estimate is also the maximum likelihood estimate. However, in our case there is censoring in the data as discussed in section 2.2, and least squares does not suffice as a statistically rigorous methodology. Instead we compute maximum likelihood parameter estimates using an expectation maximization (EM) algorithm [32] . Details regarding the use of this algorithm with ODE models can be found in [31].

We begin the parameter estimation problem by performing for each patient an a-priori sensitivity analysis at the nominal parameter values q* given in Table 1. As each patient model is evaluated at the same q∗ , the only factor that affects parameter identifiability is the patient adherence to treatment.

Before a subset specific estimate is formed, we first attempt to estimate all 22 parameters using the global optimization algorithm DIRECT with the EM algorithm. DIRECT is a bounded, sampling method based on dividing hyper-rec- tangles [34] . The termination criterion for DIRECT is only the number of iterations, and we only allow 3. DIRECT is sometimes used to determine a “better” local initial iterate for gradient based optimizers, and our approach is similar in this regard. The parameters that are not being estimated are fixed to the output of the DIRECT optimization, and it is at this point we begin the gradient based method with EM to further refine the parameter estimates on the identifiable subset.

The number of identifiable parameters range from k=8 to k=10. In addition to these parameters, all seven initial conditions were estimated for each patient. Each patient subset is given in Table 2.

Representative of the parameter estimation results are depicted in Figure 2 and Figure 3 for patients identified by number 1 and 3, respectively (for the fit of the model to other patient data see [31]). In each figure the collected clinical data are given in blue dots as well as the adjusted data (black circles) calculated through the expectation maximization algorithm.

Table 2. Patient specific identifiable subsets.

Patient	Identifiable Subset ρ
1	$d_1, k_1, k_2, m_1, m_2, N_T, \lambda_E, \varepsilon_1$
2	$d_1, k_1, k_2, m_1, \rho_1, f, N_T, \varepsilon_1, \varepsilon_2$
3	$d_1, k_1, k_2, m_1, m_2, \delta, K_b, \varepsilon_1, \varepsilon_2$
4	$d_1, k_1, k_2, m_1, m_2, N_T, \delta_E, \varepsilon_2$
5	$d_2, k_1, k_2, m_1, m_2, c, N_T, \delta_E, d_E$
6	$\lambda_2, k_1, k_2, m_2, \rho_1, c, \delta_E, b_E, K_d, \varepsilon_2$
7	$m_2, k_1, k_2, m_1, \rho_2, f, N_T, \lambda_E, \varepsilon_1$
8	$d_2, k_1, k_2, m_2, \rho_1, \delta, N_T, K_d, \varepsilon_2$
9	$\lambda_2, k_1, k_2, m_1, m_2, \lambda_E, \delta_E, d_E, \varepsilon_1$
10	$d_2, k_1, k_2, m_1, m_2, f, \delta_E, K_d$
11	$d_1, k_1, k_2, m_1, m_2, \delta, \lambda_E, b_E, K_d$
12	$d_2, k_1, k_2, m_2, \rho_1, c, \delta_E, K_b, K_d$
13	$\lambda_2, k_2, m_2, \rho_1, \delta, c, k_b, K_d, \varepsilon_1$
14	$d_2, k_1, k_2, m_1, m_2, \delta, \lambda_E, b_E, K_d$

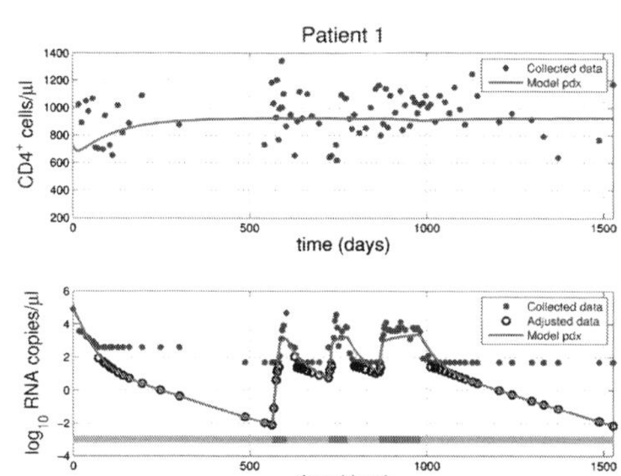

Figure 2. Collected and adjusted data with model prediction for patient 1. The red and green bars along the axis indicate patient adherence to therapy. Clinically collected data are in blue, and EM adjusted data are in black. The red trajectory is the calibrated model prediction.

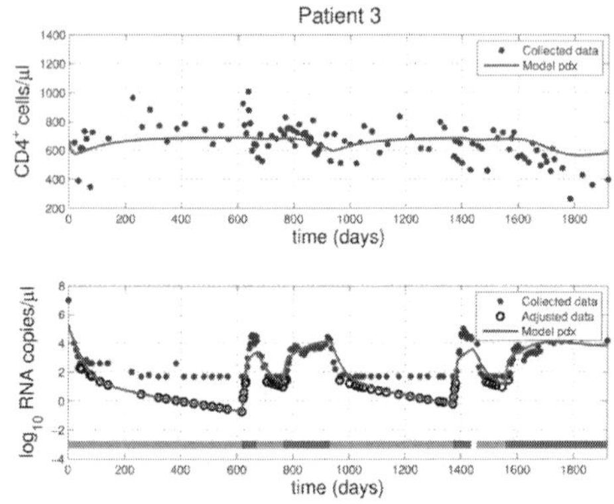

Figure 3. Collected and adjusted data with model prediction for patient 3. The red and green bars along the axis indicate patient adherence to therapy. Clinically collected data are in blue, and EM adjusted data are in black. The red trajectory is the calibrated model prediction.

The calibrated model prediction is the solid red line. Near the bottom of the figures are structured treatment interruption as prescribed by the medical doctors for each patient (green for on-treatment and red for off-treatment). In general, the model fits the clinical data reasonably well.

OPTIMAL STI THERAPY

Highly Active Antiretroviral Therapy (HAART) has changed the course of HIV treatments since its introduction. Under HAART, viral load decreases exponentially in the weeks after the start of treatment and is maintained at low levels so long as treatment is continued. Despite this exponential decline in viral load, these treatments do not completely clear the virus from the patient, and a life long therapy is necessary to maintain low viral load. Even with this kind of success, the best way to treat acutely infected HIV patients is still an open question with many approaches under investigation [1] . For many patients, long term continuous HAART is expensive and can include problems with drug toxicity and side effects, as well as increased drug resistance [35] . It has been shown that approximately 80% of patients who adhered to less than 70% of the prescribed treatment regimen experienced treatment failure, whereas patients of high adherence (>95%) experienced the best results [36] . Long term use of protease inhibitors has been associated with insulin intolerance, cholesterol elevation, and the redistribution of body fat. Because of these reasons, some HIV infected patients will voluntarily terminate HAART. Some of these patients will also interrupt the continuous prescribed therapies for short or long periods. After discontinuing HAART, patients will usually experience a rapid increase in viral load coupled with a immediate decline in $CD4^+$ counts [22] .

The canonical example of a patient undergoing unsupervised breaks in HAART is that of the "Berlin patient" [23] . In this case, the patient was able to control viral load in the absence of treatment by cycling HAART on and off due to non-related infections. When treatment was fully stopped after day 176, the patient's viral load did not immediately rebound as is consistent with going off treatment. Due to this patient, there have been a lot of interest in the use of structured treatment interruptions (STI) as a mechanism to regulate an HIV infection.

One of the key variables in the design of any STI based protocol is the criteria in which patients are removed or placed back on treatment. In some studies the viral load was the primary indicator as to when treatment would resume, whereas in other studies off periods were of a fixed length, followed by a fixed length on period. The former approach is simpler, but harder to administer as it requires a higher level of patience scrutiny with more expensive and inconvenient blood tests. The latter strategy is easier to implement in larger patient groups, but the on/off periods are still up for debate and the subject of many clinical trials. Currently the period durations are determined either in an ad-hoc style, or by trying to adapt the methodologies of other trials.

The use of mathematical modeling to determine optimal STI regimes has flourished in recent years. The survey paper [37] details the design of STI strategies using HIV models and emphasizes that the use of models may be beneficial in a clinical design scenario. In [38] the authors build upon the original work of [39] and use an in-host HIV model to simulate many possible different STI treatments. In contrast to our work however, there is no patient specific data or parameter estimates used and the STI treatments are not calculated, only evaluated; several insights into the effects of STI treatments are gained through the "virtual STI" trials.

A RHC APPROACH TO STI THERAPY

Although several control paradigms exist for the control and simulation of nonlinear systems, not many nonlinear controllers can be applied to the discrete sample-and-hold methodology of STI treatment. One method that is highly promising and is well suited to finding an optimal treatment amenable to HIV treatment is the receding horizon control (RHC) [40] . Receding horizon control has also explicitly been used to compute optimal treatment schedules in [41] , though with a very different, immune response centric model. The authors were some of the first investigators to apply RHC methodologies to biological systems.

Receding horizon, or model predictive control seeks to gain the benefits of a feedback control while maintaining the overall existing control methodology (i.e. STI) and model structure. The basic structure of the RHC methodology is shown in Figure 4. RHC is a feedback control system that operates by computing the current control from solving a finite time open loop control problem, using the current state of the system as the initial state.

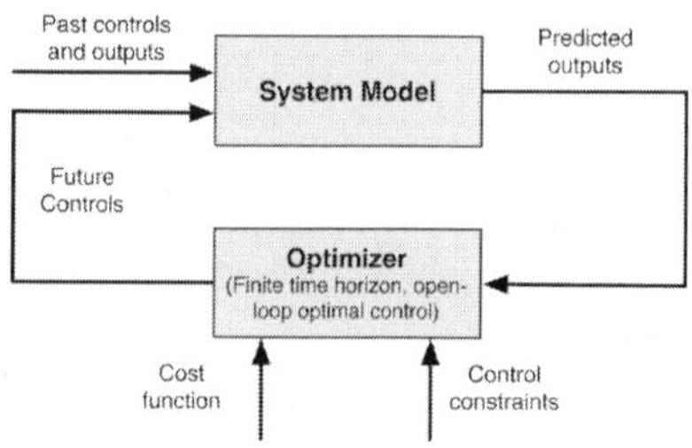

Figure 4. Schematic diagram of the receding horizon control.

This implicit optimization then yields a control for future time, and the first control in the sequence is applied to the system for a specified control window. This is the primary difference with the open loop methodologies, where the controls are computed for the entire simulation interval before simulation.

This framework is uniquely suited for the computation of controls that fall within the STI paradigm under HAART. Since the number of elements in the control sequence is finite due to the on-off nature of the STI control, the existence of an optimal control on each window is guaranteed. Moreover, this approach is model invariant, in that the HIV model can be updated or swapped out with a model with minimal modifications to the control setup. Lastly the RHC parameters such as horizon and window length, discussed later, can be easily modified based on clinical needs and observations.

There are several basic elements to the RHC system, outlined in [42]:

1) Model equations which govern the system dynamics.
2) The calculation of a sequence of optimal control laws, subject to the cost function.

3) A "receding horizon" strategy, so that on each interval or horizon, that the control is computed is shifted forward in time. The control that is computed is then only used for a portion of the horizon length.

To solidify the RHC methodology, we present the following control problem formulation. Together with the model equations (1), we consider a control problem defined by the objective function,

$$J(u(t)) = \int_0^{t_f} \left[QV(t) + R_1\varepsilon_1(t)^2 + R_2\varepsilon_2(t)^2 - SE(t) \right] \mathrm{d}t, \tag{4}$$

where ε$_1$(t)=ε$_1$u(t)ε$_1$(t)=ε$_1$u(t) , an RTI, and ε$_2$(t)=ε2u(t)ε$_2$(t)=ε$_2$u(t) , a PI. The values ε1ε1 and ε2ε2 are the patient specific values estimated in Section 2. The parameters Q,R$_1$,R$_2$Q,R$_1$,R$_2$ and SS represent the control weights for the virus, control input, and immune response, respectively. By varying these weights, the optimal control can be customized in a patient specific sense, and exact treatments can be designed. By including the control terms in (4) we attempt to minimize the systematic cost of the drugs both in the sense of physiologic side effects as well as the monetary treatment cost.

For the RHC formulation, we denote [t$_i$ t$_{i+1}$] a sequence of time intervals. Let $t_{hor,i}$ such that $t_{hor,i} \geq t_{i+1} - t_i$ be the control horizon. We denote $t_{i+1} - t_i$ to be t$_{wint}$, the current control window. Consider a sequence of control problems P$_i$,

$$u^* \in \mathcal{U} \text{ s.t. } u^* = \arg\min J(u) = \int_{t_i}^{t_i + t_{hor,i}} \left[QV(t) + R_1\varepsilon_1(t)^2 + R_2\varepsilon_2(t)^2 - SE(t) \right] \mathrm{d}t, \tag{5}$$

on the interval $[t_i\ t_{i+1}]$ subject to the model equations given by (1). The solution to each control problem P$_i$ is computed by the direct search routine as outlined in [10]. In this context, the control functions are represented as $\varepsilon_1(t) = \varepsilon_1 u(t)$ and $\varepsilon_2(t) = \varepsilon_2 u(t)$, where $u(t)$, is a binary treatment function, with a 1 representing a patient taking the drug during the given treatment interval, and a 0 meaning no treatment taken for that specific time period.

The quality of control can depend on the treatment interval, which is the minimum of time necessary to change the treatment protocol.

A sample control input is shown in Figure 5. Computing control functions of the form shown in Figure 5 is akin to calculating a series of structured treatment interruptions, rather than a continuous treatment.

Mathematically, we represent the control numerically with a pair of vectors describing the control function u(t) and the corresponding time intervals the control applies to. For example, for a treatment regimen with a treatment interval of m=15 days, a possible control could be u(t)=[1 1 0 0 1] . This corresponds to an overall treatment length of 75 days with on treatment for the first 30 days, off for the next 30, and then back on for the final 15 days of treatment. For any treatment interval with n switchings of treatment, there exists a possible 2n2n ways to define a treatment. Because this is a finite set, there exists an optimal control that minimizes (5). We denote the set of all control vectors U , with $|U|=2^n$. We then seek the optimal control, therefore n≈1400 days.

$$u^* \in \mathcal{U} = \arg\min J\left(\varepsilon_1(t), \varepsilon_2(t)\right). \quad (6)$$

On average, the data sets contain four years of longitudinal patient data,

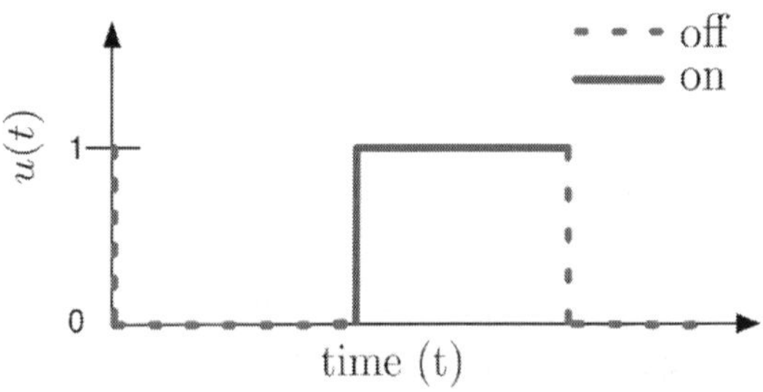

Figure 5. A sample control input for the HIV model. The switching of treatment represents a structured treatment inter- ruption.

Because n is relatively large, modeling daily changes in treatment is both impractical from a computational and clinical stand point. In practice, an interval of two to three weeks is clinically appropriate and is what we simulate.

If we assume a 30 day treatment interval, modeling the entire control interval could involve the calculation of nearly 50 control values, or switches. As the problem is defined, m=30 and n≈1400 would involve testing upwards of 250 possible treatment protocols; clearly this is not computationally tractable. To mitigate this issue, we seek to reduce the number of iterations necessary to find the optimal control. One strategy is to break the treatment interval into bins and calculate independent controls on these intervals before combining all of these controls for the entire interval. For instance, for 30 day segments we first compute an optimal control over the set $[0,30,60,90,120,150,180]$, a calculation that involves the testing of 27=128 distinct possible controls. Once this control is computed, the resulting trajectories are integrated to t=180, and a control is computed over the set [180, 210, 240,□,360] . This control is then appended to the prior control vector, and this sequence is repeated until the final time tf is reached.

Because we divide the treatment interval into several separate bins, the resulting control is only suboptimal; however in [10] they show that these results are reasonable approximations to a fully efficacious continuous therapy. In our control synthesis, we compare 10, 20, and 30 day treatment intervals.

This process is extended by RHC, outlined as follows:

1) Given an initial condition $x(t_i)$ solve the optimal control problem PiPi on the horizon interval [ti thor,i][ti thor,i] .
2) Use the control calculated in the prior step to compute the trajectory over the current control window $[t_i t_{i+1}]$.
3) Repeat this process by extending to the next control horizon to compute the next control. Terminate when the next ti>tf.

A schematic overview of this process is given in Figure 6. Note that in this system, each successive control computed on each new window is now implicitly a function of the prior window's final state-now the current window's initial condition. The window length and horizon length vary per simulation given different patient parameters, and are listed with each simulation presented.

Receding control depends on having full state knowledge in the observations of the system. Our control functions are computed after the completion of the inverse problem, so we assume our model to be accurate and predictive for each patient, therefore yielding full state knowledge at each time step.

For problems where there exists only a reduced observation of the system, a (typically) nonlinear estimation of the true state values is needed for the RHC to operate successfully. In cases such as this, the estimator is installed between the system model and the optimizer, as shown in Figure 7.

Optimal STI Results

In this section we present optimal controls and the resulting state solutions for patient 3 underutilizing differing control weights and treatment intervals.

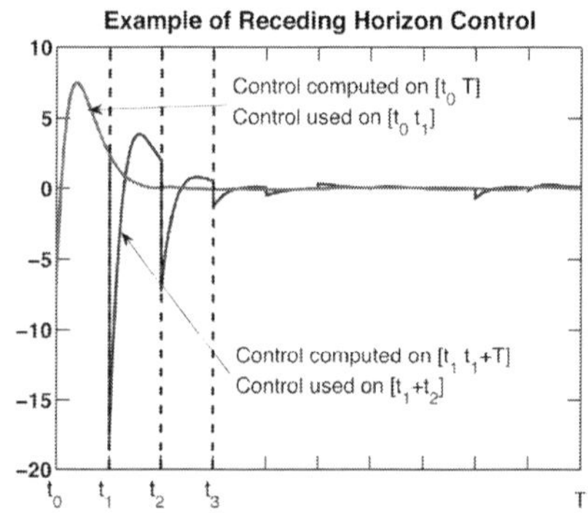

Figure 6. An example of receding horizon control. Future controls are calculated by computing controls on successive intervals.

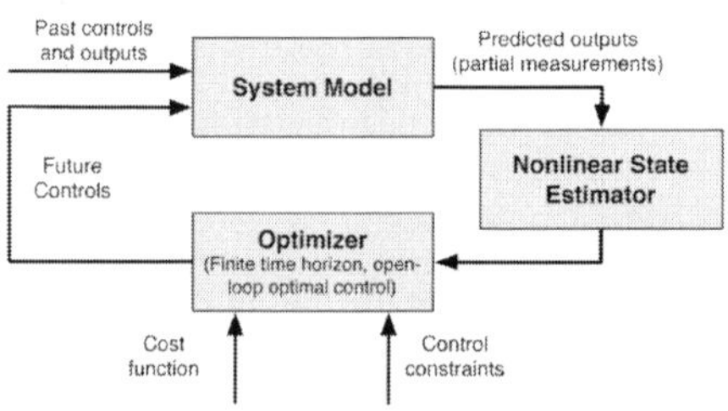

Figure 7. Schematic diagram of the receding horizon control with a non- linear state estimator.

We wish to illustrate that treatment protocols can be swayed and adjusted on a patient specific basis using the control weights. We also show cases with an "unexpected" perturbation to the optimal treatment, e.g. forced off treatment to demonstrate the feedback capability of the RHC. The control weights are presented as the vector $[Q\ S\ R_1\ R_2]$. In all of the following plots, the green and red bars at the bottom of the plot indicate clinical adherence to control, whereas the cyan and magenta at the top of the plot indicate the optimally computed control of on treatment and off treatment, respectively.

Varying Treatment Intervals

We first investigate the impact of different treatment intervals has on viral load. Figure 8 and Figure 9 differ only in the treatment interval. We first see a 20 day schedule, which results in an average viral of load of less than 1000 RNA copies/ml. The control is on for alternating periods of 60 days, followed by 40 days off, then 60 days on again.

When the interval is increased to 30 days in Figure 9 the average viral load increases to over 1500 RNA copies/ml. The control is on for the first 60 days, followed by an off treatment for 30 days, repeating periodically. Despite having a greater number of switching times, the control is off for fewer day, 30 off, versus

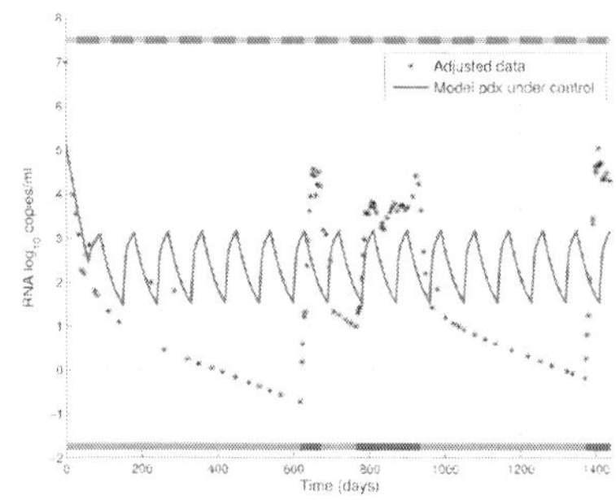

Figure 8. Patient 3, with weights [0.01 1 0.01 0.1][0.01 1 0.01 0.1] , with 20 day treatment intervals, 100 day control window, and 720 day control horizon.

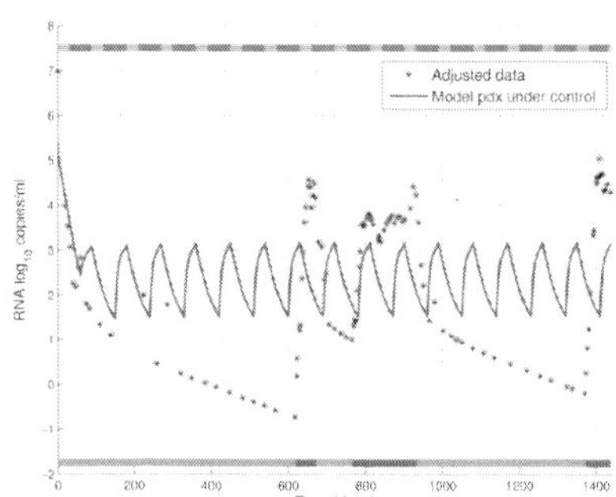

Figure 9. Patient 3, with weights [0.01 1 0.01 0.1][0.01 1 0.01 0.1] , with 30 day treatment intervals, 90 day control window, and 720 day control horizon.

40 off with m=20 in Figure 8. With 30 day treatment intervals, the viral load peaks to a level less than that of using 20 day intervals. The on/off treatment doesn't decrease the viral load to points achieved due to clinical adherence, which is constant on for nearly two years. However, when the patient goes off treatment even for a matter of days, the viral load spikes to nearly 40,000 RNA copies/ml. This kind of spike does not occur with the STI style regime produced by the RHC.

Compare these results with Figure 10, where we use a 15 day treatment interval. Treatment begins with 45 days of on treatment, before entering into a periodic switching of 30 days off, 15 days on, 15 days off, 30 days on. Due to the greater amount of time spent off control, the lowest viral load is greater than that of other treatment intervals. Through these results we see that having access to a greater number of switchings, or shorter treatment intervals, does not necessarily produce better results overall. Further, we see in general a greater amount of control used in the first 100 or so days, indicating the need to control HIV greater in the acute infection regimes.

Varying Control Weights

One advantage of the control methodology presented is being able to customize a treatment for a given patient. This can be done by varying the control weights to emphasize or deemphasize specific terms in the goal function (4). Between Figure 8 and Figure 11 we see the effect of changing the weight on viral load reduction by a factor or 10. Nearly twice as much control is used when Q=0.01 versus Q=0.001. There are currently ongoing clinical trials that are exploring STI treatments by using more frequent on-treatments compared to prior studies.

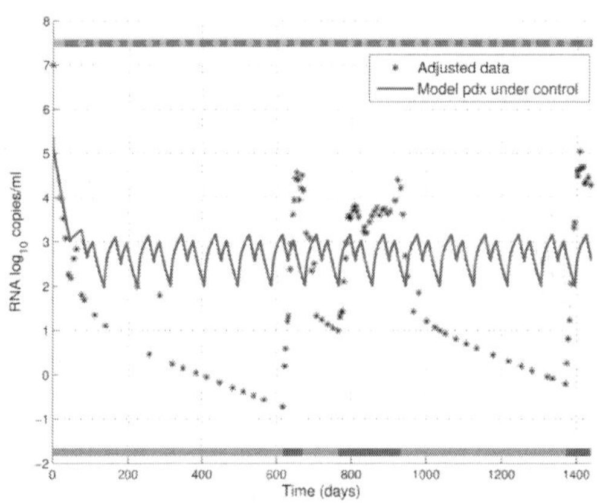

Figure 10. Patient 3, with weights [0.01 1 0.01 0.1] , with 15 day treatment intervals, 90 day control window, and 720 day control horizon.

Unexpected Treatment Perturbations

In Figure 12 we force an off treatment protocol for 100 days early in the simulation. The control returns the viral load to the same level in Figure 11, where treatment is not modified.

CONCLUDING REMARKS

In this work we have examined an in-vivo model describing the acute and chronic infection regimes of HIV. With this model, we first have performed a patient specific model calibration to clinically collected data sets consisting of CD4$^+$ count as well as viral load, which are censored.

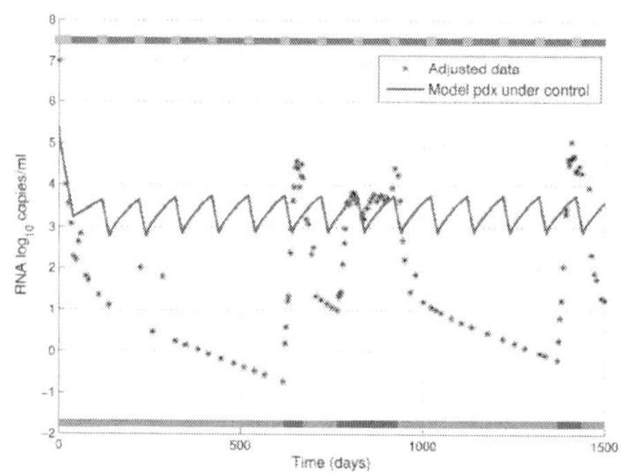

Figure 11. Patient 3, with weights [0.001 1 0.01 0.01] , with 20 day treatment intervals, 100 day control window, and 720 day control horizon.

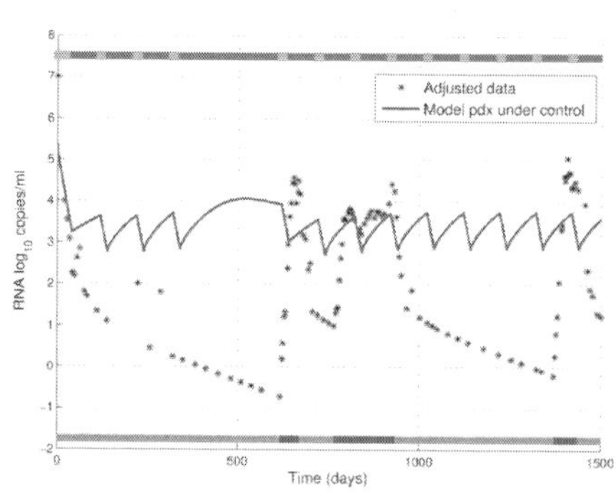

Figure 12. Patient 3, with weights [0.001 1 0.01 0.01] , with 20 day treatment intervals, 100 day control window, and 720 day control horizon. The control was fixed to zero for 100 days early on in the simulation.

We then take the first steps in investigating the construction of optimal treatment strategies, noting the lack of consensus in the best standards of treatment for acutely infected patients. To construct the treatment protocols, we use receding horizon control which computes several successive controls over a shifting interval. The broader controls are then used on short time intervals, allowing for the control to adjust to unexpected physical perturbations to the system. These controls mimic the form of structured treatment interruptions, and there are several ongoing clinical studies to assess their effectiveness against standard HAART therapy. In our control implementation, we assumed full state knowledge of the dynamic system. This is an unrealistic assumption and the use of nonlinear estimators would be beneficial. In addition, calibration and validation of more advanced HIV models could lead to greater insight into the replication processes during acute infection. For example, the development of new immune response models, an area that is currently poorly understood, could shed light into the complicated immune pro- cesses that occur post-infection. There are CD8 immune response data available, but we do not use them in this work, as the data do not match the type of immune response that we have modeled.

ACKNOWLEDGEMENTS

We thank the Editor and the referee for their comments. Research of H. Tran is funded in part by the National Science Foundation grant DMS 1022688 and by the National Institute of Allergy and Infectious Diseases grant NIAID 9R01AI071915.

Conflicts of Interest

The authors declare no conflicts of interest.

REFERENCES

1. Bell, S.K., Little, S.J. and Rosenberg, E.S. (2010) Clinical Management of Acute HIV Infection: Best Practice Remains Unknown. The Journal of Infectious Diseases, 202, S278-S288. https://doi.org/10.1086/655655
2. Perelson, A.S., Neumann, A.U., Markowitz, M., Leonard, J.M. and Ho, D.D. (1996) HIV-1 Dynamics in Vivo: Virion Clearance Rate, Infected Cell Life-Span, and Viral Generation Time. Science, 271, 1582-1586. https://doi.org/10.1126/science.271.5255.1582
3. Perelson, A.S. and Nelson, P.W. (1999) Mathematical Analysis of HIV-1 Dynamics in Vivo. SIAM Review, 41, 3-44. https://doi.org/10.1137/S0036144598335107
4. Callaway, D. and Perelson, A.S. (2002) HIV-1 Infection and Low Steady State Viral Loads. Bulletin of Mathematical Biology, 64, 29-64. https://doi.org/10.1006/bulm.2001.0266
5. Nelson, P.W., Gilchrist, M.A., Coombs, D., Hyman, J.M. and Perelson, A.S. (2004) An Age-Structured Model of HIV Infection That Allows for Variations in the Production Rate of Viral Particles and the Death Rate of Productively Infected Cells. Mathematical Biosciences and Engineering, 1, 267-288. https://doi.org/10.3934/mbe.2004.1.267
6. Rong, L., Feng, Z. and Perelson, A.S. (2007) Mathematical Analysis of Age-Structured HIV-1 Dynamics with Combination Antiretroviral Therapy. SIAM Journal on Applied Mathematics, 3, 731-756. https://doi.org/10.1137/060663945
7. Brandt, M.E. and Chen, G. (2001) Feedback Control of a Biodynamical Model of HIV-1. IEEE Transactions on Biomedical Engineering, 48, 754-759. https://doi.org/10.1109/10.930900
8. Joshi, H.R. (2002) Optimal Control of an HIV Immunology Model. Optimal Control Applications and Methods, 23, 199-213. https://doi.org/10.1002/oca.710
9. Ge, S.S., Tian, Z. and Lee, T.H. (2005) Nonlinear Control of a Dynamic Model of HIV-1. IEEE Transactions on Biomedical Engineering, 52, 353-361. https://doi.org/10.1109/TBME.2004.840463
10. Adams, B.M., Banks, H.T., Kwon, H.D. and Trani, H.T. (2004) Dynamic Multidrug Therapies for HIV: Optimal and STI Control Approaches. Mathematical Biosciences and Engineering, 2, 223-241.
11. David, J.A., Banks, H.T. and Tran, H.T. (2009) HIV Model Analysis under Optimal Control Based Treatment Strategies. International

Journal of Pure and Applied Mathematics, 57, 357-392.

12. David, J.A., Banks, H.T. and Tran, H.T. (2011) Receding Horizon Control of HIV. Optimal Control Applications and Methods, 32, 681-699. https://doi.org/10.1002/oca.969
13. Banks, H.T., Kwon, H.D., Toivanen, J.A. and Tran, H.T. (2006) A State-Dependent Riccati Equation-Based Estimator Approach for HIV Feedback Control. Optimal Control Applications and Methods, 27, 93-121. https://doi.org/10.1002/oca.773
14. Roy, P.K. and Chatterjee, A.N. (2011) Effect of HAART on CTL Mediated Immune Cells: An Optimal Control Theoretic Approach. In: Sio Long Ao, Ed., Electrical Engineering and Applied Computing, Len Gelman Springer, New York, Vol. 90, 595-607.
15. Duwal, S., Winkelmann, S., Schutte, C. and von Kleist, M. (2015) Optimal Treatment Strategies in the Context of "Treatment for Prevention" against HIV-1 in Resource-Poor Setting. PLOS Computational Biology, 11, e1004200. https://doi.org/10.1371/journal.pcbi.1004200
16. Hernandez-Vargas, E.A., Colaneri, P. and Middleton, R.H. (2013) Optimal Therapy Scheduling for a Simplified HIV Infection Model. Automatica, 49, 2874-2880.
17. Burth, M., Verghese, G. and Velez-Reyes, M. (1999) Subset Selection for Improved Parameter Estimation in On-Line Identification of a Synchronous Generator. IEEE Transactions on Power Systems, 14, 218-225. https://doi.org/10.1109/59.744536
18. Audoly, S., Bellu, G., D'Angio, L., Saccomani, M.P. and Cobelli, C. (2001) Global Identifiability of Nonlinear Models of Biological Systems. IEEE Transactions on Biomedical Engineering, 48, 55-65. https://doi.org/10.1109/10.900248
19. Xia, X. and Moog, C.H. (2003) Identifiability of Nonlinear Systems with Application to HIV/AIDS Models. IEEE Transactions on Automatic Control, 48, 330-336. https://doi.org/10.1109/TAC.2002.808494
20. Xia, X. (2003) Estimation of HIV/AIDS Parameters. Automatica, 39, 1983-1988.
21. Adams, B.M., Banks, H.T., Davidian, M. and Rosenberg, E. (2007) Estimation and Prediction with HIV-Treatment Interruption Data. Bulletin of Mathematical Biology, 69, 563-584. https://doi.org/10.1007/s11538-006-9140-6

22. Lisziewicz, J. and Lori, F. (2002) Structured Treatment Interruptions in HIV/AIDS Therapy. Microbes and Infection, 4, 207-214.
23. Lisziewicz, J., Rosenberg, E., Lieberman, J., Jessen, H., Lopalco, L., Siliciano, R., Walker, B. and Lori, F. (1999) Control of HIV Despite the Discontinuation of Antiretroviral Therapy. New England Journal of Medicine, 340, 1683-1683. https://doi.org/10.1056/NEJM199905273402114
24. Lori, F., Lewis, M.G., Xu, J., Varga, G., Zinn, D.E., Crabbs, C., Wagner, W., Greenhouse, J., Silvera, P., Yalley-Ogunro, J., Tinelli, C. and Lisziewicz, J. (2000) Control of SIV Rebound through Structured Treatment Interruptions during Early Infection. Science, 290, 1591-1593. https://doi.org/10.1126/science.290.5496.1591
25. Lori, F. and Lisziewicz, J. (2001) Structured Treatment Interruptions for the Management of HIV Infection. JAMA: The Journal of the American Medical Association, 286, 2981-2987. https://doi.org/10.1001/jama.286.23.2981
26. Adams, B.M. (2005) Non-Parametric Parameter Estimation and Clinical Data Fitting with a Model of HIV Infection. PhD Dissertation, North Carolina State University.
27. Banks, H.T., Davidian, M., Hu, S., Kepler, G.M. and Rosenberg, E.S. (2008) Modeling HIV Immune Response and Validation with Clinical Data. Journal of Biological Dynamics, 2, 357-385. https://doi.org/10.1080/17513750701813184
28. Bonhoeffer, S., Rembiszewski, M., Ortiz, G.M. and Nixon, D.F. (2000) Risks and Benefits of Structured Antiretroviral Drug Therapy Interruptions in HIV-1 Infection. AIDS, 14, 2313-2322. https://doi.org/10.1097/00002030-200010200-00012
29. Banks, H.T., Dedui, S. and Ernstberger, S.L. (2007) Sensitivity Functions and Their Uses in Inverse Problems. Journal of Inverse and Ill-Posed Problems, 15, 1-26. https://doi.org/10.1515/JIIP.2007.001
30. Miao, H., Xia, X., Perelson, A.S. and Wu, H. (2011) On Identifiability of Nonlinear ODE Models and Applications in Viral Dynamics. SIAM Review, 53, 3-39.
31. Attarian, A.R. (2012) Patient Specific Subset Selection, Estimation and Validation of an HIV-1 Model with Censored Observations under an Optimal Treatment Schedule. PhD Dissertation, North Carolina State University.

32. Dempster, A., Laird, N. and Rubin, D. (1977) Maximum Likelihood from Incomplete Data via the EM Algorithm. Journal of the Royal Statistical Society: Series B, 39, 1-38.
33. Banks, H.T. and Tran, H.T. (2009) Mathematical and Experimental Modeling of Physical and Biological Processes. Chapman & Hall/CRC, Boca Raton.
34. Finkel, D.E. and Kelley, C.T. (2004) Convergence Analysis of DIRECT Algorithm. OPT Online, 14, 1-10.
35. Phillips, A. (2005) Long Term Probability of Detection of HIV-1 Drug Resistance after Starting Antiretroviral Therapy in Routine Clinical Practice. AIDS, 19, 487-494. https://doi.org/10.1097/01.aids.0000162337.58557.3d
36. Paterson, D.L., Swindells, S., Mohr, J., Brester, M., Vergis, E.N., Squier, C., Wagener, M.M. and Singh, N. (2000) Adherence to Protease Inhibitor Therapy and Outcomes in Patients with HIV Infection. Annals of Internal Medicine, 133, 21-30. https://doi.org/10.7326/0003-4819-133-1-200007040-00004
37. Rosenberg, E.S., Davidian, M. and Thomas Banks, H. (2007) Using Mathematical Modeling and Control to Develop Structured Treatment Interruption Strategies for HIV Infection. Drug and Alcool Dependence, 88, S41-S51.
38. Bajaria, S.H., Webb, G. and Kirschner, D.E. (2004) Predicting Differential Responses to Structured Treatment Interruptions during HAART. Bulletin of Mathematical Biology, 66, 1093-1118.
39. Ortiz, G.M., Wellons, M., Jason, B., Vo, H.T.T., Zinn, R.L., Clarkson, D.E., Loon, K.V., Bonhoeffer, S., Miralles, G.D., Montefiori, D., Bartlett, J.A. and Nixon, D.F. (2001) Structured Antiretroviral Treatment Interruptions in Chronically HIV-1-Infected Subjects. Proceedings of the National Academy of Sciences of the United States of America, 98, 13288-13293. https://doi.org/10.1073/pnas.221452198
40. Garcia, C.E., Prett, D.M. and Morari, M. (1989) Model Predictive Control: Theory and Practice—A Survey. Automatica, 25, 335-348.
41. Zurakowski, R. and Teel, A.R. (2006) A Model Predictive Control Based Scheduling Method for HIV Therapy. Journal of Theoretical Biology, 230, 368-382.
42. Camacho, E.F. and Bordons, C. (2004) Model Predictive Control Advanced Textbook in Control and Signal Processing. Springer, Berlin.

SECTION 3
IT SOLUTIONS IN MEDICINE

CHAPTER 8

WIRELESS TDMA-BASED BODY AREA NETWORK PLATFORM GATHERING MULTIBIOSIGNALS SYNCHRONIZED WITH PATIENT'S HEARTBEAT

Tae Min Hwang,[1] Seol Young Jeong,[2] and Soon Ju Kang[1]

[1]School of Electronics Engineering, College of IT Engineering, Kyungpook National University, 80 Daehakro, Bukgu, Daegu, Republic of Korea

[2]School of Computer Science and Engineering, College of IT Engineering, Kyungpook National University, 80 Daehakro, Bukgu, Daegu, Republic of Korea

ABSTRACT

In the application of a body area network in medical healthcare, the process of receiving, archiving, and analyzing multibiosignals simultaneously from different devices for each body is very important. For example, to diagnose

Citation: Prieto J., Hwang T.M., Jeong S. Y., Kang Soon Ju, "Wireless TDMA-Based Body Area Network Platform Gathering Multi-biosignals Synchronized with Patient's Heartbeat", Journal of Wireless Communications, Vol. 2018, Article ID 2394384, https://doi.org/10.1155/2018/2394384.

sleep apnea symptoms, a patient must sleep with dozens of devices, including electroencephalography (EEG), electrocardiogram (ECG), photoplethysmogram (PPG), peripheral oxygen saturation (SpO_2), nasal cannula, and bands. Various wireless methods of body area network for acquisition and measurement of body signals have been introduced, but it is difficult to accurately diagnose various biosignals because their measurement frequencies are different from each other, and they are not guaranteed precise synchronization. Because each body biosignal is commonly synchronized with the heartbeat of the patient, precise synchronization of the heartbeat and other measuring cycles of each device is a critical attribute for analyzing the corelation of each biosignal in the body area network. However, it is difficult to guarantee the precise synchronization of multibiosignals by solely using carrier sense multiple access with collision detection- (CSMA/CD-) based wireless protocols, which are mainly used in existing body area networks. This study proposes a method of creating a self-organizing body area network based on wireless Time Division Multiple Access (TDMA) to guarantee the synchronization of multibiosignals and compare its accuracy with the CSMA/CD method.

INTRODUCTION

As the medical healthcare environment has changed from hospital-centered to home-centered, medical devices have changed accordingly. Classification of these medical devices can be broadly divided into wired and wireless. Wired medical devices have high precision, but they are inconvenient to wear, complicated, and difficult to use by individual patients. Therefore, these wired medical devices are not suitable for a patient living at home. In contrast, wireless medical devices are usually worn by the patient in the form of wearable devices. Because there are no wires, they are convenient to wear and using them is relatively simple. Therefore, they can be used by the patient without assistance. For this reason, interest in wireless medical devices has increased, and studies have been actively conducted. In addition, the body area network for connecting many wireless medical devices has attracted much attention.

The body area network is a short-range wireless communication technology in which devices installed inside and outside the human body can be connected and communicated. Because each device is used in contact with the human body, data such as electrocardiograms, heart rate, and acceleration can be measured according to the device. Therefore, attention has been paid to convenience and usability, and an attempt has been made to provide patient-centered medical services based on measurement of human biometric data in real life. However, for complex medical diagnosis, the following constraints must be considered.

The first is the acquisition of multibiosignals synchronized with the patient's heartbeat. To analyze two or more biosignals at the same time, it is necessary to read various biosignals from one device or several devices worn in different parts of the body. In this case, because signals arriving from several devices must be synchronized with the measured time, accurate signal analysis can be performed. Therefore, it is necessary to perform a verification process for the received signals when they are measured.

The second is user convenience. The wearable device has an advantage in that it is easy to carry and use. However, when a healthcare medical system is constructed, a user wears a plurality of devices. If many devices need to be manually operated simultaneously, the user will feel rather uncomfortable with the wearable device. Therefore, to take advantage of the wearable device, the body area network-application needs to be configured with minimal user intervention, to be simple and easy to use.

In this paper, we propose a method for constructing a wireless Time Division Multiple Access (TDMA) based body area network platform. The proposed wearable devices constitute a body area network, based on one device to store data and perform time synchronization using periodic sync-signals generated from the central device. The devices periodically receive biometric signal data through the connected peripheral devices. The user receives and stores data from different wearable devices by manipulating the central device without having to manipulate the wearable devices separately. The devices have predefined biosignal channel information, so that the devices can generate and destroy channels without having to exchange prior information about the biosignals, thereby reducing the connection time. Since data can be acquired from the devices by a simple operation, the convenience of the user can be enhanced, and the inconvenience that users may feel using the device can be minimized.

The contribution of this paper is wireless body area network (WBAN) platform that enables users to add or delete wearable devices that measure biomedical signals according to actual pathology. The proposed WBAN can measure various vital signals that are important for time synchronization with heart signal using TDMA wireless communication method. The photoplethysmogram (PPG) signal being compared with the heartbeat signal can measure the blood pressure or pathology diagnosis, so it is particularly important to confirm the time synchronized signal. In this paper, we propose a wearable device that can measure time synchronized signals and make it easy to use in real environment.

Section 2 explains the basic concepts of the method. Section 3 describes the scenario and system requirements of the synchronization method proposed in this study. Section 4 explains the structure and design of the hardware and software for implementation. Section 5 describes the implementation of the method and the scenario used for verification and explains the result of the communication loss ratio of the implemented result. In Section 6, we conclude with future research.

BASIC CONCEPTS AND RELATED RESEARCH

Body Area Network

As shown in Figure 1, sensors in the body range can be connected, and data can be collected; this data can be sent to the server side and monitored from the outside, so that it can be used in a variety of applications such as emergency situations, remote medical treatment, and exercises [1, 2].

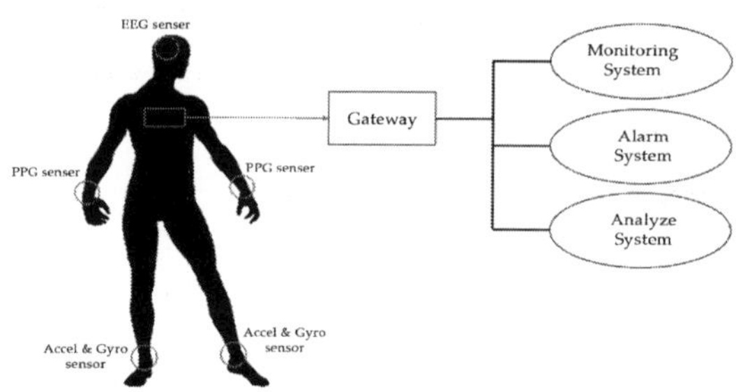

Figure 1: Body area network (BAN) structure.

However, because the sensors must be within the human body range, there is a disadvantage in that the size of the installed device is limited, and since the sensor operates in the state in which the user wears it, the consumption of the battery needs to be minimized [3]. Sensors used in the body area network typically require data rates in the order of a few kb/s to several Mb/s (body temp sensor, electrocardiogram (ECG), electroencephalography (EEG), and electromyography (EMG)). Therefore, to transmit each signal in the wireless environment, a sufficient communication protocol should be used for the bandwidth, and there are many protocols that satisfy this (such as ZigBee, Bluetooth SMART, and ANT +).

Within the body area network, sensors are attached to various parts of the body that collect biometric data and deliver it to the gateway. Signals delivered to the gateway can be connected to an external monitoring and alarm system to determine the current patient status in real time. In this study, a system is proposed in which a device attached to a human body forms a cluster; another device acts as a gateway, receiving data from the cluster and delivering it to the outside.

Wireless Communication Protocol

The communication protocol used for the wireless body area network can be either the carrier sense multiple access with collision detection (CSMA/CD) method or the Time Division Multiple Access (TDMA) method. Table 1 compares the traffic level and synchronization attribute of the protocols.

Table 1: Comparison between TDMA and CSMA/CD.

Protocol	TDMA	CSMA/CD
Preferred traffic level	High	Low
Synchronization	Depends on the latency	Depends on the traffic

CSMA/CD is a method of identifying the part where a collision can occur by detecting a carrier wave. It is possible to detect the use of communication, so that it is possible to avoid a collision between different attempts at communication, thus facilitating the configuration of a multicommunication environment constituting a body area network. As a representative MAC protocol using the CSMA/CD method, Bluetooth SMART and ZigBee are used, and body area network research is also actively performed [4, 5].

However, rather than delivering data directly, it is necessary to store the data to be sent to the queue first and to send it when communication is possible. Therefore, if the connection occurs frequently, data may not be transmitted at the desired time, and congestion may occur. Since each sender needs to perform a separate task of synchronizing the receiver with queuing data to be sent, much effort is required in synchronization [4].

The TDMA scheme is a method of using a frequency band without causing a collision, because a plurality of users use the frequency band at the same time. In the TDMA scheme, a frequency band is used only by a predetermined user during a specific period, thereby avoiding collision between users. Therefore, it is advantageous for periodic signal transmission and transmission that is not delayed. It is advantageous in comparison with CSMA/CD when data is transmitted by connecting to a plurality of UEs. Due to these advantages, many studies have been conducted on body area network using TDMA [3, 6–10]. However, if multiple slots are used adjacent to each other and the transmission timing is not accurately maintained, there is a possibility of causing a collision with a signal of another slot. Therefore, the slot between signals needs to be sufficiently large.

SERVICE SCENARIOS

Service Scenarios

In this study, each wearable device forms a cluster to read user biometric data and transmit it to the server device in real time, so that the data can be synchronized. By forming a cluster autonomously between the devices in which the user is not required to separately issue commands, the user can minimize the hassle of manipulating the devices and acquiring biosignals, so that convenience is achieved while simultaneously conducting a comprehensive analysis of the signal.

Figure 2 is an illustration of the type of service we want to provide. The user wears each wearable device on the relevant part of the body. Since the type of data that can be measured varies depending on the area in which the device is worn, the user can wear the device on other body parts depending on the purpose of the measurement.

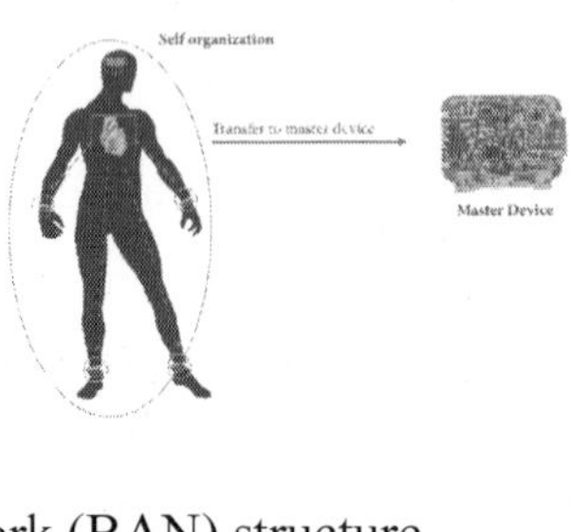

Figure 2: Body area network (BAN) structure.

The wearable devices receive the synchronization signal transmitted by the central device periodically and recognize the peripheral devices by transmitting a confirmation message. To distinguish the devices from each other, each device transmits its own device ID and is assigned an address value. Then, the devices in the created organization begin measuring by the measurement start signal of the central device. A channel for each biosignal is created, and the biosignal is transmitted through the corresponding channel.

In this case, because the transmission period for each biosignal is different, the central device first receives the biosignal from the device, stores it in the buffer, and then identifies the data of the channel to be stored in each cycle through the scheduler. The separated data is transferred to a separate analysis module and stored in the SD card or communicated with an external server to transmit data every cycle. The status of the wearer can be known by monitoring the delivered data from the outside in real time.

Design Requirements

To construct the body area network used in this study, each device must satisfy the following requirements [4].

The first is that it is easy to use. If the user operates all of the devices, the advantages of the wearable device are that it is easy to carry, which does not matter if the device cannot be utilized. Therefore, all the devices should be operable by manipulating the central device of the cluster.

The second is that it can be operated in real time. The data received from each device is inevitably delayed while being immediately transferred through the gateway. In this case, when the data is sent some time after data is accumulated in each device, the entire delay becomes large, so that it is not suitable for situations in which the user's emergency status must be immediately checked. Therefore, it is necessary to acquire each packet of data and send it to the central device immediately.

Next is communication stability. If the communication of each device is not performed properly due to a collision or other factors, incorrect data will be collected, and, if analyzed, a wrong result may be obtained. Therefore, communication should be performed in a stable manner in any situation.

Finally, the system should be secure. Since all the data acquired through the human body network is sensitive information of the individual, it is necessary to maintain the security of the learning process, measure the data, encrypt it, and transmit it to the other devices.

DETAILED STRUCTURE AND DESIGN

Device Structure

Each worn device plays a role in biometric data collection and delivery. From Figure 3, the user can separately check biometric data, reading through the user interface. Biometric data can be collected regardless of whether or not the organization is formed. In this case, since synchronization with other devices is not necessary, it is possible to measure based on the local time.

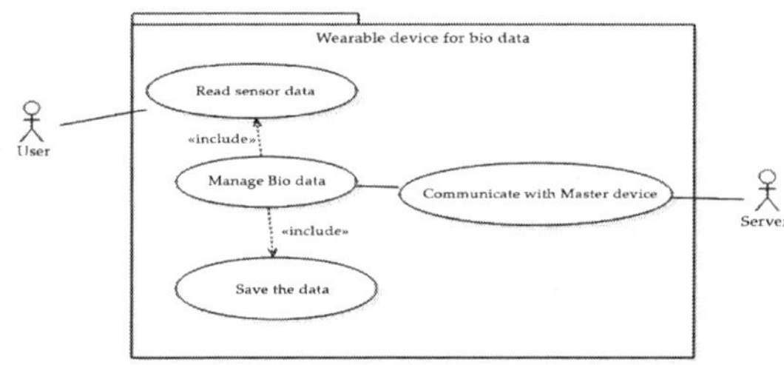

Figure 3: User biodata capture of wearable device.

Afterwards, it communicates with the center device in an organization with the external device, forms the cluster, and transmits the stored data. Since the channel information of the biometric data of the device is predefined, the devices can form a channel based on the channel information and transmit the data according to the request of the center device. In this case, each organization has a different network value in order to prevent confusion with the external organization, thereby preventing collision with the external organization.

Figure 4 shows the central device of the cluster and the devices connected to each other to receive and manage data according to the synchronization signal. Since the communication is performed by the TDMA method, when the signal transmission timing of the device deviates, there may occur a situation where a collision with a signal from the other device fails. Therefore, to prevent collision between signals, the central device periodically transmits a synchronization signal to prevent collision between the devices, preventing a collision when a new device is added. Then, according to the request of the central device, the devices form a channel to transmit the biosignal to the corresponding channel. In this case, since the center device has different periods for the biosignals, a task for managing the schedule is set separately, and the timing of receiving the data based on the respective synchronization signals is confirmed before receiving the biosignals. After receiving the signal from each device, the scheduler confirms the timing and stores the data by time. If there is no data at the scheduled time, it is determined that a loss has occurred in the transmission process and is marked separately.

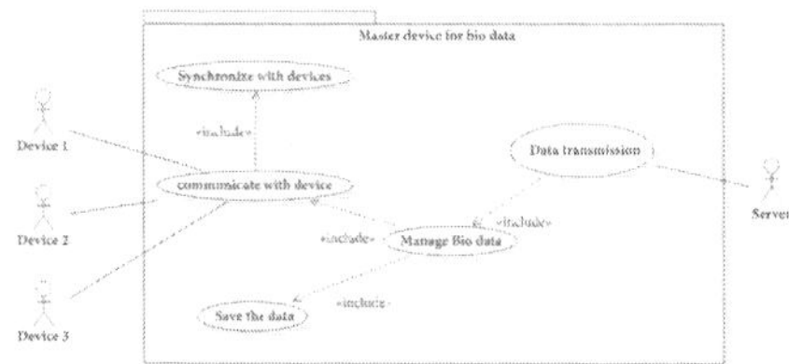

Figure 4: UseCase diagram for connection between devices and data transmission.

After that, communication with the external gateway or wired communication with the analysis module is performed to transmit data, thereby enabling data storage, monitoring, or data analysis to be performed.

Software Architecture

Figure 5 shows the software structure of the wearable device for implementation. The software of the wearable device includes a main event task to process the entire event, a user interface task to display the state of the current device, a sensing task to perform signal measurement and process communication with the sensor, and there is a communication management task to manage the time slots.

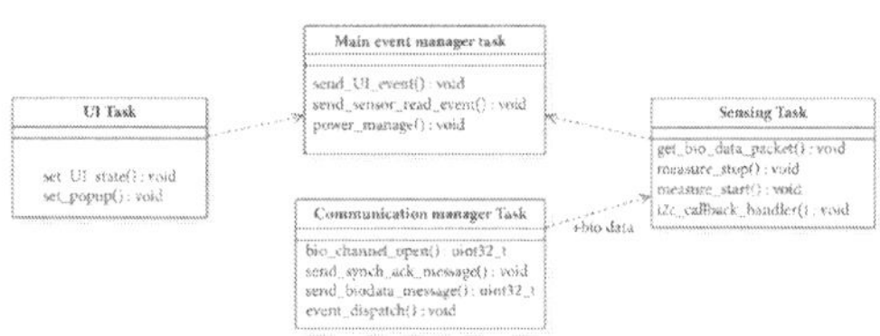

Figure 5: Software structure of wearable device.

The main event task processes the various events occurring in the device, and it handles the state change of the UI, the start and finish of the sensing task, and the button click event.

The communication management task accepts a connection request from the central device and generates a channel to transmit a biosignal. It also receives specific biometric data from the sensing task and delivers it to the central device.

Creating and Releasing Organization

The generation of the interdevice organization is based on the synchronization signal of the central device. The central device periodically sends a signal around the synchronization channel.

Figure 6 is a sequence diagram for cluster generation. The device that receives the signal can be divided into two cases, one with, and one without the assigned address. If there is no assigned address, an address allocation request-message is transmitted to the central device in order to allocate a new address. The central device receives the message, checks the empty address, and transmits the value to the device to allocate the address. After this, the device can send a message to the corresponding address. The device to which the address is allocated transmits a response message to the synchronization signal with a unique device address.

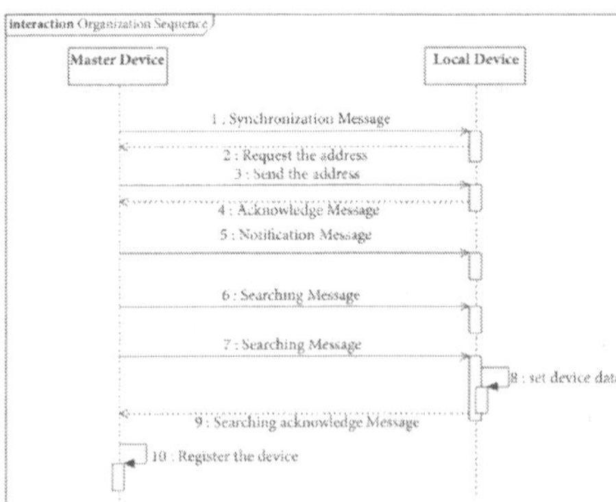

Figure 6: Organization sequence diagram.

At this time, the unique ID of the device and the sequence value of the synchronization message are stored and sent together in the response message. The central device receives the received message and checks the address of the message and the unique ID stored in the message. If the ID is not included in the organization, the central device stores the unique ID device information for the address together. By storing the device information in this way, when the device makes a data request at a later time, the device can distinguish the measurable biometric signal and make a request.

Many situations can involve the release of the organization, as shown in Figure 7. The first is the release by the decapitating signal of the central device. Like the organization creation, the central device can issue the organization release command to the device registered through the synchronization signal. Upon receiving the declassification command, the device sends a response message, closes the connected channel, and removes the registration information. Upon receiving the response, the central device releases the registration of the corresponding device.

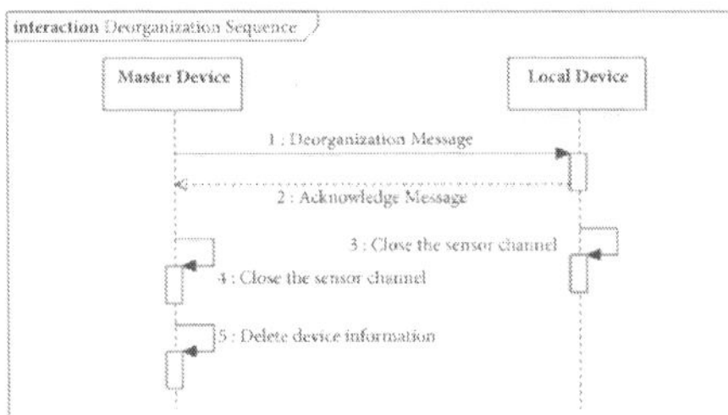

Figure 7: Deorganization sequence diagram.

The second is an unresponded state due to distance or battery shortage. The wearable device has a channel-specific watchdog timer. As shown in Figure 8, when the watchdog timer is reset by receiving the synchronization message of the central device and N messages are counted, it is determined that the connection with the central device should be disconnected without receiving the synchronization signal, and the channel connected to the central device is initialized to reduce unnecessary power consumption.

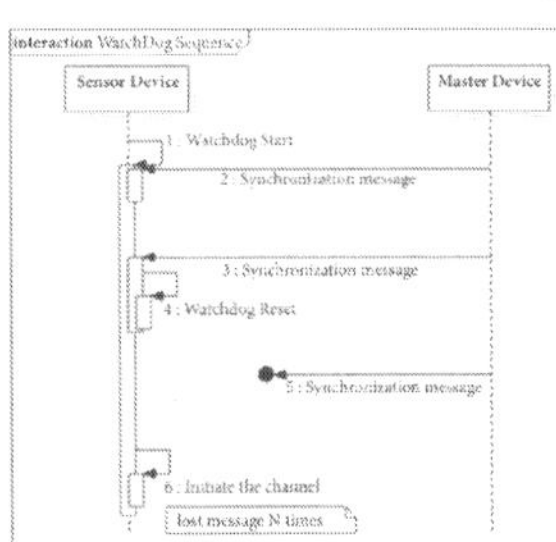

Figure 8: Sequence diagram for watchdog timer of sensor channel.

Timeslot Allocation of TDMA Scheme

In TDMA, one channel is allocated one time slot, as shown in Figure 9. The number of channels that can be connected at one time varies depending on the size of the time slot based on the synchronization signal. When the length of one cycle time is T and the length of the time slot is *t_slot*, as the synchronization signal channel always occupies one slot, the number *n_ channel* of the connectable channels can be expressed as follows:

$$n_{channel} = \frac{T}{t_{slot}} - 1$$

$n_{channel}$: *Number of channel*

t_{slot} : *Length of timeslot*

T : *Length of one cycle time* (1)

Figure 10 shows the process of transmitting data in a scheduled slot according to the synchronization signal of a central device. The central device transmits a synchronization signal to each of the devices in the first slot of the period. The devices receiving the synchronization signal store the sequence information of the current data based on this signal, and transmit the message, including the biometric data and the sequence number, to the central device side. This process is performed for each device, and as a result, the data from each device can be acquired without collision in one cycle.

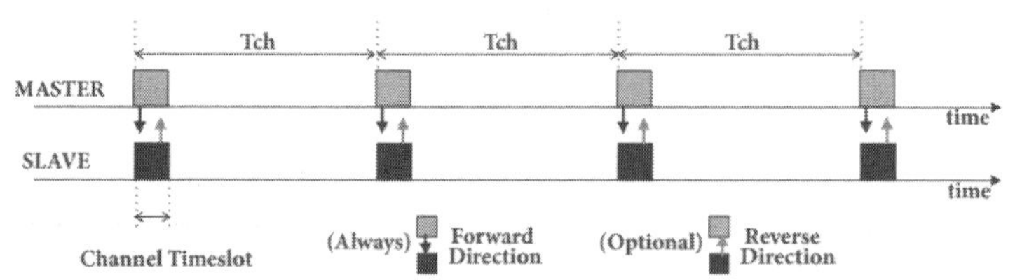

Figure 9: Time slot allocation of TDMA.

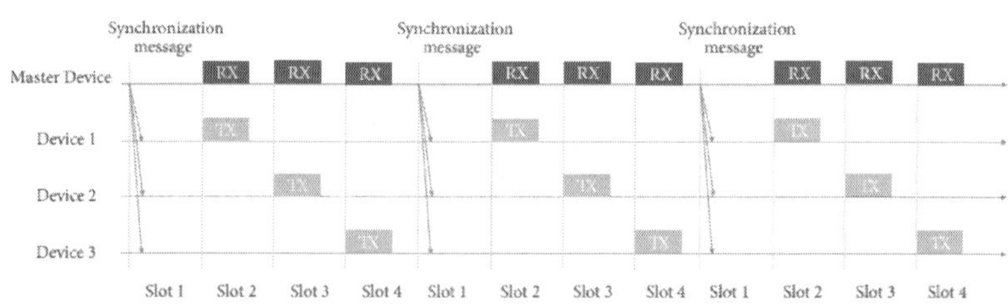

Figure 10: Example of time slot allocation in multidevice connection.

At this time, the synchronization signal has the same cycle as the cycle of the signal to be transmitted. This is to distinguish the signals in a cycle based on the synchronization signal and to prevent communication collision in the TDMA.

$$T_{Master} = T_{min}$$

$$T_{Master}: \textit{Synchronization signal cycle of the center device}$$

$$T_{min}: \textit{Cycle of the shortest signal} \tag{2}$$

Packet Structure of Synchronization Messages

In Table 2, the packet structure of the synchronization message is configured. First, messages sent to the wearable device by the central device are divided into three types—synchronization, organization creation, and organization release. The synchronization message is used for the external synchronization and device information request. The synchronization message includes an address value of a device to which a message is to be sent (an address is blank when sending a notification message to all devices) and an order value.

Table 2: Synchronization message payload.

Device	Command	Value	Bit 0	1	2	3	4	5	6	7
Main Device	Sync	0xff	addr1	addr2	0xff				sequence1	sequence2
	create channel	0x01	addr1	addr2	0x01	bio data type	device number	network num		
	delete channel	0x02	addr1	addr2	0x02	bio data type	device number	network num		

Sensor Device	Ack device info	0xff	addr1	addr2	0xff	bio data type	device id1	device id2	sequence1	sequence2
	ack channel created	0x01	addr1	addr2	0x01	bio data type	channel number			
	ack channel deleted	0x02	addr1	addr2	0x02	bio data type	channel number			
	nack channel already created	0x03	addr1	addr2	0x02	bio data type	channel number			

The organization creation and release message is a message sent to the identified wearable device to command the cluster. When sending this message, the following information is transmitted to obtain specific biometric data from each wearable device.

(i) Biometric data type: since the data rate or period required by the biometric data to be measured is different, it is necessary to define the biometric data type in advance so that the central device and the wearable device can directly transmit the biometric data, so that the channel information can be aligned with the center device.

(ii) Cluster network unique number: to prevent overlapping with the other surrounding organization when the organization is created, the unique number of the cluster network managed by the central device is transmitted, setting it as the network unique number of the cluster and preventing it from being included in the.

(iii) Timeslot assignment number: since there is no collision with the different timeslots for each device, the time slot number assigned when connected to the device is delivered.

On the contrary, when the wearable device sends a response message to the central device, the response message can be either a response to the synchronization message, an affirmative response to the organization creation and release command, or a negative response.

When a response to a synchronization message is sent, the following information is also included:

(i)Biometric data type: biometric data that can be measured according to the type of device and the part to be worn are distinguished, and this information is included in the response.

(ii) Device identification number: since the central device knows not only the address assigned to each device but also the device identification number, it can be distinguished, even if the other device responds with the same address.

Communication between Devices

Based on the synchronization signal of the central device, each device generates a channel and establishes a connection between the devices. Figure 11 shows the channel generation between the central device and the wearable device in the cluster.

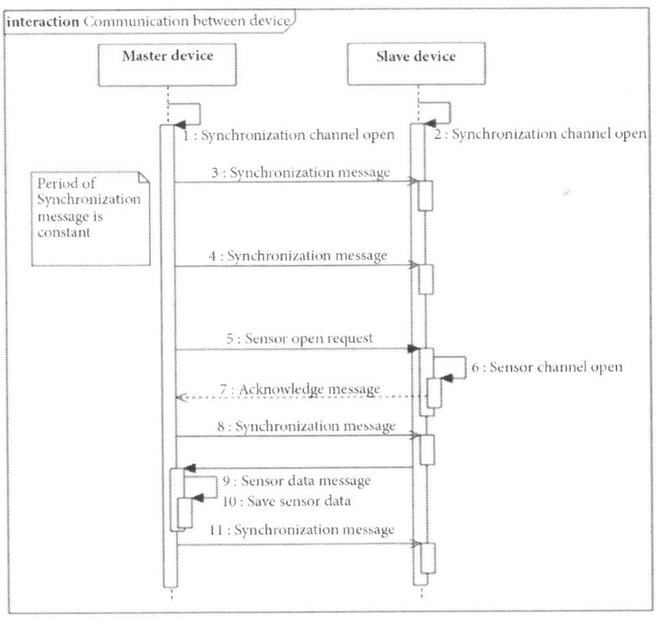

Figure 11: Sequence diagram for communication between organizations.

First, the central device periodically transmits a synchronization signal to the wearable device in a state in which the synchronization channel is open, thereby confirming the connection state and transmitting/receiving signals. If a connection is needed, the central device transmits a request to the address of the wearable device to request channel creation according to the synchronization period. Upon receiving the message, the wearable device confirms the requested biosignal type, network value, and device number within the signal, and generates a channel corresponding to the request. If it is successful, the response is transmitted to the central device. If the channel creation fails with respect to the request, the channel creation failure-message is also transmitted to the central device. The central device checks the response received from the wearable device, and when the channel is successfully created, the central device receives the data from the wearable device by connecting the corresponding channel.

The wearable device receives the user's biometric data at a predetermined period through the sensor device. Since the received data is stored in the buffer and the data is transmitted every TDMA cycle, there is no need to separately queue the data.

Signalling and Scheduling

Figure 12 shows the process of reflecting the message exchange process and scheduling between the central device and the wearable device in a sequence diagram. When the center device is connected to the wearable device, the center device registers the cycle of the corresponding biosignal in the schedule. Then, the communication task transfers the synchronization signal to the devices in the cluster. The schedule task stores the signals arriving between this signal and the next synchronization signal in one cycle. The wearable device reads and stores the wearer's vital signs, and delivers the message to the central device at every cycle.

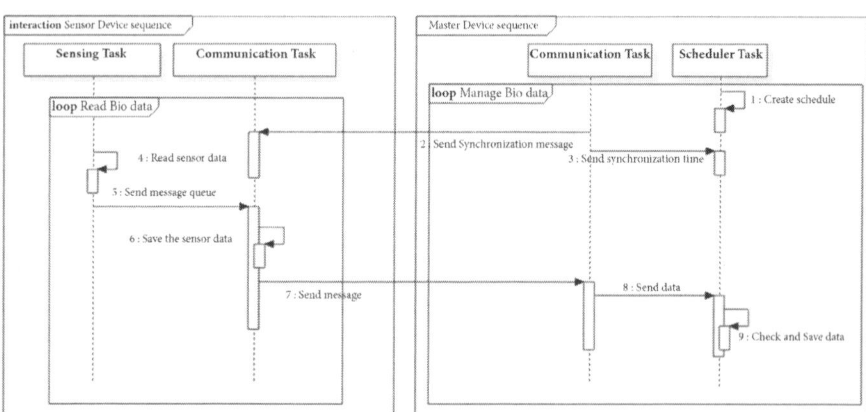

Figure 12: Sequence diagram for saving data of master device.

IMPLEMENTATION

Hardware Implementation

In Figure 13, the implementation platform is shown as follows. The photoplethysmogram (PPG) module and the acceleration sensor are connected to each wearable device in which the biosignal and acceleration data are read and stored, and data is transmitted to the central device through the RF transceiver. The status of the wearable device can be confirmed by the LCD, and the button is used when operation is required.

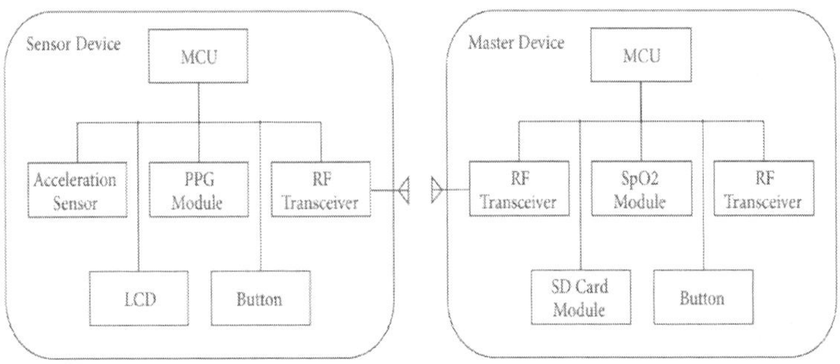

Figure 13: Implemented platform structure.

The central device is equipped with an oxygen saturation module and can measure the biomedical signal in the center device.

The measured data and the data of the wearable device are collected, and the biomedical signal data array is created and stored in the SD card or transmitted to the outside. In addition, the button is used to check the cluster creation and destruction.

The wearable device and the center device are each configured, as shown in Figure 14.

The wearable device is implemented as a wristband to be worn on the user's wrist. The PPG module is connected under the band to measure the PPG signal, and the data is received from the PPG module and transmitted to the central device.

The central device receives data from the wearable device while connected to the PC using the nRF52 development kit.

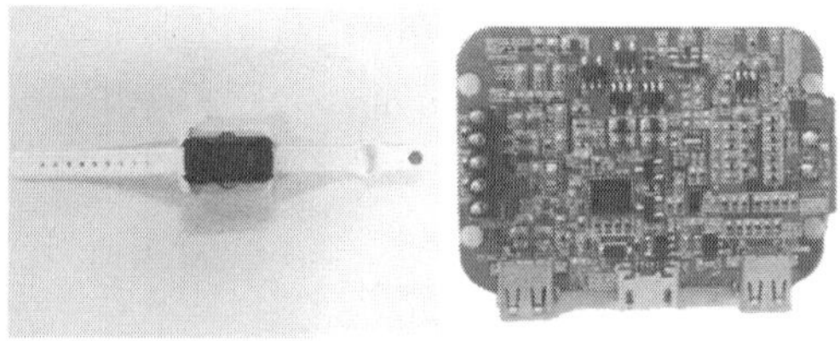

Figure 14: Implemented wearable device (left) and master device (right).

The proposed wearable medical device consists of two parts. The microcontroller unit (MCU) of master device is CortexM4-based nRF52832 chip (frequency: 64 MHz, operating voltage 3.3 V). The sensor device has the EFM32WG990F256 chip (frequency: 48 MHz). As shown in Figure 15, power consumption is an average of 76 uA in the idle state and from minimum 295 uA to maximum 52 mA (average 12 mA) in the sensing and streaming communication state.

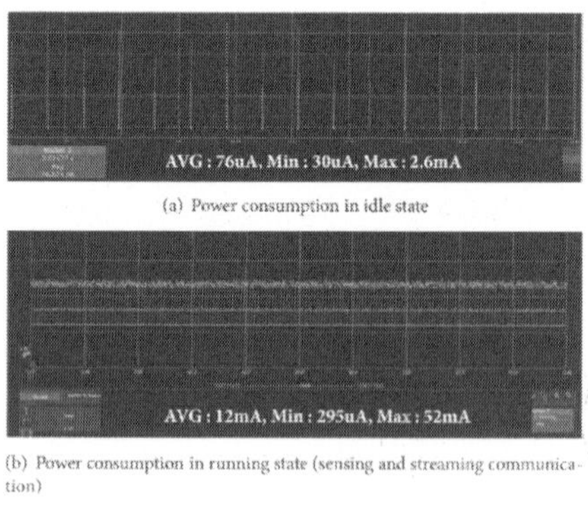

Figure 15: Low power consumption of proposed device.

ANT Communication

In this study, the ANT protocol is used to implement wireless TDMA communication. ANT is a type of communication protocol mainly used for medical and health care purposes. ANT has the advantages of simple implementation and low power consumption. It also operates in TDMA and is used within a range of less than 100 meters, similar to BLE. Its data rate was 12.8 kbits/s for broadcast and acknowledging messages and 60 kbits/s for burst mode.

Table 3 shows the performance comparison with major wireless protocols.

Table 3: Comparison between wireless protocols.

Protocol	*ANT*	*Bluetooth SMART*	*ZigBee*
Standardization	Proprietary	Standard	Standard
Topologies	Point-to-point, star, tree, mesh	Point-to-point, star	Mesh
Range	30 m at 0 dBm	10-100 m	10-100 m
Max data rate	Broadcast/Ack – 12.8 kbit/s Burst – 20 kbit/s Advanced Burst – 60 kbit/s	1 Mbit/s	250 kbit/s
Application throughput	0.5 Hz to 200 Hz	305 kbit/s	
Max nodes in piconet	65536 per shared channel (8 shared channels)	1 master and 7 slaves	Star – 65536

Compared with Bluetooth SMART and ZigBee, ANT communication transmits at 12.8 kbits/s when the data rate is broadcast/ACK message, which is somewhat lower than other communication rates. However, since the configuration of nodes is free, it is easy to form interdevice clusters, and, in the case of the system to be used in the paper, data is periodically received from the device, so that data transmission also needs to be performed periodically. Because Bluetooth SMART and ZigBee are CSMA/CD type in this respect, ANT communication is used, because there is a disadvantage in that it is difficult to guarantee the periodicity when several devices transmit signals in a short period.

PPG Signal

The PPG signal is used in the wearable device for verification. The PPG signal is a signal that indicates the change in the blood volume of the blood vessel due to the heartbeat through the return light by using the principle of absorption, reflection, and scattering by emitting light to the blood vessel. Because the signal form according to the heartbeat during measurement is clearly revealed, and the data measurement period is short, shown in Table 4, it is easy to implement the congested communication environment, and the PPG signal is measured. The PPG signal is measured once every 10 ms and is sent once every 40 ms. One piece of data has a size of 3 bytes.

Table 4: PPG (photoplethysmography) specification.

Bio-signal	**Photoplethysmography**
Required Data Rate (kbps)	24
Data size (bytes)	3
Maximum Frequency (Hz)	100
Period (ms)	40

EVALUATION

Evaluation Scenarios

The measurement environment is constructed as shown in Figure 16.

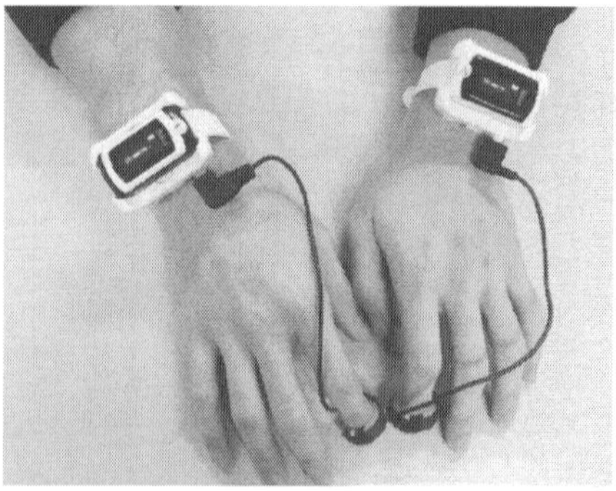

Figure 16: Wearable devices and PPG modules.

First, the user wears the wearable device on the wrist. In the module of the wearable device, the PPG infrared sensor is connected to the finger, and the PPG signal is measured from the connected PPG sensor and is transmitted to the central device. If the synchronization is performed normally, each wearable device simultaneously measures the PPG signal in real time, such that the increase and decrease in the signal will be similar.

In the ANT protocol environment, two channels are required for each PPG signal to transmit the PPG channel for sufficient performance evaluation. In the ANT protocol, since eight channels are available in one device, three wearable devices are connected in order to use the maximum number of channels. Therefore, there are six ANT channels. For comparison, the Bluetooth protocol also connects three peripherals to the central device.

The performance evaluation method is as follows. The measurement is started according to the signal of the central device when each of the devices is connected. At this time, the central device confirms the signal, and the message order value is sent from the respective wearable devices and confirms that communication has been performed for every synchronization period. After receiving the data from the wearable device for about five minutes, it checks what percentage of transmissions resulted in error messages. In addition, it confirms how the order value of the Bluetooth SMART protocol and ANT communication is changed compared to the first one, based on one wearable device, and confirms that synchronization is properly performed.

Comparison of ANT and Bluetooth SMART Communication for PPG Signals

Figures 17 and 18 show graphs displaying the PPG signals received from each wearable device using Bluetooth SMART and ANT protocols, respectively. Figures show the heartbeat signal (blue) and the PPG signals (red, green) of the both wrist. Figure 17 shows that the time synchronization does not match, even though the signal is measured at the same time. The signals of the two wrists have a heart signal and a delay time of 25~35 ms. On the other hand, in case of ANT+, which is a TDMA method, it can be confirmed that the synchronization is exactly performed every 40 ms that generated the signal. Figure 18 shows how the order value changes with time from the reference signal when the PPG signal is received in Bluetooth SMART.

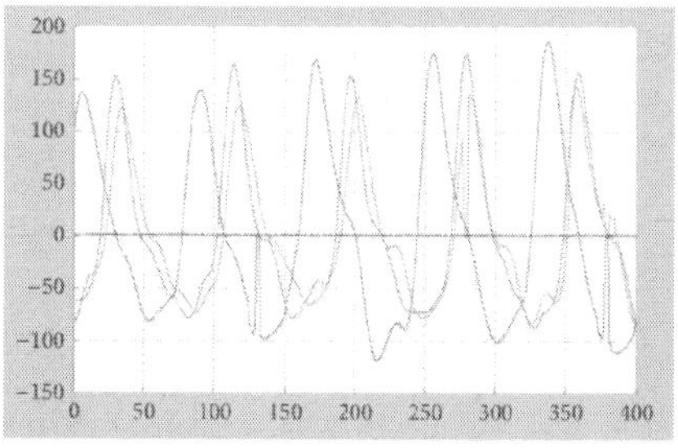

Figure 17: Multiple PPG signal with Bluetooth SMART (CSMA/CD).

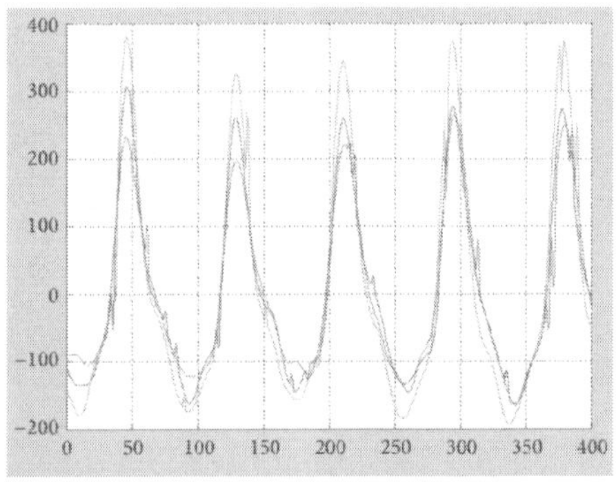

Figure 18: Multiple PPG signal with ANT (TDMA).

As shown in Figure 19, when the Bluetooth SMART protocol is used, the difference in the order value increases with time. As the number of devices increases, the cumulative delay time that is accumulated increases with time. In the case of three devices, we can see that the delay is 6.108 msec/sec. On the other hand, when the ANT protocol is used, it can be confirmed that no cumulative signal delay due to queuing occurs.

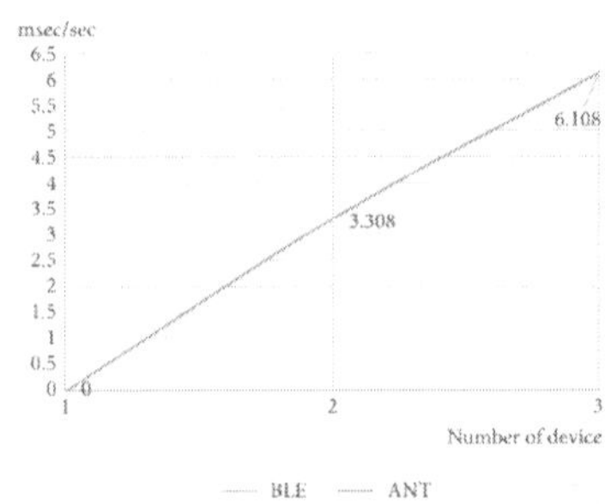

Figure 19: Difference of latency per time (msec/sec).

When the PPG signal was transmitted every 40 ms for 5 minutes, the error rate is 3.26% in ANT communication and 1.74% in Bluetooth SMART. The proposed TDMA method has a relatively small difference of error rate as compared with CSMA/CD-based Bluetooth communication.

CONCLUSIONS

In this study, based on wireless TDMA communication, wearable devices form self-organization to construct a body area network and transmit data based on a synchronization signal. To form a cluster, the central device periodically transmits a synchronization message to the periphery. At this time, the wearable device within the range receives this message and transmits a response message that includes the device information to the central device side.

Based on this response, the devices form one organization, and the organization is divided by the network key. Each wearable device learns the biosignal of the worn portion on the connected central device side and delivers it to the allocated time slot.

The central device separately checks the timing of each device through scheduling, generates a separate buffer, stores the biometric data of the corresponding period, and confirms it with an SD card or an external device.

To verify this scenario, we propose a method to transmit the PPG signal over six channels through the ANT protocol (based on TDMA), using three wearable devices and one central device. To do this, we used the CSMA/CD-based protocol and Bluetooth SMART to transmit the same size data. Experimental results show that the average data loss-rate is 2.36%. As the traffic increases, Bluetooth SMART confirms that the signal is transmitted without synchronization. In ANT communication, however, it is confirmed that the data is transmitted in the state in which the synchronization is performed, and the period of the PPG signal is matched.

The number of channels that can be connected in the future is limited, and slot collision may occur due to communication delay. Therefore, it is necessary to study more about how to overcome this problem, and it is necessary to study the process of analyzing biopsy data collected through multiple connections.

Data Availability

The data used to support the findings of this study are available from the corresponding author upon request.

Conflicts of Interest

The authors declare that there are no conflicts of interest regarding the publication of this paper.

ACKNOWLEDGMENTS

This research was supported by Basic Science Research Program through the National Research Foundation of Korea (NRF) funded by the Ministry of Education (NRF-2018R1A6A1A03025109).

REFERENCES

1. E. Jovanov, A. Milenkovic, C. Otto, and P. C. de Groen, "A wireless body area network of intelligent motion sensors for computer assisted physical rehabilitation," *Journal of Neuro Engineering and Rehabilitation*, vol. 2, no. 1, p. 1, 2005.
2. J. Jung, K. Ha et al., "Wireless body area network in a ubiquitous healthcare system for physiological signal monitoring and health consulting," *International Journal of Signal Processing, Image Processing and Pattern Recognition*, vol. 1, no. 1, pp. 47–54, 2008.
3. S. Marinkovic, C. Spagnol, and E. Popovici, "Energy-efficient TDMA-based MAC protocol for wireless body area networks," in *Proceedings of the 3rd International Conference on Sensor Technologies and Applications (SENSORCOMM '09)*, pp. 604–609, IEEE, Athens, Greece, June 2009.
4. D. Benhaddou, M. Balakrishnan, and X. Yuan, "Remote healthcare monitoring system architecture using sensor networks," in *Proceedings of the 2008 IEEE Region 5 Conference*, pp. 1–6, April 2008.
5. J. Y. Khan and M. R. Yuce, "Wireless body area network (WBAN) for medical applications," in *Proceedings of the New Developments in Biomedical Engineering*, 2010.
6. H. Alemdar and C. Ersoy, "Wireless sensor networks for healthcare: a survey," *Computer Networks*, vol. 54, no. 15, pp. 2688–2710, 2010.
7. N. Sheriff, "Time Synchronization in ANT Wireless Low Power Sensor Network," 2011.
8. R. Pan, D. Chua, J. S. Pathmasuntharam, and Y. P. Xu, "A WBAN based cableless ECG acquisition system," in *Proceedings of the 2014 36th Annual International Conference of the IEEE Engineering in Medicine and Biology Society, EMBC '14*, pp. 910–913, August 2014.
9. M. A. Hussain, N. Alam, S. Ullah, N. Ullah, and K. S. Kwak, "TDMA based directional MAC for WBAN," in *Proceedings of the 6th International Conference on Networked Computing, INC '10*, pp. 1–5, 2010.
10. R. H. Kim, P. S. Kim, and J. G. Kim, "An effect of delay reduced MAC protocol for WBAN based medical signal monitoring," in *Proceedings of the IEEE Pacific Rim Conference on Communications, Computers and Signal Processing, PACRIM 2015*, pp. 434–437, August 2015.

CHAPTER 9

SMART CARE BEDS FOR ELDERLY PATIENTS WITH IMPAIRED MOBILITY

Youn-Sik Hong

Department of Computer Science and Engineering, Incheon National University, Incheon 406-772, Republic of Korea

ABSTRACT

Most accidents occurring at medical institutions treating elderly patients with mobility impairment are bedsores and fall accidents. One of the reasons for this high rate of accidents is the lack of nursing personnel. In order to aid caregivers in nursing elderly patients who are not able to move about freely, in this paper, we propose a design and implementation of a smart bed. In this bed, several pressure sensors are deployed underneath the mattress cover

Citation: Buhari Seyed M., Hong Youn-Sik, "Smart Care Beds for Elderly Patients with Impaired Mobility", Journal of Wireless Communications, Vol. 2018, Article ID 1780904, https://doi.org/10.1155/2018/1780904.

to consider both peoples' standard physical characteristics and the specific body parts where bedsores commonly occur. To manage the pressure ulcer area and to prevent falls, the body area is divided into three vertical areas and three horizontal areas. Each microcontroller unit manages pressure-sensing information in one of the body regions divided horizontally. In this study, a real-time pressure-sensing algorithm is presented that is capable of deciding on the possibilities of bedsores and falling accidents by considering both the intensity and the duration of pressure of specific body parts. Our experimental results demonstrate that a prototype smart bed works well for several human models of various heights and weights.

INTRODUCTION

In recent years, South Korea has faced the challenge of the rapidly aging society. Therefore, the problem of the elderly patients' care becomes crucial. In addition, an increasing number of specialized medical institutions for the elderly and senior care centers (called sanatoria) have been established. However, the rapid growth of the industry related to the elderly care and the establishment of relevant institutions encounters many problems, including, among others, the lack of appropriate administration.

If an elderly individual is in the same position for too long, whether in bed or a wheelchair, the friction between the skin and the surface may stop the blood flow, causing the pressure area to receive less oxygen and thus causing the cells to die in that area. This is how bedsores will develop [1]. Pressure ulcers in elderly individuals can cause significant morbidity and mortality and are a major economic burden to the healthcare system [2].

Recent surveys [3] have estimated a huge expenditure on direct medical cost for domestic accidents (in the USA, more than US $19 billion for nonfatal falls in subjects >65 years of age; in the UK, US $1.9 billion for emergency services and hospitalization, while an Australian study reported a national healthcare cost for elderly falls of US $66.1 million). Interestingly, two-thirds of the overall medical costs are due to falls requiring hospitalization [3]. Falls are by far the leading cause of injuries among the elderly [4]. One out of every 3 seniors aged 65 and older experiences a fall each year. Falls are the leading cause of both nonfatal and fatal injuries among seniors, and 20 to 30 percent suffer moderate to severe injuries that can cause disability or increase the risk of death. From a healthcare perspective, elderly falls are a major clinical issue in terms of frequency, disability, institutionalization, and overall mortality, with an outgrowing socioeconomic burden [5].

The occurrences of bedsores and fall accidents among the elderly patients are typical problems, accounting for over 80% in such medical institutions [6]. The Ministry of Health and Welfare of Korea has introduced operational regulations for medical institutions and, using these regulations, the latter measure the risk of falls and pressure ulcers. Nevertheless, the number of occurrences of bedsores and fall accidents is still growing. The main reason behind this tendency is the lack of trained personnel.

Internet of Things (IoT) revolution is redesigning modern healthcare with promising technological, economic, and social prospects [7]. Enabled by the global connectivity of the IoT, all the healthcare information (logistics, diagnosis, therapy, recovery, medication, management, finance, and even daily activity) can be collected, managed, and utilized more efficiently [8]. Among the panoply of applications enabled by the IoT, smart and connected healthcare is a particularly important one. Networked sensors, either worn on the body or embedded in our living environments, make possible the gathering of rich information indicative of physical and mental health [9]. By the current technology status, wearable health management systems [10] provide low-cost solutions for ubiquitous, all-day, unobtrusive personal health monitoring and are expected to enable early detection and better treatment of various medical conditions as well as disease prevention and better understanding and self-management of chronic diseases. In addition, RFID technology is to provide part of the IoT physical layer for the personal healthcare in smart environments through low-cost, energy-autonomous, and disposable sensors [11].

In this paper, we have implemented an IoT-based smart bed system designed to aid caregivers to nurse elderly patients with mobility impairments. The primary goal of the smart bed system is to prevent bedsores and/or falling accidents from the bed.

For that purpose, two types of pressure sensors (*strip* and *square* type) were used to sense pressures in the specific body positions depending on sensing purposes. We used sensors regarding both the average body size by age (with reference to the Korea Agency for Technology and Standards (KATS)) and the frequent location of bedsores. Besides, the entire sensing area of a patient's body was divided into three subareas and each of them was monitored by a distinct module operating independently for fault tolerant purposes. In addition, we also introduced the pressure-sensing algorithm that accurately detects the pressure intensity and the duration of the pressure. A short version of this paper has been published elsewhere [12].

The remainder of this paper is organized as follows. Section 2 summarizes related work. In Section 3, we describe the overall architecture and detailed operations of a smart bed system. In Section 4, the experimental results used to validate the proposed method are presented. Finally, conclusions are drawn in Section 5.

RELATED WORKS

The work in [13] proposed a computer vision-based fall detection system for monitoring an elderly person in a home care application. It suffers from occlusion since subjects can sometimes be behind a sofa or furniture while being monitored [14]. Gasparrini et al. [15] developed a fall detection system using a Microsoft Kinect depth sensor. It uses two sensors, an infrared projector and an infrared sensor, to generate a 3D map of the scene [15]. The use of a 3D map allows differentiating between obstructions and the subject. It can detect a fall-down accident through the analysis of a patient's gestures. The fall-down prevention device [16] is similar to the approach of Gasparrini et al. [15]. The drawback of the above approaches is the increase in computing complexity and cost. In addition, these methods do not prevent the occurrence of bedsores.

Providing accurate and opportune information on people's activities and behavior is one of the most important tasks in pervasive computing. Lara et al. [17] survey the state of the art in human activity recognition based on wearable sensors [17]. Ozcan et al. [18] present a fall detection system using wearable cameras. Since the camera is worn by the subject, monitoring is not limited to confined areas and extends wherever the subject may go including indoors and outdoors. When a fall occurs, edge orientations in a frame vary drastically and extremely fast, as a result of this subsequent frames get blurred [14].

Another work [19] is a system of unobtrusively recognizing actions and promoting physical activities and a smart mat used for the same purpose. A mat sensor is constituted by a FSR *(force sensing resistor)* sensor, a load cell, and a piezoelectric sensor. In addition, an ultrasonic sensor, an infrared sensor, and a thermal sensor are attached outside to monitor the behavior information of a patient lying on the mat. However, since the mats require the use of numerous sensors, their application in senior care centers is too complex and expensive. Furthermore, this patent may be more problematic to apply due to its complicated structure. Among other reasons, power consumption is increased, and the mobility of the bed is not free, as the external power source must be connected. Maintenance is also difficult. However, this patent is advantageous to grasp the behavior of a person to be protected from various sensors, although there appear to be restrictions in terms of commercialization.

BodiTrak Smart Bed [20] uses its own elastic and breathable pressure-sensing fabric. As one lies on it, the system continuously monitors one's body position and pressure distribution and automatically adjusts the bed's air support for maximum comfort. It is a system that keeps pressure distribution balanced for comfortable sleep. There is similarity with the method to be proposed in this paper in terms of utilizing the pressure distribution, but both the purpose of application and the application technique are quite different.

Adaptive sleep thinking system [21] has five independent zones adjusting to relieve pressure and improve sleep quality. This system is functionally similar to [20]. The difference between these two systems is that the system [20] divides the pressure generating part of the body into five zones and independently controls each of the five zones.

MAP system [22] involves a special electronic sheet placed over a mattress that has thousands of sensors that detect the pressure distribution of the patient's body over the bed. It is very similar to our proposed method. However, our proposed system uses 1/20 times fewer sensors than MAP. In addition, depending on the upper body and lower body, different types of sensors are deployed efficiently considering the incidence of bedsores. Notice that the incidences of bedsores are relatively low in the areas with frequent movements such as legs.

THE SMART BED SYSTEM

System Overview

The primary purpose of the proposed smart bed system is to assist caregivers in nursing elderly patients who are not able to move about freely. With a smart bed, several pressure sensors installed under the mattress cover measure pressure intensity due to the weight of the patient lying on the bed. A smart bed can provide the information about pressure intensity of the points or areas of the patient's body. With this information, we know the patient's posture, that is, the supine position or lateral position, and the duration of pressure in a particular body position. This knowledge can help caregivers in terms of preventing the appearance of bedsores and/or falling accidents from the bed.

One of the most important functions of the smart bed system is that it can easily find the specific points of the patient. Based on the average body size by age (with reference to the KATS), a smart bed system is able to recognize the known points where bedsores frequently occur, that is, *occiput, scapula, superfine projections, elbow, iliac crest, sacrum, pubic bone, the Achilles tendon, heel*, etc. [23]. Figure 1 shows the block diagram of the smart bed system.

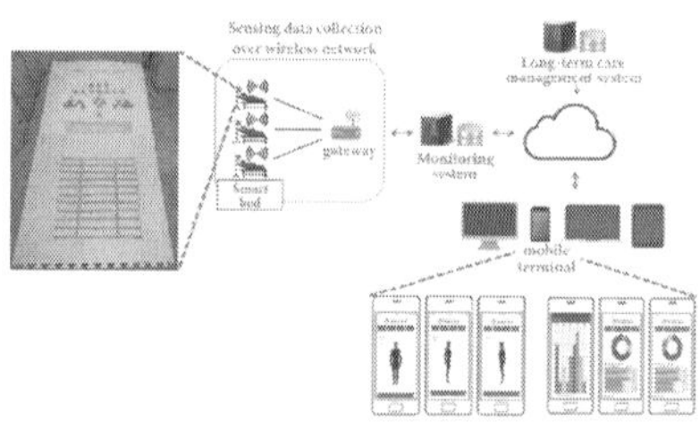

Figure 1: The H/W diagram of a smart bed system.

Design of a Smart Bed System

Our smart bed meets the standard requirements of 1,895cm x 850cm, which are the dimensions of a bed for medical purposes. The entire body area of a patient is divided into three distinct sections (see Figure 2). This classification has been performed based on pressure intensity and the location of the frequent occurrence of bedsores. The points marked as dots in each section have a similar pressure intensity and they are close to the known position of bedsores.

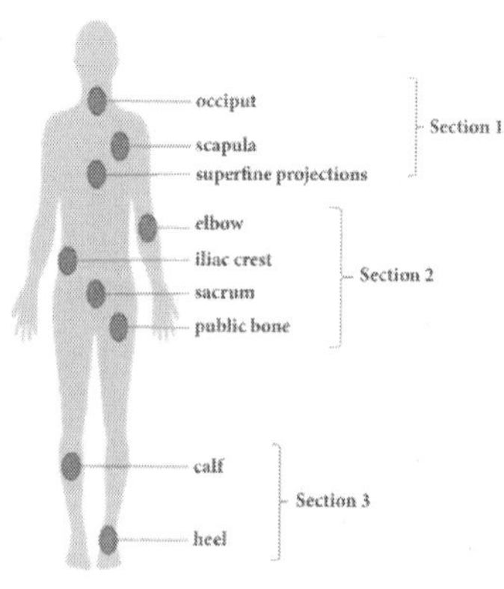

Figure 2: The three distinct sections and the positions of the frequent occurrence of bedsore.

The first section corresponds to the upper body. It consists of the head, with the three dots, namely, occiput, scapula, and superfine projections, respectively. The second section consists of arms and buttocks, with the following four dots: elbow, iliac crest, sacrum, and pubic bone. The third section consists of legs, with two dots for calf and heel (see Figure 2).

In order to collect the data on pressure intensity sent from the sensors, a microcontroller unit (MCU) is allocated in each section. It has been implemented with Arduino MEGA-2560. Since each MCU operates independently, the smart bed system performs its own work, even though one or two MCUs have some troubles or stopped accidentally.

As shown in Figure 1, the *gateway* to the monitoring system is implemented with the Raspberry PI board. It has an ATmega644 CPU and operates on the Linux operating system. The gateway communicates with three distinct MCUs via the *Master-Slave* mode [24]. Each MCU periodically transmits the pressure data to the gateway through wireless communication using Wireless LAN (WLAN). The gateway converts these raw data into the corresponding formatted data and then stores them in the local database.

These data will be sent to the long-term care management system (LCMS) and then be stored in a permanent database. Finally, they will be used as persistent data for the LCMS. In the case of a high possibility of a bedsore attack or a falling accident from a bed, an alarm message will be sent to the caregiver's smart device immediately via the Google FCM (*Firebase Cloud Messaging*) server.

Deployment of Two Types of Sensors

The pressure sensor needs to be arranged according to the average body size of each age group. In particular, if the pressure of a specific body part is to be measured, the body part dimensions for each age group should be reflected in the sensor placement process. We have deployed sensors regarding both the average body size by age, as based on the KATS, and the position of the frequent occurrence of bedsores. Doing so will make it possible to detect pressure of body positions with various body dimensions.

Our design goal for sensor deployment is to use the minimum number of sensors to detect pressure of all possible body positions. Depending on the body part, there are areas that require precise measurement of pressure and others that do not. For example, instead of measuring the pressure of a specific part of the *head* and the *lower body*, it is only necessary to measure whether or not the pressure is generated. On the other hand, the *upper* body needs to measure the pressure closely around a specific position where the pressure *ulcer* frequently occurs. In this situation, we will use two kinds of sensors: FSR-408 and FSR-406 [25]. These sensors are chosen in terms of cost effectiveness and ease of implementation. According to the data sheet [25], this force sensitivity is optimized for use in human touch control of electronic devices such as automotive electronics, medical systems, and industrial and robotics applications. The FSR-408 sensor (*strip*-type) is used to detect whether a pressure has been generated. On the other hand, the FSR-406 sensor (*square* type) is used to precisely measure the pressure of a specific area. The dimensions of FSR-408 and FSR-406 are 610mm x 5mm and 38mm x 38mm, respectively. The pressure range for the above two sensors is 0.1 ~10.2^2N (Newton).

Both FSR-406 and FSR-408 are two-wire devices with a resistance that depends on the applied force. The measuring resistor output voltage increases with the increasing force.

The FSR-408 pressure sensor can detect the pressure of a wide area with relatively smaller numbers. It knows only the strength of the pressure, whereas it does not know the exact position of the issued pressure. To use FSR-408 sensors, they are deployed in a grid pattern (see the left part of Figure 3).

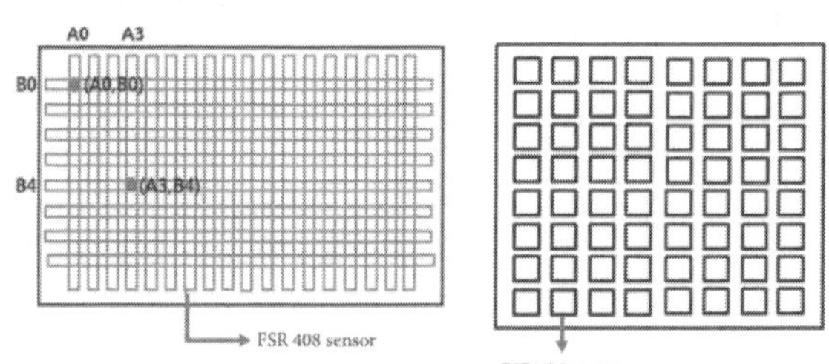

Figure 3: Deployment of FSR-406 and FSR-408 sensors.

Note that, as shown in Figure 4, they are used to detect pressures of patient head, legs, and hips. The vertical spacing between the sensors for detecting pressure of hips is 20~30mm, whereas the vertical spacing for legs is 50mm. To expect the position of issued pressure, two FSR sensors are necessary. For example, assume that two sensors, A0 and B0, in the left part of Figure 3 detect pressures simultaneously. Then, the intersection point (A0, B0) marked as a dot will be expected as the position of pressure issued. Another intersection point (A3, B4) will be the same as in the previous example.

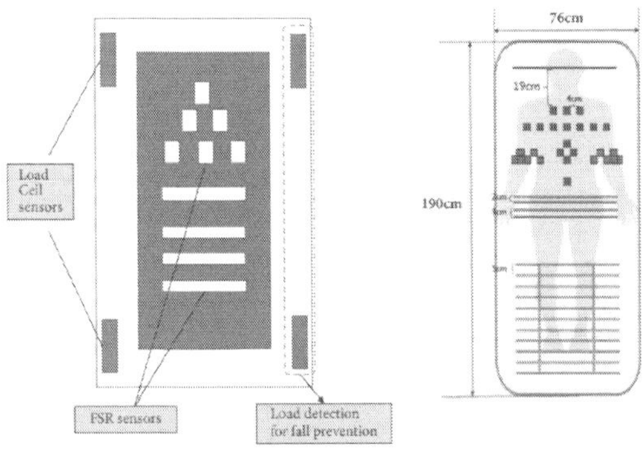

Figure 4: The placements of load-cell sensors and FSR sensors (left) and of the two types of sensors using a grid pattern and a dot pattern (right).

To detect pressure of the upper body, FSR-406 sensors are deployed in a dot pattern (see the right part of Figure 3). FSR-406 sensor does know the exact position of the issued pressure. They have been deployed by 190mm distance away from the FSR-408 sensors deployed in the back of the patient head (called *occipital area sensors*) to detect the pressure of the shoulder portion. Note that the exact dimensions are determined by using the Korean standard body dimensions from KATS. For example, this distance is measured for Koreans to amount to 190.223mm~220.44mm. FSR-406 sensors are also deployed to detect pressure of both superfine projections (*spine*) and elbow positions.

For the actual implementation (see the left part of Figure 5), a total of 45 sensors are used: 18 FSR-408 sensors and 27 FSR-406 sensors. The FSR-406 sensor and the FRS-408 sensor are priced at $10 and $25, respectively. The cost of implementing the entire system is only one-fifth of the cost of competing systems. With this implementation, 22 positions of the frequent occurrence of bedsore can be detected: 10 positions for the supine posture and 12 positions for the lateral posture. Such implementation is designed for elderly patients whose height is within the range of 150~180cm.

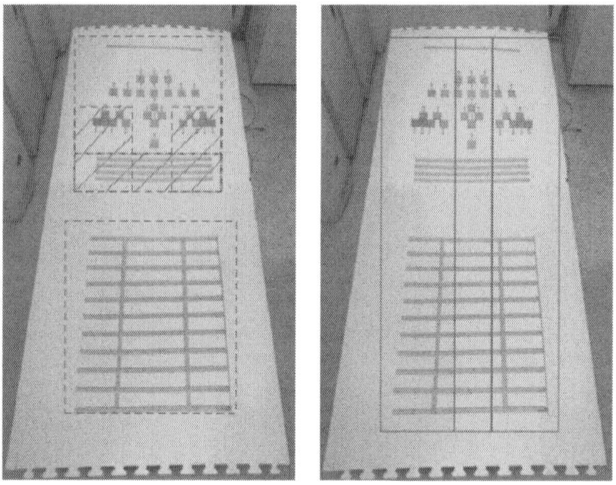

Figure 5: The 3 horizontal subsets of sensors (left) and the 3 vertical subsets of sensors (right).

Sensing Algorithm for Fall Risk Assessment and Pressure Ulcer Occurrence Warning

As shown in the left part of Figure 4, four load cells for detecting the load are placed on the edge of the bed. They can determine whether the patient is in bed and measure the patient's weight if the patient is lying down properly. In Figure 4, the dot-type (FSR-406) sensor and the strip-type (FSR-408) sensor arrangement are shown on the right. Note that the dimensions of the main parts are also shown.

The set of FSR sensors can be divided into three groups according to the sensing purpose, as shown in Figure 5, either vertically or horizontally. The left side of Figure 5 divides the FSR sensors horizontally into three subsets to measure the pressure of the major body parts. Three MCUs process the pressure information of the sensors of each subset divided in the horizontal direction. Each sensor subset in the horizontal direction is used to monitor whether the pressure at the frequent occurrence of bedsore has been maintained for a certain period of time.

As shown on the right part of Figure 5, the FSR sensors are arranged vertically in three groups: *left*, *center*, and *right*. Depending on how many sensors of one subset, as compared to the other two subsets, sense pressure, we can expect the patient's posture in the bed and thus generate the warning message against a falling accident. If over 80% of the sensors of one of the groups except for the sensors of the central group sense the pressure and, at the same time, less than 20% of the sensors of the remaining group sense the pressure, it can be decided to be one of the following two case: either the patient lying on the bed is in danger of falling or s/he is coming down from the bed. In any case, the caregiver will be immediately notified that the patient needs protection.

The system detects the patient's position every 1 minute. However, as the possibility of fall accident increases, the measurement period will be shortened to 30 seconds or less. In Algorithm 1, we present a sensing algorithm for the fall risk assessment.

```
At the initial, set the measurement cycle T_0 to 60 seconds:
While (true) do
  ΔT = 0;
  The system detects the patient's body position every T_t second;
  If N_t^left < 5% and N_t^right < 5% and N_t^center < 5% then
    The patient has gone out of the bed; T_t = ∞;    // The system will halt.
  Else If N_t^left ≥ 80% and N_t^center < 20% and N_t^right < 20% then
    Send the alarm immediately to the caregiver's smart device;
    If T_t/2 < 5 then ΔT = 5; Else ΔT = T_t/2;       // The min. cycle is set to 5 seconds.
  Else If 50% ≤ N_t^left < 80% then
    If N_t^left - N_{t-1}^left > 10% then
      Send the warning message to the caregiver's smart device;
      ΔT = T_t/6; N_{t-1}^left = N_t^left;
    Else ΔT = T_t/12;
  Else If N_t^left < 50% and N_t^right < 50% then
    If T_t + 60 ≤ 300 then T_t = T_t + 60; ΔT = 0;   // The max. cycle is set to 5 minutes.
    Else T_t = 300; ΔT = 0;
  // end of if
  T_t = T_t - ΔT;
// end of while;
```

Algorithm 1: The sensing algorithm for fall risk assessment.

Let N_t^{left} be the percentage of sensors of the left vertical group which sense pressure at time *t*. Similarly N_t^{right} and N_t^{center} are the percentage of sensors of the right vertical group which sense pressure and the percentage of sensors of the center vertical group which sense pressure at time *t*, respectively. Note that, for simplicity, Algorithm 1 describes only the detection of fall accident that occurs in the left end of the bed. In this case we assume that the safety guard on the right side of the bed is raised so that the patient cannot fall down to the right.

As the ratio of the pressure sensed by one group of sensor increases, the measurement cycle *T* starts to shorten. If the percentage of sensors of the left group sensing pressure increases by over 10% after T interval, the next cycle T will be decreased by half of the current cycle.

After a fall risk warning, if the pressure is no longer measured anywhere on the bed, it is decided that the patient is no longer in bed. It is judged that a fall has occurred or the patient has gone out of bed and moved to another place.

To prevent ulcer occurrence, perform a field test to determine the patient's posture (supine, repose, left position, right position, half position, etc.) according to the pressure pattern applied to the bed. In addition, when a patient lies in the bed, the height of a patient is calculated using the distance between the back head sensor and the farthest distance sensor based on the sensor located at the heels of the patient. In this way, the body part with frequent pressure ulcers is sought. Assume that the background data (gender, age, height, and weight) for the patient are given. A sensing algorithm for pressure ulcer occurrence warning is shown in Figure 6.

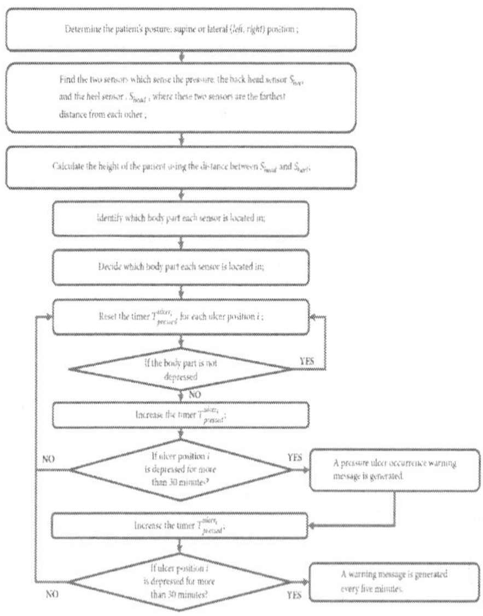

Figure 6: The sensing algorithm for pressure ulcer occurrence warning.

Finally, the system implements the following features:(1)Visualizing and displaying the duration of pressing for each body part.(2)The graph shows the current status and daily and weekly cumulative status of the patient.(3)If the same site is continuously pressed for longer than 30 minutes, a warning message will be generated.

EXPERIMENTS

The Detection Rate of the Pressures of the FSR Sensors

In this experiment, we examine whether the FSR sensors accurately detect pressure. This is because the smart bed system can accurately determine the patient's posture according to whether the pressure is properly detected. If the value sensed by a FSR sensor is below the reference value (i.e., *threshold*), it cannot be used for a determination of lying posture. In general, a FSR sensor can detect the value above the threshold if a patient lying in the bed maintains a constant posture for a certain period.

The pressure range of a FSR sensor is 0~1,023. The threshold used in this experiment is 150, where it was determined empirically. In addition, the detection rate of the pressures of the FSR sensors has been obtained when the patient was lying in the same position for more than one minute (see Figure 7). The values shown in Table 1 are the number of FSR sensors whose values were measured above the threshold. The measurements were repeated 20 times for each posture. The detection rate when lying down in normal posture (a.k.a. *supine* posture) was higher than the left or right lateral posture.

Table 1: The detection rate with respect to the lying posture.

lying posture	total no of sensors	min. no of sensors	max. no of sensors	average no of sensors
right lateral	26	23	26	24.55
left lateral	26	23	26	24.49
supine	27	24	27	25.48

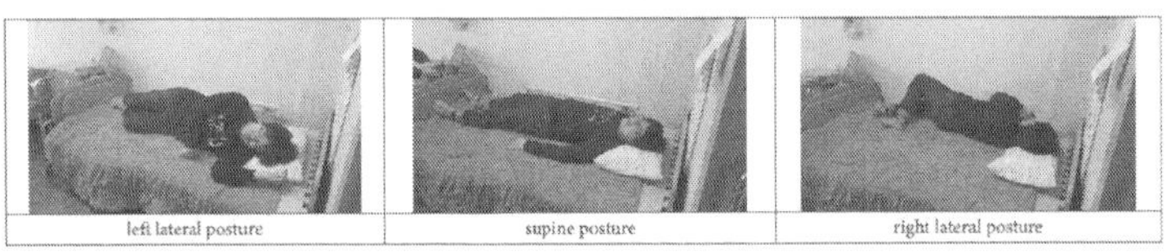

Figure 7: Measurement of the detection rate of the pressures with respect to the lying posture.

The Recognition Rate of the Lying Posture

This is an experiment to evaluate the performance of the algorithm to determine what posture the patient is lying on using the pressure values sensed by the FSR sensors. Notice that the smart bed system can determine the posture when the patient is lying in the same position for more than one minute. This delay considers all the delays due to the processing delay, the propagation delay over wireless, and the database processing delay. Experiments were conducted on elderly people in the elderly care facilities (see Figure 8).

Figure 8: Experiments for recognizing a patient's posture based on the pressures measured.

As shown in Table 2, for this experiment, three threshold values were used: 50, 150, and 300. As the threshold value becomes greater, the rate of discriminating correct posture increases. *Head*, *shoulder*, and *hip* are the body parts where their pressure values are higher than those of the other parts. The larger the threshold value, the more accurate the main body parts can be measured. If head, shoulder, and hip are recognized as straight lines based on the pressure value, the patient can be judged to be lying in the supine posture. To make such a decision, it is necessary to accurately measure the pressure values corresponding to the body part.

Table 2: The recognition rate with respect to the threshold.

threshold	no of tests	successful recognition	recognition rate (%)
50	112	85	75.9
150	128	104	81.3

300	134	117	87.3

One of the reasons for not recognizing the patient's posture is that when lying down the bed the behavior patterns and the lying postures are different for each patient. This type of the recognition error due to different behavior patterns for each patient can be effectively reduced through data accumulation and analysis. Another reason is that the patient's body size varies. When installing the system, we can reduce the rate of recognition error by adjusting the parameters to match the patient's body size. The values in Table 2 are the results of the experiments without these adjustments.

The Communication Delay over Wireless

The pressure values sensed by the FSR sensors are transmitted to the Arduino board (*Arduino Mega-2560*) as explained earlier in Section 3.2. It can communicate with the Raspberry PI board via serial communication at 9,600bps baud rate. Then it periodically transmits the stored pressure values to the Raspberry PI. Finally, the Raspberry PI wirelessly transmits them to the remote server through IEEE 802.11n WLAN. Notice that the payload data size used in the experiment is 256 Kbytes.Experiments assume a single-hop wireless transmission from the Raspberry PI to the server. We measured the time it takes for the values detected by all the FSR sensors to reach the server. This value is used as a basis for estimating the transmission time of an SMS message when an emergency such as a fall accident or a high occurrence of a pressure ulcer happens.As summarized in Table 3 and also shown in Figure 9, the wireless transmission delay is less than 2.5ms. Based on this value, it is possible to estimate the minimum period required to store the pressures values in the remote database system. In other words, the minimum interval of the data transmission for the smart bed system can be obtained. Since the processing delay is less than 1ms, the minimum period becomes 3.5ms. Since these experiments were conducted in the laboratory where there is little traffic in WLAN, it may increase in more realistic environments.

Table 3: The statistics of the communication delay over WLAN.

No of tests	142

average delay	1.616 [ms]
minimum delay	1.238 [ms]
maximum delay	2.435 [ms]

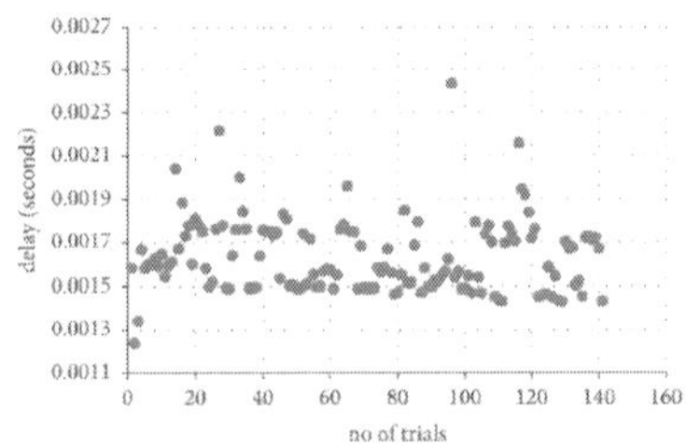

Figure 9: The distribution of the communication delays over WLAN.

However, it is not necessary to transmit the pressure values in a shorter period less than 1 minute unless there is a risk of fall accidents or occurrence of pressure ulcers. As the transmission period becomes shorter, the number of records inserted into the database increases rapidly. Therefore, it is necessary to adjust the transmission period appropriately. The transmission cycle seems to be appropriate in 3 to 5 minutes in a normal situation.

The Delay of Transmitting SMS to the Registered User

We used Google FCM, a cross platform messaging solution, to implement emergency text messaging. Performance was measured at maximum payload 4KB including dummy data. The mobile application for users is implemented on the Android platform. The number of mobile terminals to be transferred at the same time was limited to one registered terminal to protect patient information. User authentication uses the sender ID, and the message lifetime is set to only one day. Normally, the message lifetime is set to 2,419,200 seconds (i.e., 28 days). We measured message transmission time and message reception time, respectively.

As shown in the left of Figure 10, we assumed that the high possibility of falling accidents occurs and then the smart bed system sends emergency text message to the registered caregiver. The average delay is 0.74 seconds and the maximum delay is 2.64 seconds, as summarized in Table 4. This is because the variation of the delay is influenced by network traffic at the time of transmission and reception. In the performance evaluation, the measurement was made on one registered terminal, but the maximum delay was within 5 seconds even when the message was transmitted to two terminals at the same time.

Table 4: The statistics of the delays of transmitting text message to the one registered user.

No of tests	142
average delay	0.737 [s]
minimum delay	1. 096 [s]
maximum delay	2. 643 [s]

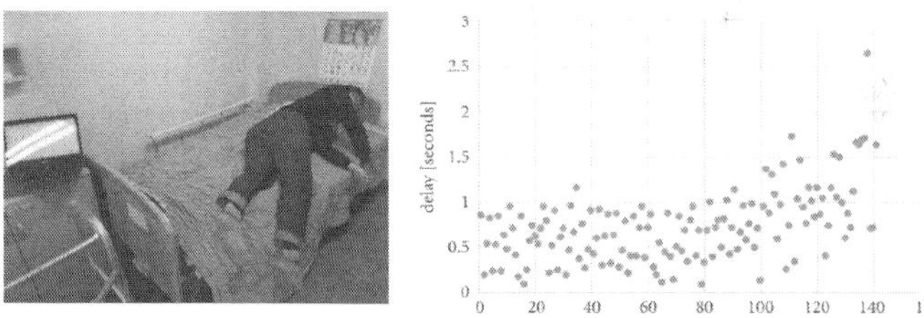

Figure 10: The experimental setup (*left*) and the distribution of the delays (*right*).

Detection of Falling Accident

We applied the prototype smart bed to two groups of patients: elderly patients who can hardly move and elderly patients with dementia who can move a little. In the case of the former group, little change in the pressure sensor value over time was observed. However, pressure changes occurred frequently in the latter group of patients. Specifically, in this group, it took at least 2.7 minutes (on average) from the time when the *left* (or *right*) pressure ratio of the bed reached 80% to the time when the patient came down from the bed. The fastest alarm cycle was set to 5 seconds, indicating that the caregiver had sufficient time to recognize the alarm and then come back to the patient. Note that, in the experiment, the caregiver was assumed to be on the same floor as the patient. Besides, the caregiver was assumed to be within the 100-meter reach from the patient.

It is not easy to analyze the relationship between detection time and prevention of falls. This is because it is hard to find out what an elderly patient will do on one side of the bed. Therefore, the proposed method only determines whether the patient's position is located one side of the bed as shown in Figure 5. It focuses on informing a caregiver as soon as possible when the patient's position reaches a dangerous zone (called *D-zone*), such as a corner of the bed, so that she (he) can identify the situation.

Experiments were conducted to investigate the effect of the size of D-zone on detection time. This is because limiting the search space can be effective for reducing detection time to prevent fall if a patient moves to one side of the bed. For the purpose of the experiment, the 3 types of D-zone are defined as shown in Figure 11. The minimum D-zone has only 10 sensors, while the maximum D-zone has 24 sensors.

(a) The minimum D-zone

(b) The medium D-zone

(c) The maximum D-zone

(a) The minimum D-zone (b) The medium D-zone (c) The maximum D-zone

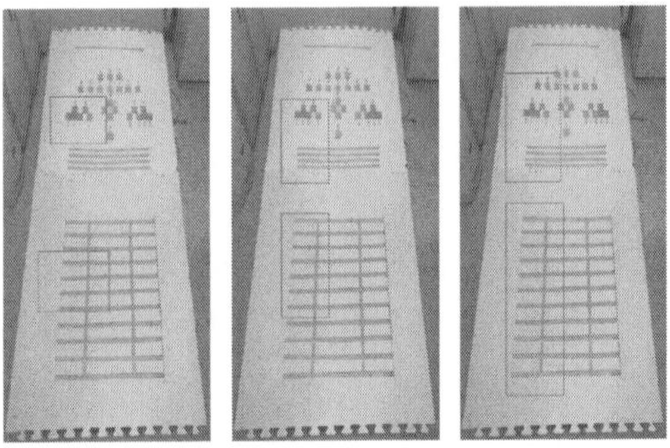

(a) The minimum D-zone (b) The medium D-zone (c) The maximum D-zone

Figure 11: Analysis of detection time with respect to D-zone setting.

Depending on the D-zone size, the processing time may vary, summarized as Table 5, but the total elapsed time heavily depends on the time it takes to send the text message to the caregiver.

Table 5: The processing time with respect to the size of D-zone.

type	no of sensors	processing time [ms] (avg.)
min. D-zone	10	0.115
medium D-zone	17	0.268
max. D-zone	24	0.412

1ms (*processing cycle*) + 2.435ms (*delay over wireless*) + 2.643s (*delay of transmitting SMS*) < 2.7s.

We set the minimum detect cycle to 5 seconds, but it can be shortened to 3 seconds.

Detection of Bedsores

If a patient is the supine position, his (her) height can be estimated by using the distance between the occipital area sensors and the sensors that are deployed farthest from the occipital area sensors. Based on the average body size from the KATS, we know which sensors are sensed which position of a patient. It is important, because, according to KATS, bedsores frequently occur in specific locations.

In order to prevent bedsore attacks, caregivers should change the patient's posture at least every 2 hours [26]. Whenever the pressure of the specific position continues for longer than 60 minutes, the smart bed system gives caregivers warning messages. When the pressure continues for 90 minutes, it sends an alarm to the caregiver's smart device to change the patient's posture as soon as possible.

Figure 7 shows the duration time with respect to the patient posture. The green, orange, and red dots indicate the duration time of 30, 60, and 90 minutes, respectively. As shown in Figure 12, our smart bed system can identify three types of patient posture: supine, lateral left, and lateral right. Figure 13 shows the patient's posture and accumulated pressure daily.

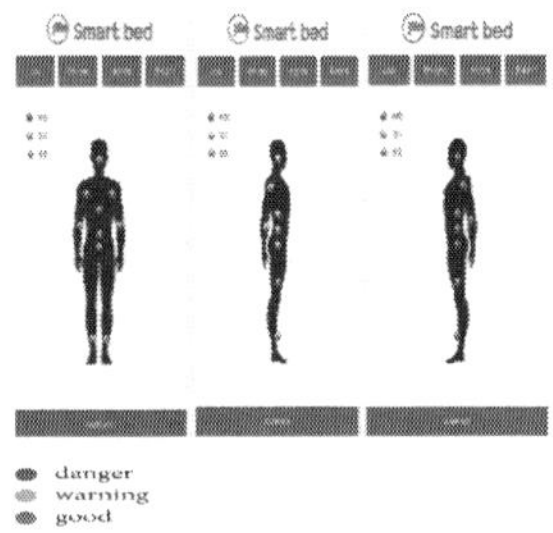

Figure 12: Visualization of the duration time of pressure with respect to the supine position (left) and the lateral position (center, right).

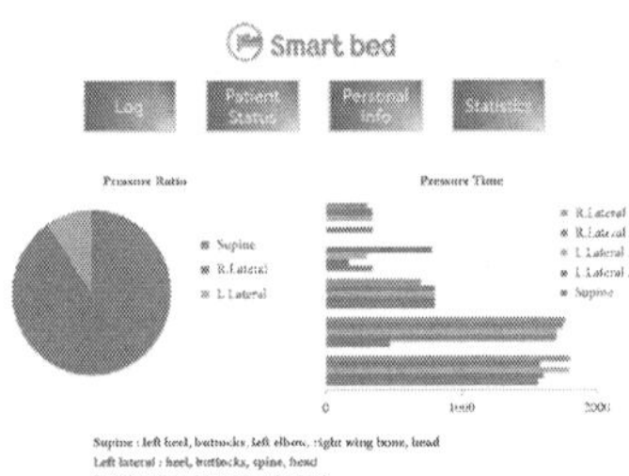

Figure 13: Patient posture and accumulated pressure daily.

Guarantee of Comfort Sleep

The commercialized model is similar to the electric plate as shown in Figure 14. The controllers such as Raspberry PI boards will be placed on the side of the mattress. The survey results showed that more than 93% of users did not feel uncomfortable when lying down because of the smart mattress. To guarantee more comfort sleep, it is necessary to consider the material of smart mattress, which is beyond the scope of this paper.

Figure 14: The prototype smart mattress (without controllers).

CONCLUSIONS

Our smart bed prototype system can sense pressure occurring on the entire body of a patient with mobility impairment at a regular interval through an efficient deployment of sensors, while using a smaller number of sensors. In addition, the proposed system can detect the position with the highest possibility of bedsore attack by finding the largest accumulated pressure. The proposed system can also provide the information about the position of the frequent occurrence of bedsore for caregivers depending on the patient's personal characteristics, for example, his (her) height or weight. Thus, it can help caregivers in terms of appropriately nursing their patients. Our system will be the one of the possible solutions to prevent bedsores and/or falling accidents and will be particularly useful in nursing homes and senior care centers.At present, our smart bed can distinguish only three postures among elderly patients lying on the bed. If a patient is lying in a bent position, it may not be able to properly locate the pressure ulcer. Thus, we are currently studying ways to find various postures of patients more effectively. In the future, we will continue to investigate methods to measure the weight of elderly patients with impaired mobility even when they are lying down.

Data Availability

The data are generated at regular interval and stored in our local database system. Thus, all the data are stored in our local database system. These data will be given for proofing the correctness of our approach to the specific interests.

Conflicts of Interest

The author declares that there are no conflicts of interest regarding the publication of this paper.

ACKNOWLEDGMENTS

This work is supported by the 2013 Grant of Incheon National University.

REFERENCES

1. "Nonstop Pressure," http://www.nursinghomeabuseguide.org/neglect/bed-sores/.
2. T. Yoshikawa, N. J. Livesley, and A. W. Chow, "Infected pressure ulcers in elderly individuals," *Clinical Infectious Diseases*, vol. 35, no. 11, pp. 1390–1396, 2002.
3. M. Sartini, M. L. Cristina, A. M. Spagnolo et al., "The epidemiology of domestic injurious falls in a community dwelling elderly population: An outgrowing economic burden," *European Journal of Public Health*, vol. 20, no. 5, pp. 604–606, 2010.
4. "Fall-Related Injuries," http://www.homecareassistancecincinnati.com/common-elderly-injuries/.
5. G. D. Velhal, "Domestic accidents among the elderly," *Annals of Tropical Medicine and Public Health*, vol. 5, no. 2, pp. 61-62, 2012.
6. Y.-O. Hwang, "Geriatric care facilities: recent trends in risk management," *Journal of the Korean Gerontological Society*, vol. 26, no. 3, pp. 505–520, 2006.
7. S. M. R. Islam, D. Kwak, H. Kabir, M. Hossain, and K. Kwak, "The internet of things for health care: a comprehensive survey," *IEEE Access*, vol. 3, pp. 678–708, 2015.
8. M. C. Domingo, "An overview of the internet of things for people with disabilities," *Journal of Network and Computer Applications*, vol. 35, no. 2, pp. 584–596, 2012.
9. S. Amendola, R. Lodato, S. Manzari, C. Occhiuzzi, and G. Marrocco, "RFID technology for IoT-based personal healthcare in smart spaces," *IEEE Internet of Things Journal*, vol. 1, no. 2, pp. 144–152, 2014.
10. M. Hassanalieragh, A. Page, T. Soyata et al., "Health monitoring and management using internet-of-things (IoT) sensing with cloud-based processing: opportunities and challenges," in *Proceedings of the IEEE International Conference on Services Computing, SCC 2015*, pp. 285–292, IEEE, July 2015.
11. A. Pantelopoulos and N. G. Bourbakis, "A survey on wearable sensor-based systems for health monitoring and prognosis," *IEEE Transactions on Systems, Man, and Cybernetics, Part C: Applications and Reviews*, vol. 40, no. 1, pp. 1–12, 2010.
12. W. Jung and Y. Hong, "A Design and Implementation of a Smart Bed for Elderly Patients," *International Journal of Elderly Welfare Promotion*

and Management, vol. 1, no. 1, pp. 1–6, 2017.

13. M. Yu, A. Rhuma, S. M. Naqvi, L. Wang, and J. Chambers, "A posture recognition-based fall detection system for monitoring an elderly person in a smart home environment," *IEEE Transactions on Information Technology in Biomedicine*, vol. 16, no. 6, pp. 1274–1286, 2012.
14. Y. S. Delahoz and M. A. Labrador, "Survey on fall detection and fall prevention using wearable and external sensors," *Sensors*, vol. 14, no. 10, pp. 19806–19842, 2014.
15. S. Gasparrini, E. Cippitelli, S. Spinsante, and E. Gambi, "A depth-based fall detection system using a kinect sensor," *Sensors*, vol. 14, no. 2, pp. 2756–2775, 2014.
16. Kei-Myung University R&DB Foundation, Fall-down prevent device, Patent No. 10-2013-0021614, 2014.8. 29 (registration date).
17. Ó. D. Lara and M. A. Labrador, "A survey on human activity recognition using wearable sensors," *IEEE Communications Surveys & Tutorials*, vol. 15, no. 3, pp. 1192–1209, 2013.
18. K. Ozcan, A. K. Mahabalagiri, M. Casares, and S. Velipasalar, "Automatic fall detection and activity classification by a wearable embedded smart camera," *IEEE Journal on Emerging and Selected Topics in Circuits and Systems*, vol. 3, no. 2, pp. 125–136, 2013.
19. HIMS Co. Ltd, System of unobtrusively recognizing actions and promoting physical activities and smart mat for the same purpose, Patent No. 10-2013-0024409, 2014. 4. 28 (registration date).
20. "Smart Bed," http://boditrak.com/products/smartbeds.php.
21. "Adaptive Sleep Thinking," http://www.elementsofrest.com/the-rest-bed/rest-technology.
22. "Mattress Sensing MAP System," https://www.medgadget.com/2013/07/mattress-sensing-map-system-prevents-pressure-ulcers.html.
23. "Symptoms of Pressure Ulcers," http://www.nhs.uk/Conditions/Pressure-ulcers/Pages/Symptoms.aspx.
24. "Arduino Forum," http://forum.arduino.cc/index.php.
25. "FSR-408 and FSR-406," https://cdn-shop.adafruit.com/datasheets/FSR400Series_PD.pdf.
26. E.-S. Kwon, *Study on the knowledge of bedsores care of a hospital nurse, recognition and execution*, Hanyang University Graduate School of Public Administration, 2005.

CHAPTER 10

A NOVEL EMERGENCY HEALTHCARE SYSTEM FOR ELDERLY COMMUNITY IN OUTDOOR ENVIRONMENT

Hui-Ru Cao[1] **and Choujun Zhan**[1]

Nanfang College of Sun Yat-sen University, Guangzhou 510970, China

ABSTRACT

By exploiting the advanced information and communication technologies, the current community healthcare systems provide digital healthcare services. However, the current healthcare framework for senior citizen in outdoor environment faces new challenges. The traditional healthcare systems are not efficient, and they do not comprise user-friendly devices and interfaces suitable for the elderly in outdoor environment. Hence, in this work, we develop an outdoor healthcare system for community

Citation: Qi H., Cao Hui-Ru, Zhan C., "A Novel Emergency Healthcare System for Elderly Community in Outdoor Environment", Journal of Wireless Communications, Vol. 2018, Article ID 7841026, https://doi.org/10.1155/2018/7841026.

senior citizens based on unmanned aerial vehicle (UAV) and Internet of things (IoT). Our system includes physical devices, wireless and wired networks, cloud and data center, and smart terminals. Further, the analysis of the proposed healthcare architecture is presented from the perspective of different layers, and an algorithm on UAV for creating high-speed communication channel and delivering medicine is provided. In addition, the healthcare UAV, related devices, and friendly APPs are designed. The proposed framework is evaluated by comparison with the current healthcare architecture. The emulating and experimental results show that our proposed system can provide a high-quality wireless communication link even at large communication distances, and in real testbed our proposal can reduce the response time by about 20% in comparison with the current methods.

INTRODUCTION

With the increase of life expectancy in many countries, the continuously growing aging trends bring a dramatic increase in the elderly population [1]. Specifically, most of the developing countries are facing a serious aging problem, and more and more senior citizens suffer from the acute conditions such as blood pressure, heart disease, and fall-related injuries [2]. On the other hand, in most developing countries, most of the younger generation move to big cities for work, and this leads to a large number of old people living alone without family. This has become a common phenomenon in many developing countries, especially in China [3]. If a senior citizen suffers from an acute disease or injury, especially in outdoor environment, he/she must be treated immediately. Hence, it is essential to develop economical, convenient, and scalable communal healthcare systems, which can effectively reduce the response time of outdoor healthcare services and support the elderly community.

Providing an effective health system for senior citizens is significant, especially for those suffering from acute conditions. Therefore, increasing researchers focus on the topic and propose a great deal of valuable works. The research works in [4–8] focused on improving the healthcare systems using technological advances. The presented architectures for the communal healthcare systems are developed by introducing advanced digital technologies such as robot technology, cloud computing, wireless communication, and IoT, into the design framework [9, 10]. These new technologies have contributed immensely to improving the existing healthcare system and providing effective health services [11, 12]. However, the existing healthcare frameworks are still not sufficient for providing an efficient service to the senior citizen community. The existing healthcare frameworks show slow first aid response time for the acute diseases or fall-related injuries of elderly due to the environment, non-user-friendly devices, traffic situations, and other obstacles. The three most important aspects of the senior citizen community healthcare system are as follows: (1) a fast response time for the first aid; it is known that if a senior citizen suffer from acute disease, the health system must respond within limited time; (2) an effective communication equipment and communication scheme; communication system is the basement for the new health framework, as effective communication equipment and scheme can promote the efficiency of whole system; (3) a set of user-friendly devices and user terminals. Lack of friendly terminal and devices is harmful for the efficiency and first aid response times. These new requirements bring new challenges for developing a healthcare system suitable for the elderly in outdoor environment, especially for response time and an effective communication system. Unfortunately, the traditional healthcare system cannot provide a fast access, efficient means, and valid communications system, which makes it difficult to meet the new requirements of the elderly healthcare system.

With the development of advanced technologies, such as smart robots, UAV, and wireless communication, it is possible to develop a new healthcare system to meet the demands of providing an efficient healthcare for elderly people in an outdoor environment. As discussed above, the existing healthcare systems are facing more challenges and cannot meet the requirements of providing highly efficient service and user-friendly devices and interface for the elderly community in outdoor environment. Hence, in this work, we propose a new outdoor healthcare system for senior citizens community by introducing the UAV and IoT. Moreover, we analyze the proposed healthcare architecture from the point of view of four layers: devices, communication, cloud, and terminal interface. Then, the proposed system is emulated in the terms of first aid response time and data communication delay in a simulation. A prototype is implemented using the designed healthcare UAV, user-friendly devices, and a related APP. Further, we build an experimental testbed and perform the experiment in a campus environment. The experimental results show that our proposed system can reduce the response time and provide a high-quality communications link. We believe that our work will shed light on outdoor healthcare system for senior citizens and accelerate the implementation of UAV and IoT-based healthcare services.

The rest of this paper is organized as follows. We present a summary of related works in Section 2. In Section 3, we introduce the system architecture and design of our proposed healthcare system for the elderly in outdoor environment and proposed an algorithm for health emergent event. We present the analysis of the proposed system and simulation and experimental results in Sections 4 and 5. Finally, conclusions of this work are given in Section 6.

RELATED WORK

Combining advanced technologies to develop a smart healthcare system is an efficient method for providing an improved healthcare for the public, especially for senior citizens in modern society. These advanced technologies and systems enhance the performance of the healthcare services significantly. In this section, we review some of the related works of recent advances in emergency care technologies and healthcare systems.

Emergency Care Technologies

In [13], the authors integrated the RFID technology, ZigBee technology, and long-range wireless communication to build an emergency care system. Similarly, a global system for mobile (GSM) based smart wearable system with different sensors is developed in [14]. The developed device is capable of detecting sudden fall situations, cardiac abnormalities, and hyper/hypotension. In [15], Robson et al. proposed a tool called intelligent detection of arrhythmic heartbeats on electrocardiograms (IDAH-ECG). The IDAH-ECG tool collects data from an electrocardiograph to analyze and classify the data to detect patterns of arrhythmic beats in the ECG signal. In [16], the authors developed a location and emergency monitoring system for providing emergency care to the elderly. In [17], for predicting ambulance arrival time in an emergency situation, a linear regression model based on the information of weather, patient characteristics, lights and sirens, daylight, and rush-hour intervals is developed, and it was implemented as a Google maps web application.

From the perspective of application level, the novel technologies for emergency care could be divided into three categories: communication, data analysis, and data mining. However, the existing works related to emergency care technologies mainly focused on the healthcare service from a prediction aspect, which suffers from two undesirable drawbacks: real-time care deficiency and lack of emotional care. By incorporating UAV, IoT, and video technology, our proposed system can overcome these drawbacks.

Healthcare System

With the development of the information and communication technologies, such as wireless networks, cloud computing, data mining, and IoT, healthcare systems have made a great progress. In [18], a novel healthcare system architecture is proposed. The proposed architecture includes three components: collaborative data collection via wearable devices, enhanced sentiment analysis and forecasting models, and controllable affective interactions. In [18], a healthcare system based on cloud computing and robotics is developed, and it comprises wireless body area networks, a robot, a software system, and cloud platform. Further, in order to improve the practicability of multimedia transmission in the healthcare system, the authors in [19] proposed a novel scheme to deliver real-time video through an improved UDP-based protocol. In [20], a cyber-physical system for patient-centric healthcare applications and services, called Health-CPS, is proposed. The Health-CPS system is built based on cloud computing and big-data analytics technologies. In [21] a new system based on IoT-aware smart architecture is developed for automatic monitoring and tracking of patients, personnel, and biomedical devices within hospitals and nursing institutes. In [22], the authors proposed a new healthcare system based on second-generation RFID systems characterized by the introduction of encoding rules that are dynamically stored in RFID tags.

From the described summary of the existing healthcare systems, it can be understood that various healthcare systems and devices are developed for accurately sensing and collecting data related to physical and mental health of users. However, there are several drawbacks for the existing healthcare systems. Firstly, the current healthcare system and the corresponding research mainly focus on a common system for everyone and lack specific concrete applications, especially for senior citizen community outdoors. Moreover, the existing research studies assume that the users move in a limited range or at home. Obviously, this assumption is one of the limiting factors. In addition, for a healthcare system, it is important to have an efficient and real-time corresponding medical emergency subsystem, particularly for the users in emergency situations in outdoor environment. Nevertheless, the current emergency healthcare system is influenced by the position of hospital or medical center, buildings, and traffic situation. Hence, in this work, we focus on UAV and IoT- based emergency healthcare system for senior citizen community in outdoor environment.

SYSTEM ARCHITECTURE

In our work, UAV and IoT will play a significant role in the proposed healthcare system for outdoor environment. For facilitating the discussion and analysis of the framework, we divide the architecture of the outdoor healthcare system into four layers: the multiple model physical layer, networks layer, cloud layer, and the smart terminals (including UAV and medical workers) layer. The data communication links the four layers from the physical layer to the terminals. In the proposed system, the healthcare UAV plays a bridging role for information delivering during senior citizens and cloud sever; meanwhile UAV deliver the medicine, bandages, and emergency supplies. Therefore, in this section, after a brief description of the proposed healthcare system, the healthcare UAV subsystem is discussed.

Framework of the Proposed System

In the proposed system, all of the status data should be gathered by the sensor nodes and the outdoor system. Next, the data is transmitted to the cloud and data center. Meanwhile, the analyzed data can be sent to the smart terminals (e.g., doctors, users, smart phones, and other smart devices). It can be seen that the information exchange plays a significant role in our proposed healthcare system; i.e., the communication network supports the whole architecture. As shown in Figure 1, the information exchange system could be divided into data gathering layer, communication layer, cloud and data center, and smart terminals (including UAV and medical workers).

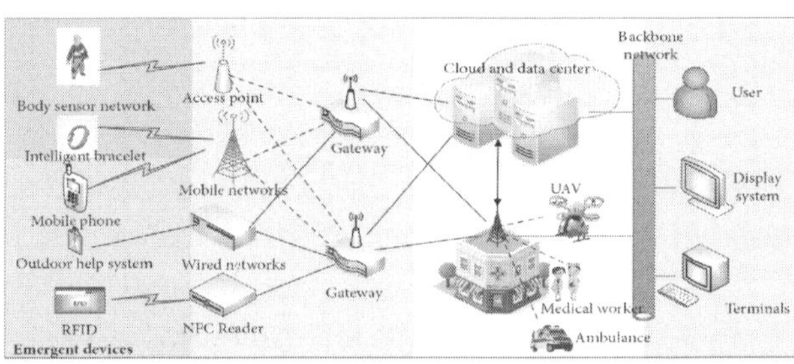

Figure 1: Architecture of network for senior citizen community in outdoor environment.

(1) *Multimodel Data Gathering Layer*. The data gathering layer determines the types of data that need to be collected by various devices in the system. The data gathering devices could be divided into two types, namely, forecasting and emergency devices. The

body sensor nodes, the intelligent bracelet, environment sensors, and other sensors form the forecasting devices. The forecasting devices mainly gather the data for the general case and forecast the health condition of the users. The emergency devices are responsible for the emergency situations such as heart attack, hypertension, and other acute diseases. The emergency devices include the mobile phone, the outdoor help system node, RFID cards, and other smart devices.

(2) *Communication Layer*. This layer is responsible for communication between the cloud and smart devices, hospital system, and the users. The communication layer uploads and delivers the sensing data, control commands, and other information. In the proposed system, the communication media platform uses both the wired and wireless communication technologies. The wired network mainly deals with the static nodes such as outdoor help system, real-time data transfer, and situations with large amounts of data transfer. For the mobile entities (such as the ambulance, UAV, medical workers, and users), wireless communication technologies such as Bluetooth, ZigBee, Wi-Fi, LTE, and NFC are used in the system.

(3) *Cloud and Data Center*. The cloud and data center perform computing to match the users' requirements and store massive amount of information. Moreover, the cloud and data center act as the processing module for all the networks. In an emergency situation, the cloud and data center create the list of the key medicines and rescue devices, by comparing the current information and the stored medical history records of a patient. The Hadoop software is used for storing massive amount of user data. After data mining and analysis, the results are delivered to users, nearby hospital, medical workers, and other smart terminals based on the priority of the message.

(4) *Smart Terminals*. The smart terminals are used to display the related information and key data using messages, web pages, or other application. This interface could provide an intuitional, effective, personal, and visual result for the elderly community and medical workers. The smart terminals can be the mobile phone, the intelligent bracelet, and the display system. For example, with the application software installed on the smart phone, the user could check the monitoring status of health conditions such

as heart-rate, blood pressure, and environment data. When real-time information is issued from data server, the reminders will be driven by sound and video.

Problem Formulation and First Aid Strategies Based on UAV

In our system, two types of data traffic are considered: (1) general data, where all of the data are delivered in normal situation; namely, the elders are not in emergency; (2), emergent data, where the data are delivered in emergent situation, that is, the elders being in a critical situation.

Assume that there are n senior citizens randomly distributed in A(L, W), where L and W are length and width of A. Let (x_i, y_i) be the position of the i-th senior citizen. For the system model, given that a senior citizen (we use current node which stands for the senior citizen) is falling into the emergent situation at the time and the first aid at time . So, the first aid response time t_0 is

$$T = t_{arrived} - t_0 \tag{1}$$

Let the coordinate of medical center be (x_0, y_0) and (x_e, y_e) be the position of emergent event. Let l denote the length of path for ambulance from (x_0, y_0) to (x_e, y_e). So, the direct length of medical center and emergent event site l_d can be described as follows:

$$l_d = \sqrt{(x_0 - x_e)^2 + (y_0 - y_e)^2}. \tag{2}$$

To better understand the solution to a problem, establish the relationship between l (real path length) and l_d, shown in the following:

$$l = (1 + \gamma) l_d \tag{3}$$

where y is path length increase coefficient and the value of y depends on different method for the emergent situation. So, the first aid response time T is formulated as follows:

$$T = t_{recieve\_RQ} + t_{arrived\_AM} + t_{data\_process} \tag{4}$$

where $t_{recieve\_RQ}$ is the communication delay for the emergency request information (ERI) arriving to medical center. $t_{arrived\_AM}$ denotes the time of the ambulance arriving at the emergent site; $t_{data\_process}$ is the data processing for dealing with the healthcare emergent event. Moreover, in the communication network, $t_{recieve\_RQ}$ can be descripted as

$$t_{recieve\_RQ} = \sum_{j=1}^{k} \left(\frac{Q}{V_{C,j}} + t_{wait,j} \right) \tag{5}$$

where Q is the data size of ERI and $V_{c,j}$ and $t_{wait,j}$ are communication rate and unload communication task time of the -th relay node. For easy understanding, let $V_{c,j}$ and $t_{wait,j}$ have the same value; namely, , $V_{c,j} = V_c, t_{wait,j} = t_{wait}$. So, (5) can be reduced to

$$t_{recieve\_RQ} = k \left(\frac{Q}{V_C} + t_{wait} \right) \tag{6}$$

Let V_m be the speed of ambulance. It is known that there is a relationship between real path length (*l*) and ambulance moving speed (V_m), as shown in the following:

$$t_{arrived\_AM} = \frac{l}{V_m}. \tag{7}$$

So, formulation (4) can simplify intoAs discussed above, in the emergent situation, we hope to get the minimum response time (MRT). So, the problem of MRT can be formulated as (9):

$$\min \quad T \tag{9}$$

$$\text{s.t.} \quad l \geq l_d \tag{10}$$

$$V_m \leq V_{m,\max} \tag{11}$$

$$0 \leq \gamma \leq \gamma_{\max} \tag{12}$$

$$Q > 0 \tag{13}$$

$$(x_0, y_0), (x_e, y_e) \in A \tag{14}$$

$$t_{wait} > 0, \ V_c > 0 \tag{15}$$

where formulations (10), (11), (12), (13), (14), and (15) are the constraints of length of medical center and emergent event site, and ambulance moving speed, path length increase coefficient, data size of ERI, position of emergent event, communication rate, and unload communication task time, respectively.

On the grounds of the processing of dealing with the healthcare emergent event and the above discussion, problem (9) can be decoupled into the following three subproblems, as being formulation as

$$\min T = \min\left(t_{recieve\_RQ} + t_{arrived\_AM} + t_{data\_process}\right)$$

(16)

According to formulations (6) and (7), the optimal problem (9) can be further simplified into (17)

$$\min T = \min(k)\left(\frac{Q}{V_C} + t_{wait}\right) + \frac{\min(l)}{V_m} + \min\left(t_{data\_process}\right) \quad (17)$$

In other words, for getting the first aid response time *T*, we can reduce the relay number of k and decrease the real path length l. Furthermore, in wireless mobile network, the receiving power p_r must satisfy the following inequality:

$$P_r = P_t - \alpha - 10\beta \lg(R) \geq P_{r,\min} \quad (18)$$

where P_t is transmitting power; R is the wireless communication radius; α and β are the attenuation at reference distance and the path loss exponent, respectively; $P_{r,\min}$ is the minimum receiving power for wireless communication. For solving the first subproblem $(\min(k))$, we can create the direct wireless communication between (x_0, y_0) and (x_e, y_e).

So, for acquiring the minimum data exchanging time, we can turn the first subproblem into searching the minimum transmitting power.

$$\min P_t = P_{r,\min} + \alpha + 10\beta \lg(l_d) \quad (19)$$

According to the above analysis, we propose a novel strategy for dealing with the health emergent event. For dealing with problem (9) with constraints of (10)-(15), we proposed the new healthcare system by using UAV, IoT, and cloud server. The strategy is shown in Algorithm 1.

Algorithm 1: First aid in emergent situation based on UAV.

Require: $Q, V_c, t_{wait}, V_m, \alpha, \beta, P_{r,min}$
Ensure: *HEA_FLAG*
(1) $HEA\_FLAG \longleftarrow 0, ERI\_flag[n] \longleftarrow 0$
(2) **for** $i = 1{:}n$ **do**
Read ERI_flag[i]
(3) **if** $ERI\_flag = 1$ & $HEA\_FLAG = 0$
(4) Read the *ERI*
(5) Acquire the position of emergent event $(x_{e,i}, y_{e,i})$
(6) $l_d \longleftarrow \sqrt{(x_0 - x_{e,i})^2 + (y_0 - y_{e,i})^2}$
(7) $P_r(i) \longleftarrow P_{r,min} + \alpha + 10\beta \lg(l_d)$
(8) Create the direct wireless communication between (x_0, y_0) and $(x_{e,i}, y_{e,i})$.
(9) Cloud and data center analysis the information
(10) Healthcare cloud server give the key medicines and rescue devices for the *i*-th patient
(11) Ambulance UAV carrying the key medicine and rescue devices directly to the emergency location
(12) **end if**
(13) **if** UAV arrived at the site $(x_{e,i}, y_{e,i})$
(14) Create the high-speed communication channel
(15) Download data from Current Node (i, D)
(16) **end if**
(17) $HEA\_FLAG \longleftarrow 1$
(18) **End for**
(19) **Return** *HEA_FLAG*

Our proposed algorithm is explained as follows. When a senior citizen is in an emergency condition, he/she and the finder could send the request (*ERI_flag*[*i*]) for help by using the outdoor help network terminal, intelligent bracelet, and other smart terminals (shown using the red line in Figure 2). Once the network receives the emergency request information, it creates a real-time wireless channel to deliver the information. By comparing the current information and the recorded history, the cloud and data center can give information regarding list of the key medicines and rescue devices for the patient. The hospital data center drives the ambulance UAV carrying the key medicine and rescue devices directly to the emergency location $(x_{e,i}, y_{e,i})(x_{e,i}, y_{e,i})$. Meanwhile, the cloud and data center inform the nearest medical workers and doctors requesting assistance at the site. When the UAV arrives at the emergency location, the wireless link will establish a connection with the hospital center, medical workers, and doctors. Meanwhile, the related emotional music will play, and the video phone will be linked, according the specific situation. Then, the finder and the nearest medical worker could give a medical care.

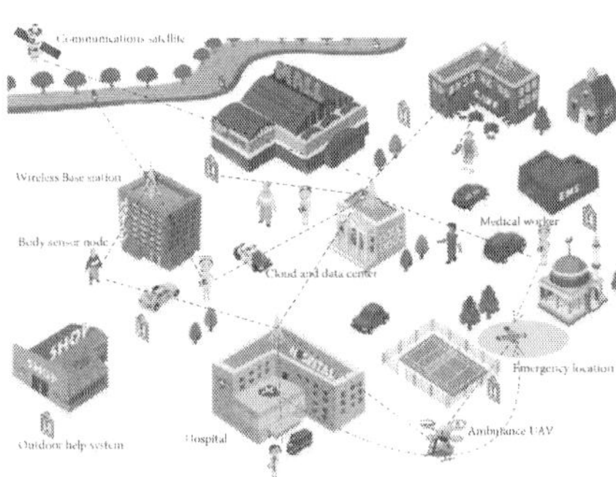

Figure 2: The outdoor healthcare system for elderly community. The red line shows the emergency situation case.

As shown in Algorithm 1, when UAV arrived at site, UAV will create the high-speed wireless channel for delivering video or other key data. Our proposal can reduce the data processing time by adopting cloud server f. Let V_c be the wireless communication rate and D be the volume of delivering data. So, we can get the communication delay, as shown in

$$T_{communication\_delay} = \theta \frac{D}{V_c} \tag{20}$$

where θ is the average number of hops for delivering data D. It is easily known that in our proposal we use UAV to create two hops for finishing the data transmitting.

PERFORMANCE EVALUATION

In this section, we will evaluate the performance of the proposed healthcare architecture and algorithm by comparing with traditional method in terms of first aid response time and communication delay.

The strategies are simulated in related software. Without loss of generality, we assume that the healthcare center is at the origin of coordinate system (namely, $(x, y) = (0, 0)$)). The distance between emergent healthcare event position and origin of coordinate system will increase for evaluating the performance index. For easy reading, we use HSUAV which stands for our proposed method and RTME and SMHS which stand for the healthcare method in [23] and [24], respectively. In the simulation setup, let speed of the ambulance vehicle of HSUAV, RTME, and SMHS be 2 m/s. The details of the remaining parameters are listed in Table 1.

Table 1: Simulation parameters.

Parameters	values	Parameters	values
(x, y)	(0,0)	α	-30
γ_{HSUAV}	0	β	2
$t_{data\_process}(HSUAV)$	10 s	$t_{data\_process}(RTME)$	10 s
$t_{data\_process}(SMHS)$	100 s	$\theta_{RTME}, \theta_{SMHS}$	2, 4
Q	1Mb	$P_{r,min}$	-100 dBm
t_{wait}	1 ms	r_{TMHC}	1~2
θ_{HSUAV}	1	l_d	100~1000 m
Vc	1Mb/s	Vm	2 m/s
D	100Mb~1000Mb	R	$50\,m$

The simulation results of *first aid response time* and *communication delay* in different healthcare frameworks are given in Figure 3. The first aid response time total time consumption is the best standard metric for different architecture. It is known that, with increase of $_{ld}$, the first aid response time T of the three strategies will be added, as shown in Figure 3(a). However, HSUAV will use less time than RTME and SMHS. When $l_d = 1000$ m, HSUAV can reduce by 30 % and 48 % first aid response time comparing with RTME and SMHS. In other words, in our proposal framework, we can get a higher efficiency for healthcare emergent event.

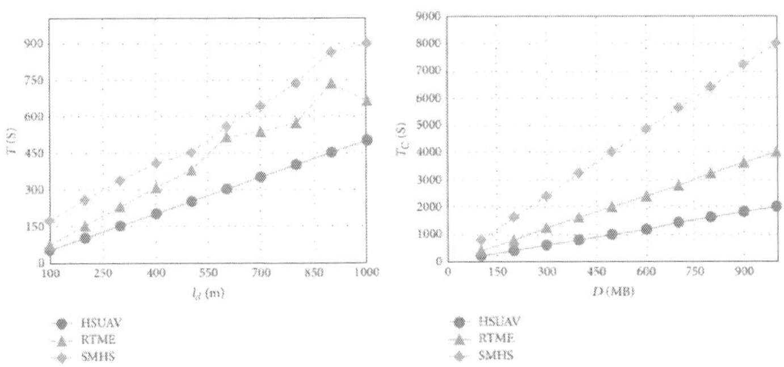

(a) First aid response times

(b) Communication delay in different loads

Figure 3: First aid response times and communication delays in different ways.

Similar performance results of *communication delay* can be observed in Figure 3(b). In general, communication delay of HSUAV, RTME, and SMHS will increase with the rising of transmission data volume. The results in Figure 3(b) indicate that HSUAV has the smaller average time consumption for data delivering. In short, our proposed method outperforms the traditional framework in terms of first aid response time and communication delay.

EXPERIMENT TESTBED

Healthcare UAV Subsystem

The ambulance UAV is used in the platform for reducing the response time. The UAV could directly fly to the emergency site, without being affected by the traffic situation. In order to implement the UAV system, dual-microprogrammed control units (MCUs) are used, as shown in Figure 4. Using PWM (Pulse Width Modulating, PWM), the MCU controls the motor, and propellers. At the same time, air velocity (MS-5611), working current, and voltage could be monitored by corresponding sensors. Further, using the universal asynchronous receiver/transmitter (UART) and serial peripheral interface (SPI), the UAV MCU configures and controls the GPS and wireless communication module for remote controlling (433 MHz DTU).

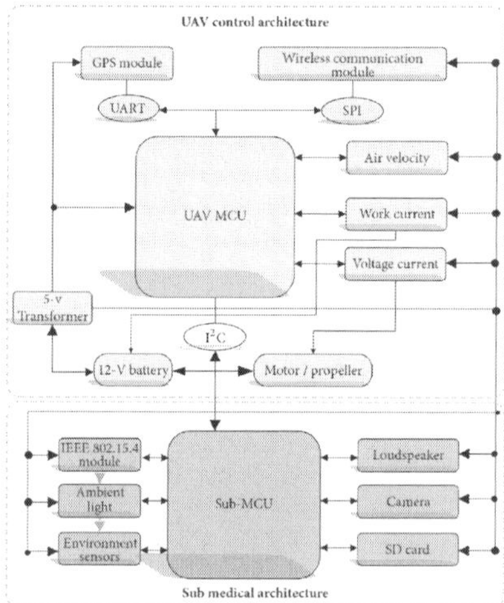

Figure 4: The UAV system hardware architecture.

The sub-MCU connects the UAV MCU using the I2C interface. The sub-MCU accesses the loudspeaker, camera, SD card, ambient light, and environment sensors for the corresponding information. When the UAV flies to the emergency site, the main MCU sends a signal from the site and then the sub-MCU begins to work. At first, the sub-MCU establishes the wireless communication links with the hospital data center and the doctor. Next, some emotional music and conversations will be sent by the program processed in the sub-MCU. Further, the sensing data, images, videos, voice, and other key parameters will be sent to the data center and other related devices.

On the one hand, the sub-MCU could receive the emergency commands from the wireless module. When an emergency command is received by the hospital data sever, after being equipped with corresponding medicine and based on the patient information, the sub-MCU sends the GPS position data to the main UAV MCU. The main UAV MCU will fly to the emergency site. On the other hand, when the UAV arrives at the site, it could transmit the real-time video to hospital, ambulance, and medical workers. Meanwhile, the UAV can play music and sound to alleviate psychological pressure. In some special situations, the doctor could give assisted help by the remote video communication from the hospital. It is important to note that the wireless communication link can be supported by outdoor help system network, Wi-Fi, or LTE.

Implementation of Prototype

In this section, we briefly introduce an effective UAV and IoT-based healthcare service prototype developed for testing in a smart campus use case scenario as shown in Figure 5. This prototype system includes serval smart devices, such as cloud data center, wireless nodes, and display screen. Meanwhile, a four-axis UAV is used as the ambulance UAV. The UAV is equipped with different sensor nodes and devices, such as GPS, wireless modules, and different kinds of sensors. The main UAV MCU is equipped with an 8-bit ATMEGA2560-16AU microcontroller unit with AVR architecture, a 256 KB RAM memory, and a CPU with 16 MHz speed. The sub-MCU board is used for supporting the functions described above. In our ambulance UAV, for reducing the energy consumption, a 32-bit ST STM32F427VIT6 microcontroller unit with ARM Cortex-M4 architecture, a 2048 KB of flash memory, a 256 KB RAM memory, and a CPU with 168 MHz speed are used. Wireless communication capabilities are provided by the IEEE 802.15.4 TI (CC2530) chip with the working frequency of 2.4 GHz. Hence, a simple ZigBee network is established on the campus.

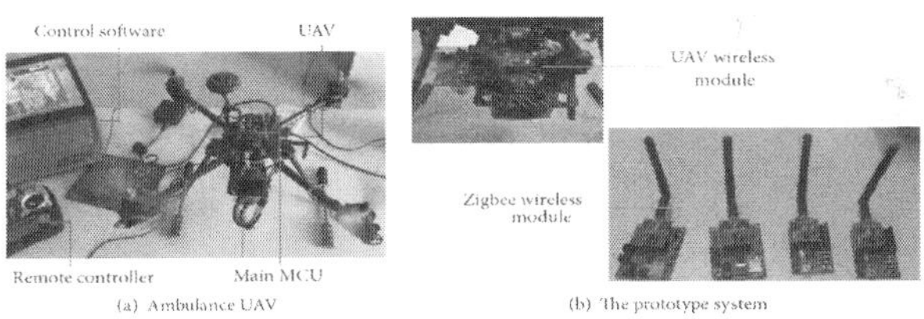

Figure 5: The platform and ambulance UAV.

The smart terminal software is developed based on the android development kit with the android operating system with version 4.5. The emergency situation information and the collected sensory data can be displayed on smart phone by the corresponding application. Figure 6 shows the environmental data and body physiological data captured by various sensors in a visualization chart. Figure 6 shows a set of screenshots of the medical application used on the phone, the application has the option to display GPS position, emergency message, heart-rate, and blood pressure information. Figure 6(a) shows main page of the user terminal, and it includes various parameters such body temperature, heart-rate, location, and environmental data. The histogram of averaging humidity per minute is also displayed as shown in Figure 6(b). Furthermore, the body temperature illustration is shown in Figure 6(c).

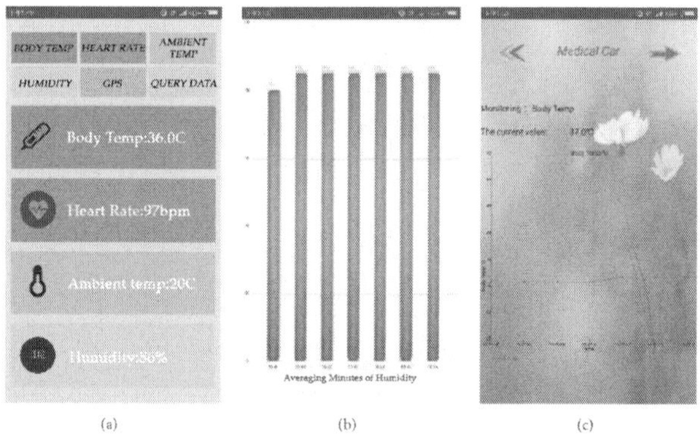

Figure 6: Screenshots of the medical app on the smart phone.

Experiment Results and Analysis

First Aid Reaction Time. For assessing the reaction time performance of our proposed healthcare system, a comparison between the proposed system and other traditional architectures is carried out in our campus. We assumed that the UAV and the traditional medical ambulance have the same speed of 36 Km/h. We choose three different distance points as the emergency sites as shown in Figure 7(a). Figure 7(b) illustrates the comparison result. From the figure, our proposed system can reduce the response time by 20%. Our proposed system has a fast reaction time compared to RTME. Results show that the proposed system outperforms the traditional architectures, which can be easily affected by building, traffic, and road network. However, the UAV could fly directly to destination without any obstacles.

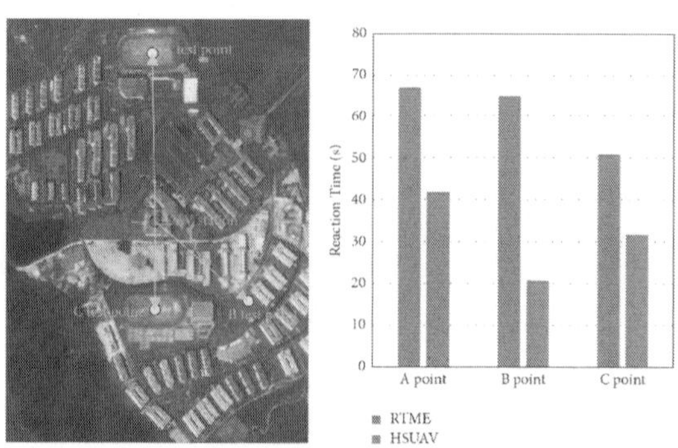

(a) The diagram of experiment location (b) The result of RT for different schemes

Figure 7: Comparison of reaction time for different systems.

CONCLUSION

In this paper, we considered the outdoor healthcare system for senior citizens in emergency situations. For reducing the response time in case of an emergency situation, a healthcare system based on UAV and IoT is designed.

The proposed system can provide real-time help to the senior citizens in outdoor emergency situations with the help of the UAV. Moreover, it can also deliver the emergency information using the communication networks and assist specialist or medical workers.

The proposed system includes four functions: sensing, communication, data processing, and medical aid. Since we used a UAV in the system, the proposed system is a closed loop system.

Moreover, we discussed the communication architecture of the proposed system from the perspective different layers. Finally, a testbed for the outdoor healthcare system has been presented and functional validation and performance validation are presented.

The experimental results show that the proposed system outperforms the traditional emergency care system architectures.

Simulation and experimental results show that the proposed system outperforms the current architectures, which can be easily affected by building, traffic and road network. However, the UAV could fly directly to destination without any obstacles.

Data Availability

The simulation results data and experimental data can be accessed from the website, https://pan.baidu.com/s/1HVw1xZ2VLrpoLW6W8tuskw, or acquired from the corresponding author upon request.

Ethical Approval

All procedures performed in studies involving human participants were in accordance with the ethical standards of the institutional and/or national research committee and with the 1964 Helsinki declaration and its later amendments or comparable ethical standards.

Consent

Informed consent was obtained from all individual participants included in the study.

Conflicts of Interest

The authors declare that they have no conflicts of interest.

ACKNOWLEDGMENTS

This work is supported by the Youth Innovation Project of Important Program for College of Guangdong Province with no. 2015KQNCX228 and Guangzhou Science and Technology Program (no. 201804010427). This work was also partly supported by the colleagues in the Department of Electronic Communication & Software Engineering Nanfang College of Sun Yat-sen University and School of Information Science and Technology, South China Agricultural University.

REFERENCES

1. W. C. Mann, "The aging population and its needs," *IEEE Pervasive Computing*, vol. 3, no. 2, pp. 12–14, 2004.
2. H. M. Holmes, M. S. Beck, and J. H. Rowe, "Geriatrics: Year in review," *Journal of Geriatric Oncology*, vol. 7, no. 5, pp. 404–408, 2016.
3. Y. Li, S. Wang, J. Li et al., "A survey of physicians who care for older persons in Southwest China," *Journal of Nutrition Health Aging*, vol. 17, no. 2, pp. 192–195, 2013.
4. P. A. Laplante, M. Kassab, N. L. Laplante, and J. M. Voas, "Building Caring Healthcare Systems in the Internet of Things," *IEEE Systems Journal*, pp. 1–8, 2017.
5. L. Wan, G. Han, L. Shu, and N. Feng, "The critical patients localization algorithm using sparse representation for mixed signals in emergency healthcare system," *IEEE Systems Journal*, vol. 12, no. 1, pp. 52–63, 2015.
6. B. P. Zeigler, "Discrete Event System Specification Framework for Self-Improving Healthcare Service Systems," *IEEE Systems Journal*, vol. 12, no. 1, pp. 196–207, 2018.
7. Y. Ma, Y. Wang, J. Yang, Y. Miao, and W. Li, "Big Health Application System based on Health Internet of Things and Big Data," *IEEE Access*, vol. 5, pp. 7885–7897, 2017.
8. A. Srivastava, N. Sankar K., B. Chatterjee et al., "Bio-WiTel: A Low-Power Integrated Wireless Telemetry System for Healthcare Applications in 401–406 MHz Band of MedRadio Spectrum," *IEEE Journal of Biomedical and Health Informatics*, vol. 22, no. 2, pp. 483–494, 2018.
9. M. M. Baig, H. GholamHosseini, and M. J. Connolly, "Mobile healthcare applications: system design review, critical issues and challenges," *Australasian Physical & Engineering Sciences in Medicine*, vol. 38, no. 1, pp. 23–38, 2015.
10. J. Wan, C. Zou, S. Ullah, C.-F. Lai, M. Zhou, and X. Wang, "Cloud-Enabled wireless body area networks for pervasive healthcare," *IEEE Network*, vol. 27, no. 5, pp. 56–61, 2013.
11. H. Qi, M. Stojmenovic, K. Li, Z. Li, and W. Qu, "A low transmission overhead framework of mobile visual search based on vocabulary decomposition," *IEEE Transactions on Multimedia*, vol. 16, no. 7, pp.

1963–1972, 2014.

12. Y. Sang, H. Qi, K. Li, Y. Jin, D. Yan, and S. Gao, "An effective discretization method for disposing high-dimensional data," *Information Sciences*, vol. 270, pp. 73–91, 2014. | MathSciNet
13. H. Shieh, C. Huang, F. Lyu, Z. Zhang, and T. Zheng, "An Emergency Care System Using RFID and Zigbee Techniques," in *Proceedings of the 2016 International Symposium on Computer, Consumer and Control (IS3C)*, pp. 65–68, Xi'an, China, July 2016.
14. S. Tewary, S. Chakraborty, J. Majumdar et al., "A novel approach towards designing a wearable Smart Health Monitoring System measuring the vital parameters and emergency situations in real-time and providing the necessary medical care through telemedicine," in *Proceedings of the IEEE Students' Conference on Electrical, Electronics and Computer Science, SCEECS 2016*, pp. 1–8, Bhopal, India, March 2016.
15. R. Pequeno, N. Carvalho, K. Galdino et al., "A Portable System to Support Electrocardiography in Emergency Care," in *Proceedings of the 2015 IEEE 28th International Symposium on Computer-Based Medical Systems (CBMS)*, pp. 256-257, Sao Carlos, Brazil, June 2015.
16. C. Park and J. Kim, "A location and emergency monitoring system for elder care using ZigBee," in *Proceedings of the 2011 7th International Conference on Mobile Ad-hoc and Sensor Networks, MSN 2011*, pp. 367–369, China, December 2011.
17. R. J. Fleischman, M. Lundquist, J. Jui, C. D. Newgard, and C. Warden, "Predicting ambulance time of arrival to the emergency department using global positioning system and Google maps," *Prehospital Emergency Care*, vol. 17, no. 4, pp. 458–465, 2013.
18. M. Chen, Y. Zhang, Y. Li, M. M. Hassan, and A. Alamri, "AIWAC: affective interaction through wearable computing and cloud technology," *IEEE Wireless Communications Magazine*, vol. 22, no. 1, pp. 20–27, 2015.
19. Y. Ma, Y. Zhang, J. Wan, D. Zhang, and N. Pan, "Robot and cloud-assisted multi-modal healthcare system," *Cluster Computing*, vol. 18, no. 3, pp. 1295–1306, 2015.
20. Y. Zhang, M. Qiu, C.-W. Tsai, M. M. Hassan, and A. Alamri, "Health-CPS: Healthcare cyber-physical system assisted by cloud and big data," *IEEE Systems Journal*, vol. 11, no. 1, pp. 88–95, 2015.

21. L. Catarinucci, D. de Donno, L. Mainetti et al., "An IoT-aware architecture for smart healthcare systems," *IEEE Internet of Things Journal*, vol. 2, no. 6, pp. 515–526, 2015.
22. M. Chen, S. Gonzalez, V. Leung, Q. Zhang, and M. Li, "A 2G-RFID-based e-healthcare system," *IEEE Wireless Communications Magazine*, vol. 17, no. 1, pp. 37–43, 2010.
23. M. M. Rathore, A. Ahmad, A. Paul, J. Wan, and D. Zhang, "Real-time Medical Emergency Response System: Exploiting IoT and Big Data for Public Health," *Journal of Medical Systems*, vol. 40, no. 12, article no. 283, 2016.
24. Y. Ren, R. Werner, N. Pazzi, and A. Boukerche, "Monitoring patients via a secure and mobile healthcare system," *IEEE Wireless Communications Magazine*, vol. 17, no. 1, pp. 59–65, 2010.

CHAPTER

11

ESKIN: STUDY ON THE SMARTPHONE APPLICATION FOR EARLY DETECTION OF MALIGNANT MELANOMA

Joanna Jaworek-Korjakowska and Pawel Kleczek

Department of Automatics and Biomedical Engineering, AGH University of Science and Technology, Krakow, Poland

ABSTRACT

Background. Malignant melanoma is among the fastest increasing malignancies in many countries. With the help of new tools, such as teledermoscopy referrals between primary healthcare and dermatology clinics, the diagnosis of these patients could be made more efficient. The introduction of a high-quality smartphone with a built-in digital camera may make the early detection more convenient. This study presents novel

Citation: Buhari S. M., Jaworek-Korjakowska, Joanna K.P., "eSkin: Study on the Smartphone Application for Early Detection of Malignant Melanoma", Journal of Wireless Communications, Vol. 2018, Article ID 5767360, https://doi.org/10.1155/2018/5767360.

directions for early detection of malignant melanoma based on a smartphone application. *Objectives and Methods*. In this study, we concentrate on a precise description of a complex infrastructure of a fully automated computer-aided diagnostic system for early detection of malignant melanoma. The framework has been customized for a dermoscope that is customized to attach to the smartphone to be able to carry out mobile teledermoscopy. The application requirements, architecture, and computational methods as well as behavioral and dynamic aspects have been presented in this paper. *Conclusion*. This paper presents a broad application architecture, which can be easily customized for rapid deployment of a sophisticated health application. Mobile teledermoscopy is a new horizon that might become in the future the basis of the early detection of pigmented skin lesions as a screening tool for primary care doctors and inexperienced dermatologists.

INTRODUCTION

Human cutaneous melanoma, a malignant pigmented lesion, is the deadliest type of skin cancer. It is characterized by a rapidly rising incidence rate among Caucasian populations and every year tens of thousands of people worldwide die of this cancer [1].

Melanoma is among the most aggressive neoplasms and rapidly metastasizes to distant organs. When it progresses to metastatic stage, it establishes powerful mechanisms to resist chemo- and radiotherapy, thus hindering the efficacy of current medical therapies [2]. However, when detected early, melanoma is treatable in nearly all cases with a simple surgical excision [3].

Apart from that, there are also benign types of pigmented skin lesions, the so-called moles that are natural parts of the skin.

Both benign and malignant pigmented skin lesions share similar visual characteristics which makes differentiating between them a challenging problem for nonspecialists [4].

This issue is particularly significant during naked eye examinations, when early stage melanomas (Figure 1(b)) often resembles benign lesions (Figure 1(a)). Due to low public awareness of the importance of skin cancer prevention and insufficient access to dermatologists in many regions of the world, melanoma is often diagnosed only after a tumor grows to a medium size (Figure 1(c)).

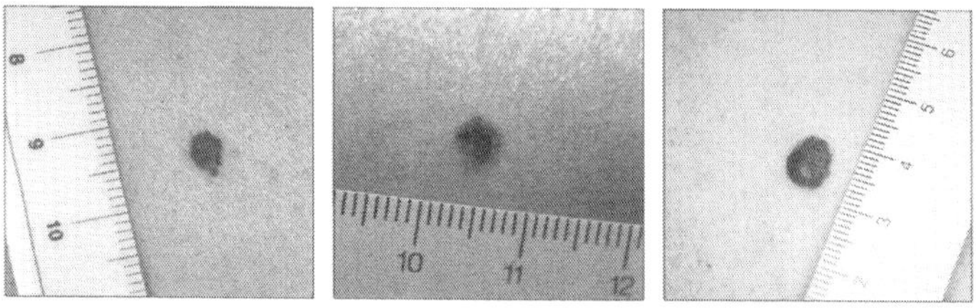

Figure 1: "Naked eye" images of melanocytic lesions [3].

In the light of the above data, prevention and early diagnosis of melanoma become extremely important issues. There is a demand to develop computer-aided diagnostic systems facilitating the early detection of melanoma which could be applied by nonexperts and the general public [5]. Based on our previous research, we propose a teledermoscopy system architecture to assess malignancy of a skin lesion as well as to differentiate between micromelanomas and developed skin moles.

The goal of this research is to provide future plans and directions for the early detection of malignant melanoma based on a smartphone application. We also summarize the state of the art in the teledermoscopy applications and outline our conclusions from previous researches. The article opens with a short introduction to the topic of the undertaken research, a clinical definition of malignant melanoma, and its epidemiology. It continues with a description of the new technology, mobile teledermoscopy (MTD), which has potential for early skin cancer detection and mortality rate reduction. Furthermore, a new robust review of applications for the detection and analysis of melanoma has been described. In Section 2, we describe a new approach to a fully automated computer-aided diagnostic system for early detection of malignant melanoma. The application requirements and architecture as well as behavioral and dynamic aspects are presented. In Section 3, the eSkin application is presented and the early experiments and results are described. In Section 4, the challenges involved in the processing of skin-lesion images acquired with mobile devices and implementation of a patient-oriented system for analyzing such images are outlined.

Clinical Definition

Melanoma (also malignant melanoma) is a malignant neoplasm, derived from cells that are capable of forming melanin, arising most commonly in the skin of any part of the body including eyes or even sore throat. The high concentration of the body's pigmenting agent, melanin, is responsible for their dark color. Although melanocytic nevi are very common, their histogenesis is not well understood and still a matter of debate [3]. All we know about the life of melanocytic nevi is based on cross-sectional or cohort studies, because it is still complicated to monitor skin lesions in vivo on a cellular level. Skin moles may be congenital or developed during lifetime. The majority of moles appear during the first two decades of a person's life.

The congenital melanocytic nevus is more likely to develop into a melanoma, because of its larger size and influence of UV radiation or chemical substances. Smaller melanomas tend to develop sporadically from a pigmented nevus and occur most commonly in fair-skinned people. Any black or brown spot having an irregular border, pigment appearing to radiate beyond that border, blue, red, or white coloration observable on close examination, or a nodular surface is suggestive of melanoma and is usually excised for biopsy [9]. Melanomas are most commonly located on the upper back and lower legs of fair-skinned and on the palms of the hands and insoles of the feet of dark-skinned individuals. Melanomas may metastasize and are among the most malignant of all cancers. Figure 2 shows the stages of melanoma evolution process.

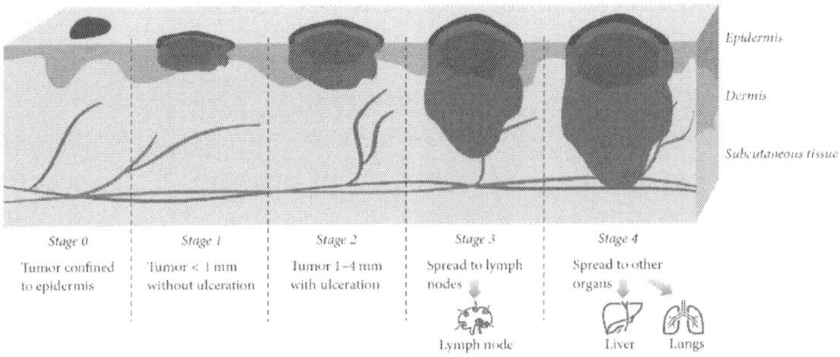

Figure 2: Presentation of five stages in malignant melanoma evolution process. Prognosis depends on the kind of melanoma, its size, and location and depth of invasion.

The most important parameter which predicts the stage of melanoma is the thickness of the examined lesion. Skin moles with the thickness less than 1 mm are nearly 100% curable [3]. Seidenari and coworkers reported the direct correlation between diameter and thickness, and as the diameter of in situ melanomas is smaller than that of invasive lesions, it is reasonable to believe that small melanomas are usually in an initial growth phase [10]. Therefore, the aim of each clinician is to detect malignant melanomas when they are still small and thin. Figure 3 shows dermoscopic images of successive stages of melanoma.

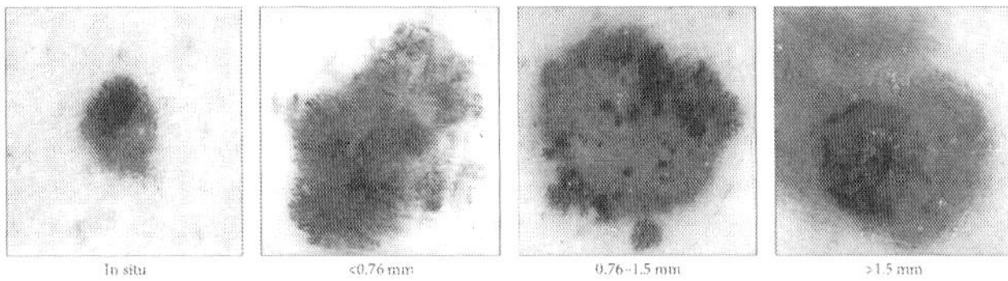

Figure 3: Dermoscopic images of successive stages of melanoma [3].

Epidemiology of Melanoma

Over the past several decades, there has been a significant increase in the incidence and mortality rate from skin cutaneous melanoma among Caucasian populations worldwide (Figure 4) [1]. Despite the fact that only about 4% of all diagnosed skin cancers are melanoma, melanoma is responsible for about 70% of skin cancer-related deaths in the United States and in Australia [11, 12]. Invasive melanoma has an estimated incidence of 73,870 and an estimated total of 9940 deaths in the United States in 2015 [13].

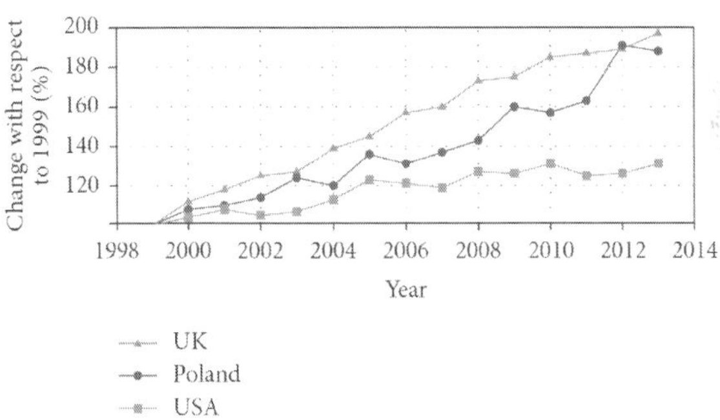

Figure 4: The increase in incidence rate of skin melanoma observed in UK, Poland, and USA between 1999 and 2013 [6–8]. The incidence rate reported in 1999 has been set as a point of reference.

One of the most important factors considered to result in melanoma is the brief, intense sun exposure pattern. Due to a constant depletion of ozone layer in stratosphere, which results in higher exposure to UV radiation, malignant melanoma is likely to become one of the most common malignant tumors in the future, with even 2–10 times higher incidence rate [1, 3]. As no effective treatment of melanoma in advanced stages has been developed so far, its early diagnosis has become an extremely important issue.

Improving Melanoma Detection Based on Sensing Technologies

Telemedicine which is also called telehealth, online health, e-health, or "medicine at a distance" is a new and rapidly developing field of medicine, providing access to medical knowledge that would be not available at a particular location and time. It is commonly defined as the use of telecommunication technologies for the exchange of medical information over a distance for the purpose of patient management (including triage, diagnosis, and therapeutic suggestions, as well as follow-up) and medical education [14]. Teledermatology has been listed in Norway among priority telemedicine specialities for large-scale implementation underlining the growing interest in this field [14, 15].

The most important question that has to be posed while supporting the early skin cancer detection is *does the teledermoscopy system achieve an adequate accuracy and is it effective?* In this research, we will analyze only two factors including diagnostic reliability and accuracy as well as economic analysis. With no doubt, the most significant parameter while using any computer-aided diagnosis system is the diagnostic reliability and accuracy which have to be compared between the diagnostic system and conventional method (human interpretation) [16]. Diagnostic accuracy assessments for dermatologic disease are still problematic. The histopathological examination constitutes the gold standard for classifying a melanocytic skin lesion as malignant. Although there exist other forms of examination (e.g., dermatoscopy), they yield lower diagnostic confidence than a histopathological examination. Still, numerous studies showed that the misdiagnosis rate of melanoma may be as high as 10–25%. Histopathologic review cannot be universally used to make a definitive diagnosis of all skin lesions. Despite this, few studies have analyzed data among patients that underwent biopsy and other diagnostic methods which made it possible to compare the teledermatology systems with the clinic-based examination [16–18]. Teledermatology systems achieved accuracy at about 70–85% which indicates that the computer-based solutions have comparable diagnostic accuracy when compared to conventional clinic-based care [16]. While implementing and deploying a teledermatology system, the economic aspects play an important role. The following criteria are taken into account: dermatology visits that have been avoided, skin biopsies skipped, and consult costs. In study [19], authors have evaluated the proportion of real-time interactive teledermatology consults that avoided a clinic-based visit to a dermatologist. Dermatology clinic visits have been avoided in 54%

thanks to the real-time interactive teledermatology. Also the decrease of the number of biopsies is a cost-saving strategy. Based on a quick evaluation of the dermoscopy image, inexperienced physicians will gain knowledge and avoid unnecessary treatment.

Related Works

According to the estimates by the American Food and Drug Administration, nearly 500 million smartphone users worldwide use eHealth mobile applications. In July 2014, there were 39 dermatology-related mobile applications aimed at general community, patient, and generalist clinician users available on the market [20]. The main functionality of over half of them was to provide information or education about melanoma, UV radiation exposure prevention advice, and skin self-examination strategies. Such applications are usually targeted at students and novice doctors. Another large group of applications were those capable of taking images of moles using mobile embedded camera, tagging them with the body location, and storing them either for review by a dermatologist or for self-monitoring to track changes in mole appearance, an important predictor of melanoma.In March 2017, there were over 45 mobile applications related to mole diagnosis available on Apple's App Store alone. Most of them (n=28) offered only educational information on melanoma, nearly half of them (n=17) allowed the user to take photos of their moles and track changes over time using simple visual comparison, and only four applications performed melanoma risk assessment or lesion classification based on image analysis (Table 1).

Table 1: A summary of mobile applications for melanoma risk assessment and diagnosis available on App Store in March 2017.

Application	Main functionality	Image analysis method
DermaCompare	Risk assessment	Image matching
Lūbax	Mole diagnosis	Content-based image retrieval
MySkinApp	Risk assessment	Unknown
SkinVision	Risk assessment	Fractal analysis

Only the authors of SkinVision and Lūbax made public the results of clinical evaluation of their risk assessment algorithm [21, 22]. Out of 4 applications summarized in Table 1, only two were certified by authorities: SkinVision received the European "CE" Marking and DermaCompare was approved by the US Food and Drug Administration.

SkinVision

The risk assessment algorithm used by SkinVision is based on the analysis of a gray-scale image of a lesion (I_G) and its associated fractal map I_{FM}. The fractal map is generated based on the weighted local fractal dimension (WLFD) proposed in [23] (the WLFD was originally used for computer tomography image enhancement, but authors of SkinVision adapted it to the context of dermatoscopy). To segment the lesion (and thus extract the lesion contour), threshold t_G and t_{FM} were obtained by applying Otsu's thresholding on I_G and I_{FM}, respectively. The following parameters are calculated on I_{FM}: percentage of pixels with WLFD lower than $t_{FM}/3$, percentage of pixels with WLFD lower than $t_{FM}/2$, number of connected regions with distinct textures found in the interval $[0, t_{FM}/2]$, and t_{FM}, and the following are calculated on I_G: number of connected regions with distinct intensities found in the interval $[0, t_{FM}/2]$, t_G, and circularity index. Based on these parameters, the SkinVision application evaluates lesions to one of the three risk classes: high, medium, or low.

SkinVision was tested on a set of melanocytic lesions images taken using iPhone 4S mobile device equipped with an 8-megapixel autofocus camera. It achieved the overall sensitivity of 73%, specificity of 83%, and accuracy of 81%. The positive and negative predictive values were 49% and 83%, respectively.

Lūbax

The skin-lesion classification system used by Lūbax consists of a proprietary database of nearly 12,000 images of diagnosed lesions and a computer algorithm based on the principles of content-based image retrieval (the algorithm compares characteristics of new images with images in the database to identify the nearest-match diagnosis).

The lesion images were taken using Celestron® (Torrance, CA) hand-held digital microscopes equipped with 2-megapixel cameras with a macro lens surrounded by a ring of white light-emitting diode lights. The consistent lighting conditions and imaging distance were ensured by attaching an opaque 10 cm tube to the front of each camera. The largest diameter for all nonmelanoma and melanoma lesions was at least 10 mm.

Each lesion image in the database was reviewed and diagnosed by at least one of three board-certified dermatologists using standard clinical criteria. The "ground truth" classification was not biopsy-proven, but based on the agreement between the reviewing dermatologists. Only 302 images of melanoma borrowed from the DermNet NZ [24] database were previously confirmed by histopathology.

The algorithm compares new images of skin lesions with the database of diagnosed skin-lesion images. It uses orientation- and artifact-independent image information on lesion size, color, shape, and texture to create a single high-dimensional signature for each image. The "malignant versus nonmalignant" classification is then performed using a k-nearest-neighbor classifier.

Lūbax was evaluated on a set of 337 images queried from the database, out of which 208 were melanomas. It scored sensitivity of 90.4%, specificity of 91.5%, and accuracy of 90.8%. The positive and negative predictive values were 94.5% and 85.5%, respectively.

DEVELOPMENT OF THE ESKIN TELEDERMATOSCOPY SYSTEM

Based on the above information, there is still a great need in the development and analysis of teledermatoscopy systems. In this paper, we propose a new approach to the analysis of nonmelanoma and melanoma lesions. The innovation is firstly based on the differentiation between micromelanomas which have diameter less than 5 mm and advanced skin moles. Secondly, we propose an additional algorithm for the skin-lesion differentiation that can be applied in a teledermoscopy system and has been described in our work [25]. In this section, we present the system overview and describe the technical requirements, application architecture, and behavioral and dynamic aspects of the system.

Concept of the System

The purpose of presenting the concept of the system is its better illustration and description of the relationships between the individual modules of the system. While composing the system, overview issues such as safe medical information transfer, fast connection availability, server choice, and database type are analyzed. Figure 5 presents the implemented concept of a system that consists of a smartphone application available to the client (client side) and the server side of the system, consisting of a general-purpose server, computing server, user's database, and images database.

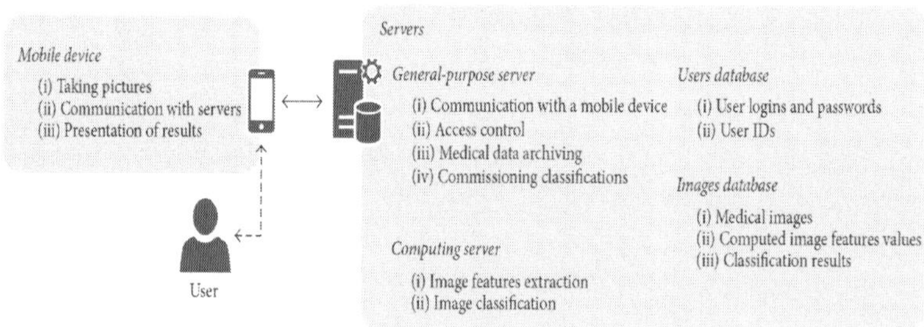

Figure 5: The concept diagram of the proposed system.

Application Requirement Specification

The most important piece of hardware is a high-quality camera system. Certain dermoscopic features of a lesion, such as pigment network or dots, are clearly visible only under magnification (usually of at least ×10). Moreover, since colors visible in a lesion are important diagnostic clues, it is desirable to take images in appropriate illumination conditions.

Most modern smartphone cameras (this is true, e.g., for all iPhone devices starting from iPhone 5S and all Samsung Galaxy devices starting from Samsung Galaxy S4) are equipped with at least 8-megapixel sensor whose pixel size is at most 1.5 μm, allowing the user to capture high-quality photos. However, smartphone cameras generally lack a quality optical zoom and are not equipped in a source of white light which would uniformly illuminate an examined lesion.

The solution to the above-mentioned deficiencies of bare smartphones is to use either a smartphone dermatoscope or a conventional dermatoscope with a mobile phone case (Figures 6 and 7). A smartphone dermatoscope is an attachment for dermoscopy that provides a detailed view of the skin through magnification and specialized lighting. Most smartphone dermatoscopes currently available on the market provide ×10 to ×40.magnification, work in both polarized and nonpolarized lighting modes, and are capable of performing examinations in both contact and noncontact mode. Some conventional dermatoscopes may be attached to a mobile phone using a special case (e.g., all dermatoscopes from 3Gen's DermLite and Canfield's VEOS series may be used with iPhone 5 and newer and 3Gen's DermLite and MoleScope products can be used with Samsung Galaxy S4 and newer).

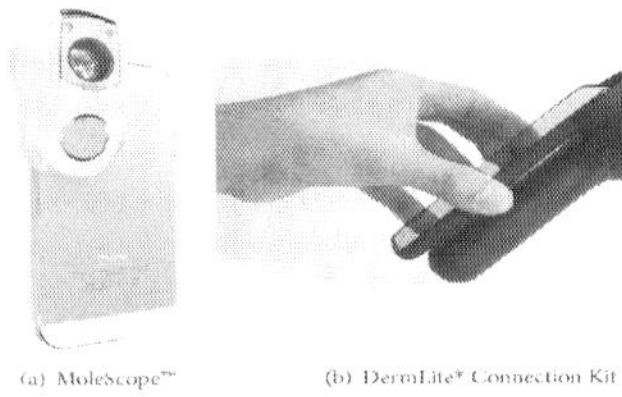

Figure 6: Examples of smartphone dermatoscopy solutions for an iPhone: (a) a smartphone dermatoscope; (b) a conventional dermatoscope attached to a smartphone in a case.

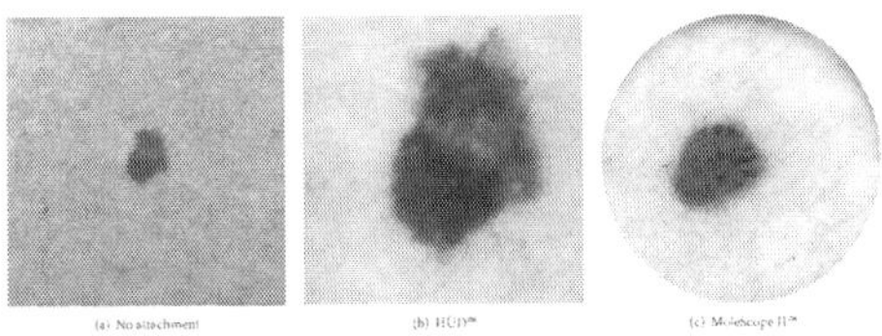

Figure 7: The comparison of the qualities of pictures taken with (a) a bare smartphone and (b, c) a smartphone equipped with a dermatoscopic attachment.

Application Architecture

Like any other complex system, software and essentially medical applications have to be built on solid foundations. During the smartphone application design process, it is important to define a structured solution that meets all of the technical and operational requirements, while optimizing common quality attributes such as performance, security, and manageability. The process involves a series of decisions based on a wide range of factors, and each of these decisions can have considerable impact on the quality, performance, maintainability, and overall success of the application [26]. The proposed system consists of two parts: mobile application and servers (Figure 8).

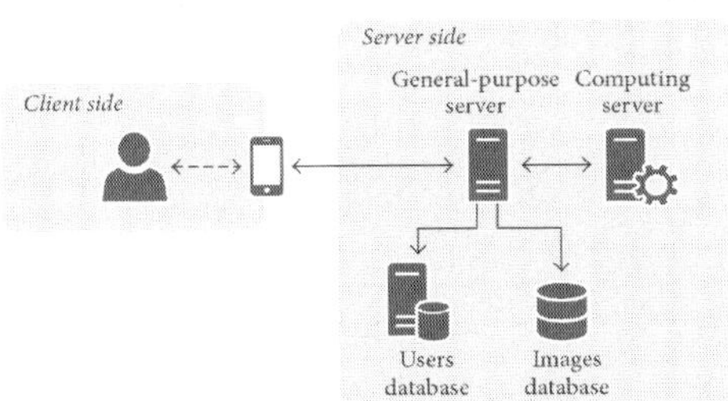

Figure 8: The system architecture diagram of the proposed system.

The tasks of the mobile application include the following:(i)Friendly user interface with the ability to log in and change basic settings(ii)The ability to take a picture of a skin mole or select from already saved pictures on the smartphone(iii)Presentation of results of classification of selected skin mole(iv)User location for UV hazard rating(v)Communication with servers including general-purpose server, image database, user database, and computing server(vi)Checking the Internet connection and data security.

The tasks performed by the server include the following:(i) Communication with the user mobile device *(general server task)*(ii)User login (username and password verification) and access control *(general server and user database task)*(iii)Calculation of feature parameters, image classification, and comparison of ratings *(computing server task)*(iv) Medical data archiving (medical images, computed skin mole parameters, and classification results) *(image and user database task)*.

Behavioral and Dynamic Aspects of the System

The activity diagram of the proposed mobile application, capturing its dynamic behavior, is shown in Figure 9. The main functionality of the application is to take photos of moles and send them to the server in order to perform melanoma risk assessment. It is also capable of archiving captured photos and browsing through past examinations. Additional features, intended to rise melanoma awareness, include ultraviolet radiation risk alerts, reminders about a subsequent examination, and a tool to easily find the nearest dermatologist.

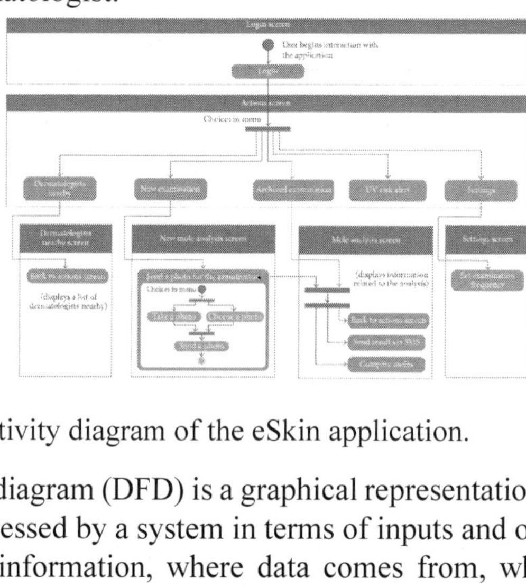

Figure 9: The activity diagram of the eSkin application.

A data flow diagram (DFD) is a graphical representation of the "flow" of how data is processed by a system in terms of inputs and outputs. It focuses on the flow of information, where data comes from, where it goes, and how it gets stored. It is a picture of the movement of data between external entities and the processes and data stores within a system. Figure 10 presents the proposed DFD diagram. A DFD diagram consists of external entities, processes, and data stores:(i)*External entities*: origin or destination of data (outside the system): user (mobile application), computing server, and general-purpose server(ii)*Processes*: work or action performed on data: image evaluation, authentication, image storage, and subcontract image evaluation(iii)*Data stores*: data that the system stores: users' database and images' database.

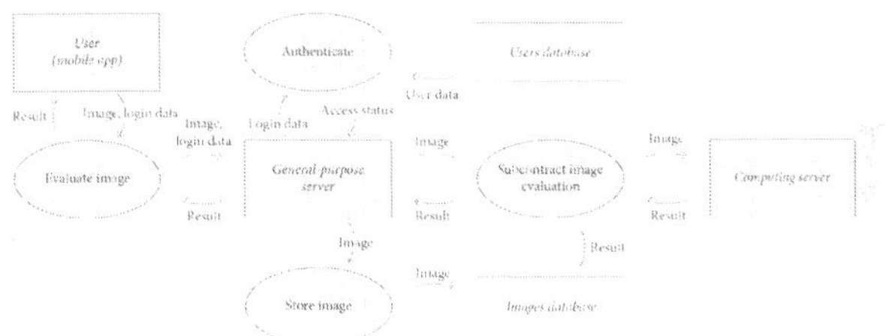

Figure 10: The data flow diagram of the proposed mobile application.

Computational Methods

Analysis and classification of melanoma skin lesions are a complex issue due to the different appearance on various levels of disease progression. Our recent research and experience in the topic of early detection of melanoma have shown that different approach to the classification process should be undertaken to improve the recognition results. The implemented and tested computer-aided diagnostic system has been presented in Figure 11. The first two steps including image preprocessing and segmentation are performed for each of the analyzed medical pictures.

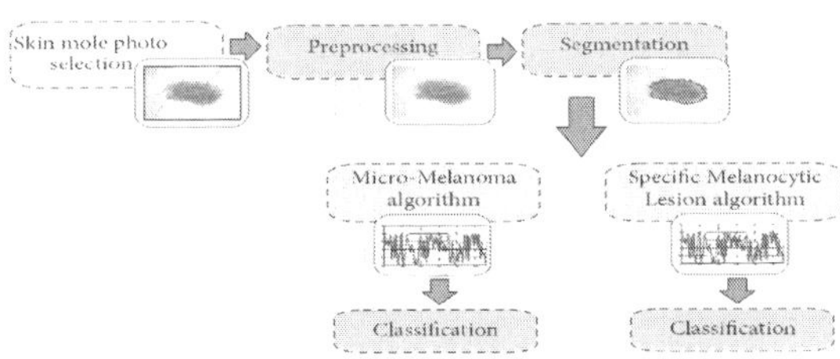

Figure 11: The schema of the implemented and tested computer-aided diagnostic system.

The preprocessing step is essential for dermoscopic images to improve the quality due to the extraneous artifacts, such as skin lines, air bubbles, and hairs which appear in almost every image. The preprocessing step contains three algorithms [27, 28]:(i)Black frame removal: black frames, introduced to the image during its digitization, are detected using lightness component of the HSL color space.(ii)Smoothing: Gaussian filter is used for smoothing of air bubbles and light hairs.(iii)Black hair inpainting: for removing black and thick hairs, we chose the white top-hat transform. Hair line pixels are replaced with values calculated on the basis of the neighborhood pixels.

A medical image is one of most complicated images to be segmented; furthermore, this step is crucial for sequential analysis and diagnosis. During our work, we have compared different segmentation methods and on the grounds of the previous outcomes the applied segmentation algorithm for the skin-lesion extraction is based on seeded region-growing algorithm [29, 30].

After the first two steps, the segmented skin mole is ordered to one of the two classification algorithms. The division is done on the basis of the mole diameter. Skin moles with a diameter lower than 5 mm are passed to the *Micro-Melanoma algorithm* and the remaining ones to the *Specific Melanocytic Lesion algorithm*.

The diameter of the lesion is provided by the user as it is not possible to assess it only based on the medical image. Micromelanomas represent a minority of diagnosed lesions, their frequency ranging from 1% to 17%. The mean diameter of in situ melanomas is around 1 cm, and invasive melanomas are usually greater than 6 mm. Despite the fact that micromelanomas are in the minority, they are responsible for most errors during the diagnosis. Separation of individual changes allows us to obtain a more accurate and reliable computer diagnosis system. The *Micro-Melanoma algorithm* and the *Specific Melanocytic Lesion algorithm* have been described in detail in [25, 28].

EARLY EXPERIMENTS

We implemented the application on an iOS smartphone, which most of the people in US use in their daily lives. This small smartphone includes all sensors that can provide enough information needed for realizing this system. The preliminary version of the eSkin application has been implemented in Swift in the Xcode development environment which is dedicated for macOS and contains a suite of software development tools for macOS, iOS, watchOS, and tvOS. Figure 12 presents the proposed version of the graphical user interface. The basic functionality including taking a medical photo and assessing the skin mole as well as medical data archiving have been implemented.

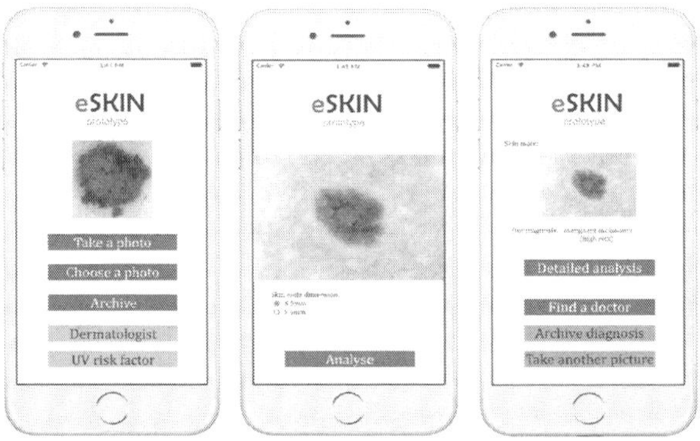

Figure 12: The proposed version of the graphical user interface.

The eSkin application uses a scientifically proven algorithm to detect and analyze the dermoscopy images for visible signs of skin cancer. To measure the diagnostic performance, we calculated sensitivity, specificity, and the area under that plot curve (AUC). The fundamental definitions of these performance measures could be illustrated as follows.

The sensitivity (also called True Positive rate) is the probability that the cell is said to be adherent given that it is.

This can be estimated by relative frequency: where TP is the True Positive answer and FP is the False Negative answer. The value of sensitivity ranges between 0 and 1, where 0 and 1, respectively, mean worst and best classification.

Specificity (also called False Positive rate), which is defined as the proportion of the True Negatives against all negative results, is defined by the following equation: where TN is the True Negative answer and FN is the False Negative answer. Value of specificity ranges between 0 and 1, where 0 and 1, respectively, mean worst and best classification.

Table 2 shows the classification results obtained with the implemented algorithms for microlesions as well as developed skin moles.

Table 2: A summary of the classification results for the medical algorithms.

Medical diagnosis	TPR [%]	TNR [%]	AUC [%]
Micromelanoma lesions	90	96	93
Blue nevus	100	100	100
Clark nevus	91	96	98
Malignant melanoma	86	96	97
Spitz nevus	94	98	98

For statistical analysis, SkinVision classified histologically proven nevi as low or medium risk and melanoma as high-risk lesion. The statistics included 144 lesions (with a minimum of 3 images per lesion) with the following histological diagnosis: 84 benign nevi (58%), 34 dysplastic nevi (24%), and 26 melanomas (18%).

Images of poor quality (e.g., due to inappropriate imaging angle or distance) and containing other elements not belonging to the lesion (e.g., hair), as well as cases with an equal number of results in two consecutive risk classes (e.g., 1 high risk, 1 medium risk, and 1 low risk result), were excluded from the analysis. In total, 26% of the images initially taken have been dismissed due to improper imaging.

The sensitivity of the SkinVision melanoma detection algorithm compared to the histological result was 73%, the specificity 83%, and the accuracy 81%.

The performance of the melanoma detection algorithm by Lūbax was assessed on a set of 337 images randomly selected from their database. The set included 129 images of nonmelanoma lesions and 208 images of melanoma lesions, all with the largest diameter of at least 10 mm. All melanoma query images were selected from the set of images acquired from DermNet NZ to ensure confirmation of the malignancy by histopathology.

The sensitivity of the Lūbax melanoma detection algorithm was 90%, the specificity 91%, and the accuracy 91%. For the melanoma classification, the sensitivity of the SkinVision algorithm compared to the histological result was 73%, the specificity 83%, and the accuracy 81%.

The conducted results achieved by the implemented classification system are much better than the results described in similar works. Our method allowed classification of skin moles very precisely and we can confirm that the classification of micro-skin lesions has to be done separately from the classification of developed skin moles. Overall, our experiments clearly show that the classification can be supported by a powerful system based on advanced machine learning techniques.

CONCLUSIONS AND DISCUSSION

In this paper, we propose a new teledermatology system for melanoma diagnosis, based on our previous research on assessing malignancy of a skin lesion as well as on differentiating between micromelanomas and developed skin moles. Our system is built in a client-server architecture and is intended for smartphone users.

In our system, the main functionality of the client application is to take photos of moles and send them to the server in order to perform melanoma risk assessment. By shifting all computations related to image assessment to the dedicated servers, we may analyze dermoscopic images using computationally demanding algorithms. Since the medical data would be archived in a central database, they would provide invaluable aid when working on improvements to the diagnostic algorithm. The client-server architecture would also make the process of implementing changes to the assessment algorithms seamless for the users, since there would be no need for client software updates.

To ensure high quality of images and good visibility of certain dermoscopic features of a lesion, the system is designed to work with smartphone dermatoscopes or conventional dermatoscopes with a mobile phone case. Such a solution would also reduce the negative impact of taking images in appropriate illumination conditions and make it possible to avoid issues with determining the size of a lesion. The latter issue is of particular importance, since our recent research has shown that depending on the size of a lesion different diagnostic algorithms should be used to improve the recognition results.

Although the client side of our system was initially developed for iOS devices, it does not use any functionality specific to either iOS or Apple's smartphones. Therefore, it could easily be ported to work with devices running the Android operating system.Due to low public awareness of the importance of skin cancer prevention and insufficient access to dermatologists in many regions of the world, there is a demand to develop computer-aided diagnostic systems facilitating the early detection of melanoma which could be applied by nonexperts. However, as of March 2017, there were only four mobile applications performing melanoma risk assessment or lesion classification based on image analysis available to the general public. With teledermatology systems achieving accuracy up to 85%, comparable to conventional clinic-based care, we are convinced that our system would fulfill that demand and allow its users to avoid dermatology visits, to skip skin biopsies, and to cut costs of consultations.

Conflicts of Interest

The authors declare that there are no conflicts of interest regarding the publication of this paper.

ACKNOWLEDGMENTS

This scientific work was supported by AGH University of Science and Technology research grant on Decision nos. 15.11.120.883 and 15.11.120.635 to J. Jaworek-Korjakowska.

REFERENCES

1. C. Garbe and U. Leiter, "Melanoma epidemiology and trends," *Clinics in Dermatology*, vol. 27, no. 1, pp. 3–9, 2009.
2. M. Campioni, D. Santini, G. Tonini et al., "Role of Apaf-1, a key regulator of apoptosis, in melanoma progression and chemoresistance," *Experimental Dermatology*, vol. 14, no. 11, pp. 811–818, 2005.
3. G. Argenziano, P. H. Soyer, V. D. Giorgio et al., *Interactive Atlas of Dermoscopy*, Edra Medical Publishing and New Media, 2000.
4. K. Korotkov and R. Garcia, "Computerized analysis of pigmented skin lesions: a review," *Artificial Intelligence in Medicine*, vol. 56, no. 2, pp. 69–90, 2012.
5. R. Tadeusiewicz, "How intelligent should be system for image analysis?" in *Innovations in Intelligent Image Analysis*, H. Kwaśnicka and L. C. Jain, Eds., vol. 339 of *Studies in Computational Intelligence*, pp. V–X, Springer Verlag, Berlin, Heidelberg, 2011.
6. *englishSkin Cancer Incidence Trends over Time*, Cancer Research UK, 2016.
7. "Zachorowania i zgony na nowotwory złos'liwe w polsce, Krajowy Rejestr Nowotworów, Centrum Onkologii, Instytut im. Marii Skłodowskiej-Curie, 2016".
8. *Seer stat fact sheets: Melanoma of the skin*, National Cancer Institute, 2016.
9. *Mosby's Medical Dictionary*, Elsevier, 10th edition, 2016.
10. S. Seidenari, C. Ferrari, S. Borsari et al., "Dermoscopy of small melanomas: just miniaturized dermoscopy?" *British Journal of Dermatology*, vol. 171, no. 5, pp. 1006–1013, 2014.
11. *Cancer Facts & Figures 2016*, American Cancer Society, 2016.
12. Australian Bureau of Statistics, *Causes of Death, Australia 2015*, 2016.
13. M. E. Celebi, J. S. Marques, and T. Mendonca, *Dermoscopy image analysis*, CRC Press LLC, 1st edition, 2016.
14. E. M. T. Wurm, H. P. Soyer, and A. C. Smith, *Telemedicine in Dermatology*, Springer-Verlag, Berlin, Germany, 1st edition, 2012.
15. J. Norum, S. Pedersen, J. Størmer et al., "Prioritisation of telemedicine services for large scale implementation in Norway," *Journal of Telemedicine and Telecare*, vol. 13, no. 4, pp. 185–192, 2007.

16. J. D. Whited, H. S. Pak, and K. E. Edison, *Teledermatology: A User's Guide*, Cambridge University Press, Cambridge, UK, 2008.
17. J. D. Whited, R. P. Hall, D. L. Simel et al., "Reliability and accuracy of dermatologists clinic-based and digital image consultations," *Journal of the American Academy of Dermatology*, vol. 41, no. 5, pp. 693–702, 1999.
18. S. Markun, N. Scherz, T. Rosemann, R. Tandjung, and R. P. Braun, "Mobile teledermatology for skin cancer screening: A diagnostic accuracy study," *Medicine*, vol. 96, no. 10, p. e6278, 2017.
19. R. Wootton, M. A. Loane, S. E. Bloomer et al., "Multicentre randomised control trial comparing real time teledermatology with conventional outpatient dermatological care: Societal cost-benefit analysis," *British Medical Journal*, vol. 320, no. 7244, pp. 1252–1256, 2000.
20. A. P. Kassianos, J. D. Emery, P. Murchie, and F. M. Walter, "Smartphone applications for melanoma detection by community, patient and generalist clinician users: A review," *British Journal of Dermatology*, vol. 172, no. 6, pp. 1507–1518, 2015.
21. T. Maier, D. Kulichova, K. Schotten et al., "Accuracy of a smartphone application using fractal image analysis of pigmented moles compared to clinical diagnosis and histological result," *Journal of the European Academy of Dermatology and Venereology*, vol. 29, no. 4, pp. 663–667, 2015.
22. R. H. Chen, M. Snorrason, S. M. Enger et al., "Validation of a Skin-Lesion Image-Matching Algorithm Based on Computer Vision Technology," *Telemedicine and e-Health*, vol. 22, no. 1, pp. 45–50, 2016.
23. A. Udrea, M. Tanase, and D. Popescu, "Nonlinear deterministic methods for computer aided diagnosis in case of kidney diseases," in *Proceedings of the 9th International Conference on Informatics in Control, Automation and Robotics (ICINCO '12)*, J. Ferrier et al., Ed., 516, pp. 31–511, SciTe Press, 2012.
24. DermNet NZ, *The dermatology resource*, https://www.dermnetnz.org/.
25. J. Jaworek-Korjakowska and P. Kłeczek, "Automatic classification of specific melanocytic lesions using artificial intelligence," *BioMed Research International*, vol. 2016, Article ID 8934242, 17 pages, 2016.
26. Patterns and Practices Developer Center, *What is software architecture?* 2009.

27. J. Jaworek-Korjakowska and R. Tadeusiewicz, "Hair removal from dermoscopic color images," *Bio-Algorithms and Med-Systems*, vol. 9, no. 2, pp. 53–58, 2013.
28. J. Jaworek-Korjakowska, "Computer-aided diagnosis of micro-malignant melanoma lesions applying support vector machines," *BioMed Research International*, vol. 2016, Article ID 4381972, 8 pages, 2016.
29. J. Jaworek-Korjakowska, "Novel method for border irregularity assessment in dermoscopic color images," *Computational and Mathematical Methods in Medicine*, vol. 2015, Article ID 496202, 11 pages, 2015.
30. J. Jaworek-Korjakowska, *Detection and analysis of local structures in malignant melanoma [Ph.D. thesis]*, AGH University of Science and Technology in Krakow, 2013.

CHAPTER

12

COMPACT MICROSTRIP LOWPASS FILTER WITH LOW INSERTION LOSS FOR UWB MEDICAL APPLICATIONS

Mohammed A. Aseeri,[1] Meshaal A. Alyahya,[1] Hatim A. Bukhari,[1] and Hussein N. Shaman[1]

National Centre for Sensors and Defense Systems Technologies (NCSDST), King Abdulaziz City for Science and Technology (KACST), Riyadh 11442, Saudi Arabia

ABSTRACT

A microstrip lowpass filter based on transmission line elements for UWB medical applications is proposed in this paper. The filter is constructed of two symmetric shunt open-circuited stubs and three series unit elements. The filter is designed to exhibit an elliptic function response with equal ripple in

---

Citation: Buhari S. M., Aseeri M. A., Alyahya M. A., Bukhari A., Shaman N., "Compact Microstrip Lowpass Filter with Low Insertion Loss for UWB Medical Applications", Journal of Wireless Communications, Vol. 2018, Article ID 8430626, https://doi.org/10.1155/2018/8430626.

the passband and the rejection band. A prototype is successfully designed, fabricated, and measured, where a good agreement is attained. The filter shows a high filtering selectivity and an ultra-wide stopband up to 20 GHz with an attenuation level of more than 20-dB. The filter is compact and has a low insertion loss and an ultra-wideband (UWB) rejection which makes it attractive for many technologies such as UWB medical applications.

INTRODUCTION

Ultra-wideband (UWB) technology has several features which makes it suitable for the application of medical monitoring such as penetrating through obstacles, high precision ranging at the centimeter level, low electromagnetic radiation, and low processing energy consumed. These monitoring applications could be patient motion monitoring, wireless vital signs monitoring of human body, and the medicine storage monitoring. One of the primary passive components of the UWB systems is lowpass filter which is necessary for blocking unwanted signals and suppressing spurious harmonics.

Lowpass planer filters with sharp roll-off, wide stopband, compact circuit size, and low insertion loss are in high demand in modern wireless communication systems and military radar receiver systems for blocking unwanted signals and suppressing spurious harmonics. A general common microstrip structure of lowpass filter is using high and low impedance (stepped-impedance) transmission lines which is known as stepped-impedance lowpass filter [1]. This type of filter has simple design methodology but it exhibits a poor skirt selectivity and a very low attenuation level at the rejection band. In order to improve the filter performance at the stopband, the low-impedance line can be replaced with a quarter guided wavelength open-circuited stub [2]. The open-circuited stub shorts can out the transmission at the resonant frequency and therefore a wider rejection band with a transmission zero can be obtained. Alternatively, a longitudinal slot can be implemented in the ground plane of a stepped-impedance filter to enhance its performance [3]. Due to the slow-wave effect of the slot-back microstrip line, the filter can exhibit a wider stopband and a sharper cut-off compared with the conventional filter. Other techniques can also be used to enhance the performance of the stepped-impedance filters such as stepped-impendence hairpin resonators [4, 5], folded stepped-impedance resonators [6], defected ground-plane structures (DGS) slot [7–12], and interdigital or semicircle defected ground-plane structures (DGS) [13, 14].

In addition, various methods and structure have been developed to enhance the performance of microstrip lowpass filters such as using circular-shaped patches and open stubs [15], rat-race directional couplers [16], stepped-impedance spiral resonator [17], combination of DGSs and a transformed radial stub (TRS) [18], T-shaped microstrip resonator cells [19], and coupled-line stub-loaded hairpin unit [20] and triangular and radial patch resonators [21].Lowpass filter can also be designed using distributed elements such as open-circuited stubs and unit elements [2]. This type of filter has spurious harmonics and therefore, it requires more elements to enhance its performance. Alternatively, a cross-coupling can be introduced between the input/output feed lines to allow the filter to exhibit additional transmission zeros at the rejection band [22]. This proposed filter can be used in many technologies such as UWB medical applications [23].A compact lowpass filter with an elliptic function response and a very wide rejection band is introduced in this paper. The filter is constructed of three series unit elements and two shunt open-circuited stubs. The filter is designed to provide an equal ripple in the passband and the rejection band. It is designed to have a passband with a sharp selectivity and an ultra-wide stopband. The proposed designed is implemented on a microstrip substrate and fabricated using printed-circuited-board (PCB). The filter design, analysis, and measurement results are demonstrated in detail.

FILTER DESIGN

The 3-dimensional view of the microstrip design of the proposed filter is shown in Figure 1 and Figure 2 illustrates its transmission line equivalent circuit model. The filter is comprised of two symmetric shunt open-circuited stubs, with a characteristic impedance of Z_s, separated by three series unit elements or connecting lines with characteristic impedances of Z_1 and Z_2. The open-circuited stub has an electrical length of θ_s while the electrical lengths of the unit elements are described by θ_1 and θ_2.

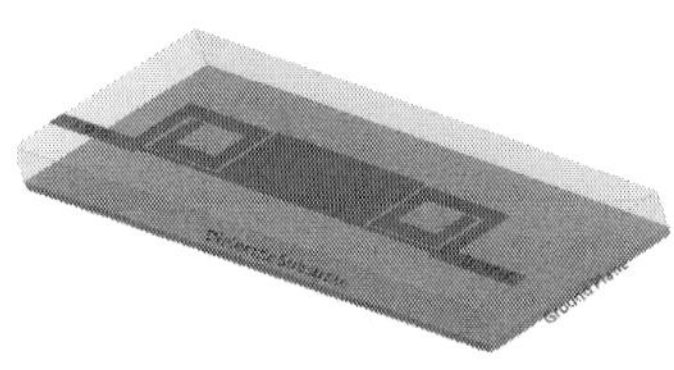

Figure 1: 3D view of the proposed microstrip lowpass filter.

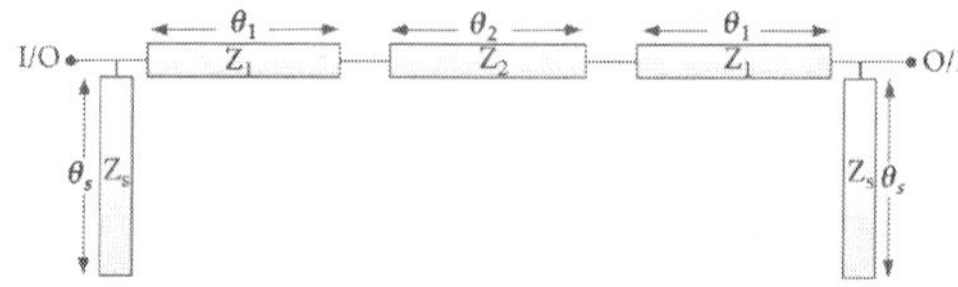

Figure 2: Equivalent circuit model of proposed lowpass filter.

The $ABCD$ matrix (M_t) of the equivalent circuit model can be written as

$$M_t = \begin{bmatrix} A_t & B_t \\ C_t & D_t \end{bmatrix} = M_s M_1 M_2 M_1 M_s, \tag{1}$$

Where M_s is the $ABCD$ matrix of the open-circuited stub and M_n is the $ABCD$ matrix for the unit elements (for $n = 1, 2$) which can be defined by

$$M_s = \begin{bmatrix} 1 & 0 \\ \dfrac{j\tan\theta_s}{Z_s} & 1 \end{bmatrix}$$

$$M_n = \begin{bmatrix} \cos\theta_n & jZ_n\sin\theta_n \\ \dfrac{j\sin\theta_n}{Z_n} & \cos\theta_n \end{bmatrix} \tag{2}$$

For a feed line impedance of z_o, the insertion loss (s_{21}) and return loss (s_{11}) responses can be computed as follows:

$$S_{21} = \frac{2(A_tD_t - B_tC_t)}{A_t + B_t/Z_o + C_tZ_o + D_t}$$

$$S_{11} = \frac{A_t + B_t/Z_o - C_tZ_o - D_t}{A_t + B_t/Z_o + C_tZ_o + D_t} \tag{3}$$

In general, a transmission line filter with quarter-wavelength elements $(\theta_s = \theta_1 = \theta_2 = \lambda/4 \text{ at } f_o)$ has all of its transmission zeros at a single frequency, e.g., midstopband frequency (f_o). Therefore, it requires more elements to enhance the selectivity and to increase the bandwidth of the rejection band. Alternatively, the circuit elements are designed to have different or unequal electrical lengths to allow the filter to exhibit three transmission zeros inside the rejection band, at $f_o/3$, f_o, and $5f_o/3$. In this case, the electrical lengths are chosen to be $\theta_s = 3\theta_1 = 2\theta_2$ at the midstopband (). In order to show the performance of this new structure, the filter is designed to have a cut-off frequency at about 3.0 GHz. The filter is also designed to have a return loss of more than 24-dB within the desired passband and an insertion loss of more than 20-dB over the whole rejection band. Furthermore, the filter is designed to generate three transmission zeros at the rejection band at 4.0 GHz, 12 GHz, and 20 GHz. In order to achieve this, the circuit model is optimized based on the above formulations and the calculated parameters are displayed in Table 1. The calculated magnitude response, of the circuit model using the parameters values in Table 1, is demonstrated in Figure 3. As can be noticed, the filter exhibits three transmission zeros which are widely separated from each other providing a very ultra-wide rejection band with high selectivity. These transmission zeros are generated by the two open-circuited stubs. This is because the length of each open-circuited stub (θ_s) is a quarter-wavelength at 4.0 GHz and therefore, its fundamental resonant frequency is generated at 4.0 GHz and it has spurious resonant frequencies occur at odd multiples of the fundamental one. Hence, the first and second spurious resonant frequencies are located at 12 GHz and 20 GHz as shown in Figure 4. Since the first three resonant frequencies of the open-circuited stubs are located inside the rejection band, the filter exhibits vey wide stopband. The filter exhibits an equal ripple for the return loss at the passband and for the insertion loss at the rejection band. Furthermore, addition, the first resonant frequency of the stub is located close to the cut-off frequency of the lowpass filter leading to a sharp rate of cut-off.

Table 1: Circuit parameters for the proposed filter at 4.0 GHz.

Parameter							
Value	50 Ω	96 Ω	170 Ω	20.2 Ω	90°	30°	60°

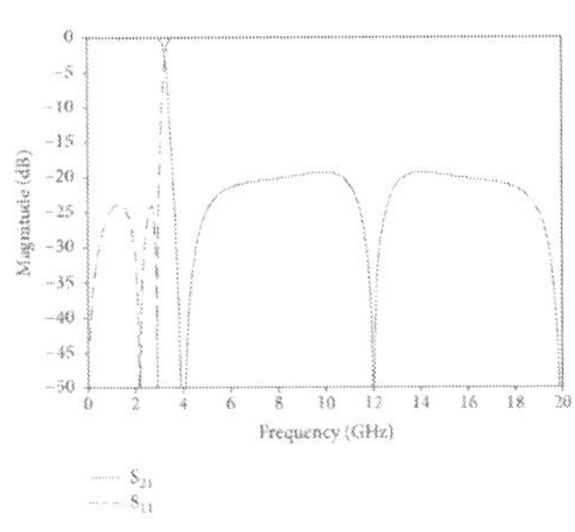

Figure 3: Calculated performance of the circuit model in Figure 2 with the parameters values in Table 1.

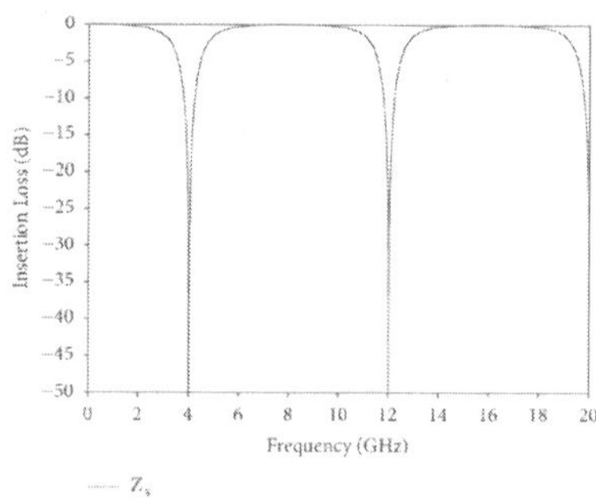

Figure 4: Calculated insertion loss of the open-circuited stub connected to 50 Ohm line.

MICROSTRIP DESIGN AND EXPERIMENT RESULTS

The proposed filter design is constructed on a RT Duroid 5880 substrate with $\varepsilon r = 2.2$ and thickness 0.254 mm and the microstrip layout is demonstrated in Figure 5. Based on the microstrip design equations in [2] with a slight tuning, the parameters of the microstrip layout are as follows: $W_o =$ 0.75 mm, $W_s = 0.7$ mm, $W_1 = 0.05$ mm, $W_2 = 3.4$ mm, $L_{s1} = 3.0$ mm, $L_{s2} = 4.65$ mm, $L_{s3} = 3.15$ mm, $L_{s4} =$ 3.65 mm, $L_{s5} = 2.3$ mm, $L_1 = 4.2$ mm, $L_2 = 8.2$ mm, $g_1 = g_2 = 0.25$ mm, and $g_3 = 0.3$ mm. The open-circuited stubs are folded in a rectangular spiral shape to reduce the filter size. The distance g_2 is optimized to have no effect on the filter performance. The microstrip layout is simulated using a commercially available tool [24] and the simulated performance is compared with the calculated results as depicted in Figure 6. Good agreement between the theoretical and simulated responses is obtained. However, there is a slight difference between the simulated and the theoretical passband. The microstrip layout can be further tuned to reduce the effect of discontinuity and to obtain a better agreement. A prototype of this filter is successfully fabricated and measured and Figure 7 shows a photograph of the fabricated filter. The fabricated filter is very small with an overall size of about 18.0 mm by 3.75 mm. The measured performance of the prototype is compared with the simulated results and demonstrated in

Figure 8. The experimental filter shows excellent results with an insertion loss of about 0.4 dB at the passband centre frequency. It also exhibits an ultra-wide rejection band up to 20 GHz with three transmission zeros and an attenuation level of more than 20-dB. The filter shows an equal ripple for the return loss at the passband and for the insertion loss at the stopband. A performance comparison between published works and proposed filter is demonstrated in Table 2. It can be noticed that the proposed filter shows wider stopband bandwidth.

Table 2: Performance comparisons between published works and proposed filter.

Ref	Relative stopband bandwidth	Rejection level (dB)	Up to
[3]	0.92	20	6.8 GHz
[4]	1.54	14	17 GHz
[5]	1.52	10	12 GHz
[7]	0.85	15	5 GHz
[8]	1.45	20	20 GHz
[9]	1.07	10	10 GHz
[11]	0.58	15	10 GHz
[12]	1.2	30	10 GHz
[13]	1.36	10	16 GHz
[16]	1.42	10	6 GHz
[17]	1.14	15	11 GHz
[18]	1.2	10	20 GHz
[19]	1.2	10	8 GHz
[20]	1.407	20	4.5 GHz
[21]	1.3	20	19 GHz
[22]	0.8	30	5 GHz
This work	*1.5*	*20*	*20 GHz*

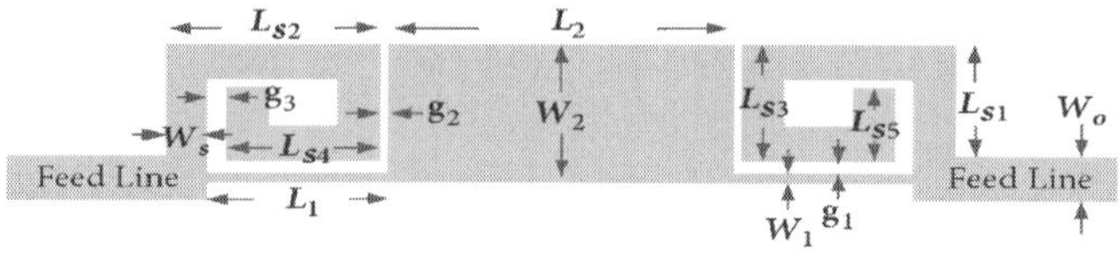

Figure 5: Microstrip layout of the proposed filter.

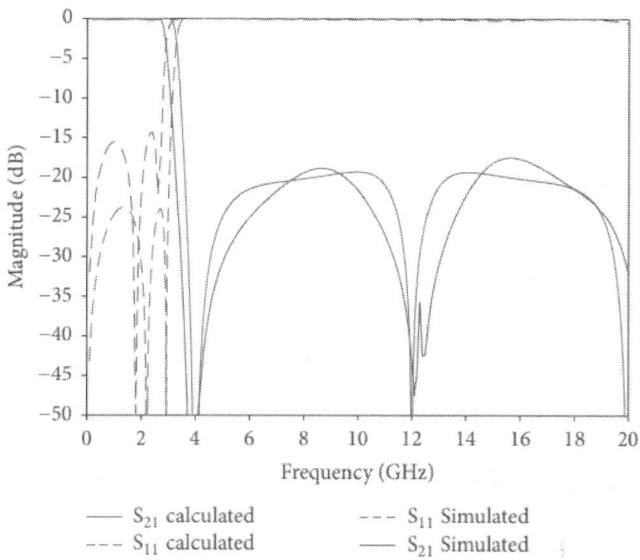

Figure 6: Calculated and simulated responses of the proposed filter.

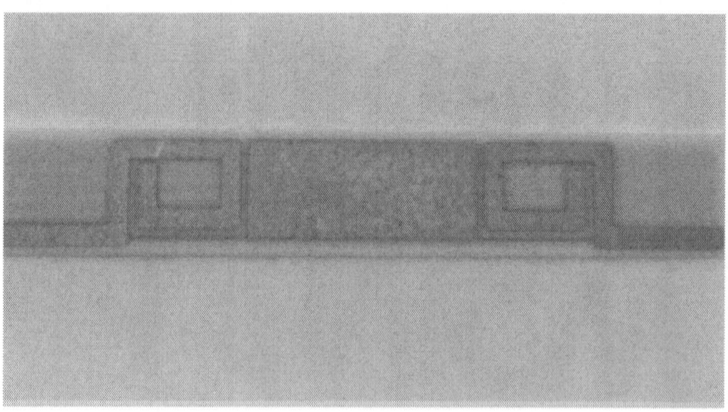

Figure 7: Photograph of fabricated filter.

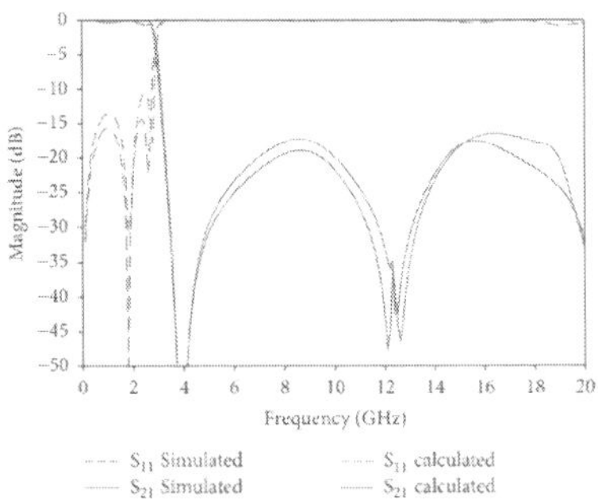

Figure 8: Simulated and measured insertion and return losses of the fabricated filter.

CONCLUSION

In this paper, a microstrip lowpass filter based on transmission line elements is proposed. The filter has been constructed of three series unit elements between two symmetric shunt open-circuited stubs. The filter has been designed to have a cut-off frequency at about 3.0GHz. In order to allow the filter to exhibit an equal ripple in both passband and rejection band, the open-circuited stub has been designed to have its first three resonant frequencies inside the stopband. A prototype has been successfully designed, fabricated, and measured, where excellent agreement between the expected and measured performances is obtained. The filter exhibits a quasielliptic function response leading to a high filtering selectivity and an extended stopband up to 20GHz with an attenuation level of more than 20-dB. Due to the small size, low insertion loss, and wide rejection band, the proposed filter looks attractive for making it attractive for many technologies such as UWB medical applications.

Data Availability

The data used to support the findings of this study are available from the corresponding author upon request.

Conflicts of Interest

The authors declare that they have no conflicts of interest.

ACKNOWLEDGMENTS

This work is sponsored by King Abdulaziz City for Science and Technology (KACST).

REFERENCES

1. G. L. Matthaei, L. Young, and E. M. T. Jones, *Microwave Filters, Impedance-Matching Network, and Coupling Structures*, Artech House, Norwood, Mass, USA, 1980.
2. J. Hong and M. J. Lancaster, *Microstrip Filters for RF/Microwave Applications*, John Wiley & Sons, New York, NY, USA, 2001.
3. S. Y. Huang and Y. H. Lee, "Compact stepped-impedance low-pass filter with a slot-back microstrip line," *Microwave and Optical Technology Letters*, vol. 50, no. 4, pp. 1058–1061, 2008.
4. F. Zhang, S. Liu, P. Zhao, M. Du, X. Zhang, and J. Xu, "Compact ultra-wide stopband lowpass filter using transformed stepped impedance hairpin resonator," in *Proceedings of the 2017 IEEE International Symposium on Antennas and Propagation & USNC/URSI National Radio Science Meeting*, pp. 2227-2228, 2017.
5. M. H. Yang and J. Xu, "Design of compact, broad-stopband lowpass filter using modified stepped impedance hairpin resonators," *IEEE Electronics Letters*, vol. 44, no. 20, pp. 1198–1200, 2008.
6. S. Pinel, R. Bairavasubramanian, J. Laskar, and J. Papapolymerou, "Compact planar and vialess composite low-pass filters using folded stepped-impedance resonator on liquid-crystal-polymer substrate," *IEEE Transactions on Microwave Theory and Techniques*, vol. 53, no. 5, pp. 1707–1712, 2005.
7. A. B. Abdel-Rahman, A. K. Verma, A. Boutejdar, and A. S. Omar, "Control of bandstop response of Hi-Lo microstrip low-pass filter using slot in ground plane," *IEEE Transactions on Microwave Theory and Techniques*, vol. 52, no. 3, pp. 1008–1013, 2004.
8. S. Sen and T. Moyra, "Design of a Chebyshev stripline based lowpass filter using open stubs and Defected Ground Structure (DGS)," in *Proceedings of the 2016 IEEE International Conference on Wireless Communications, Signal Processing and Networking, WiSPNET 2016*, pp. 936–939, Chennai, India, March 2016.
9. D. Ahn, J. Park, C. Kim, J. Kim, Y. Qian, and T. Itoh, "A design of the low-pass filter using the novel microstrip defected ground structure," *IEEE Transactions on Microwave Theory and Techniques*, vol. 49, no. 1, pp. 86–93, 2001.
10. T. Kim and C. Seo, "A novel photonic bandgap structure for low-pass filter of wide stopband," *IEEE Microwave and Guided Wave Letters*,

vol. 10, no. 1, pp. 13–15, 2000.

11. H. Fu and Y. Yu, "A novel lowpass filter based on multistage defected ground structure," in *Proceedings of the 16th IEEE International Conference on Ubiquitous Wireless Broadband, ICUWB 2016*, Nanjing, China, October 2016.
12. L.-H. Hsieh and K. Chang, "Compact elliptic-function low-pass filters using microstrip stepped-impedance hairpin resonators," *IEEE Transactions on Microwave Theory and Techniques*, vol. 51, no. 1, pp. 193–199, 2003.
13. F. Wei, L. Chen, X.-W. Shi, Q.-L. Huang, and X.-H. Wang, "Compact lowpass filter with wide stop-band using coupled-line hairpin unit," *IEEE Electronics Letters*, vol. 46, no. 1, pp. 88–90, 2010.
14. A. Balalem, A. R. Ali, J. Machac, and A. Omar, "Quasi-elliptic microstrip low-pass filters using an interdigital DGS slot," *IEEE Microwave and Wireless Components Letters*, vol. 17, no. 8, pp. 586–588, 2007.
15. G. Karimi, A. Lalbakhsh, and H. Siahkamari, "Design of sharp roll-off lowpass filter with ultra wide stopband," *IEEE Microwave and Wireless Components Letters*, vol. 23, no. 6, pp. 303–305, 2013.
16. R. Gómez-García, M.-A. Sánchez-Soriano, M. Sánchez-Renedo, G. Torregrosa-Penalva, and E. Bronchalo, "Extended-stopband microstrip lowpass filter using rat-race directional couplers," *IEEE Electronics Letters*, vol. 49, no. 4, pp. 281-282, 2013.
17. S. Majidifar, S. V. Makki, A. Ahmadi, and S. Alirezaee, "Compact microstrip lowpass filter using stepped impedance spiral resonator," in *Proceedings of the 2012 4th International Conference on Computational Intelligence and Communication Networks (CICN)*, pp. 23–26, Mathura, Uttar Pradesh, India, November 2012.
18. S. Xu, K. Ma, F. Meng, and K. S. Yeo, "DGS embedded transformed radial stub for ultra-wide stopband lowpass filter," *IEEE Electronics Letters*, vol. 48, no. 23, pp. 1473–1475, 2012.
19. K. Zhao, L. Li, and Y. Wang, "A Novel lowpass filter using three corner-cutting T-shaped compact microstrip resonator cells," in *Proceedings of the 2012 Spring Congress on Engineering and Technology (S-CET)*, pp. 1–3, Xi'an, China, May 2012.
20. V. K. Velidi and S. Sanyal, "Sharp roll-off lowpass filter with wide stopband using stub-loaded coupled-line hairpin unit," *IEEE Microwave*

and Wireless Components Letters, vol. 21, no. 6, pp. 301–303, 2011.

21. M. Hayati, S. Naderi, and F. Jafari, "Compact microstrip lowpass filter with sharp roll-off using radial resonator," *IEEE Electronics Letters*, vol. 50, no. 10, pp. 761-762, 2014.
22. H. Shaman and J.-S. Hong, "Wideband bandstop filter with cross-coupling," *IEEE Transactions on Microwave Theory and Techniques*, vol. 55, no. 8, pp. 1780–1785, 2007.
23. E. Pancera, "Medical applications of the ultra wideband technology," in *Proceedings of the 6th Loughborough Antennas and Propagation Conference, LAPC 2010*, pp. 52–56, Loughborough, UK, November 2010.
24. Sonnet Software Inc., EM User's Manual, Ver. 12, NY 2005.

SECTION 4
E-HEALTH AND M-HEALTH

CHAPTER

13

E-HEALTH AND TELEMEDICINE: CURRENT STATE AND FUTURE STEPS

Boris A. Kobrinskii

Pediatric Research Clinical Institute, Russian National Research Medical University, Moscow, Russia

ABSTRACT

The article reviews the questions related to building the e-health systems. The key element of the system is electronic healthcare record to be formed according to the modular approach in the form of primary and satellite electronic medical records. Person-centred healthcare is proposed as a foundation for e-health. Such an approach provides a potential opportunity

Citation: Kobrinskii, B. (2014), "E-Health and Telemedicine: Current State and Future Steps". E-Health Telecommunication Systems and Networks, 3, 50-56. doi: 10.4236/etsn.2014.34007.

for all the medical doctors to obtain necessary information about their patients at any time via the teleconsultations in particular. Transition to e-health is associated with the creation of new opportunities for making diagnostic and therapeutic decisions based on the use of build-in decision support modules. The computer-assisted software design or hybrid systems are considered as the fourth generation medical information systems. It is reasonable to implement the entire information space of ehealth, including the information systems of medical institutions and regional data repositories, based on cloud-optimized storage and computing solutions. This approach is expected to be implemented in Russia as a part of the unified state health information system. The authorized access to integrated databases for medical doctors of various specialties is required. In the framework of e-health, telemedicine is considered as an important component. Main elements comprise the real-time access of medical consultants to personified medical databases and remote follow-up of patients by the means of personal or home-based telemedicine. The use of personal portable devices for the control of vital signs of the organism is especially promising. Electronic stethoscopes and specialized video cameras for acquiring objective information should be increasingly used by remote consultants. Unfortunately, this trend is still underdeveloped in Russia. In perspective, e-health as unified medical space will provide a transition to the integrated analysis of population health by medical doctors of various specialties from different countries and will open new prospects for studying health based on the intelligent analysis of integrated data of patients.

Keywords:-E-Health, Person-Centred Healthcare, Electronic Healthcare Record, Telemedicine,

INTRODUCTION

E-health is a complex system aimed at solution of the entire spectrum of the health problems of the population. Transition to e-health requires an integration of the medical databases at different levels and creation of common information space of countries with an option of exchange of the required personal data within and between the countries. This is the prospect for the world's healthcare including Russia. The most advanced countries in terms of computer science have already laid the foundations for this process. In Russia at the moment the unified state health information system is being created. It is made as a three-tier system: 1) medical institutions; 2) regional systems; 3) federal system. At the regional level both personal health information and integrated data can be stored. At the federal level only integrated personal medical data will be kept, including a specific set of features. Among them is the information on chronic diseases, their treatment, and the vital characteristics of the patients. In terms of information communication, e-health is a system or an environment providing the exhaustive electronic document flow with authorized access to personal medical data, if necessary. Such a system should provide the ways for the joint remote analysis of patients' health-related data by different doctors as well as for the communication between doctors and patients in particular by using telemedical technologies. The key component of e-health is an electronic healthcare record (EHR) or health card 1, to be created at birth and filled out in every medical institution that manages the follow-ups and treatments, including medical emergency care, during the entire life of a patient. E-health requires person-centred approach 2 3 based on the authorized access to patients' personal medical data in distributed databases during the entire life of patients. Using such an approach, general practitioners, consulting physicians, emergency medical care physicians, and medical doctors of different specialities who make decisions regarding specifics and levels of necessary medical service will have all required data about the previous diagnostic results, diseases, and treatments. It is important to note that duplication of medical information in the traditional clinical records does not provide the required completeness of medical data about patients but, in some cases, leads to generation of contradicting and misleading data. However, this may be prevented using person-centred EHR. Thereafter, we will review the person-centred paradigm as a system of conceptual framework for integration of medical data of patients independent on solutions of particular diagnostic and treatment tasks being solved in certain institutions at various levels of medical help. In this case, doctors of different institutions will have a complete picture of the health status of patients throughout their disease and the effectiveness of previously applied treatments. But achieving this goal is only possible in the e-health in the implementation of person-centred paradigm.

MODULAR STRUCTURE OF HER

Person-centred approach in building the connected healthcare framework requires the presence of "primary" module containing personal identifier—PID (first and last names of patients and parents including the names changed during life; place of birth, personal data, and social characteristics).

Personal identifier is allocated at birth and used for the integration of all other EHR modules of a particular person. The use of PID is the only way to integrate all personal records and imaging studies results available in different institutions (unlike traditional independent records in each institution providing medical care). The modules of EHR can contain text files and/or associated medical images. Core module (or primary electronic medical record, EMR) should contain information necessary for doctors if a patient visits doctor's office for examination and treatment in any situation. These include data about chronic diseases and acute diseases in the past (myocardial infarction, hepatitis, etc.) as well as vital signs, essential study results, and the fact of continuous intake of medications. Satellite modules should be designed for displaying specific information regarding different diseases and conditions (pregnancy, occupational pathology, course of certain chronic diseases, etc.) and particular treatments (chemotherapy, intensive treatment, etc.) as well as for storage of radiology images, etc. Modular principle of EHR formation will enable to perform quick exchange of necessary data and to promptly acquire comprehensive information about patient's follow-up, examination, and treatment in any medical organization at a particular moment. However, it is necessary to take into account the huge volume of medical data accumulated during entire life, especially in patients with an early onset of chronic pathology. At the same time, significant amount of data has age-dependent nature. For instance, medical data, critical at early age, lose their relevance since a certain time. The same is true for major part of information concerning acute diseases and traumas. Therefore, it is reasonable to create satellite EHR in particular directions where data can be partially archived upon a certain period of life though this archiving does not prevent availability of data on demand. It is also reasonable to design satellite modules suitable for self-recording of health-related data by patients themselves and parents (development, nutrition, emotional state, stressful situations, physical exercises, etc.). The genealogy module should be maintained by the genetic centres. In the long term; it will enable an integration of genealogical information collected from different places which will enhance effectiveness of the diagnosis and prediction of hereditary diseases.

In case of modular structure formation, one may replicate EHR from central (or regional) server to the particular local modules in necessary. This will enable every medical specialist to request and receive the most essential information in a particular medical field consolidated based on patient follow-ups occurring in different medical organization (for example, cardiologist does not always need detailed records from urologist). Primary and satellite EHRs (including electronic patient record, EPR, containing reports of particular specialists) represent a background for detection of minimal health abnormalities and possible diseases in the future. The concept of organism transition state continuum serves as a theoretical background and implies practically continuous process with the absence of clear borders between the following stages: normal reactions, functional abnormalities, borderline states, and chronic diseases 4. Currently accepted concept of personalized medicine, based on the integrated analysis of information, comprises three aspects:

1) health status of a person whose data are accumulated during the entire life in EHR;
2) data about genome (combination of genes) of a person;
3) information about proteins encoded by genes.

Therefore, EHR data enable to dynamically determine the risks of hereditary predisposition and to detect early forms of diseases based on genetic studies, biochemical changes, and minimal clinical manifestations. The set-theoretical approach is proposed as the instrument for the formalization of the information system integration process. It allows creation of the territorial medical information system based on an integration of information from the different institutions and on monitoring of private and population health status data in the cohort under observation. It contains information about family components of health status, enables prompt detection of the factors affecting children's health, and identifies prenatal groups at risk of congenital diseases 5. In transition to e-health, the integrated version of personal medical information storage requires database maintenance on the server of the medical institution (for large medical organizations) or of the regional center of data processing where cloud optimized storage and computing can be achieved. Creation of EHR with the use of modular architecture requires the fulfillment of the condition of semantic interoperability. Synonymy of medical terms in this case is either excluded or accompanied by relevant database of synonyms used in all electronic medical records. Real progression of the medical information system integration is feasible only in case of standardization of medical records (EHR fields) in coordinated fashion and extent based on the unified reference data including the standards for encoding and exchanging of health status clinical characteristics.

DECISION

Support Modules Transition to e-health should provide additional opportunities for doctors in the process of diagnostic and treatment decision making via the built-in decision support modules along with access to necessary medical data of patients. We will call the information systems "hybrid" if they are built according to this principle. Such approach, also called computer-assisted software design, is used in medical information systems of fourth generation 6. Decision support modules may be activated automatically when a medical practitioner inputs particular information or by a user on demand to evaluate patient's condition or calculate infusion therapy by using data, accumulated in EHR/EMR. Such systems provide concrete help to medical doctors in managing their patients. Let us examine this approach through the examples of different orientation systems. Different decision support subsystems were incorporated as the components of the Russian National Genetic Registry 7 including subsystems for the genealogy analysis, genetic risk calculation, and selection of the methods for additional diagnostic studies. The genealogy analysis expert system for an identification of the hereditary transmission patterns in family's functions by using genetic information obtained from the registry data base upon inquiry. The result consists in a conclusion decision, received by a doctor regarding patient's chances for the presence of monogenic disease and its mode of inheritance, and is accompanied by the level of confidence. There are computational models, developed as single software packages, enabling the calculation of recurrence risk of disease in family. The intellectual module, designed for selection of the confirmatory studies, contains information about the laboratory changes specific for given diagnosis. When the inheritable metabolic disorder is suspected, this module is activated in the system upon hypothesizing the diagnosis. In Russian hybrid system, for the department of children's thermal injury, created at the Pediatric Research Clinical Institute, we developed an array of estimates and tooltips regarding the possible pathological processes upon input of certain data:

1) calculation of the injured area based on electronic graphic image of a human body;
2) calculation of infusion therapy volume depending on injury severity and patient's age;
3) detection of shock depending on input clinical data;
4) calculation of risk index for infectious complications. Based on these data, examination and treatment scheme is activated individually for each patient and all necessary information is displayed.

UNIFIED E-HEALTH INFORMATION SPACE

Currently, several Russian regions are involved in the process of integration of medical systems functioning in the individual institutions and emerging regional structures using cloud optimized storage and computing. It must be emphasized that the arrays of personal health data should be created in the first place in order to provide clinicians of all medical organizations all the information they need at any time and in any place. This should serve to improve the quality of diagnosis and treatment of patients, contribute to the prevention of unnecessary retesting. Developing information space for clinical e-health data may be considered as a background for making prompt adequate diagnostic and treatment decisions. At the same time, it will provide the way for space-time monitoring of birth, morbidity, disability, and mortality rates as well as for implementing the epidemiology studies. The unified information space represents a combination of the regional data warehouses and autonomic databases of medical information systems in clinical domain integrated into one network. Furthermore, data stored in the information systems of individual medical organizations should be referenced in the regional and federal systems. Distributed database of personal medical data should be available for all participants of the diagnostic-treatment process at any time independently on subordination and location of the institution restricted by an authorized access to particular information. Concerning software-based technical implementation of the large distributed databases, it is reasonable to use the infrastructure of computational grids 8 that provide global integration of information and computational resources. This is also true for the cloud optimized storage technology used for creation of the private clouds ensuring availability of necessary data under minimization of storage locations.

HIERARCHY ACCESS TO HER

The authorized access of various medical practitioners to the integrated databases is a mandatory requirement. Full access to data about particular patient may be given to a doctor in charge, department head, and immediate supervisor of higher level who have right to control the activity of attending physicians; full access may be also granted in case of information request from the higher-level healthcare authorities and on the resolution of the regulatory and judicial agencies. Certain restrictions for viewing information about a patient can be implemented for the medical laboratory doctors who carry out the diagnostic examinations. Higher-level restrictions are planned in regard to access to the module of genealogical data including information about health state of patient's relatives and data about certain occupational hazards. In other words, the management of access to data (authorized access or restriction of access rights) is achieved based on the consideration of identity of a subject or group where the subject is included (job/role duties). The question of protection of personal medical data by using standards is discussed in many countries entering the path of electronic healthcare. Main regime of information security complies with ISO 17799 standard approved by the International Organization for Standardization in 2000. The regime of information security is achieved:

1. at the administrative level—by organizational security policy declaring the goals and methods of achieving security;
2. at the procedural level—via the development and implementation of the information security instructions for the personnel and via physical protection measures;
3. at the software-based technical level—through the use of the approved and certified solutions and standard array of the countermeasures: data backup, firewall, data encryption.

Information security should guarantee both confidentiality (i.e. protection from the unauthorized data acquisition) and intactness (i.e. protection from the unauthorized alteration of information). At the present time, electronic signature is used for this purpose. The use of electronic signature means enables to identify the source (author) of an electronic document and to guarantee the content inalterability (the absence of data corruption in electronic document; the electronic signature loses validity in case of introduction of changes in the content). In medical information systems, data confidentiality and protection are provided based on the forced control of access which requires the use of security labels: the subject (medical worker) label describes subject's loyalty whereas object (electronic medical document) label delineates the degree of protection of information in the document. The system of user recognition, based on personal identifiers with following authentication and authorization, requires verification of the subject access rights to particular resources i.e. to the EHR sections. One of security options may consist in separate storage of personal and medical information on the different servers. In this case, particular EMR is accessible only during the period when the doctor manages it (until termination of the session and signature of given medical record).

E-HEALTH AND TELEMEDICINE

Telemedicine should be currently considered as part of e-health. In delivering teleconsultations, the role of telemedicine consists in organization of real-time access of medical consultants to personalized information of the distributed databases. This has particular significance in cases of emergency teleconsultations. Accessibility of personal medical databases for consultants enables them to promptly acquire all information necessary for making diagnostic and treatment decisions including teleconsultations in disaster medicine. Considering the availability of data about previous diseases and treatments, this will open a gate for significant improvement of the quality and promptness of medical help delivered to patients. The first experience in this direction was generated in the USA after Hurricane Katrina when the centralized electronic health records, containing information about administered drugs, were used for the organization of effective medical help for refugees while massive numbers of hard copies with medical information were lost 9. Personal or home telemedicine represents the other important direction. It reduces requests for hospitalizations under the following conditions 10:

1) remote evaluation of patient's condition by using instrumental tools and access to remote expertise via the personal computer;
2) virtual visits of patient by medical nurses, physical therapy specialists, etc.;
3) remote control of patients' physiological signs;
4) opportunity of continuous remote control of patient's condition.

Let us now review e-health or monitoring of physiological parameters of the organism by using personal portable devices (PPD). For 15 years, the Centre for E-Health and Tele-Monitoring and Maternal and Infant Healthcare Research, Oxford, has been pioneering in continuous wireless physiological monitoring for basic and clinical research as well as in service applications covering antenatal, infant, paediatric, and adult cardio-respiratory monitoring examining, in particular, the trends in development of behaviour, sleep and circadian patterns. Triad of physical activity, cardiac, and respiratory monitoring has emerged as the core measure of dysfunction in these life systems and also provided the way to quantify lifestyle and risk 11. The use of the intelligent signal processing, analysis, and mobile communication technologies (mobile telephony, PDA, GPRS, Bluetooth, inter-monitor connections, and the Internet), as a platform for widespread low-cost community-based healthcare, is the key technical development shown recently to work effectively. Vital signs monitoring by using personal portable devices is especially important for certain social groups of population. These groups comprise pregnant women, patients with chronic diseases, and individuals with limited capacities. At the present time, there is a wide range of devices for home/personal telemedicine. For example, patients can be offered monitoring of the following vital signs: heart rate, blood pressure, body weight, oxygen saturation, temperature, ECG rhythm, spirometry, and prothrombin time/INR 12. In Russia, home/personal telemedicine has not gained the widespread implementation yet unlike teleconsultations including videoconferences. At the same time, the future steps of telemedicine consist in the widespread use of the electronic equipment (electronic stethoscope), specialized video cameras (for dermatology, otorhinolaryngology, ophthalmology, gynecology, etc.), and personal portable devices for obtaining objective information by distant consultants, as well as in the organization of the digital operating rooms.

CONCLUSIONS

Looking into the future, one may predict the transition to the integrated analysis of health status of population by doctors of various specialties from different countries and the expansion of the existing trans boundary exchange of medical documents. At the same time, the synthesis of diverse information in the e-health system will provide new opportunities for making managerial decisions based on the intelligent analysis of cumulative data.

The steps of e-health for formation of the unified medical information space will guarantee:

1. improvement of the follow-up for patients and enhancement of the continuity in delivering medical care by different medical institutions;
2. increase in the effectiveness of timely detection of patients at risk of developing pathology or at early stage of disease;
3. multi factorial causal analysis contributing to reduction of morbidity, disability, and mortality. In the future, a full-scale e-health system will require:

- a unified system of identification of patients during their entire life;
- an authorized access to various sections of personal medical information for different categories of medical professionals, including the telemedicine consultations;

- an intellectual support of decision-making processes of teleconsultation (the preparatory stages, the direction and the processing of applications, formal and substantive analysis of medical records), healthcare at home and extreme situations;
- a legal coverage, software, and hardware for providing confidentiality of electronic personal medical data;
- structuring and formalization of medical records;
- congruency of information exchange mechanisms in the integrated systems;
- creation of necessary telecommunication infrastructure in the population health protection system.

It is reasonable to build the national e-health systems based on the modular formation of EHR requiring 1) integration of all necessary information through the fill-up-form module including personal identifier of an individual; 2) assembly of EMR from specialized medical organizations based on necessary standard modules; 3) modular exchange of data between information systems (database). Electronic health record enables medical workers and patients to exchange medical information with different purposes, including patient's self-control, home-based treatment with the use of sensor devices, telemedical consultations, and management of electronic registries and databases 12. The European electronic healthcare project, EpSOS (Smart Open Services for European Patients), aimed to design, build and evaluate a service infrastructure that demonstrates cross-border interoperability between electronic health record systems in Europe 13., involves access to patient's medical information, first of all, in regard to major patient's resumes and electronic prescriptions in the European healthcare systems. In Russia, the question about joining this project is currently under consideration. The Health Level Seven (HL7) standard of electronic document exchange is used to ensure compatibility of medical information systems at the data level. The HL7 standard complies with conceptual definition of application interaction approved for the seventh (applicable) level of open system interconnection: OSI/ISO reference model (user-network interface, services for data exchange between application software programs). Unfortunately, on the way to e-health we meet the cultural, national, and legal obstacles. Their solution requires a collective decision of different countries, and education of the public on the benefits of the advantages of e-health.

REFERENCES

1. Blobel, B. (2003) Interoperable Healthcare Information System Components for Continuity of Care. British Journal of Healthcare Computing & Information Management, 7, 22-24.
2. Lloyd-Williams, D. (2004) E-Health: A Dilemma for Europe. British Journal of Healthcare Computing & Information Management, 10, 20-23.
3. Mauro, A. (2008) Patient-Centered E-Health Design. In: Wilson, E.V., Ed., Patient-Centered E-Health, IGI Global, Hershey, 10-25. http://dx.doi.org/10.4018/978-1-60566-016-5.ch002
4. Kobrinsky, B. (1995) Concept of the Continuum of Intermediate States of Development: Risk Factors in Child Health. Medical Audit News, 2, 21-22.
5. Kobrinsky, B., Lupin, S. and Ponomareva, N. (2012) Integration of the Medical Information Systems for the Risk Groups of the Congenital Pathologies Formation. Bio-Algorithms and Med-Systems, 3, 315-326.
6. Dean, A.G. (2000) Computerizing Public Health Surveillance Systems. In: Teutsch, S.M. and Churchill, S.M., Eds, Principles and Practice of Public Health Surveillance, 2nd Edition, Oxford University Press, Oxford, 229-252.
7. Kobrinsky, B., Tester, I., Demikova, N., Sedov, Yu., Marjanchik, B., Taperova, L., Glukhovskaya, Yu. and Podolnaja, M. (1998) A Multifunctional System of the National Genetic Register. Medinfo'98: Proceedings of 9th International Congress on Medical Informatics, Seoul, 18-22 August 1998, 121-125.
8. Foster, I., Kesselman, C. and Tuecke, S. (2004) The Open Grid Services Architecture. In: Foster, I. and Kesselman, C., Eds., The Grid 2: Blueprint for a New Computing Infrastructure: The Morgan Kaufmann Series in Computer Architecture and Design, Morgan Kaufmann Publishers, San Francisco, 215-257.
9. Mack, D., Brantley, K.M. and Bell, K.G. (2007) Mitigating the Health Effects of Disasters for Medically Underserved Populations: Electronic Health Records, Telemedicine, Research, Screening, and Surveillance. Journal of Health Care for the Poor and Underserved, 2, 432-442. http://dx.doi.org/10.1353/hpu.2007.0040
10. Jardine, I. (2000) Telemedicine and Telecare: Addressing the Real Healthcare Issues. British Journal of Healthcare Computing &

Information Management, 5, 28-30.

11. Johnson, P. (2004) Patients' Use of Self Telemonitoring in 21st Century Clinical Care in the Community. British Journal of Healthcare Computing & Information Management, 1, 22-26.
12. Silber, D. (2003) E-Health: The Case for E-Health. EIPA 2003/E/01. http://www.eipa.nl
13. Lindén, F. (2009) EpSOS Local Data Providers. Acta Informatica Medica, 3, 142-145

CHAPTER

14

MOBIHEALTHCARE SYSTEM: BODY SENSOR NETWORK BASED M-HEALTH SYSTEM FOR HEALTHCARE APPLICATION

Fen Miao[1], Xiuli Miao[2], Weihua Shangguan[1], Ye Li[1]

[1]Shenzhen Institutes of Advanced Technology, Chinese Academy of Sciences, Shenzhen, China

[2]Taihe Hospital of Traditional Chinese Medicine, Fuyang, China

ABSTRACT

M-health, which is known as the practice of medical and public health supported by mobile devices such as mobile phones and PDAs for delivering medical and healthcare services, is currently being heavily developed to keep pace with the continuously rising demand for personalized healthcare.

Citation: F. Miao, X. Miao, W. Shangguan and Y. Li, "MobiHealthcare System: Body Sensor Network Based M-Health System for Healthcare Application,"*E-Health Telecommunication Systems and Networks*, Vol. 1 No. 1, 2012, pp. 12-18. doi: 10.4236/etsn.2012.11003.

To this end, the MobiHealthcare system, which provides a personalized healthcare based on body sensor network, is developed. The system includes various body sensors to collect physiological signals specifically for different requirements, a cell phone to facilitate the joint processing of spatially and temporally collected medical data from different parts of the body for resource optimization and systematic health monitoring, a server cluster with great data storage capacity, powerful analysis capabilities to provide data storage, data mining and visualization. Compared with existing M-Health system, the MobiHealthcare system is characteristics of low coupling and powerful parallel computing capabilities. Various healthcare applications have been implemented in the proposed system to demonstrate its effectiveness in providing a powerful platform.

Keywords: -M-Health; Body Sensor Network; Data Analysis

INTRODUCTION

Nowadays, the constraints in the healthcare of developing countries, including high population growth, a high burden of disease prevalence, low health care workforce, large numbers of rural inhabitants, and limited financial resources to support healthcare infrastructure and health information systems, accompanied with the improvement of potential of lowering information and transaction costs in healthcare delivery due to the explosively access of mobile phones to all segments of a country, has motivated the development of mobile health or m-health field.

M-health is known as the practice of medical and public health supported by mobile devices such as mobile phones and PDAs for delivering medical and healthcare services [1].

Thus, the popularity of m-health can be subjected to the development of wearable medical devices and wireless communication technology.

In order to fully utilize wireless technology between the wearable medical devices, the concept of body sensor network (BSN), which is a kind of wireless sensor network around human body, was proposed in Year 2002 with its emerging applications such as M-Health followed [2-4].

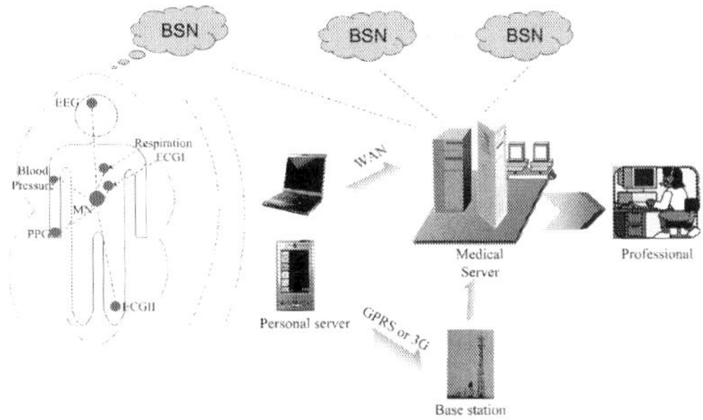

Figure 1. Illustration of body sensor network based M-Health system.

Figure 1 demonstrates a BSN based M-Health system. In a typical system, each sensor node collects various physiological signals in order to monitor the patient's health status no matter their location and then instantly transmit all information in real time to the medical server or the doctors. While an emergency is detected, the physicians will immediately inform the patient through the computer system by providing appropriate messages or alarms. Therefore, MHealth is preferred in monitoring patients in environments lack of medical doctors, such as home and workplaces.

Even though a lot of researches have been engaged in the research of M-Health system [5-8], there are a lot of key issues to be further addressed such as portable body sensors for different applications, powerful server cluster and effective data mining solution to predict the risk factor of chronic diseases, just as the theory of preventive treatment in traditional Chinese Medicine. The proposed system will integrate cloud storage, cloud computing, mobile networks and data mining technology, to realize the long-term monitoring, analysis, forecasting and management of health status at any time and any place.

The rest of this paper is organized as follows. In Section 2, the system overview is presented to provide the initial concept of the developed system. The detail components of the system for different healthcare applications are presented in Section 3. Finally, conclusions and future work are summarized in section 4.

MOBIHEALTHCARE SYSTEM OVERVIEW

The system is comprised of four main components: body sensors for collecting physiological signals, mobile device for joint processing medical information and delivering healthcare services via mobile technology, data server cluster including the database server, data mining server and graphic server in the future, and display terminals such as Television (TV), personal computer.

In the data acquisition end, vital signals such as electrocardiograph (ECG), photoplethysmograph (PPG) and blood pressure (BP) are collected for further analysis.

The collected physiological signals can be transmitted to the mobile device via Bluetooth and then to the server via Internet or 3G.

By the data server cluster, the health condition can be tracked and managed by long-term health records, and thus prevent the disease, evaluate the treatment process for the users.

Users can access the analysis result by a variety of interfaces such as personal computer, TV and mobile phone. MobiHealthcare system is designed to meet the requirements of different users. Three types of users are the main targets.

The first group is patients with heart diseases who need a long-term monitoring after recovery to prevent its relapse. The second is hypertension patients who are under the process of medicine adjustment.

The third is subhealthy people who want to have knowledge of and follow up his health conditions to prevent some kinds of chronic diseases.

SYSTEM ARCHITECTURE

In this section, four main components in the proposed system for different applications of healthcare are detailed.

Body Sensors

Body sensors developed until now for different applications are presented in Figure 2.

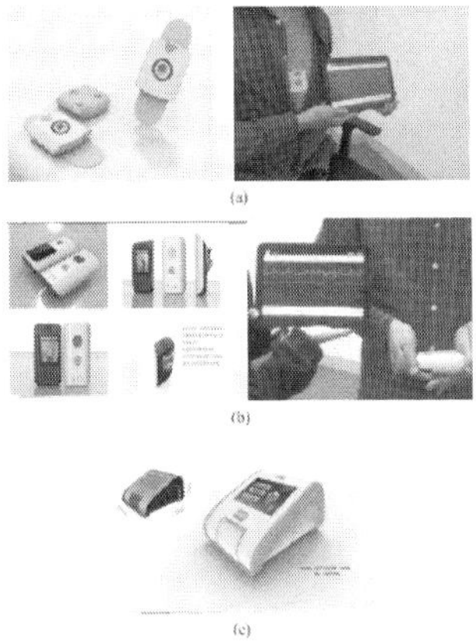

Figure 2. Body Sensors for different applications. (a) MiniHolter; (b) 3-in-1 Portable Monitor; (c) Intelligent Sphygmomanometer.

Figure 2(a) is a miniHolter characteristic of low power consumption, resistance to deviation due to movement. With a mini-Holter, long-term ECG signal such as 48 hours can be collected continuously. It is designed for the users who need a follow-up process after recovery from heart diseases and who are under the risk of sudden heart failure. **Figure 2**(b) is a 3-in-1 portable monitor which can provide ECG, PPG and SPO2 collection simultaneously for users. One can use it to monitor his physiological signals whenever and wherever without any electrodes. With a 3-in-1 portable monitor, anyone with chronic diseases can have knowledge of his current situation every day, the subhealthy people can track his physiological signals and discover some abnormal trend after long-term use. **Figure 2**(c) is an intelligent sphygmomanometer which is designed for patients with hypertension or under the risk of hypertension. There are three key advantages of the new sphygmomanometer different from traditional ones. Firstly, the new one can record one's blood pressure (BP) values for a long time and presents their direction of change with its large memory and powerful interface, while the traditional ones just record the current values.

Secondly, the new one can record the BP values of the family separately with a convenient user-identification scheme, which is impossible in traditional ones without an operating system. At last, as people, especially elder with hypertension, often forget to measure their BP or take the medicine according to the doctor's advice, the new one can remind them with a preset alarm clock. Just because of the above three advantages, the developed sphygmomanometer can be used in different applications. For example, the doctor can use it to track the information of their patients and thus adjust the medicine prescribed. The issue of obedience between the doctor and the patient can be resolved as well.

In the future, more body sensors would be developed to meet the requirements of different people, such as intelligent glucose meter for patients with diabetes.

Mobile Device

The mobile device, which aims to jointly processing medical information and delivering healthcare services, can be various forms such as the mobile phone. Anyone with a mobile phone, can install our software specifically for the platform such as Android or iPhone, and then get the preliminary analysis result such as Heart Rate, abnormalities of a single test. The software interface is presented in Figure 3.

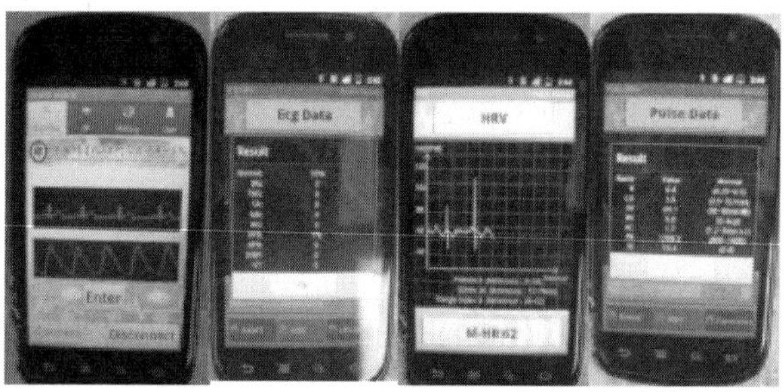

Figure 3. Mobile Device with software

Data Server

There are various released public cloud platforms, such as Amazon's EC2, Apache's Hadoop, Microsoft's Azure, Google's AppEngine and so on for data process. These systems use a proprietary cloud platform to provide a personalized service. The cloud data center specifically designed for healthcare service in our system can provide a platform for great data storage, parallel computing capabilities for data mining. It can support tens of thousands of people login and upload data simultaneously with response time of less than 1 second.

According to different applications, the system has provided different functions. For mini-Holter, which is characteristic of long-term ECG monitor, the most common forms of arrhythmia, such as bigeminy, premature, Bradycardia, and the frequency of occurrence are autoanalyzed by related algorithms. The abnormal ECG signals are labeled and presented to help the users locate the abnormality quickly. Also, the indexes of Heart Rate Variability (HRV) [9] of 5 minutes are presented to evaluate the function of autonomic regulation of the heart. Some kinds of diseases such as congestive heart failure and diabetes can also be reflected from the change of HRV indexes. To realize the above functions, an automatic R-wave detection process based on threshold detection and mathematical morphology is developed on the collected ECG signals with a recognition rate of 99%. The arrhythmia phenomenon is recognized based the standard presented in [10]. Advice is given to users according to the abnormality occurred. In the future, the risk factor of some cardiovascular diseases will be researched and presented based on long-term HRV indexes. **Figure 4” target=”_self”> Figure 4** depicts the function specifically for mini-Holter. A summary report presented in **Figure 4**(a) is given to remind the user of his health condition based the extracted features. The detail extracted information such as the abnormal ECG presented in **Figure 4**(b) and HRV indexes are presented to provide the basis for evaluation.

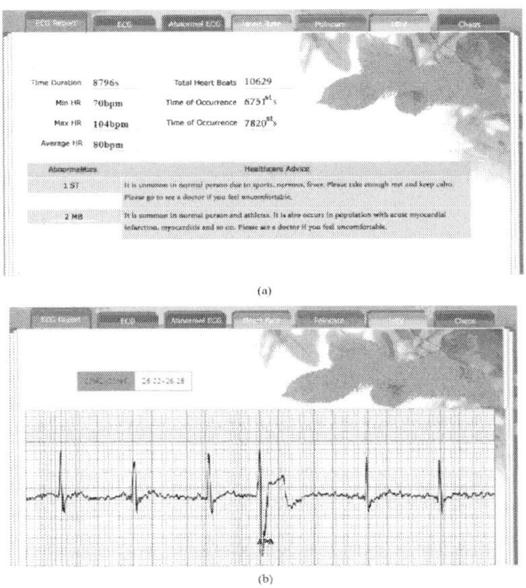

Figure 4. ECG Analysis for mini-Holter. (a) Summary Report; (b) Abnormal ECG.

For 3-in-1 portable monitor, which is characteristic of short-term multi-parameter monitor, the function includes ECG analysis and PPG analysis. The ECG analysis is similar to mini-Holter, where HRV analysis is omitted as short-term ECG can not reflect the variety of heart rate. For PPG analysis, the cardiac functional indexes such as cardiac output, cardiac index and Peripheral Vascular indexes such as Blood Viscosity, stiffness index are given. The comparison between the indexes and the normal range are presented to alert the users of their abnormalities, while advice is given. **Figure 5** depicts the function specifically for 3-in-1 portable monitor. A summary report is given to remind the user of his health condition based the extracted features. The detail indexes and the normal range are presented to provide the basis for evaluation.

For Intelligent sphygmomanometer, which is designed to track one's BP values during a long time, the blood pressure level is given according to the abnormality of BP values labeled. The advice is given according to the user's BP level. In the long-term data analysis, the tendency charts of BP values between any time duration are given to demonstrate the frequency of abnormality and thus judge the overall BP situation.

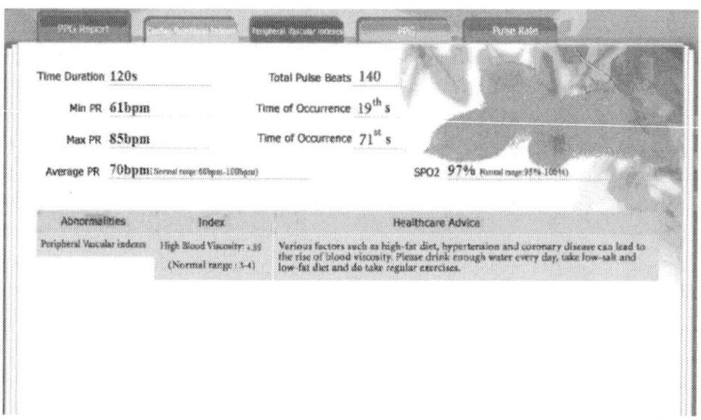

Figure 5. PPG Analysis for 3-in-1 monitor.

Figure 5 depicts the function specifically for intelligent sphygmomanometer. The single analysis is given to remind the user of his BP level, while the long-term analysis is presented to give the BP tendency during selected time duration.

In the future, the risk of some chronic diseases can be predicted based the long-term physiological signals collected with more powerful data mining solutions.

Data Visualization

There are different kinds of interfaces for the user to view his health record and the corresponding analysis results on the physiological data. For example, one can visit the health management platform, or through the TV service, as well as, he can get the analysis result and by message. The display effect on TV is shown in **Figure 7**.

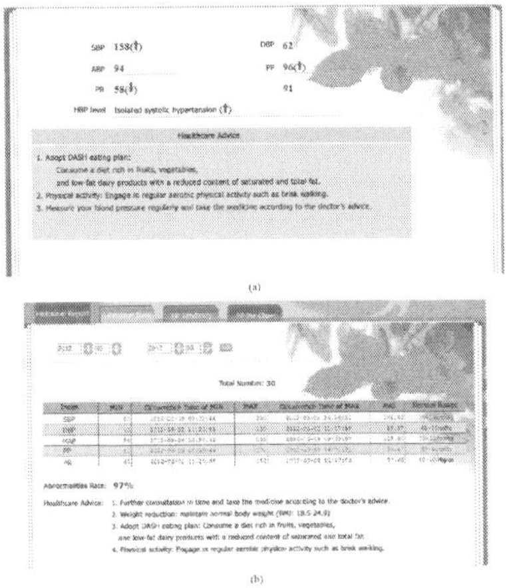

Figure 6. BP Analysis. (a) Single analysis; (b) Long-term analysis.

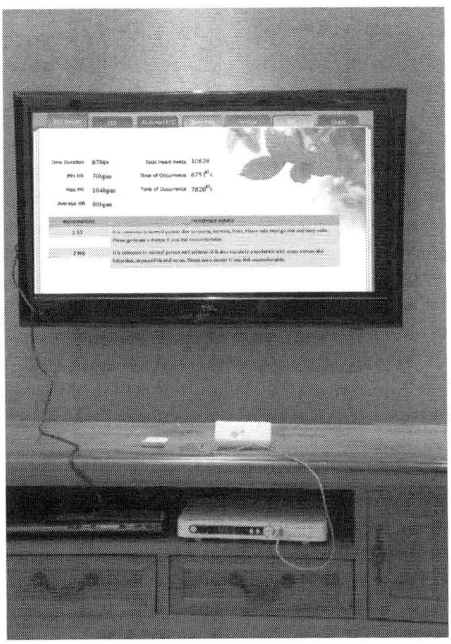

Figure 7. The display effect on TV.

CONCLUSION

The MobiHealthcare system is incorporated into multiple advanced technologies, such as precise and convenient data acquisition solution, high efficiency data storage and analysis method, to monitor the health status of users at any time and any place. Through the system, people can have knowledge of his health information and even the risk factor of some chronic diseases in the future. With our system, some acute attacks can be discovered in time and chronic diseases such as hypertensions can be prevented before onset.

ACKNOWLEDGEMENTS

Fen Miao, Xiuli Miao, Weihua Shangguan, Ye Li (No. JC201005270306A), Key Basic Research Program of Shenzhen (No. JC201005270257A), Shenzhen Technological Achievements Promotion Program (No. CG20100 7290007A) and Key Deployment Project of Chinese Academy of Sciences (No. KGCX2-yw-904).

REFERENCES

1. A. T. van Halteren, R. G. A. Bults, K. E. Wac, D. Konstantas, I. A. Widya, N. T. Dokovski, G. T. Koprinkov, V. M. Jones and R. Herzog, "Mobile Patient Monitoring: The Mobihealth System," The Journal on Information Technology in Healthcare, Vol. 2, No. 5, 2004, pp. 365-373. .
2. G. Z. Yang, "Body Sensor Networks," Springer-Verlag, London, 2006, pp. 4-13.
3. E. Jovanov, "Wireless Technology and System Integration in Body Area Networks for M-Health Applications," 27th Annual International Conference of the Engineering in Medicine and Biology Society, Shanghai, 17-18 January 2005, pp. 7158-7160.
4. E. Jovanov, C. Poon, et al., "Guest Editorial Body Sensor Networks: From Theory to Emerging Applications," IEEE Transactions on Information Technology in Biomedicine, Vol. 13, No. 6, 2009, pp. 859-863.
5. E. Monton, J. Hernandez, et al., "Body Area Network for Wireless Patient Monitoring," IET Communications, Vol. 2, No. 2, 2008, pp. 215-222.
6. K. Wac, R. Bults, et al., "Mobile Patient Monitoring: The MobiHealth System," Annual International Conference of the IEEE Engineering in Medicine and Biology Society, Minneapolis, 3-6 September 2009, pp. 1238-1241.
7. V. Jones, A. Halteren, et al., "Mobihealth: Mobile Health Services Based on Body Area Networks." In: R. Istepanian, S. Laxminarayan and C. S. Pattichis, Eds., MHealth: Emerging Mobile Health Systems, Springer, New York, 2006, pp. 36-219.
8. R. Schmidt, T. Norgall, et al., "Body Area Network BAN— A Key Infrastructure Element for Patient-Centered Medical Applications," Biomedizinische Technik/Biomedical Engineering, Vol. 47, Suppl. 1, 2002, pp. 365-368.
9. M. Malik, "For the Task Force of the ESC and NASPE. Heart Rate Variability: Standards of Measurement, Physiological Interpretation and Clinical Use," Circulation, Vol. 93, 1996, pp. 1043-1065. .
10. T. B. Garcia and G. T. Miller, "Arrhythmia Recognition: The Art of Interpretation," Jones & Bartlett Learning, Sudbury, 2004. .

CHAPTER 15

BLENDED E-HEALTH IN COGNITIVE BEHAVIOURAL THERAPY: USAGE INTENSITY, ATTITUDE AND THERAPEUTIC ALLIANCE IN CLINICAL PRACTICE

Janneke E. M. Aerts[1], Arno van Dam[1,2]

[1] Geestelijke Gezondheidszorg Westelijk Noord Brabant, Halsteren, The Netherlands.

[2] Tranzo (Tilburg University), Tilburg, The Netherlands.

ABSTRACT

Background: Though internet based cognitive behaviour therapy is proven to be effective, e-health is applied only in a minority of treatments in specialised mental health care. The low application rates are associated with therapists' attitudes towards e-health. One of the major concerns is limitations in the therapeutic relation and communication between patient and therapist.

Citation: Aerts, J. and Dam, A. (2018), "Blended e-Health in Cognitive Behavioral Therapy: Usage Intensity, Attitude and Therapeutic Alliance in Clinical Practice". *Psychology*, 9, 2422-2435. doi: 10.4236/psych.2018.910139.

Since therapist involvement is important in an effective e-health treatment, negative attitudes towards e-health can be a risk for effective e-health application. Aims: This study aimed to examine the relationship between patients' e-health usage as well as patients' attitudes towards e-health and the therapeutic alliance. The possible influence of therapists' attitudes on patients' e-health usage is also examined. Method: In an outpatient mental health setting, patients attended a blended treatment program for major depressive disorder and completed questionnaires on attitudes towards e-health and the therapeutic alliance. Therapists completed an alliance and attitude questionnaire as well. Results: Patients with more positive attitudes used the e-health application more intensively. Higher work alliance rates were related to sharing digital homework assignments and seeking contact with their therapist. Also, when treated by therapists with more positive attitudes towards e-health, patients shared more assignments with their therapist. Patients with high symptom rates at start, had more negative attitude rates and tended to use the e-health application less frequently. Conclusions: In a treatment cohesion in which therapists are positive about blended e-health, patients' attitudes are positively related to e-health usage and therefore a factor of interest in improvement of effective e-health application. Patients with severe symptoms may need extra attention like active support and iteration to promote adherence to the e-health program.

Keywords: e-Health Attitude, Therapeutic Alliance, Usage Intensity, Depression

INTRODUCTION

The practice of e-health is available in most domains of healthcare and there is growing evidence that e-health can be effective in the treatment of mental health problems (Andrews, Cuijpers, Craske, McEvoy, & Titov, 2010; Gainsbury & Blaszczynski, 2011; Karyotaki et al., 2015; Spek et al., 2008) . Several studies show that internet-based cognitive behaviour therapy (CBT) and face-to-face CBT for depressive, anxiety and somatic disorders are equally effective (Andersson, Cuijpers, Carlbring, Riper, & Hedman, 2014; Carlbring, Andersson, Cuijpers, Riper, & Hedman-Lagerlöf, 2018; Wagner, Horn, & Maercker, 2014) .

However, many therapists are reluctant to apply e-health interventions (Donovan, Poole, Boyes, Redgate, & March, 2015; Perle, Langsam, & Nierenberg, 2011) . Several authors suggest that this problem is related to therapists' assumptions involving disadvantages of e-health.

Psychologists, when indicating treatment methods, hardly ever prefer online treatment (Mora, Nevid, & Chaplin, 2008; Perle et al., 2011). The most important concerns by therapists are the limitations in nonverbal communication and problems in establishing a therapeutic alliance. As seen by these therapists, e-health is applicable for specific patients with high motivation, a high self-efficacy and lower levels of hopelessness. However, this view is inconsistent with research findings and there is no evidence that the assumed drawbacks are actual threats for treatment effects.

Although therapists tend to overlook e-health, their involvement is necessary for effective e-health practice, especially when it comes to adherence (Urech et al., 2018). Adherence problems are a threat for effective e-health application. Suboptimal usage intensity of e-health applications is related to smaller treatment effect (Donkin et al., 2011) . Specific elements in the structure of the online treatment and contact with a therapist can improve adherence and effectivity rates (Kelders, Kok, Ossebaard, & van Gemert-Pijnen, 2012) . Compared with online self-help, e-health with therapist guidance outstands treatment effect (Andersson & Cuijpers, 2009; Spek et al., 2007) . In face-to-face treatment, the therapeutic relationship is a mediating factor for therapy efficacy (Lambert & Barley, 2002) and explains a significant percentage (7% - 17%) of the variance in treatment outcome (Beutler et al., 2004) . The therapeutic relationship seems to be important in e-health too. Establishing a constructive therapeutic alliance in e-health treatment is possible, even without having face-to-face contact (Leibert, Archer, Munson, & York, 2006; Wagner, Brand, Schulz, & Knaevelsrud, 2012) .

For therapists to promote optimal e-health usage, their attitudes towards e-health may be a barrier in successfully implement e-health (Vis et al., 2018) . In comparison, research shows that lower therapists' attitudes towards a treatment protocol have a negative impact on the effectiveness of the treatment (Wiborg, Knoop, Wensing, & Bleijenberg, 2012) . Therefore, barriers like negative attitudes towards e-health should be taken seriously.

It is conceivable that this can negatively influence therapists' capability to promote patients' usage intensity. In addition to the therapists' attitude, research shows also the patients' attitude is important for e-health usage (Hardiker & Grant, 2011) . Patients' attitudes towards technology are positively related to the frequency of e-health usage (Chiu & Eysenbach, 2010) . In order to apply e-health successfully, patients' general e-health attitude should be taken in consideration before indicating e-health (Stallard,

Velleman, & Richardson, 2010). When e-health is prescribed to patients who are less positive about this method, the uptake of the program will presumably be suboptimal.Both patients' and therapists' attitude might be important in e-health treatment, but the relationship of these factors and actual usage is not yet clear for e-health applications applied in blended e-health (a combination of an internet delivered program and face-to-face treatment). Also, little is known about the relationship between e-health usage in blended form and the therapeutic alliance.

Since both expected to be important for good e-health practice and uptake, this needs to be clarified. The aim of this study is to examine the relationship between usage intensity of online modules applied as blended e-health and both e-health attitude and the therapeutic alliance.

Not only the relation between patients' attitude and e-health usage intensity, but also the possible relationship between therapists' attitude and patients' e-health usage is explored.

In consideration of previous research, we expect to find a positive correlation between usage intensity and attitudes towards e-health. In line with face-to-face treatment, we expect the therapeutic relationship to be positively related to e-health usage.

METHOD

Participants

The study sample consisted of 50 adult patients who were registered for treatment at GGZ Westelijk Noord Brabant, an institution for mental healthcare in the Netherlands. Participants were included when they met the DSM-IV (American Psychiatric Association, 2000) criteria for a major depressive disorder with a current depressive episode, there was no language barrier and participants had internet access at home.

Patients with minimal depressive symptoms according to BDI (score 0 - 13) were not included in the study. Participants suffered from moderate to severe depressive symptoms, typically treated in the specialized mental health centers, where comorbid problems are involved. Patients' descriptive characteristics are presented in Table 1.

Therapists, experienced with CBT for depression, were asked to participate in the study and apply the blended treatment program (described below). In total, nine therapists participated voluntarily.

Table 1. Descriptive characteristics study sample.

	Participants (N = 50)
Gender; Female	29 (58%)
Age (SD)	43.7 (10.41)
Range	25 - 63
Educational Level	
Low	4 (8%)
Middle	41 (82%)
High	5 (10%)

Intervention

The blended treatment program included face-to-face group therapy performed by two cognitive behavioural therapists. The treatment consisted of 12, two-hour weekly sessions and contains psycho-education, relaxation, activation, cognitive therapy and problem solving skills. Between sessions, patients gained access to an e-health program, consisting of eight sub-modules, matching the group sessions which provides information and includes exercises, registration assignments and cognitive therapy. These assignments could be shared with the therapist. Also, patients were able to communicate with their therapist through a message application. Each patient had one main therapist to contact.

Design and Procedure

This study was applied in an outpatient mental health setting with patients who attended a blended treatment program for major depressive disorder. Data collection was obtained from two different sources. Patients were asked to complete questionnaires three times. In order to determine the usage intensity, data of login frequency was registered by the e-health application. Also, the number of completed exercises and frequency of therapist contact were registered (Figure 1).

Prior to treatment start, patients were informed about the study through written and verbal information. If they were willing to participate, informed consent was obtained and patients received a baseline assessment to determine symptoms. Eleven patients refused to participate in the study but did participate in group therapy. When participants met the criteria for depressive disorder, they completed questionnaires on e-health attitudes. A questionnaire on treatment motivation was also provided in order to detect possible confounding effects. In order to take possible group differences into account, a group cohesion questionnaire was included as a post treatment measurement. Eight participants did not finish the program, two dropped out on practical reasons, five patients preferred individual treatment and one patient was referred to clinical treatment. There was no reported drop-out due to discontentment about e-health use.

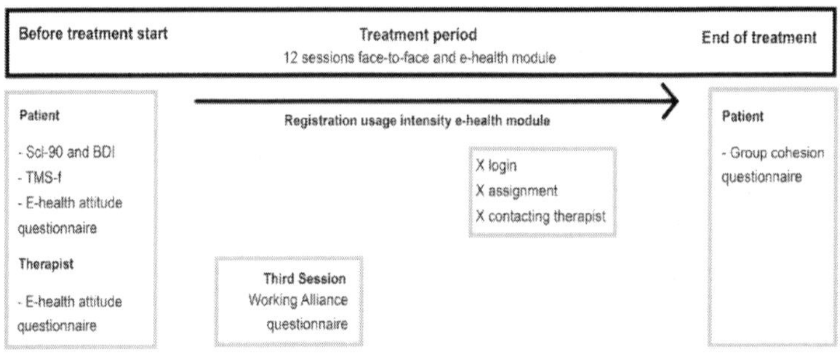

Figure 1. Flow of data collection.

For therapists, prior to treatment they completed an e-health attitude questionnaire. Therapists who participated in the study in more than one treatment group, were asked to complete the attitude questionnaire before every new treatment cycle. For the purpose of measuring the therapeutic alliance with minimalizing confounding therapy effect, patients completed the working alliance questionnaire after the third therapy session. Previous studies reported the predictive validity of the working alliance measured early on in treatment (week 3) on treatment outcome (Wagner, Brand, Schulz, & Knaevelsrud, 2012) .

Measurements

1) e-health attitude. Attitude on the use of e-health was assessed using an edited questionnaire based on the Attitude Questionnaire introduced by Addis & Krasnow (2000). This questionnaire is designed to measure attitudes on protocolled therapies. The questionnaire was adapted to the use of e-health, both items on familiarity with computer use and ideas on e-health effectivity were added. The patient questionnaire consists of 19 items that are scored on a 5-point Likert-scale. The scale internal consistency is good ($\alpha = .89$). The same scale has been used to develop a 26 item

therapists attitude scale, which consists of three components; e-health negative effects, possibilities of e-health and computer competence. Reliability scores of the scale and subscales are good (α between .83 and .89) (Aerts & van Dam, 2015).

2) Usage intensity. Usage intensity is operationalized with login frequency as a main variable. Number of completed exercises and frequency of contact with the therapist was registered for detailed analyses.

3) Work Alliance Inventory, WAI-12. An assessment of the therapeutic alliance was obtained using the Dutch, shortened version of the Work Alliance Inventory, WAI-12 (Horvath & Greenberg, 1989; Vertommen & Vervaeke, 1990) . The questionnaire is a self-report, 12 items list on emotional bond, agreement on therapy goals and therapy tasks (Stinckens, Ulburghs, & Claes, 2009). Both reliability and convergent validity are satisfactory (Munder, Wilmers, Leonhart, Linster, & Barth, 2010). For this study, patients' rating of the work alliance was obtained for the therapist couple.

4) Beck Depression Inventory (BDI) (Beck et al., 1961) . This self-report inventory measures the symptoms of a depressive disorder according to the DSM-IV present the past week. Both internal consistency and construct validity are good (van der Does, 2002) .

5) Symptom Checklist 90 (Scl-90). The presence and severity of psychopathology was assessed with the Dutch version of the Symptom Checklist 90 (Scl-90). The validity as well as the reliability of the list is good (Arrindell & Ettema, 1986) .

6) Therapy Motivation Scales (TMS-f). Treatment motivation was measured using one subscale of the Therapy Motivation Scales for forensic patients (TMS-f) (Drieschner & Boomsma, 2008), the Motivation to Engage in Treatment (MET) scale. Considering the reference to a specific forensic problem, one item was omitted. In order to obtain an acceptable reliability rate in our study, two more items were deleted (α = .74).

7) Group cohesion. An assessment of the group cohesion was obtained by the Group Cohesion Questionnaire-23 (GCQ-23) (Trijsburg et al., 2004) . Reliability statistics are satisfactory (α = .87).

Statistical Analysis

All analyses were performed using SPSS statistics 22 for Windows. Statistical significance was assumed at $p < .05$.

Before hypothesis testing, some tests are performed to check on possible confounding effects. Patients with more severe or chronic problems may have more adherence problems (Donkin & Glozier, 2012) . A Kruskal-Wallis test was performed to check if the number of depressive episodes experienced was related to usage intensity.

To rule out the possibility that differences in therapist couples might be a confounding factor on usage intensity, a Kruskal-Wallis test was performed. A Spearman's correlation test was performed on group cohesion with usage intensity, in order to invest if those two factors are related and may be confounding in the relation between e-health attitude and usage intensity.

In order to investigate whether drop outs differ from patients who completed the treatment on symptom degree at start, their motivation, e-health attitude and work alliance, t-tests were performed.

To define correlations between usage intensity and symptoms at start, attitude and work alliance, Spearman correlation tests were executed. Partial correlation tests were performed on attitude and usage intensity, in order to control for symptom degree and motivation. Both factors are hypothesized to be related to usage intensity.

To test the correlation between of therapists' e-health attitude and usage intensity, the average score of both therapists was obtained to execute Spearman correlation tests.

Partial correlation tests were performed on work alliance with sharing assignments, controlling for number of completed exercises.

Spearman's correlation tests were performed on usage intensity and both symptom inventories (Scl-90 and BDI).

A partial correlation test was used to control for effects of attitude on the relationship between symptom degree and usage intensity.

It should be noted that for the usage intensity variables, the assumption of normality is violated. Because transformation was not possible, non-parametric tests were performed when available.

RESULTS

An overview of the mean outcome measures, standard deviations, minimum and maximum scores for both dependent and independent variables are presented in Table 2. At start patients reported moderate to severe (depression) symptoms. The average BDI score indicates that patients suffer from severe depressive disorders. There is more variation between patients' attitude than in therapists' attitude.

The scores of these groups are not mutually comparable. There is a high variance in e-health usage intensity. During treatment period, 44% of the participants contacted their therapist by sharing digital homework assignments in the e-health portal more than 20 times.

First, analyses on confounding effects were performed. No correlations were found between usage intensity and the number of experienced depressive episodes ($\chi^2(3) = 5.75$, $p > .05$) or between different therapist couples ($\chi^2(3) = 4.78$, $p > .05$). Also, no significant correlation between usage intensity and group cohesion ($r = -.02$, $p > .05$) was found.Drop outs and patients who completed the program did not differ on variables measured at start and early on in treatment. They did not differ significantly on symptom degree $t(48) = 1.91$, $p > .05$, motivation ($t(48) = -.67$, $p > .05$) and e-health attitude ($t(48) = -.51$, $p > .05$).Further analysis showed that patients' e-health attitude is correlated with login frequency ($r = .28$, $p < .05$) (Table 3). There is a positive, partial correlation between patients' e-health attitude and usage intensity, controlling for symptoms and motivation ($r = .27$, $p < .05$). Patients with a more positive attitude towards e-health, used the online treatment module more frequently.

Table 2. Minimum and maximum scores, means and missing data of both dependent and independent variables.

	Minimum	Maximum	Mean	SD
Scl 90	121	433	242.84	58.61
BDI start	14	52	34.47	9.85
Attitude patient	37	95	62.32	12.17
Attitude therapist	92.5	111	100.99	6.05
Work alliance	18	54	35.28	8.88
X login	0	158	24.32	25.36
X assignment	0	444	131.14	117.86
X contact therapist	0	132	22.34	24.32

Table 3. Correlation analyses (Spearmen's rho) of symptom rate and attitude with e-health usage intensity.

	X login	X form	X contact th
Scl90	−.28*	−.16	−.11
BDI start	−.23	−.07	−.14
Attitude patient	.28	.21	.20
Attitude therapist	−.04	.16	.35**
Work alliance	.07	−.19	.33*[1]

*Significant at $p < .05$; **Significant at $p < .01$; [1]controlled for number of completed exercises.

Although no association was found between therapists' attitude and patients' usage intensity, there is a positive relation between therapists' attitude and the frequency of sharing assignments ($r = .35$, $p < .01$).

There is no significant correlation between patients' assessed work alliance and login frequency ($r = .07$, $p > .05$). However, there is a positive correlation between the therapeutic relationship and the frequency of contacting the therapist, controlling for number of completed exercises ($r = .33$, $p < .05$).

Patients' attitudes are negatively correlated to the overall level of psychopathology ($r = -.39$, $p < .01$). Although there is no significant correlation between the degree of depression symptoms and usage frequency ($r = -.23$, $p > .05$), the overall level of psychopathology and usage frequency are negatively correlated ($r = -.28$, $p < .05$) (Table 3).

DISCUSSION

The aim of the present study was to examine the relationship between attitudes towards e-health, the therapeutic alliance in blended e-health treatment and usage intensity of online modules. This study identified a positive relation between patients' e-health attitude and usage intensity. Patients with a more positive attitude tend to use the application more frequently. Therapists' attitudes are partially related to patient usage. When a therapist has a positive attitude towards e-health, patients are inclined to seek more digital contact with their therapist. The expectation that the alliance quality is positively associated with e-health usage is also partially confirmed. Patients with higher alliance rates, share a higher percentage of their digital homework assignments.

These findings generate some interesting perspectives on e-health usage intensity in a blended treatment program. In line with earlier findings on stand-alone e-health usage, a positive relationship between patients' attitudes and e-health usage appeared to be present in blended e-health. Although this study did not found causal relations, the results may suggest that patients' attitudes can be a factor of interest in stimulating intervention exposure by increasing usage frequency. With regard to the therapists' attitude, there is no relation with usage frequency in general, but there appeared to be a relationship with the frequency by which patients contacted their therapist. Therapists with a positive e-health attitude may stimulate patient's treatment involvement. Further work needs to be done to establish whether this correlation is indeed consistent. Possibly, patients feel more invited to seek contact and share their assignments with these therapists.

Our findings are in line with a study of El Alaoui et al. (2015) which showed that patients' beliefs and expectations are important for adherence in e-health, while the influence of the therapist is less distinct. Although a lot of researches focus on therapist variables, the present study raises the idea that patients variables should get more attention. Also, these results indicate that attention to patients' attitude is a part of e-health application.

The relationship between the therapeutic alliance and e-health usage in blended treatment seems to be smaller compared to attitude. Like with therapists' attitude, there is a correlation with sharing homework assignments. In a positive therapeutic alliance, patients seek more contact with their therapist and shares more assignments. This may reflect a higher treatment engagement, as described by Kelders, Bohlmeijer, & van Gemert-Pijnen (2013) . Although this seems preferable in the treatment course, it is not clear if actively seeking contact with the therapist contributes to treatment effect. Earlier studies on this topic showed positive treatment effects of guided self-help on symptom reduction, but contact frequency and support time were not correlated to this reduction (Grist & Cavanagh, 2013; Kelders, Bohlmeijer, & van Gemert-Pijnen, 2013; Tummers, Knoop, Van Dam, & Bleijenberg, 2012) . One hypotheses explaining this finding may be that, like involved patients, patients who have difficulties following the program also seek regular contact, but have less preferable outcome (Tummers et al., 2012) .

In line with previous research, this study suggests that patients with severe symptoms of depression experience more problems with adherence (Perle et al., 2011; Donkin & Glozier, 2012) . Notably, in our study this appeared to be related to e-health attitude. Patients with severe symptoms have a more negative attitude towards e-health which is related to a less frequent e-health usage. Since recent studies showed that e-health interventions can be suitable in treatment of severe depressive symptoms (Cuijpers & Riper, 2014; Meyer et al., 2015) , our findings suggest that this patient group may need extra attention. It may be valuable to evaluate if active support and iteration of psycho-education is effective in promoting adherence for patients with severe symptoms.

Overall, findings in this study show a positive relation between patients' attitude towards e-health and e-health usage intensity. This may suggest that improving patients' attitude may be profitable in order to promote efficient e-health use. Previous research showed it is possible to influence attitudes toward e-health (Ebert et al., 2015; Mitchell & Gordon, 2007) . Positive effects of a short intervention to improve acceptance of e-health for patient with depressive symptoms were reported. After displaying a video with an expert and patient providing information about internet based therapy, e-health acceptance rates increased (Ebert et al., 2015) .

This study has several methodological limitations. First, due to the small sample size, the power of the study is limited and results should be interpreted with caution. Second, the sample was relatively low educated. Though it is not yet clear which mediating factors are of significant importance, education level may affect e-health usage and the ability to benefit from it. Third, it is not clear if in blended treatment, WAI recordings are applicable in the context of an e-health program. It may be primary related to the face-to-face treatment. Jasper et al. (2014) noted differences in credibility of different aspect of the therapeutic relationship between face-to-face treatment and e-health. For the fist, "bond" seems to be more important and for the latter "tasks" seem to be prominent. Finally, the therapists in our study were practically consentient in their attitude, so possible effects were difficult to detect. The therapists in this study had positive attitudes towards e-health in comparison with a general group of therapists (Aerts & van Dam, 2015). Therefore, findings in this study are established in a treatment climate with therapists whom were positive about blended e-health. To explore effects of therapists' attitude, a more diverse therapist sample should be included.

Taken together, some recommendations towards future research arise from this study. Firstly, for a better understanding of the contribution of therapists' attitudes, the relationship between therapists' attitude and therapists' attention for e-health should be investigated. As an additive on attitude and self-rated usage, it may be interesting to use log-data of therapists' e-health usage and rate face-to-face contacts on e-health attention and possible negative signals about e-health. Also, in order to get a comprehensive view on the contribution of the therapist's attitude, a more diverse therapist group should be included.

This study on e-health usage intensity provides some insight in the correlation between e-health attitudes and patients' e-health usage. It has identified patients' e-health attitude as a factor related to e-health usage intensity, when applied by therapists with positive attitudes on e-health applications. Hence, we suggest keeping therapists' attitudes in mind when implementing e-health, in order to enable patients to get access to qualitative e-health treatment and effective support by using it. Also, patients with more severe symptoms may need extra attention in order to promote adherence. Since adherence is important in efficient e-health application, further work needs to be done to invest if improving patient's attitude before start of treatment is a good option in enhancing adherence. This may be credible, especially in patients with severe disorders. Therefore implementing and evaluating interventions on attitude could be the next step in improving e-health applications.

REFERENCES

1. Addis, M. E., & Krasnow, A. D. (2000). A National Survey of Practicing Psychologists' Attitudes toward Psychotherapy Treatment Manuals. Journal of Consulting and Clinical Psychology, 68, 331-339. https://doi.org/10.1037/0022-006X.68.2.331
2. Aerts, J. E. M., & van Dam, A. (2015). E-health Attitudelijst; Wat Drijft de Behandelaar? [E-Health Attitude Questionnaire: What Drives the Health Care Professional?] Psychopraktijk, 7, 26-30. https://doi.org/10.1007/s13170-015-0090-2
3. American Psychiatric Association (2000). Diagnostic and Statistical Manual of mental disorders: DSM-IV-TR. Washington DC: American Psychiatric Pub.
4. Andersson, G., & Cuijpers, P. (2009). Internet-Based and Other Computerized Psychological Treatments for Adult Depression: A Meta-Analysis. Cognitive Behavior Therapy, 38, 196-205. https://doi.org/10.1080/16506070903318960
5. Andersson, G., Cuijpers, P., Carlbring, P., Riper, H., & Hedman, E. (2014). Guided Internet-Based vs. Face-to-Face Cognitive Behavior Therapy for Psychiatric and Somatic Disorders: A Systematic Review and Meta-Analysis. World Psychiatry, 13, 288-295. https://doi.org/10.1002/wps.20151
6. Andrews, G., Cuijpers, P., Craske, M. G., McEvoy, P., & Titov, N. (2010). Computer Therapy for the Anxiety and Depressive Disorders Is Effective, Acceptable and Practical Health Care: A Meta-Analysis. PLoS One, 5, el13196. https://doi.org/10.1371/journal.pone.0013196
7. Arrindell, W. A., & Ettema, J. H. M. (1986). SCL-90: Handleiding bij een Multidimensionele Psychopathologie-Indicator. Lisse: Swets & Zeitlinger.
8. Beck, A. T., Ward, C. H., Mendelson, M., Mock, J., & Erbaugh, J. (1961). An Inventory for Measuring Depression. Archives of General Psychiatry, 4, 561-571. https://doi.org/10.1001/archpsyc.1961.01710120031004
9. Beutler, L. E., Malik, M., Alimohamed, S., Harwood, T. M., Talebi, H., Noble, S., & Wong, E. (2004).Therapist Variables. In M. J. Lambert (Eds.), Bergin and Garfield's Handbook of Psychotherapy and Behaviour Change (5th ed., pp. 227-306). New York: Wiley.
10. Carlbring, P., Andersson, G., Cuijpers, P., Riper, H., & Hedman-Lagerlöf, E. (2018). Internet-Based vs. Face-to-Face Cognitive

Behavior Therapy for Psychiatric and Somatic Disorders: An Updated Systematic Review and Meta-Analysis. Cognitive Behaviour Therapy, 47, 1-18. https://doi.org/10.1080/16506073.2017.1401115

11. Chiu, T. M., & Eysenbach, G. (2010). Stages of Use: Consideration, Initiation, Utilization, and Outcomes of an Internet-Mediated Intervention. BMC Medical Informatics and Decision Making, 10, 73. https://doi.org/10.1186/1472-6947-10-73
12. Cuijpers, P., & Riper, H. (2014). Internet Interventions for Depressive Disorders: An Overview. Revista de Psicopatología y Psicología Clínica, 19, 209-216. https://doi.org/10.5944/rppc.vol.19.num.3.2014.13902
13. Donkin, L., & Glozier, N. (2012). Motivators and Motivations to Persist with Online Psychological Interventions: A Qualitative Study of Treatment Completers. Journal of Medical Internet Research, 14, e91. https://doi.org/10.2196/jmir.2100
14. Donkin, L., Christensen, H., Naismith, S. L., Neal, B., Hickie, I. B., & Glozier, N. (2011). A Systematic Review of the Impact of Adherence on the Effectiveness of e-Therapies. Journal of Medical Internet Research, 13, e52. https://doi.org/10.2196/jmir.1772
15. Donovan, C. L., Poole, C., Boyes, N., Redgate, J., & March, S. (2015). Australian Mental Health Worker Attitudes towards cCBT: What Is the Role of Knowledge? Are There Differences? Can We Change Them? Internet Interventions, 2, 372-381. https://doi.org/10.1016/j.invent.2015.09.001
16. Drieschner, K. H., & Boomsma, A. (2008). The Treatment Motivation Scales for Forensic Outpatient Treatment (TMS-F): Construction and Psychometric Evaluation. Assessment, 15, 224-241. https://doi.org/10.1177/1073191107311650
17. Ebert, D. D., Berking, M., Cuijpers, P., Lehr, D., Pörtner, M., & Baumeister, H. (2015). Increasing the Acceptance of Internet-Based Mental Health Interventions in Primary Care Patients with Depressive Symptoms. A Randomized Controlled Trial. Journal of Affective Disorders, 176, 9-17. https://doi.org/10.1016/j.jad.2015.01.056
18. El Alaoui, S., Ljótsson, B., Hedman, E., Kaldo, V., Andersson, E., Rück, C., Andersson, G., & Lindefors, N. (2015). Predictors of Symptomatic Change and Adherence in Internet-Based Cognitive Behaviour Therapy for Social Anxiety Disorder in Routine Psychiatric Care. PLoS ONE, 10, e0124258.

19. Gainsbury, S., & Blaszczynski, A. (2011). A Systematic Review of Internet-Based Therapy for the Treatment of Addictions. Clinical Psychology Review, 31, 490-498. https://doi.org/10.1016/j.cpr.2010.11.007
20. Grist, R., & Cavanagh, K. (2013). Computerised Cognitive Behavioural Therapy for Common Mental Health Disorders, What Works, for Whom under What Circumstances? A Systematic Review and Meta-Analysis. Journal of Contemporary Psychotherapy, 43, 243-251. https://doi.org/10.1007/s10879-013-9243-y
21. Hardiker, N. R., & Grant, M. J. (2011). Factors That Influence Public Engagement with eHealth: A Literature Review. International Journal of Medical Informatics, 80, 1-12. https://doi.org/10.1016/j.ijmedinf.2010.10.017
22. Horvath, A. O., & Greenberg, L. S. (1989). Development and Validation of the Working Alliance Inventory. Journal of Counseling Psychology, 36, 223-233. https://doi.org/10.1037/0022-0167.36.2.223
23. Jasper, K., Weise, C., Conrad, I., Andersson, G., Hiller, W., & Kleinstäuber, M. (2014). The Working Alliance in a Randomized Controlled Trial Comparing Internet-Based Self-Help and Face-to-Face Cognitive Behavior Therapy for Chronic Tinnitus. Internet Interventions, 1, 49-57. https://doi.org/10.1016/j.invent.2014.04.002
24. Karyotaki, E., Kleiboer, A., Smit, F., Turner, D. T., Pastor, A. M., Andersson, G., Berger, T., Botella, C., Breton., J. M., Carlbring, P., Christensen, H., Graaf, E., Griffiths, K., Donker, T., Farrer, L., Huibers, M. J. H., Lenndin, J., Machinnon, A., Meyer, B., Moritz, S., Riper, H., Spek, V., Vernmark, K., & Cuijpers, P. (2015). Predictors of Treatment Dropout in Self-Guided Web-Based Interventions for Depression: An "Individual Patient Data" Meta-Analysis. Psychological Medicine, 45, 2717-2726. https://doi.org/10.1017/S0033291715000665
25. Kelders, S. M., Bohlmeijer, E. T., & van Gemert-Pijnen, J. E. W. C. (2013). Participants, Usage, and Use Patterns of a Web-Based Intervention for the Prevention of Depression within a Randomized Controlled Trial. Journal of Medical Internet Research, 15, e172. https://doi.org/10.2196/jmir.2258
26. Kelders, S. M., Kok, R. N., Ossebaard, H. C., & van Gemert-Pijnen, J. E. W. C. (2012). Persuasive System Design Does Matter: A Systematic Review of Adherence to Web-Based Interventions. Journal of Medical Internet Research, 14, e152. https://doi.org/10.2196/jmir.2104

27. Lambert, M. J., & Barley, D. E. (2002). Research Summary on the Therapeutic Relationship and Psychotherapy Outcome. In J. C. Norcross (Ed.), Psychotherapy Relationships That Work (pp. 17-32). Oxford: Oxford University Press.

28. Leibert, T., Archer Jr., J., Munson, J., & York, G. (2006). An Exploratory Study of Client Perceptions of Internet Counseling and the Therapeutic Alliance. Journal of Mental Health Counseling, 28, 69-83. https://doi.org/10.17744/mehc.28.1.f0h37djrw89nv6vb

29. Meyer, B., Bierbrodt, J., Schröder, J., Berger, T., Beevers, C. G., Weiss, M., Jacob, G., Späth, C., Andersson, G., Lutz, W., Hautzinger, M., Löwe, B., Rose, M., Hohagen, F., Caspar, F., Greiner, W., Moritz, S., & Klein, J. P. (2015). Effects of an Internet Intervention (Deprexis) on Severe Depression Symptoms: Randomized Controlled Trial. Internet Interventions, 2, 48-59. https://doi.org/10.1016/j.invent.2014.12.003

30. Mitchell, N., & Gordon, P. K. (2007). Attitudes towards Computerized CBT for Depression amongst a Student Population. Behavioural and Cognitive Psychotherapy, 35, 421-430. https://doi.org/10.1017/S1352465807003700

31. Mora, L., Nevid, J., & Chaplin, W. (2008). Psychologist Treatment Recommendations for Internet-Based Therapeutic Interventions. Computers in Human Behaviour, 24, 3052-3062. https://doi.org/10.1016/j.chb.2008.05.011

32. Munder, T., Wilmers, F., Leonhart, R., Linster, H. W., & Barth, J. (2010). Working Alliance Inventory-Short Revised (WAI-SR): Psychometric Properties in Outpatients and Inpatients. Clinical Psychology & Psychotherapy, 17, 231-239.

33. Perle, J. G., Langsam, L. C., & Nierenberg, B. (2011). Controversy Clarified: An Updated Review of Clinical Psychology and Tele-Health. Clinical Psychology Review, 31, 1247-1258. https://doi.org/10.1016/j.cpr.2011.08.003

34. Spek, V., Cuijpers, P., Nyklícek, I., Riper, H., Keyzer, J., & Pop, V. (2007). Internet-Based Cognitive Behaviour Therapy for Symptoms of Depression and Anxiety: A Meta-Analysis. Psychological Medicine, 37, 319-328. https://doi.org/10.1017/S0033291706008944

35. Spek, V., Cuijpers, P., Nyklícek, I., Smits, N., Riper, H., Keyzer, J., & Pop, V. (2008). One-Year Follow-up Results of a Randomized Controlled Clinical Trial on Internet-Based Cognitive Behavioural Therapy for Subthreshold Depression in People over 50 Years. Psychological

Medicine, 38, 635-639. https://doi.org/10.1017/S0033291707002590

36. Stallard, P., Velleman, S., & Richardson, T. (2010). Computer Use and Attitudes towards Computerised Therapy amongst Young People and Parents Attending Child and Adolescent Mental Health Services. Child and Adolescent Mental Health, 15, 80-84. https://doi.org/10.1111/j.1475-3588.2009.00540.x
37. Stinckens, N., Ulburghs, A., & Claes, L. (2009). De Werkalliantie als Sleutelelement in het Therapiegebeuren: Meting met behulp van de WAV-12, de Nederlandstalige Verkorte Versie van de Working Alliance Inventory. Tijdschrift voor Klinische Psychologie, 39, 44-60.
38. Trijsburg, R. W., Bogaerds, H., Letiche, M., Bidzjel, l., & Duivenvoorden, H. J. (2004). De Ontwikkeling van de Group Cohesion Questionnaire (GCQ). Amsterdam/Rotterdam: Universiteit van Amsterdam/Erasmus Universiteit Rotterdam.
39. Tummers, M., Knoop, H., Van Dam, A., & Bleijenberg, G. (2012). Implementing a Minimal Intervention for Chronic Fatigue Syndrome in a Mental Health Centre: A Randomized Controlled Trial. Psychological Medicine, 42, 2205-2215. https://doi.org/10.1017/S0033291712000232
40. Urech, A., Krieger, T., Möseneder, L., Biaggi, A., Vincent, A., Poppe, C., Meyer, B., Riper, H., & Berger, T. (2018). A Patient Post Hoc Perspective on Advantages and Disadvantages of Blended Cognitive Behaviour Therapy for Depression: A Qualitative Content Analysis. Psychotherapy Research, 1-13. https://doi.org/10.1080/10503307.2018.1430910
41. van der Does, A. J. W. (2002). BDI-II-NL. Handleiding. De Nederlandse Versie van de Beck Depression Inventory (2nd ed.). Lisse: Harcourt Test Publishers.
42. Vertommen, H., & Vervaeke, G. A. C. (1990). Werkalliantievragenlijst (WAV). Vertalingvoorexperimenteelgebruik van de WAI (Horvath and Greenberg: 1986).
43. Vis, C., Mol, M., Kleiboer, A., Bührmann, L., Finch, T., Smit, J., & Riper, H. (2018). Improving Implementation of eMental Health for Mood Disorders in Routine Practice: Systematic Review of Barriers and Facilitating Factors. JMIR Mental Health, 5, e20. https://doi.org/10.2196/mental.9769
44. Wagner, B., Brand, J., Schulz, W., & Knaevelsrud, C. (2012). Online

Working Alliance Predicts Treatment Outcome for Posttraumatic Stress Symptoms in Arab War-Traumatized Patients. Depression and Anxiety, 29, 646-651. https://doi.org/10.1002/da.21962

45. Wagner, B., Horn, A. B., & Maercker, A. (2014). Internet-Based versus Face-to-Face Cognitive-Behavioral Intervention for Depression: A Randomized Controlled Non-Inferiority Trial. Journal of Affective Disorders, 152, 113-121. https://doi.org/10.1016/j.jad.2013.06.032
46. Wiborg, J. F., Knoop, H., Wensing, M., & Bleijenberg, G. (2012). Therapist Effects and the Dissemination of Cognitive Behaviour Therapy for Chronic Fatigue Syndrome in Community-Based Mental Health Care. Behaviour Research and Therapy, 50, 393-396. https://doi.org/10.1016/j.brat.2012.03.002

CHAPTER 16

PERFORMANCE EVALUATION OF HEALTHCARE MONITORING SYSTEM OVER HETEROGENEOUS WIRELESS NETWORKS

Sabato Manfredi

Faculty of Engineering, University of Naples Federico II, Napoli, Italy

ABSTRACT

The wide diffusion of healthcare monitoring systems allows continuous patient to be remotely monitored and diagnosed by doctors. The problem of congestion, namely due to the uncontrolled increase of traffic with respect to the network capacity, is one of the most common phenomena affecting the reliability of transmission of information in any network. The aim of the paper is to build a realistic simulation environment for healthcare

Citation: S. Manfredi, "Performance Evaluation of Healthcare Monitoring System over Heterogeneous Wireless Networks," *E-Health Telecommunication Systems and Networks*, Vol. 1 No. 3, 2012, pp. 27-36. doi: 10.4236/etsn.2012.13005.

system including some of the main vital signs model, wireless sensor and mesh network protocols implementation. The simulator environment is an efficient mean to analyze and evaluate in a realistic scenario the healthcare system performance in terms of reliability and efficiency.

Keywords: Modeling, Simulation and Management of Health-Care Systems; Applications of Information and Communication Technologies to Health-Care Management; E-Health; Remote Health Monitoring; Telemedicine; Chronic Disease Management

INTRODUCTION

The recent increased interest in distributed and flexible wireless pervasive applications has drawn great attention to the QoS (Quality of Service) requirements of WNCS (Wireless Network Control System) architectures based on WSANs (Wireless Sensor Actuator Networks) ([1]). Wireless data communication networks provide reduced costs, better power management, easier maintenance and effortless deployment in remote and hard-to-reach areas. Although WSAN research was originally undertaken for military applications, as the field slowly matured and technology rapidly advanced, it has been extended to many civilian applications such as environment and habitat monitoring, home automation, traffic control, and more recently healthcare applications [2,3,5-8]. In particular, WBAN (Wireless Body Area Network) technology has recently significantly increased the potential of remote healthcare monitoring systems (e.g. [4,9,10]). WBAN is a particular kind of WSAN consisting of strategically placed wearable or implanted (in the body) wireless sensor nodes that transmit vital signs (e.g. heart rate, blood pressure, temperature, pH, respiration, oxygen saturation) without limiting the activities of the wearer. The data gathered can be forwarded in real time to the hospital, clinic, or central repository through a LAN (Local Area Network), WAN (Wide Area Network) or cellular network. Doctors and carers can at a distance access this information to assess the state of health of the patient. Additionally, the patient can be alerted by using SMS, alarm, or reminder messages. In a more advanced WBAN, a patient's sensor can even use a neighbor sensor to relay its data if the patient is too far away from the central server (e.g. the hospital data storage). This communication mode is called "multi-hop" wireless transmission. Generally speaking, multi-hop not only extends the communication distance but also saves energy consumption since direct sensor-server long distance wireless communication is avoided through hop-to-hop relay. WBANs will become increasingly pervasive in our daily lives. Recently, WBAN (Wireless Body Area Network) technology has significantly increased the potentiality of the remote healthcare monitoring systems [12,18]. Patient is integrated from multiple sources of measure, PoC (Point of Care) devices, enabling individuals to accurately, easily, and efficiently generate and collect healthcare data. The microelectronics industry are providing an increasing number of PoC devices that combine analysis, power efficiency and testing functionalities with a simple user interface, addressing constraints like device wearability and networking [13-17]. Transmission needs to be performed for communicating the collected physiological signals from the PoC devices to the sink node (i.e. PDA, a smart-phone, or a custom designed microcontrollerbased device) and eventually for sending the aggregated measurements to a remote medical station. PoC nodes form a cluster of Wireless Body Area Network (WBAN) and are usually in the basic configuration of a star topology, transmitting information to the sink node that provides the functionality of collecting data and routing them to the remote station (i.e. Hospital terminal) by a Wireless Mesh Network (WMN). There is a wide variety of available wireless technologies that can serve data transmission between the sink node and a remote station such as WLAN, GSM, GPRS, UMTS, and WiMAX. On the other side, wireless communication standards utilized for short range intra-BAN communication (between PoC node and sink terminal) are IEEE 802.15.1 (Bluetooth [20]) and 802.15.4 (i.e. Zigbee [19]). The Zigbee standard [19] targets low-cost, low data-rate solutions with multimonth-to-multiyear battery life, and very low complexity. Bluetooth [20] is a low-power and low-cost RF standard, operating in the unlicensed 2.4 GHz spectrum. Recently, the 802.15.6 IEEE Task Group [21] is planning the development of a communication standard optimized aimed to define BAN that works at a range even shorter than other wireless technologies that are already available in the market.

The wide diffusion of healthcare monitoring systems allows continuous patients to be remotely monitored and diagnosed by doctors. The problem of congestion, namely due to the uncontrolled increase of traffic with respect to the network capacity, is one of the most common phenomena affecting the reliability of transmission of information and the loss of packets in any network. In addition, in wireless sensor networks, it increases the dissipated energy at the sensor node. In many health care applications (i.e. fetal electrocardiogram monitoring, telecardiology), communication links carry vital information between patient and monitoring devices, that need to be transmitted in short "bursts", requiring a reliable connection. So it is a focal issue, especially in PoC health care systems, to design an appropriate protocol solution addressing reliability, energy efficiency, scalability, reduced packet losses, timely delivery without failure. By large the problem of congestion in both wireless and wired communication networks has addressed in recent years a number of research efforts (see i.e. [24-28,31] and references therein). One of the generic approaches for congestion control is to control the rate of flow of traffic to a source node (i.e. [22,23]) by allocating the available resource capacity following some fairness criteria (i.e. max min, proportional). In those cases, congestion control mechanisms are regarded as a distributed algorithm carried out by sources and links in order to solve a global optimization problem (see [29-32] and references therein). Preliminary routing based approaches to congestion control in healthcare system are presented in [33,34]. In this scenario we introduce a realistic simulator for heathcare system evaluation. Specifically, we build a realistic simulation environment including the main vital signs and wireless networks protocols modelling. The simulator environment is used to analyze and evaluate the effect of congestion phenomena on the healthcare system performance in terms of reliability and efficiency. The simulator can be used for validating novel congestion control scheme to mitigate the congestion phenomena and guarantee efficient healthcare service delivery. The rest of the paper is outlined as follows. In Section 2 the evaluation environment is described in terms of healthcare network topology, communication protocols, performance metrics and vital signals, while in Section 3 a simulation analysis of congestion effect on healthcare system performance is shown. Finally, conclusions and future work are outlined in Section 4.

HEALTHCARE SYSTEM SIMULATION AND EVALUATION ENVIRONMENT

Most of healthcare system scenario is composed of a cluster of WBANs relaying vital information to the Hospital (H) by a WMN. Each WBAN is characterized by the "many-to-one" traffic patterns with a single sink node and multiple source PoC nodes which can be considered to be affixed with the patients. In the paper we will pay our attention to such representative healthcare topology scenario in which all the PoC sensor nodes are stationary and transmit data to the Hospital terminal (H) by the sink terminal data collector. The communication between the sinks and the Hospital terminal is guaranteed by a wireless mesh network. This results in heterogeneous wireless communication network as it is composed of devices adopting different protocols such as Zigbee and Wifi. Herein we set up an evaluation environment in Matlab/Simulink-based simulator TrueTime [41], which facilitates co-simulation of controller task execution in real-time kernels and wireless network environment. The simulations are performed using the above topology of sensors randomly transmitting their information to the sink. The intra BAN protocol used for PoC-Sink communication is the standard Zigbee, while the protocol of WMN supporting sink-remote Hospital terminal communication is Wifi 802.11. Specifically, we build the simulation environment including the following models:

- The intra WBAN standard protocol Zigbee used for PoC sensors-Sink communication;
- The wireless mesh protocol Wifi 802.11 supporting sinks-remote Hospital terminal communication;
- The Ad-hoc On-Demand Distance Vector Routing Protocol (AODV) to route packets in the network;
- The models of the main vital signs such as respiration, electrocardiogram, fetal electrocardiogram, the oxygen saturation of the pacemaker control system device.

In addition, the simulation model takes the path-loss of the radio signals into account. The radio model includes support for 1) ad-hoc wireless networks; 2) isotropic antenna; 3) inability to send and receive messages at the same time; 4) path loss of radio signals modelled as 1 d^{α} where d is the distance and α is a parameter chosen to model the environment ranging in [2,4]; 5) interference from other terminals. In what follows we will describe the details of the above components and we will present the main performance metrics considered in the paper. Moreover, we have enhanced the simulation environment by introducing realistic modelling of PoC sensor power consumption.

Wifi Protocol Model Simulation

The IEEE 802.11b is modeled taking into account of the channel access method CSMA/CA (Carrier Sense Multiple Access with Collision Avoidance). Specifically, in the simulation, a transmission is modelled like this: The node that wants to transmit a packet checks to see if the medium is idle. The transmission may proceed, if the medium is found to be idle, and has stayed so for 50 μs. If, on the other hand, the medium is found to be busy, a random back-off time is chosen and decremented in the same way as when colliding. When a node starts to transmit, its relative position to all other nodes in the same network is calculated, and the signal level in all those nodes are calculated according to the path-loss formula 1 d^{α} . The signal is assumed to be possible to detect if the signal level in the receiving node is larger than the receiver signal threshold. If this is the case, then the signal-to-noise ratio (SNR) is calculated and used to find the block error rate (BLER). Note that all other transmissions add to the background noise when calculating the SNR. The BLER, together with the size of the message, is used to calculate the number of bit errors in the message and if the percentage of bit errors is lower than the error coding threshold, then it is assumed that the channel coding scheme is able to fully reconstruct the message. If there are (already) ongoing transmissions from other nodes to the receiving node and their respective SNRs are lower than the new one, then all those messages are marked as collided. Also, if there are other ongoing transmissions which the currently sending node reaches with its transmission, then those messages may be marked as collided as well. Note that a sending node does not know if its message is colliding, therefore ACK (Acknowledge) messages are sent on the MAC protocol layer. From the perspective of the sending node, lost messages and message collisions are the same, i.e. no ACK is received. If no ACK is received during ACK timeout, the message is retransmitted after waiting for a random back-off time within a contention window. The contention window size is doubled for every retransmission of a certain message. The back-off timer is stopped if the medium is busy, or if it has not been idle for at least 50 μs. There are only "Retry limit" number of retransmissions before the sender gives up on the message and it is not retransmitted anymore.

ZigBee Protocol Model Simulation

ZigBee has a rather low bandwidth, but also a really low power consumption. Although it is based on CSMA/CA as 802.11 b/g, it is much simpler and the protocols are not the same. The packet transmission model in ZigBee is similar to WLAN, but the MAC procedure differs and is modeled taking into account of the following variables:

- NB, number of backoffs;
- BE, backoff exponent;
- MacMinBE, the minimum value of the backoff exponent in the CSMA/CA algorithm. The default value is 3;
- AMaxBE, The maximum value of the backoff exponent in the CSMA/CA algorithm. The default value is 5;

- MacMaxCSMABackoffs, the maximum number of backoffs the CSMA/CA algorithm will attempt before declaring a channel access failure. The default value is 4;
- In a Rayleigh fading, the relative speed of two nodes and the number of multiple paths that the signal takes from the sender to the receiver is taken into account.

The basic battery uses a simple integrator model, so it can be both charged and recharged. We have enhanced the model by implementing the power consumption model described in [35] including the energy spent by the PoC sensor to transmit and receive packets. The main protocol simulation parameters are summarized in Table 1.

AODV Routing Protocol

The Ad-hoc On-Demand Distance Vector Routing Protocol (AODV) [11] is one common routing algorithm in ad hoc networks and is based on the principle of discovering routes as needed. AODV is a reactive algorithm that has a low network utilization, processing and memory overheads. The request is made on-demand rather than in advance, to take into account the dynamic changing of a network structure. In the AODV routing algorithm, the source node issues a route request packet to the destination node at the time a path is needed and this allows mobile nodes to pass messages through their neighbors to nodes with which they cannot directly communicate. AODV does this by discovering the routes (the discovery phase) along which messages can be passed. AODV makes sure these routes do not contain loops and tries to find the shortest route possible. AODV is also able to handle changes in routes and can create new routes if there is an error. Because of their limited range, each node can only communicate with the nodes next to it. A node keeps track of its neighbors by listening for a HELLO message that each node broadcasts periodically. When one node needs to send a message to another node that is not its neighbor, it initiates a path discovery phase by broadcasting a route request (RREQ) packet to its neighbors. The request (RREQ) message contains several fields such as the source, destination and lifespan of the message and a Sequence Number that serves as a unique ID. When intermediate nodes receive a RREQ packet, they update their routing tables for a reverse route to the source and, in the same way, when the intermediate nodes receive a route reply (RREP), they update the forward route to the destination. If multiple RREPs are received by the source, the route with the shortest hop count is chosen. If a route is not used for some period of time, a node cannot be sure whether the route is still valid; consequently, the node removes this route from its routing table. Sequence Numbers serve as time stamps allowing nodes to determine the timeliness of each packet and to prevent the creation of loops. Every time a node sends out any type of message it increases its own "Sequence Number". Each node records the Sequence number of all the other nodes. A higher Sequence Number refers to a fresher route.

The Route Error Message (RERR) allows the AODV to adjust routes when node/link failure occurs. Whenever a node receives a RERR, it looks at the routing table and removes all the routes that contain the bad nodes. When the next hop link breaks, RERR packets are sent by the starting node of the link to a set of neighboring nodes that communicate over the broken link with the destination.

If data is flowing and a link break is detected, a Route Error (RERR) packet is sent to the source of the data in a hop-by-hop fashion. As the RERR extends towards the source, each intermediate node invalidates routes to any unreachable destinations. When the source of the data receives the RERR, it invalidates the route or routes in question and performs route discovery if necessary.

Vital Signs Model Simulation

In the follows we will describe the main vital signs implemented in the simulator following the model given in the original references.

Respiration

Respiration is an important physiologic function that quantifies the physiological states by volume, timing and shape of the respiratory waveform.

It is associated with the kinematics of the chest thereby bringing about changes of the thoracic volume.

Among sensors used to measure respiration there are ones based on inductive plethysmography ([36]) or magnetometers ([37]). Recently, a wearable based piezo-resistive sensor has been developed [38]. This signal requires a reporting rate ranging from 10 Hz to 50 Hz [39]. An example of breath signal implemented in the simulator is shown in Figure 1.

Table 1. ZigBee and Wifi protocol main parameters.

	ZigBee (802.15.4)	Wifi (802.11 b/g)
Path loss exponent	3	3
Sink/wifi Router Transmission Power	0 dbm	20 dbm
Sink capacity	30 pkt/s	-
Sensor Transmission Power	–3 dbm	-
Receiver signal threshold	–48 dbm	–48 dbm
Sensor Buffer Size	30	-
Sink/wifi Router Buffer Size	300	500
Retry Limit	3	3
Ack timeout	0.000864 sec	0.000864 sec
Packet size	150 byte	2.5 MB
Data rate	250,000 bit/s	10 Mbit/s

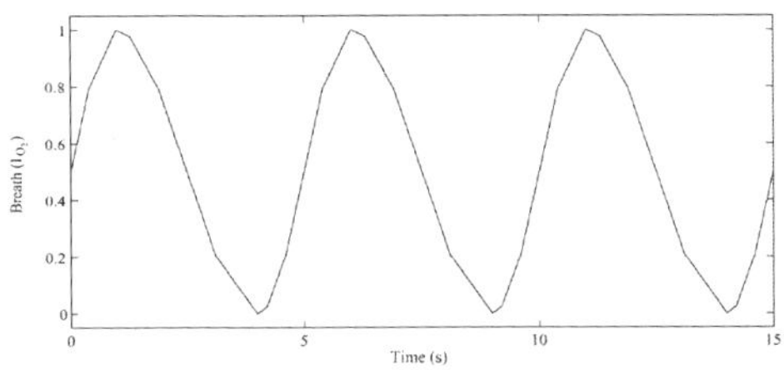

Figure 1. Respiration vital sign dynamic evolution.

Electrocardiogram

The electrocardiogram (ECG) is a time-varying signal reflecting the ionic current flow which causes the cardiac fibres to contract and subsequently relax. The ECG surface is obtained by recording the potential difference between two electrodes placed on the surface of the skin. Here, for simulation purpose, we have used a dynamical model proposed in the literature [40], based on three coupled ordinary differential equations which is capable of generating realistic synthetic electrocardiogram (ECG) signals. Standard clinical ECG application can require reporting rate from 200 Hz to 300 Hz [39]. In Figure 2 it is shown the dynamic of ECG signal implemented into the proposed simulator by using the above model.

Performance Metrics

Depending on the type of target application, QoS in healthcare system can be characterized by, among other factors, reliability, energy efficiency, timeliness, robustness, availability, and security. Among the different performance indices measuring the level of QoS, the following are particularly significant and will be evaluated by the evaluation environment discussed above:

- Throughput is the effective amount of data transmitted in a specific unit of time. In healthcare monitoring, to provide a better observation of a patient's health condition, a sensor can transmit data at a high reporting frequency and then use a high data rate to send out the large amount of data sensed.
- Delay is the time elapsing from the departure of a data packet from the source node to its arrival at the destination node, including queueing delay, switching delay and propagation delay, etc. Delay sensitive applications are common in healthcare environments requiring the monitoring system to deliver the data packets in real-time in order to fulfill specific timing requirements.
- Reliability is the packet reception ratio (the number of "received" packets divided by the number of "transmitted" packets), related also to the two above performance indices.
- Energy consumption is the energy spent in the time to permit the network to work. The nodes must be capable of playing their role for a sufficiently long period using the energy provided by their battery. Consequently, energy efficiency is one of the main requirements of WBANs. Packet collision at the MAC layer, routing overhead, packet loss, and packet retransmission reduce energy efficiency.
- System lifetime. It is strictly related to the nodes average and variance of the energy consumption and it can be defined as the duration of time until some node depletes all its energy.
- Network coverage. It is related to the nodes average and variance of the energy consumption and it means that the entire network space can be monitored by the sensor nodes.
- Packet loss rate is the percentage of data packets that are lost during the process of transmission. It can be used to represent the probability of packets being lost. A packet may be lost due to

e.g. congestion, bit error, or bad connectivity. This parameter is closely related to the reliability of the network.

- Scalability. This is the ability of the healthcare system to guarantee acceptable performance (i.e. a reliability >80%) with the increasing number of patient sensors. It indicates if the healthcare system will be suitable for a large nursing system.

EVALUATION OF CONGESTION EFFECT ON HEALTHCARE SYSTEM PERFORMANCE

Firstly we analyze by using the simulator exploited above, the effect of congestion phenomena on the healthcare network performance degradation. Notice that for each signal at each PoC sensor, we appropriately package the sampled piece of vital sign information into packet to be sent to the Hospital terminal. We have evaluated the network reliability and scalability by increasing the number of the PoC sensors (and so the overall reporting rate) accessing to the sink. As we note from Figure 3, there is a threshold of 30 pkt/sec for the overall PoC sensors reporting rate that produces network congestion with reducing reliability and scalability, and increasing of packet loss: this threshold corresponds to the capacity C = 30 pkt/s of the sink to manage packets. In the same way there is an increasing of time delivery (Figure 4). The worsening of the performance in terms of reliability is mainly due to the buffer overflow and collision packet losses. On the other side the time delay for the delivered packet is due to the time of packet spent waiting at the sink queue before to be transmitted to the Hospital. Indeed, if we consider an overall sensors reporting rate close to sink capacity of 30 pkt/s, it results a time delay of 10 time unit (see Figures 5 and 6) corresponding to the backlog delay at the sink queue of $Buffer_{\text{sink}}/Rr_{PoCs} \simeq 300/30 = 10$. For increasing value of the input reporting rate, it will be a collapse of sink with heavy reduction in reliability and time delivery performances due to the increasing of packet losses, packet retransmission and collision effects. The increasing of packet losses and packets retransmitted increases the PoC sensors average energy (Figure 7) and its variance (Figure 8) consumed by the nodes with consequently heavy reduction of network life time and network coverage. The main effect of the congestion at the sink bottleneck node on the healthcare system performance is the reduction of the quality of the vital signs received at the Hospital. This makes hard to reassemble the vital signs at the Hospital server as so as the estimation of the patient pathologies by doctor. Indeed an increasing of reporting rate and therefore of traffic in the network leads to a worsening of the quality of vital signs, even at the high priority, that requires more bandwidth as it appears from Figure 10 for the case of the ECG signal. On the other side, the Breath sign presents low degradation level although it requires low priority and bandwidth requirements (Figure 9). Therefore, the shape of the signals with high bandwidth requirement can strongly deteriorate loosing significant characteristics for the correct patient diagnosis. For instance the congestion effect on the quality of ECG is the loss of many peaks (e.g. compare Figures 2 and 10) that are of main importance for the correct patient diagnosis about the cardiac pathologies (e.g. ventricular tachycardia, and ventricular fibrillation). Moreover, as shown in Table 2, the average latency is the same irrespective of the different bandwidth/priority requirement of the vital signs (i.e. ECG signal requires more bandwidth and more responsiveness than the respiration sign one). We remark that also for low reporting rate, might occur packets loss due to MAC error and/or collision. For instance, in this case, the overall packet loss due to the collision effect is about of 24% as shown in Table 2.

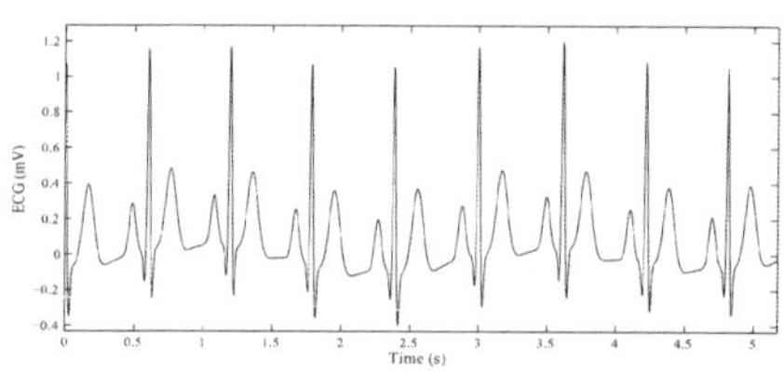

Figure 2. ECG vital sign dynamic evolution.

CONCLUSION AND FUTURE WORK

Due to the "many-to-one" nature of the traffic patterns in healthcare system architecture, congestion at the sink bottleneck node can occur when the PoC nodes traffic increases with respect to the sink capacity. So, it is a focal issue for health care application to design an appropriate sink capacity allocation strategy addressing reliability and timely delivery without failure. We have built a realistic simulation environment for healthcare remote system evaluation including the main vital signs and wireless network protocol modelling. The simulator is used to analyze and evaluate the effect of congestion phenomena on the healthcare system performance in terms of reliability and efficiency. The proposed simulator is suitable to support and validate the design of a novel management control law for healthcare applications that is object of ongoing work.

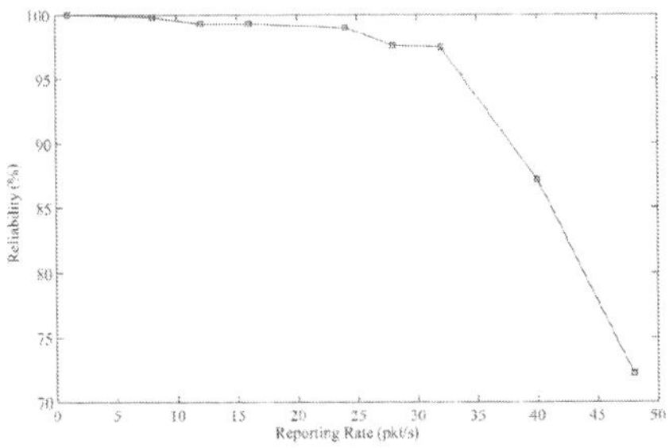

Figure 3. Healthcare remote system reliability as function of the PoC sensors reporting rate.

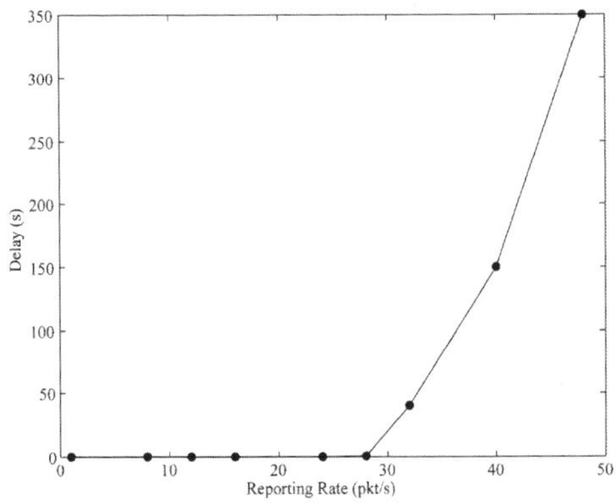

Figure 4. Time delivery delay as function of the PoC sensors reporting rate.

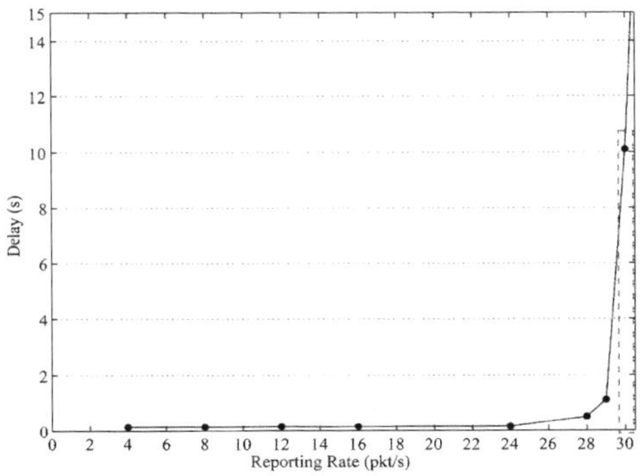

Figure 5. Time delivery delay for PoC sensors reporting rate close to the sink capacity of 30 pkt/s.

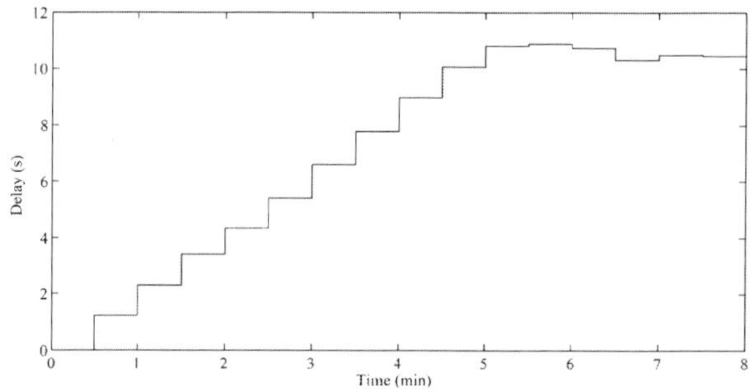

Figure 6. Time delivery delay dynamic for PoC sensors reporting rate close to the sink capacity of 30 pkt/s

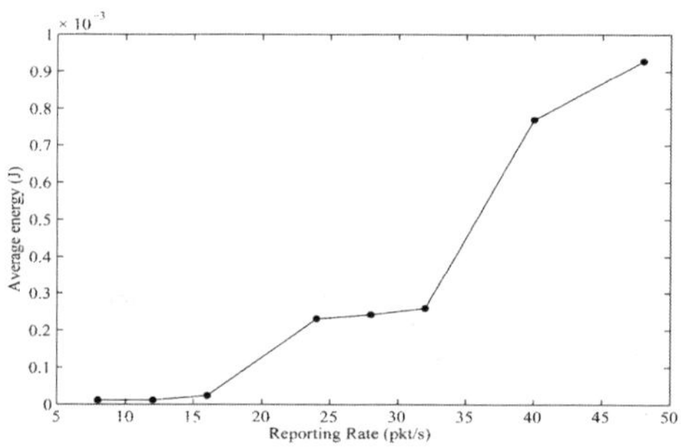

Figure 7. PoC sensors average energy consumption as function of the reporting rate.

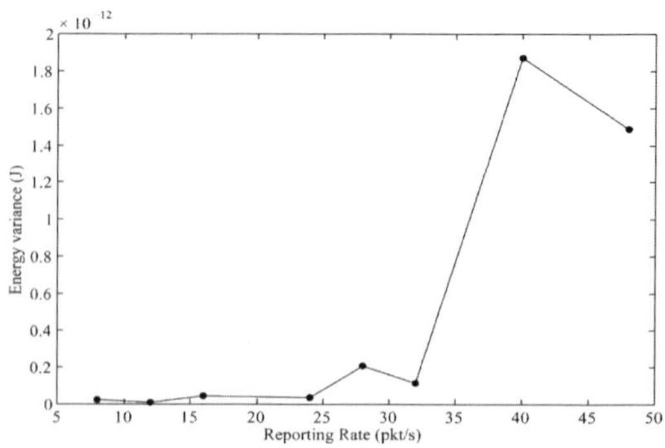

Figure 8. Variance of sensors energy consumption as function of the reporting rate.

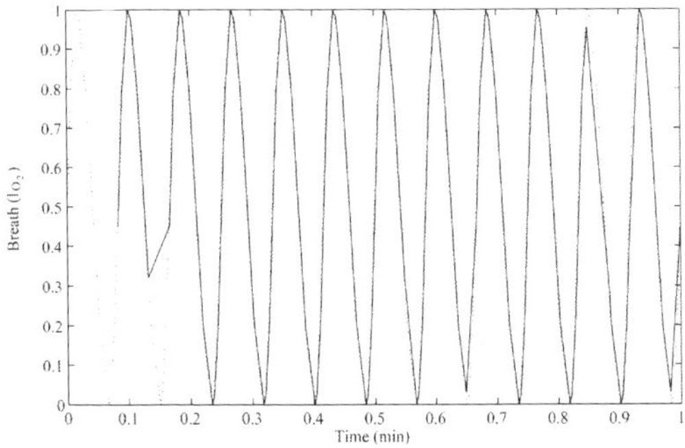

Figure 9. Breath vital signal received at the Hospital (continues line), breath vital signal sampled at the PoC sensor (dashed line).

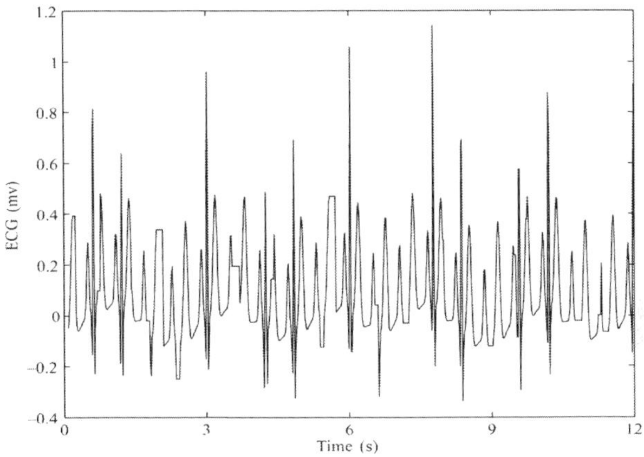

Figure 10. ECG signal received at the Hospital.

Table 2. Time Delivery to the Hospital terminal of each vital sign class with different priority.

Signal/Priority	Delay
Breath/1	40 s
ECG/10	40 s
Packet Collision loss	24%

REFERENCES

1. U.S. DOE, "Industrial Wireless Technology for the 21st Century," Report, Technology Foresight, 2004.
2. K. Hung and Y. Zhang, "Implementation of a WAPBased Telemedicine System for Patient Monitoring," IEEE Transactions on Information Technology in Biomedicine, Vol. 7, No. 2, 2003, pp. 101-107. doi:10.1109/TITB.2003.811870
3. E. Jovanov et al., "Stress Monitoring Using a Distributed Wireless Intelligent Sensor System," IEEE Engineering Medicine and Biology Magazine, Vol. 22, No. 3, 2003, pp. 49-55
4. E. Jovanov, A. Milenkovic, C. Otto and P. C. de Groen, "A Wireless Body Area Network of Intelligent Motion Sensors for Computer Assisted Physical Rehabilitation," Journal of NeuroEngineering and Rehabilitation, Vol. 2, No. 1, 2005, pp. doi:10.1186/1743-0003-2-6
5. T. Gao et al., "Vital Signs Monitoring and Patient Tracking over a Wireless Network," IEEE Proceedings of the 27th Annual International Conference of the Engineering in Medicine and Biology Society, Shanghai, 17-18 January 2006, pp. 102-105.
6. Kafeza et al., "Alerts in Mobile Healthcare Applications: Requirements and Pilot Study," IEEE Transactions on Information Technology in Biomedicine, Vol. 8, No. 2, 2004, pp. 173-181. doi:10.1109/TITB.2004.828888
7. U. Varshney, "Wireless Networks for Enhanced Monitoring of Patients," International Journal of Healthcare Technology and Management, Vol. 6, No. 4-6, 2005, pp. 489-499. doi:10.1504/IJHTM.2005.007009
8. C. Poli, A. Pietrabissa, D. G. Ferriero and M. Grigioni, "An Optimization Framework for Hospital Assets Tracking with Sensor Networks," 2012.
9. T. O'Donovan, J. O'Donoghue, C. Sreenan, P. O'Reilly, D. Sammon, K. O'Connor, "A Context Aware Wireless Body Area Network (BAN)," Proceedings of the Pervasive Health Conference, London, 1-3 April 2009, pp. 1-8.
10. K. Yazdandoost et al., "Channel Model for Body Area Network (BAN)," Proceedings of the Annual International Conference of the IEEE Engineering in Medicine and Biology Society, 20-25 August 2008, pp. 1549-1552.
11. Y. Zhang and T. A. Gulliver, "Quality of Service for Ad Hoc On-Demand Distance Vector Routing," IEEE International Conference on

Wireless and Mobile Computing, Montreal, 22-24 August 2005, pp. 192-196

12. Age Data, "U. S. Census Bureau Statistics," 2010. http://www.census.gov/population/www/socdemo/
13. L. Gatzoulis and I. Iakovidis, "Wearable and Portable eHealth Systems," IEEE Engineering in Medicine and Biology Magazine, Vol. 26, No. 5, 2007, pp. 51-56. doi:10.1109/EMB.2007.901787

CHAPTER 17

IMPACT OF USING M-HEALTH APP ON IMPROVING UNDERGRADUATE STUDENTS' SPORTS AND HEALTH HABITS AND THEIR ATTITUDES TOWARD ITS USE

Ali Al Musawi, Wajeha Al-Ani, Mohamed Al-Aghbari

College of Education, Sultan Qaboos University, Seeb, Oman

ABSTRACT

This study aims to explore the Sultan Qaboos University undergraduate students' perceptions and attitudes towards using m-Health app and its impact on improving their sports and health habits. Triangulation was used by applying a questionnaire and focus groups interviews to answer the research questions. The survey sample was (20) male and female students from four science and humanities colleges. Both quantitative and qualitative findings

Citation: Musawi, A, Al-Ani, W. and Al-Aghbari, M. (2019), "Impact of Using m-Health App on Improving Undergraduate Students' Sports and Health Habits and Their Attitudes toward Its Use". *E-Health Telecommunication Systems and Networks*, **8**, 1-9. doi: 10.4236/etsn.2019.81001.

unequivocally reveal the students' positive perceptions and attitudes toward the use of the mobile health app. No statistically significant differences were found between the responses of either males or females, or the science and humanitarian colleges of the sample students. In light of these findings, the study set forth its conclusions and recommendations.

Keywords: Mobile Health Apps, Sultan Qaboos University, Students, E-Health

INTRODUCTION

Advantages of mobile phone use in physical activity can be seen by the increasing use of the m-Health apps. Individuals are increasingly using mobile phones to monitor their health and physical fitness. Mobile health apps (m-Health apps) are categorized to: 1) fitness and general health apps and 2) disease management apps [1] . It seems that m-Health apps are important to use in the curriculum of science-based colleges, medicine and nursing in specific [2] [3]. [4] explains that many mobile apps offer advice on a range of physical exercises for both women and men. These apps are able to measure all sports statistics such as distance, speed and calories consumed. They add that there are also specific apps that allow the use of the smartphone as a pedometer to calculate the number of steps a user walks daily by subject. The study shows that these apps are able to positively influence behavior change in the individual using these apps and obtain instant data. Other studies show that m-Health apps send text messages to manage disease and are used for depression treatment and psychological support [5] [6] [7] .

[8] shows that mobile health (m-Health) has emerged as an important area for managing various diseases and evaluating health behavior and interventions. Various mobile techniques have been adopted in many health fields because they offer new methods of measurement and intervention methodologies. This study proved the effectiveness of mobile apps in terms of cost and change of health behavior and treatment through providing a permanent reminder and instant feedback in a timely and adaptive manner. [9] conducted a study about of mobile health apps interface characteristics and usefulness and showed the importance of the ease of navigation and simplicity of customization. They add that aesthetics are important too.

In India, [1] found that obtaining information and guidance is the mostly preferred feature by the majority of users. Healthy young users were interested in using health apps to support their health-related behavior change. Other users expected these apps to be able to record and track goals and behaviors. In Sweden, [10] found that there is a lack of knowledge and awareness about m-Health apps and the respondents do not differ between various kinds of apps but show their willingness to use them if they had more information about them.

In Oman, [11] illustrates that employing technology has a crucial impact for E-health progress in the country because people, organizations and technologies influence its development. Sultan Qaboos University (SQU), the only public university in Oman, was established in 1986. The University sets plans to realize its vision and future role. At present, SQU prepares its undergraduate students to be able to apply the knowledge and skills relevant to the specialization; and communicate effectively and use information and communication technologies [12] . Therefore, the students are well versed in using new technologies such as social media and mobile apps to improve their learning and lives [13] .

This study attempts to explore the SQU undergraduate students' perceptions and attitudes towards using m-Health app and its impact on improving their sports and health habits. The following sections explain the study questions, objectives and importance. The methodology section shows the methods, population, sampling techniques, instruments and procedures used. Findings, results, conclusions and recommendations are then discussed in details.

STUDY QUESTIONS

The study attempts to answer the following questions:

1). What are the perceptions of SQU undergraduate students on the impact of using m-health app on improving their sports and health habits?

2) Does the m-health app use differ by gender and college variables?

3) What are the attitudes of SQU undergraduate students towards the use of m-Health app?

STUDY OBJECTIVES

There is a need to investigate how and to what extent m-Health app use exists in the Omani Society, specifically among young users. This study also aims to find out the perceptions of SQU undergraduate students on the impact of m-Health app on improving their sports and health habits and explore their attitudes toward its use.

STUDY IMPORTANCE

The rapid progress in the use of technology innovations in mobile app technologies, m-Health apps in specific, has been a major influence in the daily lives of individuals and society alike. The study is one of the first studies that provide important data about SQU students' views on how the use of m-Health apps changes and improves their sports and health habits.

METHODOLOGY

Method

The descriptive approach was applied combined with focus group interviews. Authors preferred to use more than one instrument because literature shows that it is challenging to investigate their use merely through traditional surveys because individuals' activities and motivations to use them are varied [14] .

Population and Sample

The study community includes all the SQU undergraduate students. However, the fieldwork, for both the questionnaires and focus group interviews, is based on a purposive sample consisted of (20) male and female undergraduate students, ages 18 - 24, divided equally, with 5 students from each college, into two humanities colleges (Education and Arts) and two colleges of scientific studies (Science and Agriculture). Although small, the purposive sample is most effective when one needs to study a certain cultural domain and can be used with a number of techniques in data gathering such as a survey [15] .

Instruments

1) A questionnaire was adapted from Jain, Udinia and Sahoo, 2017; reviewed and used as a tool for collecting data about the perceptions and attitudes of the students towards the use of the m-Heath app.
2) Focus group interviews were conducted to address the perceptions and attitudes in terms of behavior change, features, and reasons for continued use in an in-depth manner and to triangulate the quantitative findings.

Validity and Reliability

A panel of experts validated the questionnaire. It was then modified in light of their comments and feedback. Then, the reliability coefficient was calculated and Cronbach's alpha was at (0.688) and considered as a satisfactory reliability level. Focus groups interviews were recorded, transcribed, analyzed; and categorized in themes.

Procedure

The following steps were implemented:

1) The sample individuals were asked to walk or jog everyday using the "Health®" app on their mobile phones for a week.
2) They were asked to record their observations daily by monitoring their health performance, heart rate and calorie data.
3) After the week period of use, the questionnaire was administered to the study sample.
4) The focus group interviews were conducted after additional week of reflection on the practice.

Statistical Treatment

For the quantitative part of the study, theoretical means, standard deviations and t-test were used.

FINDINGS AND DISCUSSION

Research Question 1

To answer the first question, the sample individuals were asked to rate their responses regarding their perceptions on the impact of the use of m-Health app by responding to (12) statements of the questionnaire. Their responses to the instrument items range from (5) which mean they strongly agree the statement to (1) which means they strongly disagree. Table 1 shows the means and standard deviations of undergraduate students' responses to the instrument items.The results in Table 1 shows positive perceptions of the students on the impact of the use of m-Health apps on their health and sport habits since most responses are higher than the theoretical mean (3.0). The "students' ability to access medical and health information is what makes them use the health software" was ranked as the first statement on their perceptions of the m-Health app use. This finding coincides with [4] [8] and [1] on the importance of using the mobile app in terms of providing instant information and data.

Research Question 2

To answer the second question of the study which states that "Does the m-Health app use differ by gender and college variables?" paired sample T test was used to test for differences if any. Table 2 shows the results. The results in Table 2 show no statistically significant differences between the responses of either males or females, or the science and humanitarian colleges of the sample students. This demonstrates that the gender or college does not influence students' perceptions of their use of m-Health app in general. These findings partially substantiate [2] and [3] on the m-Health apps for science-based colleges.

Research Question 3

To answer the third question, the sample individuals were asked to rate their responses regarding their attitudes toward the use of m-Health app by responding to (7) statements of the questionnaire. Their responses to the instrument items range from (5) which mean they strongly agree the statement to (1) which means they strongly disagree. Table 3 shows the means and standard deviations of undergraduate students' responses to the instrument items.

Table 1. Perceptions of undergraduate students on the impact of the use of m-Health app*.

Statement	Mean	Standard Deviation
My ability to access medical and health information is what makes me use the health software	4.35	7.45
Graphical and statistical data in the health software helped me to get a clear and understandable summary of my daily performance	4.20	0.616
I think that there is a need to design a system in the health software to reward the user for his/her health and athletic progress	4.20	0.951
Comparing information and data every day helps me improve my physical performance	4.10	0.718
I believe that having a mobile phone is my main drive to use the health app	4.05	0.686
I think that the lack of interest and knowledge by members of the community about the health software forms a barrier for its use	4.05	0.887
I see that data provided by the health software are useful and reliable	3.90	0.852
I see that the daily watching of the health tracker in the software improves my health and fitness	3.90	0.912
It is better to provide the health software with lessons on how to use it before you start using it	3.80	1.196
I use multiple health apps to exercise and monitor my fitness and health	3.45	0.686
I find it difficult to navigate between health software data and screens	3.05	1.050
Physicians and nurses encourage me to use the health software	2.70	1.081

*Theoretical Mean = 3 (Source: adapted from Jain, J., Udinia, P. and Sahoo, 2017).

Table 2. T test for paired sample of m-Health app use.

Variable	Test for Equality of Variances		T-test for Equality of Means	
	T	Df	F	Sig.
Gender	1.526	18	0.011	0.916
College	2.359	18	3.425	0.081

Table 3. Means and standard deviations of students' responses regarding their attitudes toward the use of m-Health app.

Statement	Mean	Standard Deviation
I think exercise, jogging and calorie/weight control are the common reason for using m-Health app	4.25	1.020
I think that m-Health app contributes to the improvement of general health care among members of the community	4.10	0.553
I think using the health software is useful to check my fitness and health and to reduce the cost of visiting clinics and doctors	3.85	1.040
Health software has become a part of my daily life	3.70	0.979
I feel stress when using the health software and understanding its data	3.35	0.587
I feel that health does not help me to follow up on my health and sports	3.05	0.759
I think the design of the health software is inconvenient to enable the user to monitor his/her data on a daily basis	2.95	0.686

Responses in Table 3 were positive on all statement that measure the students' attitudes toward the use of the mobile health app in terms of content, design and use, as most responses are higher than the theoretical mean (3.0). These findings are consistent with the results of [4] study on positive attitudes toward m-Health apps and their impact on users' behavior after using them.

Qualitative Analysis

Inductive thematic analysis of the above qualitative data was conducted. Four main themes were recognized in terms of students' perceptions towards using m-Health app as it 1) increases health performance, 2) plays a stimulating role, 3) provides support for physical fitness, 4) stands good chance for future use. The followings explain these themes:

- Theme 1: m-health app increases health performance: Most students generally substantiated the quantitative findings by stating that the use of such software keeps them informed about their health and physical level along with their heartbeat rate and calories loss. They also said that the app encourages them to walk longer distances and reduce dependence on the vehicle at simple distances. One student reiterated the same idea saying that: "It increases my physical performance… because it makes me aware of how far distances I have walked/ran". These findings generally corroborates the results of [1] study.

- Theme 2: m-health app plays a stimulating role: One student said, "It motivates me more to exercise continuously and orderly". Some students stated it reflects positively on their psychological and physical state and make them pay more attention to their daily routines and unhealthy habits. Another student interestingly commented that: "It stimulates the individual to do more by comparing his activity day after day and gives a good impression of the individual health as well as it encourages us to continue our sports effort for more goal achievement competing with our previous results".
- Theme 3: m-health app provides support for physical fitness: A student expressed his satisfaction with the health software "the app is excellent and the sign of my satisfaction with it is that I highly depend on this app". Another female student said, "This is the first time I have used a healthy app but I am very encouraged to use these apps and take advantage of them".
- Theme 4: m-health app stands good chance for future use: Some students recommended the software for community members and patients as it makes them more committed to sports activities. Another student said that she "told all her family members that these apps are useful and advised them to use them". On the contrary, her colleague emphasized, "I have used this app for years and I have been following it continuously". Some said they connect them to wearable devices while walking. The majority of the sample students do not see any obstacles to continue using the m-Health app. These findings agree to some extent with [10] and [16] .

CONCLUSION

The primary objective of this study was to explore the Sultan Qaboos University undergraduate students' perceptions and attitudes towards using m-Health app and its impact on improving their sports and health habits. In general, respondents were positive in their responses to all statements that measure their attitudes towards mobile health app. However, the study was limited to the campus students besides some research and technical limitation concerning the small size of the sample and the various software versions used. Therefore, drawn conclusions should be carefully considered when intended for wider scale application.

RECOMMENDATIONS

According to the above findings, the study recommends the followings:

1) Raise the awareness of the university and the local community members toward the importance of using mobile health apps to improve their health.
2) Encourage individuals to use these apps by the medical and health authorities.
3) Design advanced m-Health apps with programmed personal health and medical data of their users.
4) Conduct the same research but on the public audience and local community.

ACKNOWLEDGEMENTS

The research team would like to thank the students of the study sample for their participation in the fieldwork.

Conflicts of Interest

The authors declare no conflicts of interest regarding the publication of this paper.

REFERENCES

1. Jain, J., Udinia, P. and Sahoo, PK. (2017) Qualitative Study to Analyze the Pros-Cons and Consumer's Perception towards mHealth Apps. The Pharma Innovation Journal, 6, 43-48.
2. George, T., DeCristofaro, C. and Murphy, P. and Sims, A. (2017) Student Perceptions and Acceptance of Mobile Technology in an Undergraduate Nursing Program. Healthcare, 5, 1-8. http://www.mdpi.com/journal/healthcare
3. Subhash, T. and Bapurao, T. (2015) Perception of Medical Students for Utility of Mobile Technology Use in Medical Education. International Journal of Medicine and Public Health, 5, 305-311. https://doi.org/10.4103/2230-8598.165959
4. Ber, F., Giacometti, M., Gualano, M., et al. (2014) Smartphones and Health Promotion: A Review of the Evidence. Journal of Medical Systems, 38, Article ID: 9995. https://doi.org/10.1007/s10916-013-9995-7
5. Bexelius, C., Lof, M., Sandin, S., Lagerros, Y.T., Forsum, E. and Litton, J.E. (2010) Measures of Physical Activity Using Cell Phones: Validation Using Criterion Methods. Journal of Medical Internet Research, 12, e2. https://doi.org/10.2196/jmir.1298
6. Free, C., Phillips, G., Galli, L., Watson, L., Felix, L., Edwards, P., Patel, V. and Haines, A. (2013) The Effectiveness of Mobile-Health Technology-Based Health Behaviour Change or Disease Management Interventions for Health Care Consumers: A Systematic Review. PLoS Medicine, 10, e1001362. https://doi.org/10.1371/journal.pmed.1001362
7. Grassi, A., Gaggioli, A. and Riva, G. (2009) The Green Valley: The Use of Mobile Narratives for Reducing Stress in Commuters. CyberPsychology & Behavior, 12, 155-161. https://doi.org/10.1089/cpb.2008.0156
8. O'Reilly, G.A. and Spruijt-Metz, D. (2013) Current mHealth Technologies for Physical Activity Assessment and Promotion. American Journal of Preventive Medicine, 45, 501-507. https://doi.org/10.1016/j.amepre.2013.05.012
9. Ericsson, A., Pettersson, J. and Sjogren, F. (2018) Perceived Usefulness of User Interface Characteristics for Mobile Health Applications. Orebro Universitet, Handelshogskolan-Informatik.
10. Altmann, V. and Gries, M. (2017) Factors Influencing the Usage

Intention of mHealth Apps: An Empirical Study on the Example of Sweden. MA Thesis, Business Administration, Karlstad Business School, Sweden.

11. Al-Maskari, G. (2004) Exploiting Internet Technologies in Health Care of Sultanate of Oman, BSc Information Systems with Management Studies 2004/2005. https://minerva.leeds.ac.uk/bbcswebdav/orgs/SCH_Computing/FYProj/reports/0405/Al-Maskari.pdf
12. SQU (2018) Graduate Attributes. Sultan Qaboos University. https://www.squ.edu.om/About/About-SQU/SQU-Graduate-Attributes
13. Al Musawi, A. and Ammar, M. (2015) Students Use of the Internet and Social Networking Sites for Learning and Other Activities at Sultan Qaboos University. International Journal of Social Media and Interactive Learning Environments, 3, 142-161. https://doi.org/10.1504/IJSMILE.2015.070775
14. Bol, N., Helberger, N. and Weert. J. (2018) Differences in Mobile Health App Use: A Source of New Digital Inequalities? The Information Society, 34, 183-193. https://doi.org/10.1080/01972243.2018.1438550
15. Tongco, D. (2007) Purposive Sampling as a Tool for Informant Selection. Ethnobotany Research & Applications, 5, 147-158. https://scholarspace.manoa.hawaii.edu/bitstream/10125/227/4/I1547-3465-05-147.pdf https://doi.org/10.17348/era.5.0.147-158
16. Hongu, N., Going, S.B., Orr, B.J., et al. (2014) Mobile Technologies for Promoting Health and Physical Activity. ACSMs Health Fit Journal, 18, 8-15. https://doi.org/10.1249/FIT.0000000000000050

INDEX

F

G

H

T

U

V

W